Gender Politics in Sudan

Gender Politics in Sudan

Islamism, Socialism, and the State

Sondra Hale

WestviewPress
A Division of HarperCollins*Publishers*

Copyright © 1997 by Westview Press, A Division of HarperCollins Publishers, Inc.

Published in 1997 in the United States of America by Westview Press, 5500 Central Avenue, Boulder, Colorado 80301-2877, and in the United Kingdom by Westview Press, 12 Hid's Copse Road, Cumnor Hill, Oxford OX2 9JJ

Library of Congress Cataloging-in-Publication Data
Hale, Sondra.
  Gender politics in Sudan : Islamism, socialism, and the state /
Sondra Hale.
    p. cm.
  Includes bibliographical references and index.
  ISBN 0-8133-3370-9 (pbk.)
  1. Women in politics—Sudan. 2. Women and socialism—Sudan.
3. Women in Islam—Sudan. 4. Feminism—Sudan. I. Title.
[HQ1236.5.S73H35 1997]
305.42´09624—dc21   97-9394
                                                                      CIP

The paper used in this publication meets the requirements of the American National Standard for Permanence of Paper for Printed Library Materials Z39.48-1984.

10   9   8   7   6   5   4   3   2   1

For Asma, Samira, Nahid, Bushara, Nabeela,
Huda, Mimi, Hafiz, Hisham, Musa, Hussein,
Leila, and Idris

you know your importance in my life
and why I am dedicating this book to you

Contents

Tables

Acknowledgments

This research is based on years of fieldwork in Sudan and short periods in Egypt and Eritrea. The Sudanese scholars, friends, and government officials to thank number in the hundreds; some I cannot name at this point in Sudan's political history, as it would put them at risk.

There are specific people to be thanked here. I have concentrated my thanks on those who helped or influenced me during my 1988 field trip (from which most of the material on Islamism derives). However, since chapter 5 on the Sudanese Communist Party and Women's Union is based on my 1970s research, and some of the gendered labor and economics data on 1981 research, I want to thank my research assistants for all three periods: Omer Baba, Fatma Khalid, Sunita Pitamber, Amal Abdel Rahman, William Young, and Sherifa Zuhur.

Those who hosted me at the University of Khartoum were Fahima Zahir and Taj el-Anbia el-Dawi, who served as Heads of the Department of Anthropology, and many other colleagues associated with the department. I gained significant insights from conversations with Samia el-Nagar, Balghis Badri, Amal Hassan, and especially Zeinab el-Bakri and Idris Salem el-Hassan. Others at the university who guided me in my research were Fawzia Hammour, Abdallahi An-Na'im, Abdallahi Ali Ibrahim, Gilal el-Din el-Tayib, and from Omdurman Ahlia University, Farouk Kadouda and the late Mohamed Omer Beshir (who inspired so much research on Sudan).

Outside of the university milieu many helped by setting up interview contacts or by being interviewed themselves: my longtime friend Judge Nagwa Kamal Farid, Suad Ibrahim Ahmed, whose work I have followed for decades, and Fatma Ahmed Ibrahim, Sudan's best-known woman political leader. None I have named should be held responsible for my views.

Many of my ideas were developed in association with organizations and groups around the world: the now dormant Socialist-Feminist Network of Southern California, the various women's and African/Middle Eastern studies programs with which I have been associated—most recently, UCLA's—the Association of Middle Eastern Women's Studies (especially Suad Joseph, Mervat Hatem, Judith Tucker, Julie Peteet, Mary Hegland, Erika Friedl, and Leila Ahmed), Feminist Focus on Middle East and Africa (among them Nancy Gallagher, Sherna Gluck, Sherifa Zuhur, Sherry Vatter, Nayereh Tohidi, Tsion Gad, Cheryl Dandridge-Perry, Amina Adan, Pat Kabra, Monhla Hlahla, and Soraya Altorki), UCLA's International Gender Study Group (among them Nikki Keddie, Ned Alpers, Jasamin Rostam, Lloys Frates, Christine Ahmed, and Sandy de Grijs), and the Center for the Pacific-Asian Family (especially Linda Ikeda-Vogel), to name only a few. Valentine Moghadam, whose work has been important to my own, invited me to Helsinki for a breakthrough workshop on identity politics and women that resulted in a provocative volume.

For support networks, in addition to the above I want to acknowledge Emily Abel, Sharon Bays, Carole Browner, Sandra Harding, Katherine King, Valerie Matsumoto, Karen Sacks, and Miriam Silverberg—my UCLA family—which also includes a group of very smart and creative graduates and undergraduates in Middle Eastern/African and women's studies.

The recognition of my intellectual and political indebtedness to my two teachers, Hilda Kuper and Leo Kuper, now deceased, would fill a separate volume. I remember them often in my daily life and in my work, as I do my late close friend, Linda Hackel.

The manuscript itself benefited from very close readings by Sherna Gluck, Ellen Gruenbaum, and Victoria Bernal. Sherna's feminist insights combined with her knowledge of women's resistance movements informed this book, as did Ellen and Victoria's knowledge of Sudanese women's studies. My dear friend, Mary Beth Welch, read an early draft and made many useful suggestions, and Sandy de Grijs assembled the bibliography. Ed Corey was the final copy editor and helped beyond my expectations to raise the level of the work. I am deeply indebted to him and to Alison Hamilton, who worked with us. The very patient Westview Senior Editor Barbara Ellington took an early interest in the manuscript, and guided me through the publishing process. As usual I am indebted to Gerry Hale, this time for suggestions on chapter 5 and for helping me surmount a "writer's block," and to Mohamed Omer Bushara, one of my longtime collaborators, for the cover artwork.

Like all extensive research agendas, this one was funded by a number of different agencies and units, and I thank all of them for their support: Fulbright-Hays, American Research Center in Egypt, The American Association for University Women, the National Endowment for the Humanities, California State University, Northridge, UCLA Center for the Study of Women, the Gustave E. von Grunebaum Center for Near Eastern Studies, and the James S. Coleman African Studies Center.

My family provides me with an environment that nurtures my writing and creativity in that it is safe and loving. For that haven I thank Gerry, Alexa Almaz, and Adrienne Nabeela ("Bulbul") Hale.

My extensive Sudanese family, some of whom I name in the dedication, includes two namesakes (the "two Sondras"), one in the northern Sudan, the other in the south. I hope I will see all of them again one day.

A Note on Arabic Transliteration: I have used a nonclassical, popular form of transliteration from the Arabic, hoping to make the book more accessible to a broader readership. Spelling inconsistencies have been unavoidable. One problem is that authors with Arabic names often vary the spelling of their own names, thwarting my attempt to accomplish two things at once: spell their names as they have chosen and be internally consistent.

Sondra Hale

PART ONE

Introduction

1

Theory, Living Fieldwork, and Autobiography: An Introduction

Setting the Problematic

As gender issues and studies in the late twentieth century have moved from the fringes to center stage of social discourse, they have become increasingly politicized. Community and national leaders, intellectuals, and ordinary women and men all over the world have taken up these issues. So central have they become that the [post]modern state, its apparatuses, political parties, and interest groups (even those in seeming opposition to the state) have put gender on the agenda and currently attempt to shape gender identity and politics to serve whatever priorities head their programs.[1] Consequently, all too often, gender researchers find themselves having to take these state agendas, institutions, and activities into serious account. In so doing some are finding that states and parties are serving their agendas by manipulating the social and cultural identities of women, positioning them within the culture often to their detriment.

Of course, women are social actors, not just passive receptors of state or party actions. So, located at the center of gender discourse is how women respond, adapt, ignore, redirect, or even subvert such state and party activities and projects intended to shape their behavior, lives, and thoughts. Here, too, researchers have to delve into a highly politicized terrain in order to discover how women, as agents of their own being and becoming, negotiate and determine their roles.

In the "North" (i.e., the advanced capitalist world) as well as in the "South" (i.e., the periphery) it is becoming clearer that the debates, actions, and struggles of the state and women are not homogeneous or universal. This suggests that researchers of gender issues, more specifically social scientists and humanists, now have to pay close attention to what they bring to the field, to what they find there, and to their subjective and interactional experiences in that locality. We are learning to be careful about our own assumptions, about those built into the conceptual apparatuses of our disciplines, about what we are learning, for whom, and for whose benefit.

What do we need to examine about ourselves and our methodologies in relation to our research topics and to the people who become our research subjects? To stand apart from the fray and perceive oneself as uninvolved but somehow highly informed seems wrongheaded. It seems desirable instead to acknowledge one's involvement with the subject and the ways in which both personal and political experiences have contributed to the construction of one's perceptions. For that reason I locate myself and the book within an autobiographical frame: not in the mode of the new reflexive ethnography where the anthropologist becomes a character in the work, but in the sense that the researcher is not abstracted away.

What kinds of anthropological analyses and bodies of knowledge do we need in order to understand how gender identity and politics in an African Muslim society like Sudan have been and are still being constructed by modern political institutions like the state and political parties?

Political Institutions, Gender, and Identity Politics

This research is an analysis of the relationship of gender to the state, a perspective that has been dealt with by very few scholars working on northern Sudanese gender topics.[2] In fact, the subject is relatively new for Middle Eastern women's studies.[3] Some of the more provocative questions within recent Marxist-feminist scholarship point to the relationship of gender to the state. Such questions arise perhaps more dramatically and vexingly in the Middle East (including Israel) and in Islamic societies than anywhere else because of the politicization of gender. The causes of this politicization can be traced to the relationship of the state and its apparatuses to religion, to the particular expression of gender in Islam, to the politicization of Islam itself, and to forces outside the Middle East, such as international capital and its accompanying culture.

In raising questions about the relationship of the state to issues of gender, ethnicity, class, and religion, I have analyzed the mechanisms employed by the state and/or party to achieve political and cultural hegemony.[4] In Sudan this has meant examining the identity politics that are often strategies or by-products of, or reactions to, state/party hegemonic processes.

In proposing the importance of the uses of "traditional" culture by the state and other institutions to recreate gender ideology, I hope to dispel some myths proliferating about the perplexing phenomenon of Islamism and its impact on women.[5] Islam, I argue, is but one area of "traditional" culture used to re-create identity politics through the maintenance of gender alignments.[6] It is, however, necessary to bear in mind that gender is a major variable and people are actors, not just the "receptacles" of Islamic doctrines and prescriptions.

Northern Sudanese women's studies is rich in theoretically significant material, in part due to the following processes, institutions, and historical events and situations.[7]

To begin with, northern Sudan is an Islamic society that remains steeped in indigenous and oftentimes contradictory traditions. Within that Islamic framework, discussed in greater detail in chapter 3, the Sufi-Sunni interaction has been highly complex and the sectarian identity politics emanating from this religious history remain active. Currently there is a vigorous Islamist movement, which some scholars argue is an outgrowth of these politics.

The social heterogeneity of Sudan is staggering. For example, northern Sudan is at once "Arab/Nubian" and African, with the complexity that that entails in terms of ethnicity and identity politics. Even the legal system is pluralistic: *sharia* (Islamic religious law), civil, and customary law have coexisted for nearly a century.

There are also pluralistic political traditions. Coexisting with religious and sectarian movements is a recent, but well-developed, socialist tradition, from which originated a vigorous leftist women's movement. The "urban" labor movement is only quasi-urban; it is shored up mainly by the small-town and village workers on the railways and ports. Instead of the urban proletariat, Marxist-Leninist socialism in Sudan has been supported mainly by these railway workers, some agrarian syndicates, and some intellectuals and students. Peasant class formation is highly complex, as are the ethnic and regional power realignments of the last few decades that have changed Sudan's class structure.

A variety of governments have ruled within the last two centuries: colonial regimes (e.g., Ottoman and "Anglo-Egyptian"), Islamic states (e.g., the Funj, the Mahdist), parliamentary democracies (1956–89), military regimes, and now an incipient military theocracy. Since 1972, multinational corporations, nongovernmental organizations, and foreign aid projects (Arab, European, and American) have intervened in Sudan's "natural" political process, dominated Sudan's economy, altered its class structure, and challenged the gender arrangements and culture of many Sudanese. Withal, Sudan is one of the poorest twenty-five countries in the world and endures persistent civil war. These conditions profoundly affect women's lives and the nature of their activism.

As previously mentioned, women's rights and/or emancipation have been on the political agendas of various groups for some time. In fact, feminist programs have been state sponsored, but with the inevitable, mixed results. Furthermore, women have participated in several kinds of movements, and a strong and vibrant women's culture exists that simultaneously empowers and marginalizes the women who are the actors in it.

Because one of my focuses is on the ways men have positioned women within male domains, I have constructed a somewhat artificial dichotomy of Islamists and secularists, condensing their political ideologies, goals, and strategies to show the similarities in the cultural positioning of women to serve their respective movements.

Among the goals and strategies of the Islamists in Sudan are (1) to manipulate religious ideology toward a more "authentic" culture,[8] (2) to represent, reiterate, or reinforce the centrality of women within that "authentic" culture, (3) to create a new trend in the gender division of labor or to stem recent changes within that labor system, and (4) to purge from (i.e., purify) an "authentic" women's culture particular non-Islamic customs that "weaken the morals" of women (e.g., the *zar*).[9]

The goals and strategies of many secularists (such as the Sudanese Communist Party [hereafter, SCP or the Party] and its affiliate, the Sudanese Women's Union [WU or Union]) may look different, but there are underlying similarities to the Islamists'. Members and cadres may often acknowledge Islamic culture as the "authentic" culture of northern Sudan's "working class" and peasantry. In the SCP's and WU's political oppositional work, cadres often make attempts to coexist with Islam or to work within an Islamic framework, although Islam is relegated to the private spheres of Party members. The SCP's secularist view of women as future workers, mothers of workers, and half the population (and therefore a potential political force) necessitates the rhetoric of the centrality of women in the political process. Another similarity to the Islamists is SCP and WU activism also aimed at eradicating "negative customs" from women's culture.

In contemporary northern Sudan, therefore, as in many other areas of the Middle East and North Africa, we find two seemingly antagonistic forces juxtaposed: "secular" forces, usually associated with the nationalist era; and Islamic forces, having older historical roots. Concomitantly, there are two types of women's movements: one represented by the secular left of the WU, and the other by the cultural nationalists (including the Islamist women of the National Islamic Front [hereafter, NIF]). In both cases we see women positioned to serve men's movements. Both lay claims to elevating the position and status of women, the former by placing the "woman question" and the emancipation of women at the forefront of the political struggle, the latter by also placing women and the family at the center of the culture as the instruments for revitalizing Islamic culture.

Sudanese, like many other groups, have always defined "in" and "out": weeding out customs that detract from what they see as uniquely Sudanese at the same time that there is a gathering in of history and culture as part of group self-definition. But these tendencies of inclusion and exclusion have intensified in the past two decades, a response perhaps to the deepening economic crisis. Regardless of the causes, both secularists and Islamists are now engaging in politics of authenticity. Communists ask: Who are the true Sudanese "masses"? Islamists ask: What are the authentic roots of Sudan's Islam? In a search for authenticity—for an identity that is "uniquely" Sudanese in the face of international interlopers—a tendency to essentialize has emerged in the rhetoric and testimonies of most Sudanese. Nowhere is this new essentialism,[10] which is also a part of state ideology, more apparent than in the attempts to generate icons of women and women's roles in Sudan's past, present, and future. These politics of authenticity focus on women more than on any other group. The identity politics that result from the search for authenticity are proactive: the male-controlled political institutions—religious and secular—manipulate women's participation in or disengagement from particular cultural practices or economic activities, all in the name of the ideal woman—an essentialized category.[11]

Kandiyoti commented on cultural authenticity and the focus on women in the Middle East:

> Anti-imperialist pronouncements about the West are often a thinly disguised metaphor to articulate disquiet about more proximate causes for disunity. These include the existence of indigenous social classes with different cultural orientations and conflicting interests, and the coexistence of religiously and ethnically diverse collectivities in the very bosom of the nation. *Discourses on women's authenticity are therefore at the heart of a utopian populism* which attempts to obliterate such divisions by demarcating the boundaries of the "true" community and excluding the "Other within" ... [including] Muslims themselves.[12]

To Kandiyoti women represent "the focal point of kinship-based primary solidarities as against a more abstract and problematic allegiance to the state."[13]

The utopian populism of current northern Sudanese politics is the backdrop for the state/party's manipulation of religious ideology and the re-creation of identity politics, the centrality of gender in these processes, and the impact on the gender division of labor and other gender arrangements.

Within Middle Eastern studies, at least, subaltern studies of women and of gender and the state have been seen by scholars as incompatible levels of analysis. Nonetheless, although my perspective privileges the state as the salient variable, I make reference to women as among subaltern groups. For example, when I trace state/party rhetoric to show the strategies used to generate a model woman that reflects state ideology and activity, I argue that women are given a generative and transformative role by the state/party and that this positions them at the core of any social movement. The analyses of state/party manipulation of women's roles and identities, and women's reactions and actions, are at the heart of this study.

Women—not Islam, the state, or the party—are the subject of my study. Moreover, I argue, the zar practitioners, the women activists of the NIF and the WU, and the like, are the subjects of their own lives—both contributing to and subverting the political economy of the state and its hegemonic forces.

A Question of Methods:
Reveries of a Reluctant Interventionist

Although feminist theory is the guiding framework of the research, it is not only feminism that has shaped my thinking, actions, and research choices and strategies as a Euroamerican woman. Within anthropological research for and about women, I have been struggling with such ideological issues as cultural imperialism and ethnocentrism, and with such personal issues as loyalty, betrayal, and abandonment. Years of personal and political change and many years of "fieldwork" in northern Sudan have developed my standpoint. I briefly describe some of the contradictions, ironies, dilemmas, and problems I have encountered.

While my goal is to analyze contemporary gender politics in northern Sudan, I also have another, more personal agenda: to end the self-silencing that for many years has plagued my writing on Sudan. To explain the silence, I present some of my methodological, personal, and ethical dilemmas that are far more complex than suggested by Oakley's assertion that interviewing women is "a contradiction in terms," or Riessman's suggestion that gender congruence may not be sufficient when women interview women.[14] My dilemmas move beyond Oakley and Riessman's problems of subjecting *women* to research scrutiny and thereby possibly objectifying them. My ethical predicaments also include issues of race, class, and ethnicity; "Third World" versus "First World"; and the colonized and the colonizer. In this work, I have tried to position the research in relation to my long personal history in Sudan and to my equally long and problematic academic connection with anthropology. I have come to recognize that my complex personal, ethical, and methodological dilemmas are the product of shifting paradigms and ideologies.

This will not, one hopes, be seen as an exercise in self-indulgence. I expect that my own experiences will raise some troubling questions for others about the applicability, when crossing race, class, and cultural boundaries, of not only anthropological but "feminist" methodology.[15]

No personal history is simple. My Sudan connection has spanned some thirty-five years, involving six trips and six years of residence. In all of my research trips I engaged in what most anthropologists would refer to as "participant observation," but I have mainly relied on formal interviewing and informal oral testimony. In my last two field trips, focused entirely on women, I relied heavily on interviews. But aspects of the interview process have given me considerable pause, as has anthropological fieldwork in general.

The angst of anthropological field-workers has been well documented in the last two decades. It is not my intention to augment our library of such testimonies[16] or to offer more than an implied critique of the ethnocentrism and self-delusion of "participant observation" or to do more than comment on the strange concept of "doing fieldwork."[17] My purpose is to examine some of my long-standing dilemmas, which have been not only academic and political but also ethical and personal, just as my long contact with Sudan has been both professional and personal. To accomplish this, I have tried to locate myself historically and socially—i.e., to *name* my positionality—vis-à-vis the Sudanese nation-state, its people, classes, and institutions.

In 1961, when I began research on social and political changes among northern Sudanese women, I was an unconscious and unself-conscious liberal whose intellectual life had been greatly influenced by Freudianism. I was also socialized by my mother to embrace a generic egalitarianism, and I internalized an unconscious populism that emanated both from my childhood urban working-class environment and from the rural, farmworker populism of the surrounding Iowa countryside.

During my first Sudan stay, "interviewing" took the form of conversations with hundreds of women and girls over a period of three years.[18] I developed many intense friendships, and many of these friends encouraged me to identify as an "insider." This encouragement took the form of constant Sudanese statements that I did not "seem like an American." (It was a wonderful validation. Besides, as an American [i.e., not British] I was spared being classified as a colonial or even an ex-colonial; and the concept "neocolonialist" was not yet common.) Even newspaper articles—usually about my tennis, theater, or teaching accomplishments—proclaimed me an honorary Sudanese.

I was Sudanese; they said it
as they transfused my blood.

I was Sudanese; they wrote it
in the newspapers:
"You are one of us,"
(they said),
"We will always keep you
among us; drink the waters
of the glorious Nile.
Return to us; we are one."[19]

Embraced by a women's community and given special treatment, I led
a charmed life in still-colonial Khartoum. Being accorded high status was
an unusual experience for someone from a working-class background. In
my innocence at the time I did not fully comprehend why I was accorded
such privilege, but I relished it. I dreamed of staying there forever, of
being Sudanese.

At the same time, I was becoming more politically aware of the problems and politics of Sudan. The nation had been independent only five
years when I first arrived, and the headiness of the nationalist period was
still in the air. The Algerians and Vietnamese had ousted the French colonials, and the nationalists and leftists of the Third World were vocal about
socialism, colonialism, imperialism, and the significance of the Bandung
Conference of 1955. Sudanese voices were often poetic. Singer/composer
Abdel Karim el-Cabli put to music the Arabic lyrics of communist poet
Taj el-Sirr el-Hassan, *Asya wa Afriqia* ("Asia and Africa"), words that
stirred the nation and me:

[I will sing] To the reflection of the shadows
of the Blacks in Kenya forest [Mau Mau]
To my comrades in the Asian countries,
In Malaya and Dia Bandung, to Ethiopia,
To the happy young nights in new China,
For which I sing in my heart a thousand songs.
Oh, my friends who are creating glory for my people,
You who are like candles whose green light is my heart.
Wahran [reference to the Algerian war] has come
To life again and is walking ...
And the glorious canal [Suez after nationalization],
The waters are like blood through my veins.
And I in the heart of Africa [Sudan] am a saboteur.
I do not know my friends; I have not visited Indonesia,
The land of Sukarno.

But the morning light is in the new Africa,
The slight light drinks from the faraway star [China].

I have seen *the* people; I have also seen Jomo;
I have seen Jomo [Kenyatta] like the light of the dawn
Against the light of the whole day.[20]

In Sudan such ideas were being played out against a backdrop of extreme poverty. Along with Taj el-Sirr, other socialist-realist poets, among them Jaily Abdel Rahman, Mohamed el-Faituri, and Mohi el-Din Faris, used the language of the left in writing against capitalists and the exploitation of the masses. Faituri, not unlike Fanon, voiced race consciousness, anticolonialism, and a call for resistance:

An old hag wrapped in incense,
A ditch filled with fire....
The dance of the naked Blacks
Singing in black happiness ...
To the white of this age,
The master of all ages.

Or,

Africa awake. Wake up from your black dream.
Yes, our turn has come, Africa,
Our turn has come.[21]

Salah Ahmed Ibrahim, moved by the political injustices of a colonized Africa and the rancidness of internalized colonialism, wrote:

Have you ever tasted the humiliation of being coloured
And seen the people pointing at you, shouting:
"Hey, you, black nigger"....
Have you one day tasted the hunger in a strange land
And slept on the damp ground.[22]

These ideas, which were in the foreground of Sudanese intellectual and cultural life at the time, entered my consciousness through the lyrics and poems recited and simultaneously translated for me at social gatherings. These political lyrics served not only as entertainment but also to integrate me into the milieu of the Sudanese left intelligentsia.

In 1964 I returned to the United States, which was being rocked by its own tumultuous social movements. The New Left and countercultural 1960s made an impact on me. These were my graduate years in African studies and anthropology at the University of California, Los Angeles. I was a campus and community activist profoundly influenced by the student, civil-rights, and antiwar movements and the ideas of the New Left.

Along with others in my progressive milieu I was questioning the morality of the academic enterprise. African studies and anthropology, like all academic fields, were being heavily scrutinized and criticized, anthropology being referred to as "the child of imperialism,"[23] and the anthropologist as "reluctant imperialist."[24]

Sudan offered a very good example of the "child of imperialism" argument. When it was a British colony, it had a highly respected Sudan Service staffed by government anthropologists of considerable repute (E.E. Evans-Pritchard, S.F. Nadel, Godfrey Lienhardt, Ian Cunnison, C.G. Seligman, among many others), who figured prominently in this critique. This was partially evidenced by a major work, *Anthropology and the Colonial Encounter*, edited by a Sudanist anthropologist and including other Sudanists.[25]

Before I returned to Sudan, I was forced to question my right to carry out research there, to objectify its people for my own career ends—indeed, even to *be* in Sudan. Anthropologists were compelled to rethink the history of our field and its suspect origins and purpose.[26] The people we had objectified were demanding that we be made accountable to those we claimed to serve.

Until the 1960s anthropology had been spared such scathing critiques and self-critiques, perhaps because the field had been shrouded by the romance of fieldwork, the "exotic" adventure that, magically anointing the "marginal native,"[27] served as the anthropologist's initiation. The mere act of living in an exotic culture surely meant that one was open, adaptable, and tolerant of others. It took a while for the romance of the "marginal native" to be replaced by charges of racism and exploitation.[28] For me, personally, these developments meant that I had to face the subtle racism of my romantic attachment to Sudan.

In the 1960s critics were calling for a *reinvention* of anthropology[29] that involved rewriting its history, trying to serve the people who are the subjects of its research, challenging the elitism of the academic enterprise, "studying up" instead of constantly objectifying the poor and powerless,[30] focusing on and doing fieldwork in our own culture, and writing more truthful accounts of the fieldwork experience.

Positivism was under attack. Some scholars began to recognize the importance of subjectivity and the realization that the researcher/interviewer should not be abstracted away, two elements of the critique of positivism that emerged in this period. In short, many anthropologists called for a more reflexive and critical anthropology,[31] greater social responsibility,[32] and the recognition that all knowledge is political.

These challenges prefigured the development of feminist methodology as part of an intellectual and activist vocabulary that had a considerable effect on my approach to the ethics of social science methods. In the early 1960s the native populism and cultural relativism[33] that I carried with me to Sudan mandated that I respect my "informants," which included protecting their anonymity.

While doing research in the 1970s on the responses of Nubians to relocation, I was sincere about informing the people I interviewed of the exact nature of my research. My populism and cultural relativism demanded honesty and directness. I refrained from using many of the techniques of deception that I learned in graduate school, especially in survey research courses: tricking people into exposing themselves or others, leading them into contradictions, and in general manipulating them to obtain the "truth" and the "facts." At that time I was comfortable with one solution to all ethical dilemmas: being open and honest with everyone. Such an innocent approach, however, created a new set of problems, and I had to make some very uncomfortable choices.

On one occasion, for example, I had to obtain a research permit from a government that at the time was suspicious of Nubian political activities. I still wished to be honest with everyone, but I naively took it for granted that my *first* responsibility was to serve the Nubian community.[34] I did not realize the full ethical and political implications of the fact that there were competing segments of "the Nubian community." In my research on Nubian ethnicity under threat, one of my hypotheses was that the accentuation of Nubian ethnicity was partially a result of the upper-class Nubian elite manipulating Nubian cultural reassertion for its own political and economic gain. Most of my interview subjects were working-class or former small farmers and merchants; most of my Nubian hosts, one of whom was my sponsor (the person responsible to the government for my conduct), were upper-class. I had to decide how much duplicity and connivance on the part of some elite Nubians I could, in good conscience, reveal. What followed was my first formal exercise of self-censorship.

The most profound personal impact of the critique of positivism during the 1960s and 1970s was my recognition that *I* was part of the problem. The research outcome was affected by my very presence, my charged and intimate interactions with Sudanese only adding to the complicated field situation.

Some anthropologists have maintained that feelings of uncertainty increase in the field-worker "with the greater degree of difference in cultural expectations between his hosts and himself."[35] I suggest, instead, that the closer the culture of the host group to the anthropologist's, the greater the uncertainty. Everything in the field-worker's experience is inescapably influenced by a whole range of subjective phenomena, not the least of which is that the members of a society allow one to study only what they choose. Although I lived in what seemed a small-town society (Khartoum) and mingled across classes, my closest friends were elites—

"Westernized" Sudanese whose culture and material culture did not seem very different from my own. Still, I did not quite belong, which exacerbated the potential for "insider"/"outsider" confusion. The problem was made worse by the friendly Sudanese claim that I did not seem like an American.

Inevitably, my social and historical location profoundly affected my approach to Sudanese studies; consequently my claims to objectivity, if I ever had them, were mistaken. I soon began to comprehend that I could not be a completely objective observer, because the form and content of each interview and observation were affected by what I had already experienced, how people already viewed me, and the fact that most of my knowledge came from living there and unconsciously acting out my roles within an intricate social network (teacher, tennis player, confidante, actor in the local theater, researcher, etc.). I was not only very visible, but also, to some, suspect. Many Sudanese were puzzled as to why I seemed to like Sudan so much and how I could be so well-integrated into Sudanese society.[36]

The above personal dynamics were intermingled with a number of new ideas I had internalized from the changing field of ethnography. Mainly I am referring to the self-reflexivity that has become a code of behavior for postmodern anthropologists and others and has made it more acceptable in academic writing to express one's anguish in the field: those feelings of inadequacy, heightened by the constant self-questioning and doubts about the worth of one's contribution, the validity of the data, and the "morality" of the anthropological enterprise.[37]

Nonetheless, despite the newly acquired sensitivity to the ethical and political issues of research that affected the progressive anthropologists (and others) of the late 1960s, the belief remained that some degree of distance was desirable, that we students of the social sciences were the authorities, that there is a truth "out there"—or at least some universals—and that, although we might speak of integrating theory and practice, the stress should be on theory, as distinct from experience, ideology, opinion, rhetoric, and emotions. It was not until later that I began to question the privileging of Theory.

With this ambivalent background, I began exploring feminist theory and methodology.

In the early years of women's studies, Euroamerican feminists too often historically decontextualized feminist methodology; i.e., we were frequently arrogant in claiming some ideas and methods as our own inventions. For example, in the late 1960s feminism revived a number of political methods and strategies new to me and others; e.g., the use of criticism/self-criticism for self-awareness and community-building and the use of small consciousness-raising groups—strategies that some

Euroamerican feminists commonly refer to as "feminist process." But as we know, the stress on consciousness-raising and criticism/self-criticism in general was a highly influential method of the left (especially of Chinese revolutionaries), carried over into feminism.[38]

As feminist theory and methodology developed, feminists began to challenge dichotomous constructs and binary oppositions—among them subject/object, insider/outsider, observer/observed, public/private, and oppressor/oppressed.[39] Feminists also critiqued the linear process whereby the out-group, for example, was depicted as assimilating to the in-group (e.g., the "Oriental" becoming "Western")—rarely the reverse. However, without seeing the contradictions, we anthropologists had always depicted ourselves as experiencing "culture shock" or "cultural alienation," and sometimes as "going native," in the process of conducting our fieldwork.

Another counterconventional development that influenced feminist scholars was the process of the Outsider writing back,[40] a response to Westerners for centuries studying and speaking for the rest of the world. Now, Orientalism was being subverted;[41] the Western gaze was being met,[42] just as the male gaze would soon be met.

Decentering the patriarchy has paralleled the decentering of the West. Questions of authenticity were raised: Who has the authority to speak for any group's identity? Can our statements be valid when we are writing about something or someone outside our cultural experience? How have the articulated self-identifications of groups set apart by anthropologists and others as "different" affected research and analysis? The ensuing recognition of multidimensional identities and ideologies has led to the recognition that we all have different socially mediated constructions of reality.[43]

Before my 1981 field trip another strain began to develop within Marxism and Marxist-feminism. Western feminists on the left, in particular, had become impatient with the relationship between Marxism and feminism and with left organizations' responses to feminist ideas. The critique began to be referred to as the "unhappy marriage of Marxism and feminism."[44] Some who held this perspective often called for the abandonment of Marxism altogether; others called for feminists, and all on the left, to move "beyond the fragments."[45] This theme of the critique of socialism by feminists has been revisited in a collection edited by Kruks, Rapp, and Young, *Promissory Notes*.[46] My critique in chapter 5 of one socialist party is in the tradition of this collection.

The critiques mentioned above affected the way I looked at my field research with Sudanese women.[47] By the 1980s, however, I had already grown critical of a number of the ideas of Euroamerican feminism, including the credo that feminist studies is the study *for* women. That credo—along with the notion of "empowerment" (as it usually implies that the teacher or researcher has established a context whereby a powerless person/woman becomes empowered)—began to sound patronizing and manipulative to me.

An aspect of the notion of empowerment that has made a great deal of sense to me, however, is that the woman/person being interviewed is the narrator of her own life: She is central. Her testimony is her truth. The feminist researcher, then, takes that truth and others, and attempts to propose a theory that can be translated into action. In the process the researcher makes a contribution to empowerment. The researcher (listener/recorder/synthesizer) and narrator act as partners, becoming agents rather than one of them—the research subject—being the object of change (or recipient of largesse or reform).

Although a significant number of feminist scholars and activists have railed against the 1960s' and 1970s' tendency within social science and positivism to privilege Method, we too—by trying to validate *how* something is done and valorizing means over ends, process over product—sometimes privilege it.

Renate Duelli Klein and Marcia Westkott, for example, privilege method in the form of *conscious subjectivity* (the validating of each woman's subjective experience) and *intersubjectivity* (the dialectical relationship between subject and object of research), respectively.[48] These methods entail the interviewer constantly comparing her work with her own experiences as a woman and a scientist while simultaneously sharing these ideas with the narrator, who then adds her opinions to the research, which in turn might change it.[49]

Klein also discusses "faking," a process that conventional researchers attempt to avoid and devise tricks to eliminate. Faking is the narrator giving responses that she thinks the listener wants to hear. Klein reminds us that, for women, faking has been necessary for survival and needs to be included as valid input in our research.

Much of feminist methodology is dynamic and unmeasurable: the interaction, the interrelationship of acts and feelings, statistics and intuition, the obvious and the hidden, the behaviors and the attitudes.[50] Ideally, a woman (interviewee, narrator, autobiographer, oral historian of her own life) should be given the space to be herself, not only in the sense of being frank, but also, if she chooses, of not remaining anonymous; to be the subject of her own life, to express her feelings, to relate her personal experiences, to reinvent herself, to reinvent history (especially to interject herself into history), and to act. Her answers will not always fit *his* questions, nor "ours" either.[51]

In the course of thirty-five years of interaction with Sudanese, I developed and maintained friendships with dozens of women, some of whom

I count among the closest friends in my life. This presented a major problem when I shifted into women's studies in the mid-1970s and began to write for and about women.[52]

When I began to carry out feminist anthropological research, my natural, obvious entree into Sudanese women's communities was through my women friends. But I was loath to "use" them as research contacts or subjects. For years I had avoided interviewing or questioning my close friends about my particular research topic, even if they were experts on some area of the research. I insisted on interviewing "strangers" exclusively and thus could rationalize using more-conventional interview techniques.

But eventually I came to question whether it is any more justifiable to objectify strangers.

During my last field trip (1988), I shifted strategies and began to converse with my friends about many topics, including the effects on their lives of the Islamic Trend government and the growing Islamism of the Sudanese middle class. I asked feminist friends about their coping mechanisms within a more conservative milieu. I became more straightforward in the personal questions I asked some old friends, e.g., about their being circumcised, about their divorces, about their lives while their husbands were in prison, and about their relationships with the men in their lives.

A few friends and acquaintances had changed their lives considerably since my last visit. Some, for example, had become observant Muslims, which they partially expressed by donning the *hejab* (modest Islamic dress). We had long conversations about the personal reasons behind the changes (explored more fully in chapter 6).

To my surprise, a number of friends stated or implied that they had always thought of me as disinterested or uninformed about some of the important personal issues in their lives, and as mostly interested in politics, theory, and intellectual matters. Although ostensibly acting on their behalf, by avoiding most of the subjects I thought too personal I inadvertently had separated the personal and political.

Even though I partially resolved the dilemma of asking sensitive personal questions, new issues arose regarding the interview material obtained from hejab-wearing Islamist women. I have had to ask myself whether I have a right to interpret their lives in print or even in the classroom.

Because of my feminist biases, I have been concerned with how to reconcile my political discomfort with the Islamic Trend government (and Islamism in general) and my respect for the decisions and activities of the women I interviewed. Was it betraying Islamist women to write a critique of the state's manipulation of religious ideology (and, thus, gender ideology) and the potential negative impact on women? Was it possible to facilitate an opportunity for Islamist women to "write back," or was that frame of reference too peculiarly my own? The new Islamic militancy is, indeed, an effective pattern of resistance to the West. Does their history of being colonized carry more weight than our common histories as oppressed women? Even though I may not have resolved all these questions in chapter 6, the testimonies of women in the NIF about their central activist role in the movement impelled me to raise in my writings the spectrum of contradictions between Marxian notions of "false consciousness," Euroamerican feminist goals of empowerment for women, and Western ethnocentric ideas about the oppression of women under Islam. These contradictions emerged as I *listened* to what my friends were telling me about the satisfaction they felt in their lives since becoming active in the new Islamic movement.

The experience of interviewing women on the left was also problematic. On a personal/experiential level, I began to fear that I would self-censor as I had done for years: i.e., not publish anything critical about Sudan, especially the left.[53]

I feared that publishing my critical account of the relationship of the SCP and the WU would be a betrayal. How could I be critical of the movement I had wholeheartedly supported all these years? The few Sudanese feminists I discussed this issue with did not see why I was agonizing over it; they urged me to use my material to stimulate a discussion on the direction of the WU. But I had had that experience with Sudanese feminists before—i.e., being encouraged to publish something critical partially based on information given me by them—only to have them "abandon" me when I did.[54] I began to understand that one can be used as a conduit or a surrogate for making public certain criticisms, and that the urging to be critical is not insurance against abandonment. The problem with that abandonment is that I was left with the feeling not only of having been politically incorrect, but of inadvertently betraying Sudanese.

But is the antidote to self-censorship a disregard for circumspection about what one publishes? Is the antidote of following one's own agenda perhaps amoral at best?

What I see as a quandary may be an artificial dilemma. Analyzing the interviews, I became aware that privileging one's research agenda might negate the validation process that the feminist interviewer may be trying to effect, so I struggled internally to minimize imposing abstract theoretical, methodological, and ideological principles on a *real* person's life. I had to start with acknowledging my interviewees' different feminisms and agendas, which effectively blunted my theoretical or ideological disagreement with the content of the interviews. In other words, I engaged in a running self-critique and a critique of Western feminisms, mainly the dominance of process, which I have discussed elsewhere.[55]

An important sphere of self-criticism relates to my expectations and feminist assumptions. For example, I had assumed that, as my left-feminist friends and colleagues and I were from the same general backgrounds (i.e., middle-class professionals and political activists), with the same general agendas (i.e., emancipating women and facilitating the Sudanese socialist revolution), my "interviews" with them would be interactional and intersubjective—i.e., more akin to "dialogues." As it turned out, in some cases it was almost as if we held opposing agendas. The interviews often turned into debates, or were situations in which I was expected to listen to a monologue and not interject.

For example, when I interviewed Fatma Ahmed Ibrahim (hereafter, Fatma),[56] I felt she offered only politically correct responses, perhaps because she saw me as able to forward positive propaganda about the WU. Whatever the motivation, she described only the successful or courageous periods of the WU and only her positive acts. In essence, I was given a portrait of a lifetime of work in which there were no contradictions, no mistakes, and no moments of human frailty. Our agendas, occasionally overlapping, were distinct: Hers was to convince me of the validity of her cause and her crucial and effective role in it so that I would write it in just that way.[57] Mine, of course, was to carry out research for which she was one of the sources. (Such a cynical interpretation flies in the face of the women's studies credo of research *for* women, but any other claim seems disingenuous.) I also wanted information that would validate my views on some of the problems of women's movements in the Third World, in order to assess the potential for women's emancipation. As a feminist activist, I, too, think of myself as having a cause. But it was presumptuous of me to think that Fatma and I shared the *same* cause and that she would acknowledge and affirm my role in it.

Furthermore, I had assumed we had the same basic "constituency": leftists and feminists. But it was more complicated than that in terms of who our listeners/readers are. During the course of the exchange Fatma had to take into consideration her professional/political reputation, as I did mine. She was carrying the load of Party expectations and needed to think about who would be hearing the interview. We both had to be aware of what others might expect from the interview: the Union and Party wanted to come out of the situation whole, and readers of my research wanted a critical appraisal. We both were protecting the political reputations of others: she, the heads of the SCP and members of the WU; I, certain left-feminist Sudanese with whom I have been associated for years.

The interaction and intersubjectivity were undermined by different concepts of modesty, authority, self-disclosure, and honesty. Besides, as many of us engaged in race and feminist scholarship and politics know very well by now, when the oppressed is in dialogue with a representative of the oppressor and they are both feminists, for the former, "national" goals sometimes outweigh "feminist" goals, at least for the moment of the interview; and the product may outweigh the process. Fatma likely saw me as a conduit to forward a cause she has worked for all her life. And I, despite my guilt in the role as representative of the colonizer, felt that both my populist sentiments and my particular style of feminist process had been subverted.

Clearly, I had overdrawn expectations, derived from the particular kind of feminist process that I had internalized. However, the problem is even more complex: my long and complicated history with Sudanese and my location in Sudanese society, as well as my location in U.S. society, were all relevant to the interview. The disappointment I experienced may have come from my commitment to the progressive movement in Sudan, but it is also a product of vestigial arrogance about being considered an "insider." In my mind, I was not just *any* interviewer or researcher: I had been given honorary membership. Besides, by that time I had carried out nearly three decades of research on Sudan, which I thought would qualify me as someone with whom a Sudanese feminist might want to engage in dialogue (as *I* was defining it).

Somewhat more convoluted were our class locations. Fatma, like a number of the Sudanese left feminists whom I interviewed, is from a privileged class, if not economically, at least in traditional status. And although she may have seen me as privileged, as an American professor, as white, as the neocolonizer, the exploiter—my *self*-image is working-class. My location in the American left also had relevance. A persistent problem I have had with Sudanese leftists is their disdain toward the American left, even in terms of the ideas we may bring into a dialogue.

Analytically, the experience of interviewing some of Sudan's most outstanding women of the left can be seen as illustrative of the flaws in certain Western feminist ideas about methodology. The colonizing of the product by the process can profoundly affect our scholarship, that is, our ability to create distance, to evaluate the narrator's life as separate from our own, and to assume a critical attitude without personalizing. Interactional female identification and the power of shared experience may be relied on in certain situations, but there may be a contradiction between facilitating a situation where the interviewee is the narrator of her own life (therefore holding center stage), and the interactional process.[58] To put it in the Sudan context, when there are class and/or racial differences, or when the interviewer represents the colonizer and the narrator the colonized, it is probably not reasonable for the interviewer to expect to be equally validated in order to fulfill a Western idealization of an interactional process. Was it logical for me, a white Western feminist interviewing a Sudanese, to expect to be acknowledged or validated as *myself*, when I may represent so many other categories to her?

Is it feasible for any interviewer/biographer/facilitator to avoid imposing what or who they are? If we are committed to particular theories and methodologies, is it authentic to practice otherwise? On the other hand, if we are more than conduits, do we automatically become cultural imperialists when we attempt to control the direction and content of the interview?

So much of what anthropologists do in the field is calculated, even participant observation, that intense centerpiece method wherein we live in a community and informally participate in its life, all the while (ideally) keeping our distance and documenting the process. The interview is conventionally classified as a quite different method, mostly calculated, formal, and prestructured. Feminist researchers, however, with the stress on interaction and intersubjectivity, have redefined the interview as something more akin to participant observation. In the redefined situation, the interviewer/interpreter/biographer sets up the situation and then participates in it. Being and doing are important to both the narrator and her interpreter. It is possible, however, that the small but significant degree of distance demanded in conventional participant observation is inevitably denied to the interactional and intersubjective interpreter of another woman's life. At the same time, in the feminist interview, the closeness and intersubjectivity frequently remain artificial and temporary, frustrating expectations and potentially creating tensions between women espousing different feminisms.

Serious methodological problems plague "woman-centered" analyses. In recent years, feminist researchers and others have tried to avoid context-stripping that includes abstracting away the researcher as part of the context. Still, interjecting oneself in the process is fraught with problems. These are only some of the dynamics of my research process in Sudan and the philosophical, theoretical, and methodological undergirdings of this work.

Locating the Work

The preceding section was a statement of my positionality as it relates to theory and methods. I have tried to move away from the assumption of oppression, instead presenting Sudanese women as political actors, even where our assumptions tell us we are least likely to find them: for example, in the NIF. By de-emphasizing ethnographic description (while being culturally specific) and refusing to privilege veiling, female circumcision, or Islam, I attempt to subvert "othering." Because of the Western framework, however, I acknowledge the improbability of total success.

Although I stop short of becoming a character in the story, I have not erased myself from the work; I have engaged in some self-reflexivity. With regard to the narrators, I variably center them as individuals or members of specific interest groups. This flexible approach is most apparent in the discussion of female, as contrasted to feminist, consciousness. However, while I have avoided universalisms (e.g., oppression of women), they remain apparent in assumptions about the hegemonic character of the state and international capitalism, which comprise the backdrop for the study of the interrelationships of socialism, nationalism, Islamism, and feminism.

Development of the Argument

I have divided the book into three parts, with concluding comments in the final chapter (chapter 7). Part One (chapters 1 and 2) is an introduction: theory, methods, and epistemology. In chapter 2 I contextualize Sudanese women's studies within African/Middle Eastern studies in general, and within African/Middle East women's studies and feminist scholarship in particular. Part Two (chapters 3 and 4) gives a background on northern Sudan and Sudanese women. Chapter 3 is a historical, ethnographic, and geographical background that includes analyses of northern Sudan's political economy, urban environment, and sectarian politics that culminated in the rise of Islamism and the Islamists coming to power in 1989. Chapter 4 is an analysis of the conditions of contemporary northern Sudanese women's lives.

In Part Three (chapters 5 and 6) I present two case studies of gender and revolutionary organizations. Chapter 5 focuses on gender relations in the communist movement. Following an overview of the SCP and other socialist movements, I question whether or not the "secular" Marxist movement in Sudan has addressed gender (women's) interests as distinct from the interests of the peasants or workers; whether or not women are creating their own movement through their own cultural institutions; and whether or not culture (including Islam) is being used as a powerful force for determining gender arrangements that serve male-controlled institutions, namely, the SCP and the state. In chapter 6 I analyze the rise of Islamism in current Sudanese politics (1971 to the present). I develop the ways in which the NIF uses women as the centerpiece for rebuilding a "modernized" but nativistic culture. Although the chapter is aimed at dispelling a number of myths in the literature about a superstructural Islam determining women's lives, the fact is that the women are *chosen* (positioned) by the men of the NIF to be the nexus of the new Islamic culture and movement.

The concluding remarks in chapter 7 revisit the cultural positioning of women by men in both the SCP and the NIF. After outlining potential spheres for political mobilization neglected by the SCP, I turn to socialist stances toward aspects of culture as an explanation for that neglect, ending with a discussion of the paradoxical role of culture in the oppression and emancipation of women in general and Sudanese women in particular.

Notes

1. It is not the purpose here to debate the nature of the state, e.g., whether or not the precapitalist state was an autonomous entity separate from its class base or is an extension of the ruling class. It should be clear that I am using a revisionist approach to the latter, one that derives from the ideas of Antonio Gramsci (*Selections from the Prison Notebooks* [London: Lawrence and Wishart, 1971]; *Selections from Political Writings, 1910–1920* [London: Lawrence and Wishart, 1977]; and *Selections from Political Writings, 1921–1926* [London: Lawrence and Wishart, 1978]), but borrows from others, e.g., Perry Anderson, *Lineages of the Absolutist State* (London: New Left Books, 1974), and *Passages from Antiquity to Feudalism* (London: New Left Books, 1974); and Nicos Polantzas, "The Problem of the Capitalist State," *New Left Review* 58 (1969): 119–33. I have also found useful Bob Jessop's "Recent Theories of the Capitalist State," *Cambridge Journal of Economics* 1 (1977): 353–73, and *The Capitalist State: Marxist Theories and Methods* (New York: New York University Press, 1982). My ideas on state apparatuses were stimulated by Gordon Clark and Michael Dear, *State Apparatus: Structures and Language of Legitimacy* (Boston: Allen and Unwin, 1984).

There are segments of this book where I conflate party and state, e.g., as in reference to the National Islamic Front, the Islamist/military "state/party" that has been in power since 1989, virtually constituting a one-party state. It goes without saying that there are often parties in opposition to the state (e.g., the Sudanese Communist Party since the 1940s). Nonetheless, for much of Sudan's political history, sectarian ruling parties have ideologically dominated the state—with the military enforcing and reinforcing that ideology.

2. Ellen Gruenbaum's work on gender, health, and the state is an exception. See "Medical Anthropology, Health Policy and the State: A Case Study of Sudan," *Policy Studies Review* 1, no. 1 (1981): 47–65. Lidwien Kapteijns' work (e.g., "Islamic Rationales for the Changing Social Roles of Women in the Western Sudan," in *Modernization in the Sudan: Essays in Honor of Richard Hill*, ed. M.W. Daly [New York: Lillian Barber Press, 1985], 57–72) also deals with gender, economy and the state, as does some of Fatma Babiker Mahmoud's work (e.g., *The Role of the Sudanese Women's Union in Sudanese Politics* [M.A. thesis, University of Khartoum, 1971], and "Capitalism, Racism, Patriarchy and the Woman Question," *Africa's Crisis* [London: Institute for African Alternatives, 1987], 79–86).

3. See Deniz Kandiyoti, ed., *Women, Islam and the State* (Philadelphia: Temple University Press, 1991). The collection, which focuses on the relationship between Islam, state projects, and gender relationships, is not confined to the Middle East, but includes South Asia. Sudan is not represented.

4. See note 1 above.

5. I use the term "Islamism" to mean political Islam. "Cultural nationalist" mechanisms are often used by the state/party to advance political goals, but the terms "Islamist" and "cultural nationalist" are not synonymous. The former is a kind of identity politics within the latter. See chapter 7.

6. "Traditional" is a highly problematic term, basically drummed out of African studies in the 1960s. I use it here reservedly to refer to a body of customs and beliefs extant in the precolonial (pre-British) period. However, referring to Islam as "traditional" is dubious and raises historical questions. (The coming of Islam to Sudan is discussed in chapter 3.) Some of my later statements raise the question but do not resolve the contradiction between referring to Islam as "traditional" and "modernist." See chapter 7, note 24, for definitions of "antecedent," "indigenous," and "traditional" culture.

7. When I use the term *northern* Sudan, it is more than a direction or a region. It is a statement about *culture*, because, to the informed reader it means that I am writing about the "Arab," mainly Muslim, north, and not about the "Black African," partially Christianized, south. There is a further discussion of this topic at the beginning of chapter 3.

8. Islamists I interviewed used the terms "authentic," "true," and "real" interchangeably. Asked for definitions, their responses varied and were vague. Hasan el-Turabi, de facto leader of the National Islamic Front, refers to a "pure" Islam unfettered by ethnic (i.e., Arab) customs. The "authentic" culture is an Islamic one, based on sharia. Therefore, pre-Islamic customs such as the *zar* (see note 9 below) are deemed not "authentic." Islamists began to delineate which aspects of culture are "legitimate," i.e., includable within an Islamic framework.

9. The *zar* is classified in any number of ways in the literature, e.g., as a women's spirit possession cult and as a healing ritual, among others. Mentioned throughout this work, the zar is discussed in chapter 7 as one of the examples from "women's culture" of a prefigurative political form.

10. By "essentialism" I am referring to something being presented as if it has a basic and singular nature and as if it is monolithic, immutable, and undifferentiated.

11. Elsewhere I suggest that particular institutions where we may detect elements of potentially liberatory cultural identity and practices (e.g., the zar) may be consciously thwarted by both secular and Islamist interest groups, while aspects of culture with oppressive or nonemancipatory aspects for women are either consciously encouraged, accepted, or rationalized. See Hale, "Transforming Culture or Fostering Second-Hand Consciousness? Women's Front Organizations and Revolutionary Parties—the Sudan Case," in *Arab Women: Old Boundaries, New Frontiers*, ed. Judith Tucker (Bloomington: University of Indiana, 1993), 149–74.

12. Kandiyoti, *Women, Islam, and the State*, 8; italics mine.

13. Ibid., 9.

14. Ann Oakley, "Interviewing Women: A Contradiction in Terms," in *Doing Feminist Research*, ed. Helen Roberts (London: Routledge and Kegan Paul, 1981), 30–61; Catherine Kohler Riessman, "When Gender Is Not Enough: Women Interviewing Women," *Gender & Society* 1, no. 2 (1987): 172–207. Riessman's analysis is closer to my own, however, as she examined contrasting interviews of two women—an Anglo and a Puerto Rican—and concluded that gender congruence does not help an Anglo interviewer make sense of the working-class Latina's account of aspects of her life.

15. Many of these ideas were first worked out in my "Feminist Method, Process, and Self-Criticism: Interviewing Sudanese Women," in *Women's Words: The Feminist Practice of Oral History*, ed. Sherna Gluck and Daphne Patai (London: Routledge, 1991), 121–36.

16. John Middleton used the expression "paradox and expectations" in *The Study of the Lugbara* (New York: Holt, Rinehart, and Winston, 1970).

17. "Fieldwork" is an odd term. Some anthropologists and other scholars use it to refer to a suspended state in which, using formal techniques—the tools of our trade—we observe the "other." It is the way we, having undergone this rite of passage, achieve credibility in our trade. It is also supposed, by some, to mark a certain personal transformation, our having imposed a marginality upon ourselves (in many cases, *another* marginality).

18. Some of this material was published in my "The Nature of the Social, Political, and Religious Changes among Urban Women: Northern Sudan," *Proceedings of the Third Graduate Academy of the University of California, UCLA, April 11–12, 1965* (Los Angeles: The UCLA Graduate Student Association, 1966), 127–40. Although for many years it was nearly the only study of northern Sudanese urban women and as a consequence was much cited, I have often used this study as an object lesson in ethnocentrism.

19. From my poem "The Return," *Africa Today* (special issue on *The Sudan: 25 Years of Independence*) 28, no. 2 (1981): 99.

20. Sondra Hale, "Arts in a Changing Society: Northern Sudan," *Ufahamu* 1, no. 1 (1970): 70–71. Mahi Ismail, cultural critic and ethnomusicologist, worked with me on the project and translated these lyrics.

21. Hale, "Arts in a Changing Society," 73–74. The translations are by Muhammad Ibrahim el-Shoush, *Some Background Notes on Modern Sudanese Poetry* (Khartoum: University of Khartoum Extra-Mural Studies, 1963).

22. Ibid.

23. For example, see Kathleen Gough, "Anthropology: Child of Imperialism," *Monthly Review* 19, no. 11 (1967): 12–27.

24. Wendy James, "The Anthropologist as Reluctant Imperialist," in *Anthropology and the Colonial Encounter*, ed. Talal Asad (London: Ithaca Press, 1973), 41–69.

25. Talal Asad, *Anthropology and the Colonial Encounter.*

26. For a good bibliography of these critiques, see Peter Forster, "A Review of the New Left Critique of Social Anthropology," in Talal Asad, *Anthropology and the Colonial Encounter*, 23–38.

27. "The anthropologist has been a marginal man for most of anthropology's history ... he almost invariably 'came on' as marginal to society. To members of his family he was 'the strange one' who was more interested in primitive rituals ...

than modern rituals." Morris Freilich, ed., *Marginal Natives: Anthropologists at Work* (New York: Harper and Row, 1970), vii. For some of the same themes, see Hortense Powdermaker, *Stranger and Friend* (New York: W.W. Norton, 1966).

28. Forster, "A Review of the New Left Critique," cites a number of these works.

29. Term borrowed from Dell Hymes, ed., *Reinventing Anthropology* (New York: Vintage, 1972).

30. For example, Laura Nader, "Up the Anthropologist—Perspectives Gained from Studying Up," in Hymes, *Reinventing Anthropology,* 284–311.

31. For example, Bob Scholte, "Toward a Reflexive and Critical Anthropology," in Hymes, *Reinventing Anthropology,* 430–57.

32. In 1968 a Social Responsibilities Symposium was published in a special section of *Current Anthropology* 9, 5: 391–436. See especially Gerald Berreman, "Is Anthropology Still Alive?" as well as his "'Bringing It All Back Home': Malaise in Anthropology," in Hymes, *Reinventing Anthropology,* 391–96, 83–98.

33. By the 1970s I was cognizant of the left critique of cultural relativism (e.g., Hymes, *Reinventing Anthropology*), but that criticism was later made more succinct by feminist theory and ideology.

34. This ethical choice was dramatized after I returned to the U.S. in 1972 and found a letter from the Sudanese Ministry of Interior demanding my recorded interviews and/or the transcriptions of interviews with sixty-seven Nubian men and women. I felt compelled either to deny or ignore the request (opting for the latter), risking not being allowed to do research in Sudan again.

35. Middleton, *Study of the Lugbara,* 71.

36. I deal with these processes at some length in my Ph.D. dissertation, *The Changing Ethnic Identity of Nubians in an Urban Milieu: Khartoum, Sudan* (University of California, Los Angeles, 1979), 35–40.

37. Although by the 1970s it was becoming more common to write in a personal way about one's field experiences or to talk personally about the field—e.g., Paul Rabinow, *Reflections on Fieldwork in Morocco* (Berkeley: University of California Press, 1977); Rosalie Wax, *Doing Fieldwork: Warnings and Advice* (Chicago: University of Chicago, 1971); Jean Briggs, *Never in Anger* (Cambridge, MA: Harvard University Press, 1970); Peggy Golde, ed., *Women in the Field: Anthropological Experiences* (Berkeley: University of California Press, 1970); Middleton, *Study of the Lugbara*; Powdermaker, *Stranger and Friend*; David Maybury-Lewis, *The Savage and the Innocent* (Cleveland: World Publishing Company, 1965); and as discussed in a review article by Dennison Nash and Ronald Wintrob, "The Emergence of Self-Consciousness in Ethnography," *Current Anthropology* 13 (1972): 527–42—when anthropologist Laura Bohannan wrote so personally in 1954, she not only felt she had to write under a pseudonym, but she fictionalized her experience. Her account of totally subsuming her identity as an American and immersing herself in Tiv (Nigerian) culture to the point of nearly "losing herself" read like a horror story to me, a graduate student entering anthropology in the 1960s. Elenore Smith Bowen [pseud.], *Return to Laughter* (New York: Harper & Row, 1954).

38. To some extent, I have conflated "feminist process" and "consciousness-raising," while, in fact, they are different, but overlapping methods. Feminist process is a method of making decisions, usually in small groups. Therefore, it is a

consensus-based group process. Consciousness-raising is a method of "conscienti-zation," e.g., the coming into awareness that the personal is political. Portions of "second-wave" feminism have staked claims to this particular form of conscious-ness-raising as part of the methodological and political base of feminism. I am indebted to Mary Beth Welch for this distinction.

39. Cynthia Nelson, "Public and Private Politics: Women in the Middle Eastern World," *American Ethnologist*, 1 (1974): 551–63.

40. I am indebted to James Clifford, *The Predicament of Culture: Twentieth-Century Ethnography, Literature, and Art* (Cambridge, Massachusetts: Harvard University Press, 1988), for reminding me of the works by Michel Leiris on anthropology and colonialism, which, in 1950, introduced the concept of "writing back." Michel Leiris, "L'Ethnographe devant le Colonialisme," *Les Temps Modernes* 58 (Paris: Mercure de France, 1966). This tradition has recently been most eloquently revived by Edward Said, *Orientalism* (New York: Pantheon, 1978).

41. Said, *Orientalism*.

42. Clifford, *The Predicament of Culture*, 256.

43. Soheir Morsy has written powerfully on this subject in "Toward the Demise of Anthropology's Distinctive-Other Hegemonic Tradition," in *Arab Women in the Field: Studying Your Own Society*, ed. Soraya Altorki and Camillia el-Solh (Syracuse: Syracuse University Press, 1988), 69–90.

44. The term is taken from essays by Amy Bridges and Heidi Hartmann pub-lished in 1975 and 1977 and a version in *Capital and Class*, no. 8 (1979). However, the best-known version is "The Unhappy Marriage of Marxism and Feminism: Towards a More Progressive Union," which appeared under only Hartmann's name in *Women and Revolution: A Discussion of the Unhappy Marriage of Marxism and Feminism*, ed. Lydia Sargent (Boston: South End Press, 1979), 1–41. Others had used similar expressions, e.g., Batya Weinbaum, *The Curious Courtship of Women's Liberation and Socialism* (Boston: South End Press, 1978).

45. See, for example, Hartmann, "The Unhappy Marriage of Marxism and Feminism," and Sheila Rowbotham, Lynne Segal, and Hilary Wainwright, *Beyond the Fragments: Feminism and the Making of Socialism* (London: Merlin Press, 1979).

46. Sonia Kruks, Rayna Rapp, and Marilyn Young, eds., *Promissory Notes: Women in the Transition to Socialism* (New York: Monthly Review Press, 1989).

47. Although the use of "with" in reference to research in the 1970s and early 1980s is an anachronism, the reasons for its use here will become clearer below.

48. Renate Duelli Klein, "How to Do What We Want to Do: Thoughts about Feminist Methodology," in *Theories of Women's Studies*, ed. Gloria Bowles and Renate Duelli Klein (London: Routledge and Kegan Paul, 1983), 94; Marcia West-kott, "Feminist Criticism in the Social Sciences," *Harvard Educational Review* 49 (1979): 422–30.

49. Klein, "How to Do What We Want to Do," 94–95. This is not dissimilar to Paulo Freire, *Pedagogy of the Oppressed* (New York: Seabury Press, 1970).

50. Ibid., 98.

51. A play on Hilary Graham's "Do Her Answers Fit His Questions? Women and the Survey Method," in *Public and Private*, ed. Eva Gamarnikov, June Purvis, Daphne Taylorson, and David Morgan (London: Heinemann, 1983), 132–46. "Ours," in this case, refers to Western scholars, male or female.

52. As a graduate student at UCLA from the mid-1960s to the mid-1970s I had resisted doing research on women. My Ph.D. chair, Hilda Kuper, had urged me many times to take advantage of my contacts with Sudanese women. I resented, however, that on the basis of my gender I was being relegated to the lowly status of studying women. At the time I was convinced that "important," hard-core, rigorous theory was being written by men about men.

53. I had several experiences that contributed to my refusal to publicly critique aspects of Sudanese society. For example, I had studied the north-south civil war for many years; had, in fact, delivered an early paper on southern Sudanese as "strangers" in the north (Sondra Hale, "Southern Sudanese: Strangers in a Plural Society" [paper presented at the Southwestern Anthropological Association, San Francisco, 1966]). I began noting that, often, encouragements to present my work on the south were extended by those writing or speaking within an anti-Arab or anti-Muslim framework, disguised or not as scholarship. As a consequence, I published only one article on the civil war, a cautious and abstract piece that might have been written by anyone who had read the secondary sources, not by someone who had spent years in Sudan (Sondra Hale, "Sudan Civil War: Religion, Colonialism, and the World System," in *Muslim-Christian Conflicts: Economic, Political, and Social Origins*, ed. Suad Joseph and Barbara L.K. Pillsbury [Boulder: Westview Press, 1978], 157–82).

54. I tested the waters with the publication of "The Wing of the Patriarch: Women and Sudan's Revolutionary Party," *MERIP Middle East Report* 16, no. 1 (1986): 25–30. Two episodes only reinforced my concern: first, one of the primary sources of my information about the relationship of the SCP and the WU dissociated herself from the article; next, the person who had been considered the "cultural ideologue" of the SCP when it was underground confronted me in tears about the injustice I had done the late secretary-general of the SCP, whom he claimed was highly enlightened about gender issues.

55. Hale, "Feminist Method, Process, and Self-Criticism."

56. Fatma Ahmed Ibrahim, whom I interviewed 12 July 1988 at her home in Omdurman, Sudan (a conversation that will be discussed in the fifth and seventh chapters), is a political folk hero in Sudan. As the leading activist in the main women's organization, the Women's Union, for over thirty years, she has been Sudan's most visible woman politician. In 1965, running as an independent, she became the first woman elected to Parliament. As a member of the SCP she has been in the vanguard of nearly every collective action carried out against the various repressive governments and has been jailed many times. I refer to her by her first name in this chapter because I know her, because this is a personal statement of the subject, and because it is acceptable and respectful in Sudanese culture to do so. I refer to her as Ibrahim in all following chapters.

57. The irony was that, as a strong SCP and WU supporter, and Fatma being one of the only true-life heroes I had, I went into the interview with that attitude already in mind. I thought she knew that. Her supporters had checked me out before she agreed to the interview.

58. Hale, "Feminist Method, Process, and Self-Criticism."

2

Locating Sudanese Women's Studies

Introduction

Studies of northern Sudanese women straddle the fluid borders between African and Middle Eastern studies. Their epistemological location depends sometimes on which social or political institution or custom the researcher privileges; i.e., if Arab or Islamic identity is privileged, publishers tend to place the work in their Middle East catalogs; if the research focuses on kinship, ritual, or ceremony, Africa may be its niche. My rule of thumb has been to use people's self-identification, and most northern Sudanese self-label as "Middle Eastern" and/or "Arab." In this I have acquiesced, though as discussed in the next chapter, such nomenclature is problematic because Sudan is clearly in *Africa*. However, gender studies of the Middle East are at an exciting and dynamic juncture, and exploring one's research topic within the context of such a volatile field is rewarding.

In this chapter I offer a general discussion of the problematics of gender studies, particularly feminist scholarship, within Middle Eastern studies. I highlight particular themes (such as women as political actors), explore the work of some of the new critical ethnographers, and conclude with an assessment of the place of Sudanese women's studies.

Gender and Middle Eastern Studies

Recent ethnographic and sociopolitical literature emerging from Middle Eastern women's studies has critiqued not only colonial perspectives, but Marxist-feminist theory as well, calling into question concepts of private and public, and of autonomy; interpretations of power relationships within the family; the function of religion in women's everyday lives; definitions of political activism and emancipation; and interpretations of the relationship of gender to the state—thus, the nature of politics itself. Ideas emanating from Middle Eastern women's studies have also toughened the challenges to "false consciousness" as a rationale for the nonconformity of non-Euroamerican women to Euroamerican concepts of oppression, equality and liberation.

Most literature on the Third World is highly charged and politicized; literature on the Middle East is especially problematic.[1] Significant for feminist scholars is that women and gender arrangements are at the core of the considerable ethnocentrism. Put another way, the concept of gender is highly charged and politicized precisely because Western social scientists and Western-trained scholars from the Middle East have given what has been called for some time an "Orientalist" interpretation to data on Middle Eastern women.[2] The charged nature of the subject matter has resulted in works being reactive, especially some of the works by Middle Eastern women in the 1970s and 1980s.

The internal and external politics of the Middle East and the dynamics between American and Middle Eastern scholars make gender studies a very difficult subject. To compound matters, following a long period of little or no dialogue, quite a degree of tension emerged between Western feminists and Middle Easternists (not mutually exclusive categories). Within Middle Eastern studies, as within other regional studies, numerous scholars assert their own "feminisms" and resent the ethnocentrism of aspects of Western feminist ideologies. Furthermore, some feminist Middle Eastern scholars have raised questions about Western appropriation of Middle Eastern culture in the forms of scholarly research and publication.[3]

There are also problems in dealing with one Middle Eastern society within a Middle East framework. The area is strikingly diverse in economy, culture, ethnicity, race, language, class, ideology, *and* religion. Further confounding scholarship, the ways that class, ethnicity, race, gender, and religion intersect often do not fit our Marxian or feminist models. The interaction of indigenous religions, economies, and cultures with British (and many other) imperialisms adds further complexities. Inevitably, how colonialism and neocolonialism in their various forms affect gender relationships differs by region, culture, and economy.[4]

By the 1980s, analyses of these complexities' relationships to everyday life began to change the face of regional studies and, therefore, the social sciences, especially anthropology. Until very recently, Middle Easternists represented women as if encapsulated in bounded groups or categories; e.g., households, lineages, tribes, ethnic or sectarian groups. Male researchers often left the data collection on women to their spouses[5] or failed to gather such data altogether. The politics of Western knowledge of the Middle East exaggerated the gender partition. Because of how the "seclusion" of women was perceived, male scholars were able to rationalize the exclusion of women in their analyses. It has partially been the historicist-Arabist-Islamicist legacy[6] of Middle Eastern studies that, until the late 1970s, impeded the development of women's studies in the region and virtually relegated feminist studies to a backseat. Suad Joseph explained that: "Functionalism, Orientalism, sexism, and certain feminist approaches have enforced one another in depicting Middle Eastern women as confined to their kin, tribal, ethnic, class, or national boundaries; as isolated from men; and as passive actors in the public domain."[7] Joseph further contended that anthropological models, dominated by functionalism and reinforced by pluralism, looked to "an ethnic division of labor in which interethnic relationships occur only in the marketplace" (2). Furthermore, "Perhaps in no area of the world have Western gender biases more emphatically polarized male and female images than in Middle Eastern studies" (3).

The privileging of various dichotomies (best seen as heuristic devices but often reified through the privileging process) has meant that studies are constructed of binary oppositions: honor/shame, patron/client, and public/private. These theoretical, ideological, and methodological constructs have limited studies of Middle Eastern women to dress, segregation, polygamy, and genital surgeries as they relate to the overarching cultural (superstructural) determinant: Islam.

The privileging of Islam in women's behavior and status is a special problem in the literature, made more onerous by historical writings linking Islam and sexuality. Waines has argued that Europeans from the seventeenth century wrote of a lascivious Islam, of a culture embedding a repugnant sexual morality. To those early observers, the "tyrannical nature" of "Oriental" society was reflected in ruler over subject, which included "man's wanton possession of woman as object," the secluded, mysterious, erotic Muslim woman.[8] Dramatic representations of this Euroamerican view of Middle Eastern women can be found in *The Colonial Harem*, a collection of photographs (some of which were used as postcards) of overeroticized, -exoticized Algerian women.[9]

By the 1990s we can still find a significant body of literature that "assumes *a priori* the existence of a universal Islam which mysteriously molds behaviour 'from above.'"[10] One reason for this monolithic approach to Muslim women may be that sharia (Islamic law), where it is applied, has promoted a great deal of superficial uniformity. Thus, since the *Quran*, the *hadiths*, and sharia strictly formalize gender relationships, since many Muslims see these religious and legal doctrines as universal, and since many segments of these doctrines often technically deem women unequal, most outsiders see women as enduring universal subordinate status.

This assumption has proven very difficult to debunk. As early as 1978, Beck and Keddie cautioned against a too simplistic view of the impact of Islam on women:

> The question is not why traditional Islamic culture has been more discriminatory toward women than other major cultures ... the real question, which contains policy implications for population control, improved child rearing, educational development and economic change, is why Islamic society has been more conservative in its maintenance of old laws and traditions in this area than have other societies.[11]

Some fourteen years later Lila Abu-Lughod still found it necessary to make clear that Islam is only one aspect of "Bedouin"[12] women's experience: "not all events or utterances can be explained by reference to Islam."[13] She elaborated:

> The stories in this book bring out numerous tensions that relate to this identity: between practices and their justifications, between ideals and behavior, between simple prescriptions and multiple interpretations, between sense of the universal and the complexity of local and individual experience. It is hoped that these stories will help draw out the distinction between reference to and determination by Muslim traditions.[14]

Related to the overprivileging of Islam in Middle Eastern women's studies and within "Third Worldism"[15] in general is the assumption of oppression, challenged by Lazreg in her work on Algerian women.[16] Arguably, no one group of Middle Eastern women has been so relegated to the role of failed selves. They have been used as metaphors for failed revolutions and seen as incarnations of the female mired in mysterious and immutable culture.[17] Palestinian women activists in the intifada (uprising) proclaimed regularly, "'We will not go back. We will not be another Algeria.'"[18] Gluck reported being relieved when they would quickly add the caveat, "'otherwise, we will make another *intifada*—for women!'"[19] Women activists of the National Islamic Front (NIF) would make similar comments. Arching their eyebrows at my questions about women being left out of the revolution in the end, they seemed to assume that most of my questions were headed toward the suggestion that they might become like Algerian women. Many researchers, Western and Middle Eastern alike, activists and academics, have used Algerian women as a symbol of failed emancipation, which is logical, perhaps, when one begins with the assumption of oppression.

Assumptions of oppression in Middle Eastern studies of women often rely on such dubious indexes as dress (i.e., the veil), genital surgeries, and sexuality.

Research on the veil is very problematic.[20] There are few, if any, regions of the world where *one* element in the culture still symbolizes so much to scholars and observers as does the veil in the Muslim Middle East. It conjures up the exotic, the erotic, the process of seclusion, the harem,[21] marginalization, modesty,[22] honor and shame, social distance, gender segregation, and, of course, the subordination of women. Middle Eastern feminists, especially those trained by Europeans, by foreign missionaries, or schooled in Europe, often were influenced to treat the veil as a symbol of their oppression.[23] Throughout the 1980s and into the 1990s the word "veil" appeared more than any other word in the titles of works about Middle Eastern women. The veil is privileged whether or not the authors differ greatly in their politics. Euroamerican or indigenous, male or female, religious or not:[24] regardless of the positionality of the author, the image of the veil is pervasive. So pervasive, that:

> The act of cultural observation and understanding is like drawing back a veil in order to grasp the meaning of cues and symbols of other cultures, rather than imposing meaning upon such symbols from behind the seclusion of one's own cultural veil. For too long the western observer, accustomed to gaze through a veil darkly, has accepted formless shadows as tangible objects of reality.[25]

Even if one were to accept the proposition that the veil yields important information about Middle Eastern women, privileging it tends to totalize them. But there is more to the question than veiling or not veiling. The type of veil, the occasion it is worn, the category of person veiling (class, region, type of occupation), and the politics of it (as in Iran) are exciting variables too rarely analyzed. Whether donning the veil is for the purpose of enacting seclusion (social distance from men), making a statement about sexuality (social control), or affirming Islam (modest dress for women and men); if it is for fashion or national dress (sometimes as an abrogation of Western style and values, as in Iran), or is simply deemed more practical or economical than other modes of dress (because it uses local material rather than imported goods)—the reasons for veiling are seldom explored. Besides, the word "veil" is used indiscriminately to describe variations ranging from a "moderate" hejab (modest Islamic dress, which might be a long skirt and sleeves with a head scarf) to more thorough covering (cover-all gowns from head to foot, only the eyes showing; gloves) to a wraparound to a simple filmy covering for the face.

These are variable modes of dress inter- and intranationally, among classes, urban or rural, according to religion, sect, or ethnicity. Most significantly, the choice is often up to the woman and may reflect her everyday life. In the documentary *A Veiled Revolution* Egyptian women explain their voluntary adoption of modest Islamic dress (which varies appreciably in the film) in terms of their differing degrees of compliance to the faith, will power, determination, and other factors such as fashion, economy, and ease of movement in physical jobs.

For a century, most Muslim women in northern Sudan have worn a loose, wraparound, filmy gown referred to as the *tobe*, which they wear in public or around male strangers in private. Some women used to cover their faces with a piece of the tobe, but the common Western reference to this dress as "veiling" is a misnomer. The reasons women state for wearing the tobe are as varied as the reasons listed above, and in recent years many have stopped wearing it. The tobe now is often little more than the modest "national dress" of a large portion of the population, and for some middle-class women in the urban area, the outfit for ceremonial occasions. For a minority of Islamists, the tobe has been replaced by the hejab, which varies in severity. Women gave me a multitude of reasons for wearing the hejab, ranging from vague "religious reasons" to "it's cheaper and more accessible than the tobe," which consists of eleven yards of expensive imported cotton. By many, the tobe is now seen as more progressive or modern, with some Sudanese resenting the imported idea of the hejab. Seldom was I told either that the purpose of the tobe or hejab is to hide or seclude women, or that these modes of dress function to inhibit sexuality. Women mentioned "self-respect," "modesty," and "protection from leering men" (strangers), and always stressed the voluntary nature of their dress decisions. Uses of and attitudes toward the tobe and hejab have changed historically and differ demographically. Moreover, individual choice magnifies variation.[26] Lazreg's argument that silence is an eloquent cultural statement suggests that the "veil" may also be seen as a form of eloquent silence.[27]

One reaction to the veiling-equals-submission formula has been to show veiled women as active members of society, including politics. Zuhur and MacLeod, for example, have given us provocative though very different works that try to break the mold by presenting veiled women as engaged in resistance, protest, and accommodation.[28] A more common new tendency, however, is to de-emphasize the importance of veiling or not mention it at all.[29]

Another mode of cultural behavior that some researchers use to symbolize the lowly status of women in the Middle East is "female circumcision," a term that refers to various forms of female genital surgeries (now also frequently referred to by Westerners and Middle Easterners as the more charged "female genital mutilation").[30] Great alarm has accompanied the "discovery" by Westerners of this custom, which arguably has its most extensive use in Sudan.[31] That we have mistakenly associated this custom with Islam, thereby generalizing for the entire Middle East, further stereotypes the women of the area and inextricably links Islam to issues of sexuality and subordination.[32] The invalidity of the link is dramatized by the omission, on the part of scholars and activists dealing with female circumcision, of information on the performance of such genital surgeries on women in the United States in the twentieth century:

> Doctors' attitudes toward women reflected their anxiety about female emancipation and changing sex roles. The specialty of gynecology emerged in significant part as a reaction to female emancipation. The strong surgical emphasis in American gynecologic practice has continued. The operations, clitoridectomy and female castration, were intended to reimpose the traditional sexual order (the term "castration" and "female circumcision" implied women had become men).[33]

The interface of Middle Eastern and Mediterranean themes of veiling, sexuality, subordination, and Islam with the dichotomous model of "honor and shame" was first eloquently forwarded in Peristiany's collection.[34] Interpretations of gender relations were thereafter frequently framed in terms of the passive ideals of chastity, virginity, and femininity for women, whereas for men there were the more active concepts of valor, machismo, revenge, manliness, and brotherhood. When we investigate the theoretical and empirical research on the Mediterranean, southern Europe, and the Middle East, we see that the code of honor and shame is assumed to be the dominant value system in small, communal societies.[35] Researchers writing during this period often borrowed the model uncritically.

Scholars writing within the context of a new literature (some of which is discussed below) are helping us recognize diversity, variability, historical and political dynamics, and resistance. As Joseph has remarked, "Only if we understand clearly the specificities of Middle Eastern states, classes, and ideological formations can we apprehend the necessary context for evaluating women's place in politics today."[36]

Feminist Scholarship on the Middle East

Against this backdrop one can see progressive new trends in writings—much of it being done by anthropologists—by and about women in the Middle East.[37] We will see below that the Sudan literature exhibits these trends in important ways.

By the 1980s two important changes appeared in a field that first excluded representation of women altogether and then represented them only as encapsulated in social institutions such as tribes or kin groups. The first trend consisted of studies that emphasized how women were changing the face of the society (e.g., by their entrance into the workforce in larger numbers, through their influence on the national polity, and through their participation in social movements). In other words, partially in response to changes within international feminist discourse, women began to be seen as possessing agency. Since the early 1980s, there has emerged a second trend, which I refer to as the "New Ethnography": a combination of critical ethnography and greater cultural specificity.[38]

Two indicators of the maturation of a field of study are, first, the appearance of theoretically framed anthologies and, second, the conversion of the objects of study into actors. In the latter case, Middle Eastern women began, in print and in English, to be the narrators of their own lives.[39]

By 1988 we witnessed an English-language, Arab-edited collection by Arab women, most still living in the Middle East at the time. It is the first such volume edited by a Sudanese, and for the first time, writers from Egypt and Sudan were preponderant, accounting for nearly half the articles. *Women of the Arab World* presents contributions from seven regions, and is definitely feminist in its stance.[40] The collection is also striking in its subject choices. Only two articles of fourteen relate to Islam, and one of those very indirectly (by the distinguished Moroccan sociologist Fatima Mernissi). The volume asserts that there is simply more to Muslim and Middle Eastern women's lives than Islam and the veil: namely, problems in their material lives, especially regarding health issues. The papers "range from the philosophically contemplative [Mernissi], [to] the statistically precise [Rima Sabban on Lebanon] to first-hand personal experiences" [the Giacaman and Oden article on Palestine].[41] The politics, too, vary from liberal to rather classical Marxist (Fatma Babiker Mahmoud's article on Sudan).

Far from being the usual monolithic treatment of the Arab world and women in it, this collection has sharp contrasts. For example, el-Saadawi's victimology is almost diametric to Mernissi's suggestion that Arab women stop complaining and release the past. Mernissi also is skilled at placing Arab women's situation within the international feminist context, proclaiming for example, that what differentiates the patriarchy of the Arab world from most societies is not the form, but "the perpetuation of this system as an incontestable model and an ideal, while in other societies it is open for discussion."[42]

Feminist literature on Middle Eastern women is not unified epistemologically, ideologically, and theoretically. There are those still writing within the philosophical framework of cultural relativism,[43] others writing more apologetically,[44] and others writing within a feminist "universalistic" framework of women's subordination.[45]

One of the most active schools of feminist thought to emerge from Middle Eastern women themselves is one that examines the grounds for women's emancipation embedded in the Quran, the hadiths, and sharia. Mernissi investigated the original texts in an effort to turn traditional interpretations on their heads.[46] Using a different twist, Sabbah (a pseudonym) examined two main discourses: the religious-erotic and the orthodox. In raising the question of "Why are silence, immobility, and obedience the key criteria of female beauty in ... Muslim society,"[47] she saw the female body presented as the product of male pleasure in the religious-erotic discourse and as the product of male sacred power in the orthodox. Her concluding chapter on female beauty as a mirror of male fantasies is a feminist tour de force.[48]

Leila Ahmed's 1992 historical survey *Women and Gender in Islam* heralded another step forward for Middle Eastern feminist studies.[49] It has Ahmed's important signature—an exploration of Muslim women's contested relation to Western feminisms.

Two important but divergent themes to emerge in the recent sociological literature are (1) the integration of gender and politics (political economy/universalistic) and (2) the "New Ethnography."[50] One of the primary periodicals to promote the former is *MERIP* (Middle East Research and Information Project) *Middle East Report*, the foremost American left journal on the Middle East. The MERIP Editorial Collective has consistently examined issues relevant to women factory and migrant workers and to the gender division of labor.

Even within feminist scholarship there is a lingering problem. Middle Eastern feminists themselves omit the voices of their subjects. Most researchers speak *for* the women they are researching. As Soha Abdel Kader argues in a review of research on women in the Middle East: "Instead of arguing whether Islam is beneficial or detrimental to women's roles, it might be best to study what aspects of religion women practise, and what aspects of it they think is of importance to their lives."[51] Even feminist anthropologists have often forgotten aspects of their own feminism and its process (giving voice) when writing on the Middle East.

By the late 1970s there emerged a number of new ethnographies (e.g., by Makhlouf, Wikan, Altorki, Dorsky, and Abu-Lughod), some written by Middle Eastern women or those with close kin ties.[52] We were able to see in some of them a movement away from speaking *for* women, to presenting women speaking for themselves.[53] These demonstrate a growing sophistication in the use of the personal as expressive of the values and ideologies of the society. Women are beginning to emerge as real: as individuals and as members of kin and extra-kin social groups.

Probably the one recent anthropological work that best illustrates the use of the personal as it reveals the society, from the voices of the women themselves, is Friedl's *Women of Deh Koh*.[54] Using stories by Iranian village women, Friedl illuminated childbearing, use of space, barrenness, wealth and poverty, engagement, marriage, marital rifts, rape, and every-day occurrences. In trying not to intrude, either as a facilitator or as an anthropologist, Friedl, though departing from conventional ethnographic forms, still did not resort to the usual ethnographic practice of fictionaliz-ing. What emerged were seamless portraits of women coping with the material and social conditions of their lives. Women in Deh Koh show defiance, resistance, and well-honed negotiating skills.

Feminist oral history, sociology, and autobiography characterize Middle East women's studies in the late 1980s and 1990s. One of the most striking works is a rare, nonsensational, and uplifting look at the life of a Berber woman; another the capturing of the memoirs of "an Arabian princess from Zanzibar."[55] Many others have emerged, making Middle Eastern women's studies one of the more active in the field of feminist oral history.

The new ethnographies, oral histories, and autobiographies are not only giving us testimony of women's everyday lives, but can be useful in ana-lyzing different concepts of household management, varied mechanisms and strategies for negotiating ideologies, complex individual responses to religion—from everyday observances to ideological thought—gender dynamics as symbolized by seclusion and the veil, ideas about kinship, and information on women's bonding. These works also lead us to new ideas about the political/public roles of Middle Eastern women.

A Feminist Theme: Women as Political Actors

Only men were portrayed as political actors in analyses of political hierarchies and processes, class stratification, and resistance strategies (including participation in social movements). In Middle Eastern studies the situation was exaggerated. Recent research on Middle Eastern women has changed that.

One breakthrough came in 1986, with *MERIP's* special issue on *Women and Politics in the Middle East.*[56] The subject matter pertained to different levels and types of political activity—not just the clichéd "private" domain, with women exerting only informal political power through men. Rather, women are involved in the same kinds of political activity as men and not restricted to informal power gained only through gossip or political songs.[57]

Joseph analyzed the differing ways women have been mobilized in the Middle East and showed how this has been interpreted by women themselves, by men, and by the state. She maintained that "women become a subject of mobilization, targets of political action programs, a mass to be welded into citizens or political followers,"[58] and asked if the nature of women's political participation differs if it is initiated by the state (as in Turkey and Iraq), by nationalist movements (as Peteet presented in her article on Palestinians), by communist parties (my Sudan article), or by spontaneous revolt (as in Tucker's Egyptian study or Hegland's study of Iran). My article, "Wing of the Patriarch," explored the potential uses of "traditional" culture to mobilize women against their oppression as women (a theme I further develop in this work).[59] These studies examined the relationships of feminism, nationalism, socialism, and the state.

The literature now includes studies of the individual woman not only as political actor, but as *leader* or *hero*. In analyzing the relationship between feminist movements and social transformation, Nelson drew a portrait of Egyptian feminist Doria Shafik, an activist who from 1945–57 worked for the full political rights of women.[60] Shafik founded the first post-World War II feminist journal published in Arabic, *Bint el-Nil* ("Daughter of the Nile"), and later formed a political party under the same name. In 1948 she organized a demonstration to seize Parliament by women![61] She campaigned all her life, organizing others and also engaging in individual acts of defiance and resistance. Prior to Nelson's work, Shafik's activism—like most of Egyptian women's feminist political activism in the decades between Huda Shaarawi and Nawal el-Saadawi—was virtually unknown to Egyptians and to the international public.[62]

An article by el-Messiri contained a startling sliver of data on woman-as-leader. She analyzed the role of the *futuwwa* (pl. *futuwwat*), a word that denotes a strong, bold *man*, but also carries the connotation of a religious or outlaw orientation. She said, "By definition the *futuwwat* are young men, yet among them were several *futuwwa* women, such as ... 'Aziza al-Fahla of al-Migharbilin."[63] These futuwwat were neighborhood heroes; as bosses or protectors they were expected by Caireens to exemplify size, strength, and hardiness. These qualities are reflected in the nicknames of some of the better-known futuwwat such as *al-fahl al-kabir* (the big animal), *zalat* (the stone), *al-husan* (the horse). El-Messiri reproduced a description of 'Aziza al-Fahla from the memoirs of 'Mahmud al-Miligi:

> I saw 'Aziza al-Fahla who was at the top of all the *futuwwat* of al-Migharbilin. A giant lady who possessed extraordinary strength. Around her arms were tons of gold (i.e. bracelets). One blow from her hand was enough to knock any man to the ground. A blow with her head would split a stone. She was married to a man called *al-fahl al-kabir*, the big animal. He used to support his wife in any quarrel, but this was rare because 'Aziza was always capable of gaining victory alone. By becoming one of 'Aziza's follower [*sic*], I learned my first lesson in *fatwana* (i.e. the brave deeds of the *futuwwat*).[64]

One of the most impressive anthropological works that portrayed woman-as-political-actor, even hero, and one of the most influential on my approach here, is Peteet's ethnography of Palestinian women in Lebanon during the resistance (1968–82).[65] She focused on the (national) culture of resistance, that is, struggle-as-culture. Her aim was to study both "ordinary" and politically active women of the Shatila refugee camp: the growth of their political and feminist consciousnesses, their processes of mobilization into organizations, the specific work they perform, and the implications of this political activism for concepts of gender and gender relations.

Peteet begins with an overview of pre-1948 Palestine, but the heart of the work covers the experience of exile in Lebanon, and she presents a description of the early women's movement and its relationship to the national movement. Important to the present study are the two chapters in which Peteet examines various forms of consciousness (class, national, and feminist), their transformation through crises, and the mobilization of women in the process.[66]

Peteet's theory interrelates political economy, practice, and cultural ideologies. Her methods include participant observation, collection of life histories, and in-depth interviews. The authentic tone emanates partially from what she describes as an "ethnographic encounter" in which empathy with the "other" is heightened under danger. She skillfully interweaves historical narration, cultural description, and portraits of daily lives, using testimonies of the women themselves.

Palestinian studies present us with theoretical and methodological challenges. For example, it is difficult to analyze a culture that is geographically fragmented and under military threat. Peteet's study also underscores the complexity of a pariah culture's presentation of itself: that is, the process of objectifying one's own culture as political agenda, as well as the dialectic of wanting people to know the agenda, while fearing that the knowledge may be used against you. In fact, similar to my own reservations in the first chapter are Peteet's self-criticisms about doing research in the midst of a culture that has been both denied and expropriated (18).

While making women central, Peteet nonetheless was skilled at integrating genders within the broader context. Like many feminist works, including my own here, there is a tension between outlining the suffering ("victimization") of women, and facilitating their emergence in print as strong, surviving, and indispensable actors. An integrated study of class and culture, Peteet's ethnography of Palestinian women remains one of the few works of Middle Eastern women's studies that does not center religion (namely, Islam) as the determinant of the entire culture, as puppeteer of women's behavior.

Peteet addresses many significant questions of gender and social change. For example, she demonstrates that militancy often has an uneven impact on women's status and that, with the decline of traditional mechanisms of control (e.g., segregation), new ones (e.g., ridicule) may emerge to maintain or reproduce domination (156).

Peteet's greatest contribution to the literature on social change—and to my own work—is her delineation of different forms of women's political consciousness. Drawing on the ideas of historian Temma Kaplan, Peteet differentiates female and feminist consciousnesses. Kaplan, in such work as her case study of female collective action in Barcelona, developed a theory of women's agency in social movements:[67]

> Female consciousness, recognition of what a particular class, culture, and historical period expect from women, creates a sense of rights and obligations that provide motive force for actions different from those Marxist and feminist theory generally try to explain. ... Those with female consciousness accept the gender system of their society.[68]

By contrasting female and feminist consciousnesses, one can avoid the imposition of a feminist model, while drawing distinctions in forms of consciousness.

Since the Iranian revolution in the late 1970s, feminist writers have had to contend with a need to sharpen our analyses to account for "cultural reassertions" and identity politics in feminist form. Recent political phenomena have frequently turned conventional categories of revolutionary and conservative on their heads, not to mention confounded conventional Western definitions of feminism and provoked reappraisals of the relationships between socialism/communism, nationalism, and Islamism, very much the heart of this work. Moghadam is among the scholars asserting that class is being analytically occluded by "culture," and that there is a necessity to keep our analyses within the framework of international capitalism.[69]

The Challenges of the New Ethnography

It is very difficult to deal with subject matter related to Islam, sexuality, seclusion, veiling, and concepts of honor and shame without committing the sins of our fathers and mothers. The reintroduction of oral tradition avoids most of the usual pitfalls. This type of research is not only a viable means of literary expression, but is also an ethnographic method for exploring gender relations.[70] In Abu-Lughod's *Veiled Sentiments*, based on two years of living with Awlad 'Ali Bedouin women of Egypt, she suggests ways of looking at the veil and seclusion with heightened sensitivity.[71] "For the Awlad 'Ali Bedouins, the bonds of womanhood that integrate the world of women have much to do with shared suffering and longing for [men]."[72] Although the women are segregated from the men and oriented toward other women, they develop deep affective bonds with men, revealed primarily through the women's love poems. Thus, shunning the usual simplistic binary construct of segregated men and women, Abu-Lughod presents a more gender integrative study, one that includes views by women about men.[73]

Taking the same tack on the honor and shame dichotomy, Abu-Lughod offers an explanation of *hasham* (propriety):

> Those who are coerced into obeying [social rules] are scorned, but those who voluntarily defer are honorable. To understand the nature, meaning, and implications of voluntary deference we must explore the concept of *hasham*. Perhaps one of the most complex concepts in Bedouin culture, it lies at the heart of ideas of the individual in society. ... In its broadest sense it means propriety.[74]

Her decoding of hasham leads Abu-Lughod to a sophisticated explanation for veiling:

> The best test of the validity of this interpretation of *hasham*—that denial of sexuality is equated with deference—is its power to explain the pattern of women's veiling. Bedouins consider veiling synonymous with *hasham*. ... Symbolizing sexual shame as it hides it, veiling constitutes the most visible act of modest deference.[75]

As mentioned above, veiling is usually interpreted as a symbol of women's subordination—a view that runs contrary to some recent and respected works, such as Abu-Lughod's. The veil can be seen simply as (and is often considered by most Middle Eastern women to be) a statement about modest deference, which men may display as well. Or it may be seen as a mode of communication that, e.g., the woman is beautiful, modest, and honorable. It is also a major visible symbol of marital status in many areas (e.g., Oman).[76] Abu-Lughod's research in a highly segregated society allows us to reconsider ideas about seclusion (whether there are positive aspects), the subordination of women (whether that may not be the woman's self-image), female associations and bonding (whether these give them strength and raise self-esteem), and gender relationships in a Middle Eastern context (whether these can be expressed passionately). Abu-Lughod not only explodes misconceptions about male/female relationships in the Egyptian Bedouin context, her work puts the honor/shame dichotomy within a cultural relativist framework.

In her second "ethnography," *Writing Women's Worlds: Bedouin Stories*, Abu-Lughod offers us research that, while working against itself as ethnography, reinvents itself in the process. An experimental ethnography emerges: open, dynamic and contradictory.[77] For Abu-Lughod, a self-described "halfie" (Arab/American), "[P]ositionality cannot be escaped" (36); nor can the power of anthropological language, emerging as it did from colonialism (8). "The world from which I write still has tremendous discursive, military, and economic power. My writing can either sustain it or work against its grain" (36).

Abu-Lughod tries to work against the grain of the bread-and-butter concepts of anthropology/ethnography—namely, *culture* and *difference* (as in *cultural differences* and *a different voice*)—as well as against certain aspects of Euroamerican feminism and its assumptions that Western academic interpretations and analyses are superior to other kinds of cognition. For example, as chapter headings for Bedouin women's (and men's) storytelling, she uses concepts emanating from Orientalism and academic feminism ("patrilineality," "polygyny," "honor and shame"), only to undermine them in the stories that follow. As for Islam, which Western readers expect to loom large as a determining element in Bedouin women's lives, Abu-Lughod makes clear that it is only one aspect of experience (23).

Abu-Lughod presents some of the methodological dilemmas within the new critical ethnography and feminism. Acknowledging the limitations of the standard anthropological monograph, she wonders if there were some style of ethnographic writing that might "better capture the qualities of 'life as lived' in this community" (2). She had decided to write an ethnography "in a different voice" (echoing Carol Gilligan).[78] Not only would the ethnography be written in the voice of Bedouin women, "more important, it would be in the voice of a woman ethnographer."[79] But she soon challenged even that approach:

> First came a discomfort with the notion of a specifically female voice. ... [The process] foundered on false essentialism and culture blindness. Feminist anthropologists had done too much excellent work on the variety of women's experiences and the variability of gender systems for anyone to imagine that there might be some universal "woman's experience" or "woman's style" (3–4).

Abu-Lughod then aspired to writing a "feminist ethnography"; but "if feminism ... implied some sort of emancipatory project applied to the subjects of the ethnography, it would not fit [the Bedouin]" (4). As in many Third World societies, both women and men see themselves locked into a shared struggle for survival, and occupy a subject position far less powerful than that of the (usually) Western feminist anthropologist.

Therefore, using the postmodernist ideas and methods (e.g., "the situatedness of all knowledge")[80] of such scholars as Aihwa Ong, Marnia Lazreg, Chandra Mohanty, Gayatri Spivak, and Donna Haraway, Abu-

Lughod settled for writing an ethnography aimed at the world of feminist scholarship, her audience (6).

In the section "Writing against Culture," a critique of ethnography and representation, Abu-Lughod describes how ethnographic generalization has invented "otherness" and "difference." She writes:

> What became for me the most troubling aspect of ethnographic description was that it, like other social scientific discourses, trafficked in generalizations ... our goal as anthropologists is usually to use details and the particulars of individual lives to produce typifications. The drawback ... is that generalization can make these "others" seem simultaneously more coherent, self-contained, and different from ourselves than they might be ... This in turn allows for the fixing of boundaries between self and other (7).

Whereas we in the West have *families* and *ethnicity*, we anthropologists have created *tribes*, *clans*, and *kinship* for the *Native*. We have, in fact, created cultures. Our "good works," with our anthropological language of power, have succeeded in essentializing, homogenizing, and fixing people in time, with the ultimate effect of exaggerating our differences (7–9). "Others" are different from the self, and the self is privileged (13).

Abu-Lughod's general goal is to unsettle the culture concept and, thus, subvert othering. Nowhere is this agenda more warranted than in Middle Eastern women's studies—the cradle of feminist and anthropological exotica. Abu-Lughod argues that Bedouin women, central in *Writing Women's Worlds*, are the narrators of their own lives; they are not the subjects or objects of ideas projected by the ethnographer's imagination. Abu-Lughod uses humanist strategies in an antihumanist era. She uses a narrative form, focusing on one or two people in each story, neither erasing herself nor making herself an intrusive character. (I have tried to strike this balance as well.)

Women and men talk about their lives, composed as memories of significant events. They relay these not in the (self-centered-narrative) way a Westerner would, but through folktales, narratives, songs, and poetry. The stories are not supposed to represent to the Western feminist/anthropologist/Middle Easternist reader anything that typifies "the culture." In fact, not only do the chapters on patrilineality and polygyny subvert our acceptance of the universal preference for and unchanging dominant position of boys and men, the narrators in each section express much ambivalence and individuality, and offer different interpretations of crucial questions.

Abu-Lughod did not have to tell us that Bedouin ideas and behavior are very complex; she simply quoted her hosts in their expressions of complicated beliefs about such topics as pregnancy and birthing, and procedures used in these. There is no official answer; the women debate each other about beliefs and procedures (133–38).

For all of her effort, however, to decolonize a people in writing and to subvert the usual preconceived ideas the Western reader brings to studies of Arabs and Muslim women, there is much in this work that remains anthropological and colonial—due partly to that power of Western language to name, frame, and transfix. There is also the problem of political decontextualization, thus carrying the culturally specific too far. Abu-Lughod did acknowledge the "basic configuration of global power on which anthropology is based" (26), but in her work and in that of most experimental ethnographers, there is no analysis of the West's and capitalism's impact on the Bedouins. Although it is, indeed, refreshing to move away from a familiar portrait of victimization so prevalent in the metanarratives of Marxism and feminism, the forced resettlement and partial absorption into a market economy experienced by the Bedouin have appreciably altered their economy and class structure. Not dealing with world capitalism's effect on a former pastoral, nomadic people runs the risk of our seeing them as isolated, outside of history and culture, and, ultimately romantic.

Sudanese Women's Studies

The cliché of Sudan's "splendid isolation" has often been evoked to express the process whereby Sudan is excluded from both Middle Eastern and African scholarship and politics. Certainly, until the 1980s, exclusion was the key word in describing Sudanese women's studies, especially *northern* Sudanese.

To digress for a moment, one should add that this exclusion of *northern* Sudanese women's studies, in anthropology, is an extension of the slower development of the anthropology of the north in general. British colonial anthropologists found southern Sudan far more interesting (read, "primitive"). Besides, because the south was administered more directly than the north, the people were more accessible as objects of study.[81] As a consequence, the literature on the south was among the most distinguished in British social anthropology.[82] It was not until the 1960s that Ian Cunnison's work on a group of northern Arab nomads was published, and a bit later, Talal Asad's study of the Kababish Arabs.[83] These works had little to do with women.

Such exclusion has been a mixed blessing. One can take the position that Sudanese women—both in the north and south—have been spared the kind of objectification that characterized some early anthropology. Also, for the most part, with the exception of a very few scattered articles, northern women were spared "Orientalist" descriptions.[84] Conversely, the body of literature on gender in the Middle East, and on gender in general, has suffered as a consequence of the exclusion of northern Sudanese women.

More recently, however, for geopolitical and epistemological reasons (including a spillover from the crowded field of "Third World" and women's studies) Sudan has been seen as a very important area of new scholarship to Africanists and Middle Easternists. At the same time that the field of Sudan studies is growing, there is an expanding interest in Middle Eastern and Muslim women and in Islam, as evidenced by the above discussion. It was perhaps inevitable that Sudanese women's studies would also attract greater attention. A new generation of "government anthropologists," using the phrase generically, was one of the noticeable consequences. External influences on Sudan have grown appreciably in the last two decades, culminating in the late 1980s with scores of governmental and nongovernmental agencies establishing bases there.

Above and beyond the proliferation of interest in Sudanese women is the potential for fresh interpretations to emerge from Sudanese women's studies. Moreover, indigenous researchers, many of them social anthropologists, have now begun to undertake some of the most useful research being done on northern Sudanese women.[85]

Besides anthropologists, there are many other Sudanese academics, medical doctors, lawyers, and journalists writing about gender issues.[86] Two of the most influential are Fatma Babiker Mahmoud, a political scientist, and Dina Shiekh el-Din Osman, a legal scholar.[87] One of the better and more original popular treatments is *Sisters under the Sun*, Bakhita Amin Ismail's collaboration with Marjorie Hall.[88] Although not entirely about northern Sudan, its focus is strongly northern and urban. Recently, Susan Kenyon collected summary articles based on Sudanese theses and dissertations housed in the Graduate College, University of Khartoum. The anthology, *The Sudanese Woman*, the first of its kind published in Sudan, is skewed toward the north.[89] Mahasin Khider el-Sayed's work represents an important new field for Sudanese women writing on gender in the north: rural economics.[90]

A number of non-Sudanese feminist and Marxist scholars, among them Diana Baxter, Victoria Bernal, Janice Boddy, Carolyn Fluehr-Lobban, Ellen Gruenbaum, and Lidwien Kapteijns, are now working in areas of the north.[91]

There is one major work within northern Sudanese women's studies that I consider an example of the New Ethnography: Janice Boddy's *Wombs and Alien Spirits*, a study of women's culture in a northern village.[92] Although her work is highly abstract and theoretical (falling loosely into postmodernism), it never loses sight of women's everyday experiences and their expressions of their own lives. It is perhaps the richest piece on Sudanese women yet written. She deconstructs the language of the zar and maintains:

> When read, in part, as allegory, ethnographies contain a wealth of potential messages about the culture they silently imply: some critical, others clearly supportive. Their power, like that of other allegorical genres, lies in their capacity to contextualize the world from which they spring. ... Whatever else ethnography is and has been, perhaps it, like the *zar*, is a form of subordinate discourse whose elusive, yet allusive "said" confers the possibility of expanded consciousness, even therapeutic realignment (359–60).

Boddy's poetic study of the subaltern interweaves descriptions of everyday life and the metaphoric variations on its themes. Using ideas of Raymond Williams, Antonio Gramsci, and Fred Halliday, she refers to the zar as an "antisociety" with an "antilanguage." The antisociety is counterhegemonic in that it is an alternative view of the world held by the subordinate group in response to an elite's discourse of domination. In the village of Boddy's research the ideology of Islam legally and materially privileges men. "The subaltern group which constitutes an antisociety is nonetheless constrained by the system of meanings it shares with society at large; yet it is concerned to articulate those meanings from its own, unprivileged, perspective" (157).

Boddy's deconstruction of an institution of women's culture, the zar, is important to my own analysis, as is her stimulating material on "creating female persons." In the introductory chapter I introduced the theme of shifting essentialisms as part of my analysis of hegemonic men's culture. Boddy's account of the social construction of gender is a departure from most social-constructionist gender studies because she asserts that female circumcision is one of the ways appropriate feminine dispositions are being inculcated in young girls so that they are inscribed "not only physically, but also cognitively and emotionally." However, she argues that the trauma of circumcision is insufficient to shape the feminine self and illuminates how meaning about the self is built through the use of metaphors and associations. Boddy's notion that women are oriented toward their "all important generative and transformative roles" in the village is set in opposition to the fact that in order "to achieve this gender identity, women implicitly repudiate their sexuality" (57).

The feminist research discussed in the previous section is my inheritance, as is the rich literature on Sudan. My research on northern Sudanese women augments, affirms, challenges, and revises many of the above themes. Although I do not pretend to cover all of these themes, my findings nonetheless raise a number of implications for Middle Eastern and women's studies.

Notes

1. The term "Middle East" is itself problematic. Dale Eickelman's concept of the "Middle East" relies on "the presence throughout the area of key cultural symbols and their variants and ... shared historical circumstances [that justify] that this region can ... be considered as a single sociocultural area" (*The Middle East: An Anthropological Approach* [Englewood Cliffs, N.J.: Prentice-Hall, 1981], 4). While remaining critical of the term, Eickelman maintains that it is the best available and that one simply has to acknowledge its limitations and avoid glossing over the extensive differences, variations, and contradictions. Edward Said would have us recognize the Orientalist and Eurocentric aspect of the term. *Orientalism* (New York: Pantheon, 1978).

2. Said, *Orientalism*. I first introduced the ideas for the following section within the framework of a literature review: "The Politics of Gender in the Middle East," in *Gender and Anthropology: Critical Reviews for Research and Teaching*, ed. Sandra Morgen (Washington, D.C.: American Anthropological Association, 1989), 246–67.

3. See, e.g., Leila Ahmed's review of Margot Badran's translation and editing of Huda Shaarawi's *Harem Years: The Memoirs of an Egyptian Feminist (1879–1924)* (New York: Feminist Press, 1987), in "Women of Egypt," *Women's Review of Books* 5, no. 2 (1987): 7–8.

4. Although for heuristic purposes I have been referring to the Middle East as one area, it is important to avoid treating the cultural region as a monolith (see note 1 above). To use Sudan as just one example, there may be as many as 582 ethnic groups and 110 separate languages. (Sudan, Ministry of Social Affairs, *First Population Census of the Sudan, 1955–56* [Khartoum: 1958].) The country is often classified as Arab, but this is really a misnomer; one of the most culturally significant groups in the north, the Nubians, although Muslim, are not Arab. Even using the term "Muslim" can be misleading, as much of the southern Sudan is not Muslim, and there are pockets of Christians in the north and south. As one might imagine, the cultural histories are very complex, especially the Islamic histories and the histories of the Arabization processes. There are also dozens of sects and brotherhoods (*turuq*; singular, *tariqa*), many highly politicized. Such complexity is typical of Middle Eastern countries.

5. E.g., Hildred and Clifford Geertz, Margaret and John Gulick, Elizabeth and Robert Fernea, Mary Hoogland (aka Hegland) and Eric Hoogland, Christine and Dale Eickelman.

6. When I think of Middle Eastern studies as "conservative," my reference point is a field dominated, until recently, by historians of antiquity, ancient-art historians, classical-linguistics/language specialists (especially Arabists), and Islamicists: i.e., the "Orientalists" proper. Studying contemporary society and politics has never been considered the most prestigious academic enterprise.

7. Suad Joseph, "Working Class Women's Networks in a Sectarian State: A Political Paradox," *American Ethnologist* 10, no. 1 (1983): 2.

8. David Waines, "Through a Veil Darkly: The Study of Women in Muslim Societies," *Comparative Studies in Society and History* 24, no. 4 (1982): 643–44.

9. Malek Alloula, *The Colonial Harem* (Minneapolis: University of Minnesota, 1986).

10. Waines, "Through a Veil Darkly," 652.

11. Lois Beck and Nikki Keddie, eds., *Women in the Muslim World* (Cambridge: Harvard University Press, 1978), 27.

12. Although I have followed Abu-Lughod's use of *Bedouin* (capitalized) as an ethnic term, I am uncomfortable with using a term that denotes a way of life (nomadic) as ethnic nomenclature.

13. Lila Abu-Lughod, *Writing Women's Worlds: Bedouin Stories* (Berkeley: University of California Press, 1992), 23.

14. Ibid., 25.

15. A term I first encountered in Reza Hammami and Martina Rieker, "Feminist Orientalism and Orientalist Marxism," *New Left Review* no. 170 (1988): 93–106.

16. Marnia Lazreg, *The Eloquence of Silence: Algerian Women in Question* (New York: Routledge, 1994). Whereas silence is a behavior conventionally associated with oppression, Lazreg describes how Algerian women have used it as a resistance strategy.

17. The tone was set in the 1960s and 1970s by such writers as Germaine Tillion (*The Republic of Cousins: Women's Oppression in Mediterranean Society* [London: Al Saqi Books, 1983]) and Juliette Minces, who commented (*The House of Obedience* [London: Zed, 1980], 86), "Independence [for Algeria] was finally won in July 1962, and the women were sent back to their homes." This image was etched into the minds of Middle Easternist feminists.

18. Sherna Berger Gluck, *An American Feminist in Palestine: The Intifada Years* (Philadelphia: Temple University, 1994), 149.

19. Ibid.

20. In fact, Minces, *The House of Obedience*, 49–54, subtitles her chapter on "Everyday Forms of Oppression": "Two Symbols of Women's Oppression: The Veil ... Circumcision of Women."

21. See Leila Ahmed's discussion of "Western Ethnocentrism and Perceptions of the Harem," *Feminist Studies* 8, no. 3 (1982): 521–34.

22. For a discussion of modesty see Richard Antoun, "On the Modesty of Women in Arab Muslim Villages: A Study in the Accommodation of Traditions," *American Anthropologist* 70, no. 4 (1968): 671–97, and M. Abu Zahra, "On the Modesty of Women in Arab Muslim Villages: A Reply," *American Anthropologist* 72 (1970): 1079–92. See also Valerie Hoffman-Ladd, "Polemics on the Modesty and Segregation of Women in Contemporary Egypt," *International Journal of Middle Eastern Studies* 19, no. 1 (1987): 23–50.

23. See, e.g., Nazirah Zein ed-Din, "Removing the Veil and Veiling" (1928, trans. Salah-Dine Hammoud), in *Women and Islam*, ed. Azizah el-Hibri (New York: Pergamon, 1982), 221–26.

24. Some contemporary examples are Evelyne Accad, *Veil of Shame* (Sherbrooke: Naaman, 1978); Waines, "Through a Veil Darkly"; Amal Rassam, "Unveiling Arab Women," *The Middle East Journal* 36, no. 4 (1982): 583–87; Anne Betteridge, "To Veil or Not to Veil," in *Women and Revolution in Iran*, ed. G. Nashat (Boulder: Westview, 1983); Carla Makhlouf, *Changing Veils* (Austin: University of Texas, 1979); Fatima Mernissi, *Beyond the Veil* (Cambridge: Cambridge University Press, 1975); Unni Wikan, *Behind the Veil in Arabia* (Baltimore: Johns Hopkins University Press, 1982); Mervat Hatem, "Lifting the Veil," *Women's Review of Books* 2, no. 10

(1985): 13–14; Lila Abu-Lughod, *Veiled Sentiments: Honor and Poetry in a Bedouin Society* (Berkeley: University of California Press, 1986); Sherifa Zuhur, *Revealing Reveiling: Islamist Gender Ideology in Contemporary Egypt* (Albany: State University of New York, 1992); Elizabeth Fernea's film, *A Veiled Revolution* (New York: First Run/Icarus Film, 1982); and many others. By suggestion, the title of one of the most famous pieces by a Middle Easternist refers to veiling. See Nawal el-Saadawi, *The Hidden Face of Eve*, trans. Sherif Hetata (London: Zed, 1980). Her works deal with a number of themes I have referred to here as problematic. Saadawi's work deals with female circumcision through the eyes of an indigenous (Muslim) feminist and nationalist. Her first major work on the subject of women was published in Arabic in 1972 in Beirut, after she had been subjected to censorship in Egypt. I was in Cairo just after the book was published and was able to experience the "shock waves" in a society not used to women (or anyone) discussing sexuality so frankly. See her *Woman and Sex* (in Arabic) (Beirut, 1972). Compare it to Abdel Wahab Bouhdiba's *La Sexualité en Islam* (Paris: Presses Universitaires de France, 1975). See Jon Anderson's "Social Structure and the Veil," *Anthropos*, 77 (1982): 397–442, for a fairly typical contemporary treatment of the function of the veil.

25. Waines, "Through a Veil Darkly," 643.

26. This is not to deny that forms of dress, such as veiling, can be used to subordinate women or may symbolize that subordination. There may also be elements of coercion, as in Iran and Saudi Arabia. In these situations and others, veiling may be a statement by men about women, made through mandatory women's dress.

27. Lazreg, *The Eloquence of Silence*.

28. Arlene Elowe MacLeod, *Accommodating Protest: Working Women, the New Veiling, and Change in Cairo* (New York: Columbia University Press, 1991); and Zuhur, *Revealing Reveiling*.

29. See, e.g., Julie M. Peteet, *Gender in Crisis: Women and the Palestinian Resistance Movement* (New York: Columbia University Press, 1991).

30. American legal scholar Isabelle Gunning uses one term and Sudanese medical doctor Nahid Toubia uses another. Gunning, "Arrogant Perception, World-Travelling and Multicultural Feminism: The Case of Female Genital Surgeries," *Columbia Human Rights Law Review* 23, no. 189 (1991–92): 189–248; Toubia, *Female Genital Mutilation: A Call for Global Action* (New York: Women, Ink., 1993).

31. See my "A Question of Subjects: The 'Female Circumcision' Controversy and the Politics of Knowledge," *Ufahamu* 22, no. 3 (1994): 26–35.

32. See el-Saadawi, *The Hidden Face of Eve*. Although these works are variable in their quality, readers interested in female circumcision in Sudan can consult literature by Sudanese doctors and lawyers and North American anthropologists. See, e.g., Nahid Toubia, "The Social and Political Implications of Female Circumcision," in *Women and the Family in the Middle East*, ed. Elizabeth Fernea (Austin: University of Texas, 1985), 148–59; Toubia, *Female Genital Mutilation: A Call for Global Action*; Ellen Gruenbaum, "Reproductive Ritual and Social Reproduction," in *Economy and Class in Sudan*, ed. Norman O'Neill and Jay O'Brien (London: Gower, 1988), 308–25; Asma el-Dareer, *Woman, Why Do You Weep? Circumcision and Its Consequences* (London: Zed, 1982); Rose Hayes, "Female Genital Mutilation, Fertility

Control, Women's Role and the Patrilineage in Modern Sudan," *Ethnologist* 2, no. 4 (1975): 617–33; Janice Boddy, *Wombs and Alien Spirits: Women, Men, and the Zar Cult in Northern Sudan* (Madison: University of Wisconsin Press, 1990); and Asma M. Abdel Haleem, "Claiming Our Bodies and Our Rights: Exploring Female Circumcision as an Act of Violence," in *Freedom from Violence: Women's Strategies Around the World*, ed. Margaret Schuler (New York: United Nations Development Fund for Women, 1992), 141–56.

In reviewing three works for a feminist publication, Mervat Hatem included Ann Cloudsley's study of Sudanese women, *Women of Omdurman: Life, Love and the Cult of Virginity* (London: Ethnographica, 1983; New York: St. Martin's Press, 1985). Hatem referred to this book as a "good example of the 'Objectionable Orientalist' approach which presents Middle Eastern women as an 'alien' and 'exotic' group that is 'separate' and 'different' from the rest of us." "Lifting the Veil," *The Women's Review of Books* 10, no. 2 (1985): 13–14.

33. Ben Barker-Benfield, "Sexual Surgery in Late-Nineteenth-Century America," *International Journal of Health Services* 5, no. 2 (1975): 279. The practice was common in the nineteenth century, and continued on into the twentieth. As late as the 1950s, instances of the operation were reported. I am surprised that Cloudsley, *Women of Omdurman*, a British nurse writing with horror about female circumcision in Sudan, did not seem to know the history of gynecology in her own culture.

34. J.G. Peristiany, ed., *Honour and Shame: The Values of Mediterranean Society* (Chicago: University of Chicago Press, 1966). Obviously, the honor/shame motif is salient in the writings on Mediterranean societies. See, e.g., Jane Schneider, "Of Vigilance and Virgins: Honour, Shame and Access to Resources in the Mediterranean Societies," *Ethnology* 10 (1971): 1–24; and David Gilmore, "Anthropology of the Mediterranean Area," *Annual Review of Anthropology* 11 (1982): 175–205. It is significant, however, that the honor/shame motif disappears from the scene in a relatively new anthology edited by Monique Gadant, *Women of the Mediterranean*, trans. A.M. Berrett (London: Zed, 1986 [1984]).

35. See Forouz Jowkar's lively challenge to conventional "honor/shame" approaches, in "Honor and Shame: A Feminist View from Within," *Feminist Issues* 6, no. 1 (1986): 45–65; and Sally Cole's critique of this dominant paradigm of southern European gender relations, *Women of the Praia: Work and Lives in a Portuguese Coastal Community* (Princeton, New Jersey: Princeton University Press, 1991).

36. Suad Joseph, "Women and Politics in the Middle East" (Introduction), *MERIP Middle East Report* 16, no. 1 (1986): 7.

37. Although there is a dependence here on works in English, it goes without saying that there are a number of works on Middle Eastern women in French and Arabic. Some of the major ones, e.g., el-Saadawi, *The Hidden Face of Eve*, and Tillion, *The Republic of Cousins*, have been translated. Works on Sudanese women are still mainly in English, with a few in Arabic.

38. By the 1980s anthropologists had begun to assert themselves in a field that had traditionally been dominated by the ancient historians, classicists, and "Orientalists." I am using the term "new ethnography" as my own term to refer to a renewed emphasis on description and on culture-specific studies. I acknowledge that the term is also used, e.g., by G. Marcus and M. Fischer, *Anthropology as Cul-*

tural Critique: An Experimental Moment in the Social Sciences (Chicago: University of Chicago Press, 1986), to refer to postmodernist anthropology. These authors are referring to a new reflexive ethnography and also to new types of experimental ethnographic writing. I have subsumed critical ethnography under the "new ethnography." With the work of Janice Boddy, discussed below, these two uses intersect.

39. The first anthology in English, of Middle Eastern women writing about their lives, *Middle Eastern Muslim Women Speak* (Austin: University of Texas, 1977), was edited by American and Middle Eastern feminists Elizabeth Fernea and Basima Qattan Bezirgan, respectively. See also Beck and Keddie, *Women in the Muslim World*; and Margot Badran and Miriam Cooke, eds., *Opening the Gates: A Century of Arab Feminist Writing* (Bloomington: Indiana University Press, 1990). In 1985 *Women and the Family in the Middle East: New Voices of Change,* ed. Elizabeth Fernea (Austin: University of Texas, 1985), was the first American-published anthology to include a contribution by a Sudanese woman (Nahid Toubia).

New collections have emerged in the 1990s in which Middle Eastern women are among the primary contributors. To name just a few: Nikki Keddie and Beth Baron, eds., *Women in Middle Eastern History: Shifting Boundaries in Sex and Gender* (New Haven: Yale University Press, 1991); Judith Tucker, ed., *Arab Women: Old Boundaries, New Frontiers* (Bloomington: Indiana University, 1993); Deniz Kandiyoti, ed., *Women, Islam and the State* (Philadelphia: Temple University Press, 1991); and Valentine Moghadam, ed., *Gender and National Identity: Women and Politics in Muslim Societies* (London: Zed, 1994).

40. Nahid Toubia, ed., *Women of the Arab World: The Coming Challenge* (London: Zed Press, 1988). There is one male contributor.

41. Ibid., xii.

42. Ibid., 37. Consonant with these thoughts is Hisham Sharabi's *Neopatriarchy: A Theory of Distorted Change in Arab Society* (New York: Oxford University Press, 1988).

43. E.g., Fernea, *Women and the Family;* Unni Wikan, *Life among the Poor in Cairo,* trans. Ann Henning (London: Tavistock, 1980 [in Norwegian, 1976]).

44. E.g., in *Women and Islam,* ed. Azizah el-Hibri (Oxford: Pergamon Press, 1982).

45. Some examples are el-Saadawi, *The Hidden Face of Eve;* Tillion, *The Republic of Cousins;* Amal Rassam, "Towards a Theoretical Framework for the Study of Women in the Arab World," Cultures 8, no. 3 (1982): 121–37, and "Unveiling Arab Women," *The Middle East Journal* 36, no. 4 (1982): 583–87; Juliette Minces, "Women in Algeria," in Beck and Keddie, *Women in the Muslim World,* 159–71, and Minces, *The House of Obedience;* Fatna Sabbah [pseud.], *Woman in the Muslim Unconscious* (New York: Pergamon Press, 1984); and some of my own earlier work, e.g., "Women and Work in Sudan: What Is Alienated Labor?" Proceedings, *Conference on Women and Work in the Third World* (Berkeley: Center for the Study, Education and Advancement of Women, University of California, 1983), 245–50; "The Wing of the Patriarch: Sudanese Women and Revolutionary Parties," *MERIP Middle East Report* 16, no. 1 (1986): 25–30; and "Transforming Culture or Fostering Second-Hand Consciousness? Women's Front Organizations and Revolutionary Parties—

the Sudan Case," in *Women and Arab Society: Old Boundaries, New Frontiers,* ed. Judith Tucker (Bloomington: Indiana University Press, 1993). To a great extent, this last essay and the present work represent my movement away from the universalistic subordination theme.

46. Fatima Mernissi, *The Veil and the Male Elite: A Feminist Interpretation of Women's Rights in Islam* (Reading: Addison-Wesley, 1991 [1987]).

47. Fatna Sabbah, *Woman in the Muslim Unconscious,* 3.

48. Ibid. A later and arguably even more sophisticated work in this genre of using early Arabic texts to translate contemporary women is Fedwa Malti-Douglas, *Woman's Body, Woman's World: Gender and Discourse in Arabo-Islamic Writing* (Princeton: Princeton University Press, 1991). In it she argues that women in the classical period often spoke through the body, whereas contemporary Arabo-Islamic women's writing turns corporeality into a literary weapon to assert power over discourse.

49. Leila Ahmed, *Women and Gender in Islam* (New Haven: Yale University Press, 1992).

50. See note 38 above.

51. Soha Abdel Kader, "A Survey of Trends in Social Sciences Research on Women in the Arab Region, 1960–1980," in *Social Science Research and Women in the Arab World* (London: UNESCO, 1984), 160.

52. E.g., Carla Makhlouf, *Changing Veils: Women and Modernization in North Yemen* (Austin: University of Texas Press, 1979); Wikan, *Behind the Veil*; Abu-Lughod, *Veiled Sentiments*; Soraya Altorki, *Women in Saudi Arabia: Ideology and Behavior among the Elite* (New York: Columbia University Press, 1986); and Susan Dorsky, *Women of 'Amran: A Middle Eastern Ethnographic Study* (Salt Lake City: University of Utah, 1986).

53. In Mahklouf's case, however, it is from a male poet's point of view. Makhlouf, *Changing Veils*.

54. Erika Friedl, *Women of Deh Koh: Lives in an Iranian Village* (Washington, D.C.: Smithsonian Institution Press, 1989).

55. Fadhma Amrouche, *My Life Story: The Autobiography of a Berber Woman,* trans. Dorothy S. Blair (New Brunswick: Rutgers University Press, 1988 [1968 in French]; and Emily Ruete, *Memoirs of an Arabian Princess from Zanzibar* (New York: Markus Wiener, 1989). Amrouche, mother of French cultural figures Jean Amrouche and Marguerite Taos, was a Christian Kabyle poet and singer who lived from 1882–1967. Her stunning autobiography is a clear picture of life as a religiously and ethnically marginalized North African woman.

56. *MERIP Middle East Report* 16, no. 1 (1986). Suad Joseph introduced the issue with an overview on "Women and Politics in the Middle East." Historian Judith Tucker examined the interesting case of "Insurrectionary Women: Women and the State in 19th Century Egypt." Three anthropologists documented the political roles and participation of Iranian (Hegland), Palestinian (Peteet), and Sudanese women (Hale).

57. Although Mary Hegland does refer to the fact that "the roles of Aliabad [Iran] women in community politics retained their indirect, protected, supportive and secondary character even after their participation in the revolution," her anal-

ysis puts women squarely in the political realm. "The Political Roles of Iranian Village Women," *MERIP Middle East Report* 16, no. 1 (1986), 46.

58. Ibid., 3–4.

59. An article by Rokhsareh S. Shoaee, a professor at the Free University of Iran, dispelled any notion we might have had that Muslim women are passive in national politics. Her study of Iranian women supporters of the Mujahidin-e Khalq is a direct challenge to the notion that Islam, women, and national political activity are incompatible elements. "The Mujahid Women of Iran: Reconciling 'Culture' and 'Gender,'" *The Middle East Journal* 41, no. 4 (1987): 519–37.

60. Cynthia Nelson, "The Voices of Doria Shafik: Feminist Consciousness in Egypt, 1940–1960," *Feminist Issues* 6, no. 2 (1986): 16.

61. Ibid., 22.

62. Historian Margot Badran has translated and introduced Huda Shaarawi's memoirs, *Harem Years: The Memoirs of an Egyptian Feminist* (New York: Feminist Press, 1987). Shaarawi is often referred to as Egypt's first feminist activist. El-Saadawi is an activist doctor and writer.

63. Sawsan el-Messiri, "The Changing Role of the Futuwwa in the Social Structure of Cairo," in *Patrons and Clients*, ed. Ernest Gellner and John Waterbury (London: Duckworth, 1977), 237.

64. Ibid., 243.

65. Peteet, *Gender in Crisis*.

66. Peteet describes women's management of "the opposition generated by their open challenge to normative traditions of gender." Ibid., 8.

67. Temma Kaplan, "Female Consciousness and Collective Action: The Case of Barcelona, 1910–1918," in *Feminist Theory: A Critique of Ideology*, ed. Nannerl O. Keohane, Michelle Z. Rosaldo, and Barbara C. Gelpi (Chicago: University of Chicago Press, 1981), 55–76.

68. Ibid., 55.

69. See, e.g., Valentine Moghadam, *Modernizing Women: Gender and Social Change in the Middle East* (Boulder: Lynne Rienner Publishers, 1993); Moghadam, ed., *Gender and National Identity: Women and Politics in Muslim Societies* (London: Zed, 1994); and Moghadam, ed., *Identity Politics and Women: Cultural Reassertions and Feminisms in International Perspective* (Boulder: Westview, 1994).

70. See Lila Abu-Lughod, *Veiled Sentiments*. In his *Daughters of Yemen* (Berkeley: University of California, 1985), Mishael Maswari Caspi translated the poetry of Yemenite Jews, revealing many of the same modes of expression and ideas as the Abu-Lughod work.

71. Lila Abu-Lughod, "A Community of Secrets: The Separate World of Bedouin Women," *Signs* 10, no. 4 (1985): 637–57; and *Veiled Sentiments*.

72. Abu-Lughod, "A Community of Secrets," 657.

73. Using fiction, Elizabeth Fernea did the same in *Guests of the Sheik: An Ethnography of an Iraqi Village* (New York: Doubleday, 1969); Friedl, *Women of Deh Koh*, did the same, using women's stories.

74. Abu-Lughod, *Veiled Sentiments*, 105.

75. Ibid., 159.

76. From Omani material we can learn that "the *burqa* [veil] beautifies in a spiritual sense." The woman becomes beautiful because the burqa is beautiful, a trea-

sured ornament. A woman's beauty is enhanced all the more by wearing it. Wikan, *Behind the Veil*, 101.

77. Abu-Lughod, *Writing Women's Worlds*.

78. Carol Gilligan, *In a Different Voice: Psychological Theory and Women's Development* (Cambridge: Harvard University Press, 1982).

79. Abu-Lughod, *Writing Women's Worlds*, 3.

80. This term is from Donna Haraway, "Situated Knowledges: The Science Questions in Feminism and the Privilege of Partial Perspective," *Feminist Studies* 14 (1988): 575–99.

81. For a discussion of some of these points and for a general idea of the relationship between colonialism and anthropology in Sudan, see discussions by Wendy James, "The Anthropologist as Reluctant Imperialist," and Abdel Ghaffar M. Ahmed, "Some Remarks from the Third World on Anthropology and Colonialism: the Sudan," in *Anthropology and the Colonial Encounter*, ed. Talal Asad (London: Ithaca Press, 1973).

82. E.g., E.E. Evans-Pritchard, Godfrey Lienhardt, and S.F. Nadel all did their major work in southern Sudan.

83. Ian Cunnison, *Baggara Arabs: Power and the Lineage in a Sudanese Nomad Tribe* (Oxford: Clarendon Press, 1966); Talal Asad, *The Kababish Arabs: Power, Authority, and Consent in a Nomadic Tribe* (New York: Praeger, 1970).

84. Examples that come immediately to mind span four decades: e.g., Sophie Zenkovsky's two-part "Marriage Customs in Omdurman," *Sudan Notes and Records* 26, no. 2 (1945): 241–55, and 30, no. 1 (1949), 39–46; or Cloudsley, *Women of Omdurman*. Both works dwell on exotic descriptions and, especially in the latter, exploit the women who are their subjects.

85. Fawzia Hammour has written a who's who of Sudanese women's studies, "Sudanese Professional Women Series: Who—Is—Who in Women Studies" (paper presented at the Workshop on Women's Studies in Sudan, National Council for Research, Sudan Family Planning Association, Khartoum, 7–9 February 1989). There are some fine Sudanese anthropologists and sociologists working in women's studies now. Zeinab el-Bakri was publishing for some time at the Hague in the Netherlands through ISIS (e.g., "On the Crisis of the Sudanese Women's Movement," forthcoming), and has produced a monograph with el-Wathig Kamier (aka Kameir), Idris Salim el-Hassan, and Samya el-Nagar, *The State of Women Studies in the Sudan.* (Khartoum: Development Studies and Research Centre, Faculty of Economic and Social Studies, University of Khartoum, 1985); also with Kameir, "Women and Development Policies in Sudan: A Critical Outlook" (paper no. 46, presented at the 2d OSSREA Congress, Nairobi, 28–31 July 1986); and with el-Haj Hamad M. Khier, "Sudanese Women in History and Historiography: A Proposed Strategy for Curriculum Change" (paper presented at the Workshop on Women's Studies in Sudan, National Council for Research, Sudan Family Planning Association, Khartoum, 7–9 February 1989). Samia el-Nagar is working on a monograph based on her Ph.D. dissertation, "Patterns of Women [*sic*] Participation in the Labour Force in Khartoum" (University of Khartoum, 1985), and has published a number of articles in Sudan, e.g., "Women and Spirit Possession in Omdurman," in *The Sudanese Woman*, ed. Susan Kenyon (Graduate College Publications No. 19, University of Khartoum, Khartoum, 1987), 92–115. Balghis Yousif

Badri (aka Belgis Y. Bedri) has published in *The Ahfad Journal: Women and Change* (Omdurman, Sudan); also "Food and Differential Roles in the Fetiehab Household," in Kenyon, *The Sudanese Women*, 67–91; and elsewhere. Asha Mustafa, working in the Wad Medani area, has written "Role of Women in the Traditional Food Systems of Drought-Affected Environments—A Study of Kordofan Region—Sudan," *Research Report* (Khartoum: Women in Development Programme, Development Studies and Research Centre, University of Khartoum, [1985–88?]). These anthropologists also participate in various government conferences, e.g., Samira Amin Ahmed, Inaam A. Elmahdi, Belgis Y. Bedri, Samya el-Hadi el-Nagar, and Amna Badri, "Population Problems, Status of Women and Development" (paper presented at the Third National Population Conference, University of Khartoum, Khartoum, 10–14 October 1987).

86. See, e.g., (Dr.) Nahid Toubia, "Female Circumcision"; *Female Genital Mutilation*; Toubia, *Women of the Arab World*; and Toubia, ed., with Amira Bahyeldin, Nadia Hijab, and Heba Abdel Latif, *Arab Women: A Profile of Diversity and Change* (New York: Population Council, 1994); see also (Dr.) Asma el-Dareer, *Woman, Why Do You Weep?*; and Abdel Haleem, "Claiming Our Bodies."

87. Although Mahmoud's best-known published work, *The Sudanese Bourgeoisie: Vanguard of Development?* (London: Zed, 1984), is definitely not about gender, she did an early study, "The Role of the Sudanese Women's Union in Sudanese Politics" (M.A. thesis, University of Khartoum, 1971), that has served as a foundation for many of us working on the Sudanese women's movement. Lately she has been writing on women again. See, e.g., "Capitalism, Racism, Patriarchy and the Woman Question," *Africa's Crisis* (London: Institute for African Alternatives, 1987), 79–86; and "The Role of Alienation and Exploitation of Women in the Origins of State and Capitalism in the Sudan," in Toubia, *Women of the Arab World*, 139–47. See also Dina Shiekh el-Din Osman, "The Legal Status of Muslim Women in the Sudan," *Journal of Eastern African Research and Development* 15 (1985): 124–42.

88. Marjorie Hall and Bakhita Amin Ismail, *Sisters under the Sun: The Story of Sudanese Women* (Essex: Longman Group, 1981), 264.

89. Kenyon, *Sudanese Women*.

90. See "Women in Sudanese Agriculture," ibid., 116–33. She uses as her starting point the fact that 87% of Sudan's female labor force is in agriculture (117–18) and focuses on the north where so much of that agriculture is done. Other agricultural and rural economists are represented in Diana Baxter, ed., *Women and the Environment in the Sudan* (Environmental Research Paper Series No. 2, Institute of Environmental Studies, University of Khartoum, Khartoum, 1981), 142, appendix; and in Food and Agricultural Organization of the United Nations, *National Conference on the Role of Women in Agriculture and Rural Development in the Sudan, Interim Report* (Shambat, Khartoum North: Khartoum Polyechnic and FAO-Project GCP/SUD/030 (FIN), 18–22 January 1987), 142.

91. Examples of their work are Baxter, *Women and the Environment*; Bernal, "Losing Ground—Women and Agriculture on Sudan's Irrigated Schemes: Lessons from a Blue Nile Village," in *Agriculture, Women, and Land: The African Experience* (Boulder: Westview, 1988), 131–56; Boddy, *Wombs and Alien Spirits*; Carolyn Fluehr-Lobban, *Islamic Law and Society in the Sudan* (London: Frank Cass, 1987), 320; and

many others that deal more directly with women; Gruenbaum, "Reproductive Ritual"; and Lidwien Kapteijns, e.g., "Islamic Rationales for the Changing Social Roles of Women in the Western Sudan," in *Modernization in the Sudan: Essays in Honor of Richard Hill*, ed. M.W. Daly (New York: Lillian Barber Press, 1985), 57–72.

92. Boddy, *Wombs and Alien Spirits*.

PART TWO

Background to Sudan and Sudanese Women

3

History and Political Economy: Gender, Ethnicity, Religion, and the State

Situating the Study

Sudan is a one-million-square-mile, ethnically heterogeneous, poor, rural, sparsely populated agricultural country with an overcrowded capital (the "Three Towns") of some two million people.[1]

With a World Development Report total population estimate of 25.8 million in 1991, Sudan's annual gross national product per capita is an estimated $300–$420.[2] The population is young and fertile, but not very healthy. Forty-six percent are under fifteen years old, the birthrate is 45 (per 1,000 live births), the infant mortality rate is 107 (per 1,000 population), and the mortality rate for children under five years old is 181 (per 1,000 live births). The life expectancy for females is 51.0 years; for males, 48.6.[3]

The central riverain cultural area of the Sudan[4] is the focus of this work, for it is there we see the greatest concentration of urban areas and settled life; where many colonial efforts focused, where capital-intensive investments have been most common, where consumer culture predominates, where many labor and religious migration depots are, and where northern Sudan's largest agricultural scheme (the Gezira) is located. It is the center for the arts, the media, and educational, religious, and national-political life,[5] and where I lived and carried out research for some six years.

This study situates itself in the contemporary urban life of northern Sudan, for its deeper focus is on the conurbation at the juncture of the Blue and White Niles, referred to as the "Three Towns," "the tripartite capital," or "Greater Khartoum"—consisting of Khartoum (the capital), Khartoum North (an industrial and residential city), and Omdurman (known as the "traditional" cultural/political/economic center)—connected by three bridges and river traffic. In recent decades the greatest manifestations of identity politics—ethnic, gender, religious, and national—have been at this juncture of the two Niles. I return to this sprawling city below.

To say that this book is about *northern* Sudan is, ostensibly, to make a statement about *culture*, because to the informed reader it means that I am writing about the "Arab," mainly Muslim north, and not about the "Black African," partially Christian south. This positioning situates northern Sudan in a "Middle Eastern" framework and southern Sudan in an African one. However, my propensity over the years has been to consider Sudan *African*, deeming other interpretations suspect in the sense of the implicit racism that removes the Arabs of Egypt (and by extension, northern Sudan) from the African continent, in essence denying Africa recognition for the considerable historical contributions of *African* Egypt and Nubia to the development of human societies. As a corollary of this racist framework, Nubians of northern Sudan and southern Egypt become "Hamitic" or "Cushitic" instead of African, placing their advanced iron-age civilization (of Cush/Kush or Meroe) in the artificial "Middle East."[6]

Nearly every published piece on the social or historical aspects of Sudan at least mentions the social and cultural diversity of the area and stresses its record of ethnic migrations, invasions, displacements, and mixing. Sudan has been called a "crossroads" between African and Arab worlds, "a corridor to Africa," "an African frontier zone," an "Afro-Arab state," "Black Arab," "Islamic-African," and the like.[7] The literature is, in fact, full of clichés about Nubians, Arabs, and the ethnic groups of the Nile valley, such as: "The Nile valley, from the junction of the Blue and White Niles to the first Cataract had become a *sinuous vial into which many racial stocks were poured*."[8] Trimingham, in a classic European work on Islam in Sudan, exemplifies the difficulty of delineating northern and central Sudan's ethnic diversity. Trying to be exact, he reaches the ridiculous in his labels: "Semitized-Hamites or Semitized Negroes, but more clearly ... Semitized Negroid-Hamites ... or Semitized-Hamite-Negroids."[9]

History and Ethnography

No work on Sudan can proceed without commenting on its protracted north-south civil war, one sphere of Sudan's ethnic and religious power structure. Afterwards I offer a brief history of Sudan's well-known intruders before concentrating on northern Sudan, whose "core culture" I analyze, eventually generalizing gender arrangements within its ethnographic and historical framework.

The "North-South" Division

Sudan's civil war, one of the most brutal in twentieth-century African history, is a major manifestation of the politicization of religious differences.[10] Hostilities have existed since 1955, despite a brief accord reached in 1972 (the Addis Ababa Agreement). The historical roots of the war are too complex for the scope of this book, but it is instructive to acknowledge the exacerbating effects of various colonial regimes. The colonialisms have helped shape Sudanese class formation, religious behavior and institutions, the structure of the state, political dynamics, and gender arrangements.

Since the seventh century, foreign intrusions of Arabs, Ottomans, Egyptians, and British have transformed indigenous economies, leading in the north to today's powerful, landed, Muslim aristocracy and bourgeois commercial administration, and in the south to a small Christian elite. Unequal regional development fostered class antagonisms articulated in religious terms. This conflict is commonly presented in the Western media and in some academic literature as a struggle between a "Muslim" north and a "Christian" south; more specifically, that Christianity is being suppressed by Islam or that Christians are being annihilated by Muslims. But the dynamic is far more complex, as migrations, missionary activity, settlement, and colonialism have had profound influences.

The effect of forty years of the resulting war has left a depleted, devastated, and nearly depopulated south and a legacy of such hatred that it is difficult to imagine resolution. The divisions between north and south, originally artificial, are now real. For example, even though scholars hypothesize the south to be as Muslim as Christian, the ideology of elite southerners is that the south is Christian; accordingly, they treat Muslims as intruders. At the same time, the identity politics of northerners has become more rigidly Muslim and "Middle Eastern."

Migrations, Colonialism(s), the Mahdiyya, and Gender Relations

Arabs migrated sporadically into Sudan from the seventh to the fourteenth centuries. Bedouin tribes led the way, peacefully migrating into Nubian areas along the Nile and penetrating southward, assimilating to varying degrees with indigenous cultures.[11] Later, enduring Muslim states (the Funj Kingdom of Sennar [1504–1821] and the Fur Sultanate in Darfur [1650?–1916]) established themselves in the Arabized areas.

Only with the founding of the Funj state, with its capital at Sennar, was there a powerful enough institution that could marshal the resources to carry Islam into the southern Sudan.[12] Besides providing a political, military, and economic center, the Funj Kingdom fostered the spread of Arabic language, culture, and forms of social organization, as well as Islam. But while Funj missionaries fresh from their religious education in Mecca were preaching Islam, other Muslims were enslaving local populations. Still, vast areas of Sudan remained unaffected by Islamic proselytization and economic exploitation.

Early in the sixteenth century an expanding Ottoman Empire was subjugating Arab populations and incorporating their territories. Egypt was annexed in 1517, but its upper reaches and the Sudanese reaches beyond were too distant and, thus, largely ignored. Only much later, in the early nineteenth century, did Sudan become the object of Turkish/Egyptian expansionism. Not only did the semi-autonomous Ottoman viceroy of Egypt, Mohamed Ali, regard Sudan as rich in slaves, gold, ivory, and wood, but its conquest would eliminate dissident Mamluks who had fled Egypt after its Ottoman conquest in 1811.[13] Sudan was relatively easy to conquer, its people religiously and politically fragmented into small Muslim states and "pagan" tribal territories.[14]

From 1821 to 1881, a time referred to as the "Turkiyya," armies of the Turco-Egyptian colonial regime plundered Sudan, charging heavy tribute and taking the toll in slaves. The slave trade was a state monopoly until 1850. It is difficult to know the slave trade's full effects upon Sudan's economy or ethnic and gender relations. We do know that the Turks extended their power deep into southern Sudan by 1849, establishing fear and hostility toward Islam among Black Africans, who referred to most intruders with lighter skin as "Turks," an unflattering term still in use.[15]

It was not only among southerners that class, color, and ethnic differences became salient during the Turkiyya. Albanians, Kurds, Circassians, Bosnians, and Magyars were among the many Ottoman agents ruling northern Sudanese. Ottoman tax collectors were called *Kushaf* (after the Arabic word for "lists"), an ethnic label still used by many Nubians. These "Turks" established patron-client relations, which along with slavery controlled the labor element in their economy. Ethnic groups such as Nubians and riverain and northeastern Arabs, e.g., the Shaygiyya, were favored in this feudal system, creating new ethnic tensions and divisions and introducing European-influenced Ottoman patriarchal relations into indigenous Sudanese gender relations.

The "Turks" tried to force upon the people a rigidly and formally doctrinaire Islam promulgated by el-Azhar University-educated religious scholars. Its rigid orthodoxy characterized the teachings of local holy men *(faqis)* and the methods of Quranic schools *(khalwas)*.[16] The colonial regime suppressed the populist, less hierarchically structured Sufi Islam of the Sudanese masses, and a potential unifier of ethnic groups—Islam—

became instead a source of friction and division. This was true of gender relations, as the patriarchal character of the Islam superimposed on Sudan subverted local conditions; any vestiges of matrilineal descent to be found among Nubians were eradicated and any syncretism that could have occurred, didn't.

If the intruders' form of Islam was not palatable even to the already Islamized northern Sudanese, the economic and psychological effects on parts of the south were devastating. Not only were many southern people conditioned to suspect and reject all lighter-skinned Muslims, forced conversion to Islam created further disorientation, causing more ethnic cleavage and general disorganization. Those groups most affected by slave raiding were forced to retrench and reorganize. Despite this resilience, their economies were assailed by exploitative petty traders and large-scale merchants (*jallaba*). For southerners the ethnic stereotype of the jallaba is that they are Nubians, usually Danagla.[17] These merchants, invariably racist as well as parasitic, were the precursors of the capitalist system.

Early Capitalism and Ethnic and Gender Dynamics. Before the Turkiyya, communal modes of production predominated. Market production was limited to some small-scale cash cropping and rudimentary manufacturing like the iron foundry in Kordofan. Consumption was mostly local, and little of what was produced entered into long-distance trade.[18] Not until the early nineteenth century, when as a periphery of Ottoman Egypt it was drawn into the latter's economy, did Sudan begin to be linked to a European-dominated, globalizing economy. What followed inexorably was a profound economic, religious, and sociocultural transformation.

The replacement of communal production and social relations by semifeudal ones commenced unevenly, occurring most intensively in northern riverain localities and in substantial areas in the west, and gradually expanding southwards. Through slaving, ivory hunting, and gold mining, the Turco-Egyptian regime began disrupting and destroying social life, production, and settlement in selected areas ever farther from the Nile as it sought to construct an export-oriented, dependent, and colonialized economy. Elites from Egypt, Nubia, and elsewhere captured people, land, and resources, and organized them in an attempt to monopolize the export trade; in so doing they dispersed or fragmented many local communities.

After 1850 the Turco-Egyptians and their riverain petty-trader and jallaba allies left the slaving mostly to nomadic Sudanese, whose social and political organization became more territorial and dominated by warrior nobles. On the fringes of the south and in extensive areas in the west slaving had disruptive effects on non-Arab communities as well. In areas more directly controlled by the Turco-Egyptians, *sheikhs* were appointed and made responsible for tax collection, thereby fostering the growth of a small but better-off stratum of peasants. As a result, some cultivators and semipastoralists lost their land or animals; some became attached to the property and households of Egyptian *beys* and Sudanese sheikhs; and still others, hunted by nomads and impoverished, fled to the few towns to be drawn into an incipient wage-labor market.[19]

This disruption and reorganization of the economy and society of central Sudan and its outliers set in motion the emergence of a weak and fragile class of wage laborers, typically in the few cash crop areas along the Nile as well as in the few towns that stood as nodes in the network linking the periphery (Sudan) with its Turco-Egyptian core. Commercialization and privatization of production and land helped push and/or draw some cultivators/craftspeople into places where they could earn wages.

Commercial, communications, and transportation infrastructures were developed and extended to facilitate the flow of commodities and to step up the turnover of capital. In this climate trading companies flourished. By the mid-nineteenth century, Sudan was an exploited frontier on the periphery of the world system.[20]

In all the areas affected by the Turkiyya, changes in gender relations, particularly in the gender division of labor, were underway. Traditionally, women had performed their valued share of agricultural and pastoral labor, engaging, along with men, in a subsistence (use-value) economy and carrying out some trade. The core-periphery social relations of production pulled a small number of men of the periphery into income-generating commodity production (both crops and crafts), whereas women were relegated to domestic labor. The relationship that women had to this income-generating activity was through their spouses or other male relatives. Where there was systematic, large-scale slavery, women were shunted into domestic labor and men into the fields. Slavery, forced labor, and commodity production (i.e., the exploitative labor processes of capitalism and its corollary, colonialism)—all generated a profound imbalance in the gender division of labor.

The above interpretation, which views the economic dynamic in the north as socially fragmenting, challenges many writings about the north during the Turkiyya.[21] Although there were many ethnic groups and economies, the conventional approach to the social, ethnic, and religious composition of the north is that the region was unified by religion (Islam) and language (Arabic), and any division of the people was viewed as merely sedentary versus nomadic. This gloss, which overlooks extant ethnic antagonisms by privileging Islam, results in the rarely acknowledged fact that Turco-Egyptian economic interests intensified these extant divisions. The most common representation of Sudan's ethnicity is of a sharp ethnic division between north and south. Even some grim enact-ments of colonialism and slavery—the impressment of southern men into the Egyptian army and the appropriation of women as domestic servants or concubines—are discounted by the notion of a hegemonic Islam that swept aside all other differences, both forcibly and peacefully incorporat-ing everyone into a dominant northern population and culture.[22]

Most sources identify the 1870s as the time of serious European pene-tration into the Sudan, primarily in the form of mercenary-adventurers in the Turco-Egyptian army. They gained control over wide areas in the inte-rior at a time when in Egypt itself European financiers were helping to drain the country of its financial resources.[23] The Turco-Egyptian presence in Sudan was weakening, and high taxation and other perceived oppres-sive measures led to growing unrest and resistance—all of which pre-saged the next political epoch, the Mahdiyya (1881–98), the last time for more than a half century that Sudanese would be independent.

Multiple processes and events precipitated the rise of the Mahdi, the leader who was the eponym of the religiopolitical movement and histori-cal period known as the Mahdiyya. During the Funj period local forms of Islamic teaching and practice, often derived from Arabian orders, arose, and these opposed the more formal Sunni Islam imposed from Egypt. The Mahdists aimed at overthrowing Turco-Egyptian rule and its sanc-tioned religious institutions and practices, and at superseding all other local orders (brotherhoods).[24]

In their efforts to establish and maintain dominance, the Turks exploited ethnic, tribal, and religious divisions to advantage when and where they could. Importantly, they used religious sheikhs as political administrators and in so doing intensified tribal animosities. In particular, the Turco-Egyptians patronized the Khatmi order (Mirghani family)—whose adherents included many northeastern groups such as Nubians, Kassala Arabs, and especially the Shaygiyya Arabs—at the expense of other orders and social groups. This favoritism created a religious and political cleavage between the Mahdists (Ansar) and Khatmis that still influences Sudanese religious and ethnic relations today.

The Mahdiyya. The Turco-Egyptian regime was believed to be highly corrupt;[25] repressive economic conditions, the inability of Turco-Egyptian authorities to gain the loyalty of indigenous Sudanese, and the peculiar synthesis of Sufism and pietistic Sudanese orthodoxy—all contributed to the rise of the Nubian mystic, Mohamed Ahmed.[26] Because the Khat-miyya was so closely associated with the Turco-Egyptian regime, the rise of the Mahdi automatically pitted Mahdists against Khatmis—a schism extant in contemporary Sudanese politics and to which I return below.

The Mahdists succeeded in unifying some northern groups for a con-siderable period. The Dongola-born Sufist, Mohamed Ahmed, proclaimed himself the Mahdi[27] and marshaled a desert guerrilla army that not only drove out the Turco-Egyptians, but succeeded in holding off British interests for some time while an indigenous state flourished, one of the few successful African/Middle Eastern states to resist colonialism.

The Mahdist victory and establishment of an indigenous state can be attributed to three allied elements: (1) ascetic pietists, (2) a jallaba class of dispersed Jaaliyyin and Danagla middle-class merchants who were malcontents deprived of the fruits of the slave trade, and (3) Baggara groups from the western Sudan.[28] Although their power base was disaffected peasants and nomads, the Mahdists formed alliances with petty chiefs and tribal leaders in the west, east, and even small areas of the south, to achieve a modestly integrated Islamic state.

This was, however, a crucial negative period for north-south relations, as the Mahdists, intent on spreading Islam, often used repressive methods.[29] One lasting effect of these actions was to create fear and hatred among southerners for northerners.[30] It is not unfair to say that, by its oppression and violence, the Mahdiyya jihad checked the spread of Islam in the south.

The Mahdiyya did, however, stimulate a socioeconomic revolution in northern Sudan, even though aspects of the regime furthered class cleavages and regional inequities. Centralization of authority and economic activity produced growth in Omdurman, for example, and since the Mahdiyya this Greater Khartoum area has thrived at the expense of the hinterland. When the Mahdi's successor, the Khalifa, took power, the Sudanese economy became semifeudal. The Ansar (see note 27) and Khatmis formed two new landed aristocracies that still exist and control part of Sudan's economy.

The Mahdist revolution not only failed to stem religious frictions that have stood as an obstacle to unification; it failed economically. It was parochial, conservative, peasant-based and short-lived, succumbing inevitably to the dynamics of imperialism and the world-capitalist system. The new class system that emerged continued, albeit in another form, the exploitation of the hinterland peasantry and the extraction of raw materials for a European market.

We know very little about gender relationships before and during the Mahdiyya. Based on what we know about Ottoman history, speculations about these relationships under Turco-Egyptian rule are problematic, to say the least. In writing on women and politics in medieval Sudan ranging from the Keira sultanate in the far west to an area near the present Ethiopian-Sudanese border, el-Hag Hamad Mohammed Kheir (aka el-Haj Hamad M. Khier) deals mainly with the ruling class. He considers the prominence of matrilineal descent in the ancient northern and central kingdoms and its effect on politics—e.g., women serving as queens: "In spite of the rise of the Islamic Kingdoms with their emphatically patrilineal systems of succession, there have also been powerful queens of Sudan, ruling over large tracts of territory."[31]

Hall and Ismail tell us that women took part in the struggle against the Turks as couriers, delivering messages from Aba Island, the Mahdi's stronghold. Not citing their sources, the authors maintain that once the revolt was more formalized and recognized, "the Mahdi selected a few women in whom he recognised special qualities suitable for the task. During the battles that followed, women helped to tend the wounded, acted as spies to report enemy movements and dispositions, and generally rallied the men."[32] This characterization could be representative of any number of past or present societies: what I have described later in this chapter and in chapter 5 as the "women-as-Greek-chorus" syndrome. To their credit, however, they, unlike Kheir, depict ordinary life, not queen-envy:

> With the exception of these few devotees of the Mahdi whose activities appeared to be restricted to rural areas where, because of economic conditions, women always had more social freedom than those in the towns, the female position was, to say the least, unenviable. Muslim society at that time was exclusively a man's world, and the ideal status to which almost every male aspired was to have the means to maintain a polygamous household and to keep his womenfolk shut away behind closed doors ... Veiled from puberty and generally never seen by anyone except her close male relatives, his wife lived with other female members of the family in the women's quarters ... it was unusual for a woman to be seen in public ... Such a rigorous system of seclusion effectively removed women from public life, and lack of educational facilities condemned them to a state of ignorance ... they had no concept of a wider horizon and therefore they offered little resistance to the tradition which relegated them to an inferior position and a negative existence.[33]

Although the Sudanese woman coauthor is complicit, this quote exemplifies some of the problems of Sudanese (and much of Middle Eastern) women's studies. It is difficult to know, for example, if the above description is particular to the Mahdiyya or portrays some sort of universal suffering under Islam. In terms of historical method, it is unclear if these ideas come from contemporary archival sources, from oral testimonies of women of the period (some of whom might still have been alive) or from extrapolations of the present. We do not know if these were exclusively urban women or what class they represented. The statement is totally decontextualized, though (except for the implication of "false consciousness") vaguely familiar to me as a description of *some* lower-middle and middle-class women of the capital as late as the 1960s.[34] It is hard to imagine that the situation I observed for some women in 1961 was the same during the Mahdiyya. Regardless or perhaps *because* of such descriptions, our knowledge of gender relations during the Mahdiyya is severely limited.

Writing as a committee, some of Sudan's leading women's studies scholars recently summarized gender relations under nineteenth-century regimes in this way:

> Women in heavily Islamic areas tended to be secluded, isolated from public life, especially if they belonged to the developing upper landowning and merchant classes. Women in less Islamic areas (e.g. western Sudan) were economically more independent, legally more responsible for themselves and socially more free than has been usual or acceptable in many other Muslim societies.[35]

Their rendition of gender relations under the Ottomans adds only slightly to our understanding:

> The Turco-Egyptian invasion of 1821 brought with it a heavier emphasis on the seclusion of women and the ideology of domesticity and the harem. This development was strengthened by the spread of the slave trade in this period. Large numbers of slaves were women. These took on most household chores, and the "free" women of the privileged classes were consequently expected to dedicate themselves totally to their husbands. These changes did not affect peasant or pastoral women, who remained involved in productive activities (176).

Conditions for women seemed to worsen during the Mahdiyya:

> This spontaneous movement had its roots in the peasant classes. It called for social reforms. The trade in male slaves was forbidden. Female slavery continued. The Mahdi strove to create an Islamic state. Women's economic independence, where they still were independent, was curtailed, and a strict sex-segregation was imposed, also on classes which previously did not adhere to this custom (176–77).

El-Bakri and Khier point out that periodization itself, e.g., the Mahdiyya, "is primarily concerned with the basis of the superstructure without serious consideration of the basic material structure on which these periods developed."[36] They remind us that Western scholars established this periodization model and mainly male Sudanese and expatriate scholars followed it. About the Mahdiyya and gender relations they suggest that, in terms of social emancipation, "[Mahdism] was restrictive ... especially as relates to women, ... even more restrictive than 'Orthodox' Islam."[37]

We have, expectably, more documentation of material life under British colonialism, but data on gender arrangements are still fragmentary. Are we to consider "patriarchy" a constant, and that women's lives did not change drastically in the abrupt transition from Mahdist to British rule?[38]

In a dramatic confrontation with the Mahdists, the British, in arms with the French, managed by 1899 to "reconquer" Sudan for emerging capitalism. European politicians who saw Sudan as a focus of colonialism and capitalist expansionism in Africa promoted the reconquest and shaped what was to be called the Anglo-Egyptian Condominium (1899–1956).[39] Under British hegemony, administrative and military priorities prevailed over economic development. The British formed policy and appointed Egyptians to lower administrative positions; in the colonial process a new northern Sudanese elite was created and co-opted.[40]

Northern and Southern Women under Colonialism

Although it was ruled as one colony, Sudan was not administered as an integrated territory.

In the north the British bolstered the Islamic religiocultural structure through their policy of "indirect rule"; at the same time, they impeded Muslim unification. Fearing another Mahdist revolt, they at first supported the rival Khatmiyya order—a key colonial strategy for neutralizing religious resistance. Later, when the threat seemed moot, colonialists favored the Mahdi's descendants as useful in indirect rule.

Such British support developed a British-controlled indigenous landlord class based on plantation agriculture (namely the Gezira Scheme, the largest cotton plantation in Africa). Mahdists became a semifeudal aristocracy loyally supported by an irregular militia. Administration, political power, military organization, economics, ethnicity, and religion were, therefore, intricately related in British Sudan.

Hierarchies that were established not only among ethnic groups patronized or suppressed by the colonials (expectably, preserving traditional authority in order to normalize colonial rule) had ramifications for gender relations: in regulating, routinizing, and codifying as many aspects of "traditional" northern Sudanese society as possible. British colonial rule in effect codified patrilineal and patriarchal practices, establishing a gender hierarchy as well—which reflected British chauvinism.[41]

According to el-Bakri et al., not all gender relations were rigidified:

The British did not interfere in those areas in which women's position was low. However, they regarded those areas where relations between the sexes were relatively egalitarian as "uncivilized". Thus, women's position varied widely by region and class, and more specifically with the degree of

Islamization. The effect of colonialization has equally been different for different groups of women, although colonial policy in general was dictated by the desire to extract as much surplus as possible. In order to facilitate this, where women were already markedly subordinate to men and a severe public/private dichotomy existed the colonialists did not interfere. In other situations where women shared relatively equal status with men, they lost this status under the pretext of "civilization". In this the colonial male bourgeois mentality played an important role.[42]

These chauvinistic attitudes often translated into policy. For example, when the British decided to school Sudanese so that they might serve in the lower rungs of the civil service, they selected boys for those schools and for those jobs.[43]

By disjoining northern and southern Sudan, Condominium rule had the inadvertent effect of separating northern and southern women. Although fewer numbers of southern women are formally educated and active in wage-earning occupations, in subsistence labor they are more economically active than central riverain women. Their performance in primarily transhumant economies, not to mention the participation of many in civil-war-related work, has advanced southern women in terms of autonomy and self-worth. We see the same pattern of greater women's autonomy among the pastoral or nomadic people of the northern Sudan. Among the riverain agriculturalists and urban dwellers the pattern is different, however; women are more removed from the public arena.[44] Had the two areas been more integrated over the last century, the influence of freer "southern" gender relations might have been a factor in modifying the impact of European and Arab patriarchal structures.[45] In assessing the degree of the hegemony of Arab/Islamic culture in the various regions of Sudan, el-Bakri and Kameir maintain that "women's status has generally been higher (... they have a larger role in production, are socially freer, have more say in public affairs, etc.) in areas where Arab/Islamic influence has been the least ... southern Sudan."[46]

Capitalism and Class Formation

There are various ways one might periodize Sudanese history, but because it allows me to highlight the congruence of particular regimes with certain modes of Islam, I have followed a rather conventional classification of the history of Sudan: according to the political systems that governed. Mahmoud, however, borrowing from Amin,[47] and constructing a political-economic history based on more orthodox Marxist approaches, claimed there were

three main periods [namely, Turkiyya, Mahdiyya, and the Condominium], each of which represents a juncture of transformation in: 1) the means and relations of production; 2) the forces of production; 3) the class formation; 4) the contradictions between country and town; 5) the level of the integration of the non-capitalist production in the capitalist market; 6) the reproduction of the producing and the appropriating classes; 7) the imposition of economic laws by the government and 8) the relation of the Sudanese economy to the international market.[48]

We know for sure that Sudan was drawn into the world system of capitalist exchange as early as Turco-Egyptian domination. Class formation in Sudan during the last two centuries has been the logical outcome of the Turkiyya and the Mahdiyya; these periods witnessed the emergence of the merchant/administrative class and the landed aristocracy. The British nourished both of these classes and the former "played an important role in the process of encapsulation of the Sudan into the economic and political structure of the British Empire."[49] By the time the British colonized Sudan there was considerable world competition for cotton, and British industries were looking for areas within the empire to produce it. Sudan, a likely source of raw materials, was also strategically located to protect the trade route to India.

From 1919 to 1925 the British set up the administration and physical plan of the Gezira Scheme. Developed, the scheme accounted for nearly the entire modern economy of the colony. But the scheme did not develop Sudan; it instead created dependency on a cotton monoculture. Uncertain world markets for cotton threw the Sudanese into continual crises. Caught up in these world market forces, the colonial administration, the operating syndicate, and the independent state that followed after 1956 ceaselessly exploited the tenant farmers so as to maintain the artificially cheap costs of production to sell the all-important crop in the competitive world market.[50] By the late 1950s, 75 percent of all government expenditure went into the Gezira district.[51] While this went on in the north (namely, in the central riverain district), other areas (especially the south and west) were virtually ignored in terms of capital investment.

The Mahdists still draw much wealth from north-central riverain estates and the Khatmis dominate the peasants of the northeast. Second to the landed aristocracy in this north-central riverain area are the urban elites: the commercial, industrial, bureaucratic, and petit bourgeoisie. This class now controls the commercial sector of the economy and maintains the various external links to the capitalist world system.[52]

Twentieth-century colonial and postcolonial developers have used a growth-pole strategy, that is, the concentration of investment in a favored region to create centers of growth.[53] The rationale has been that there would be a spread—a trickle-down effect—to peripheral areas. In Sudan, as in most other areas with pronounced core-hinterland disparities, this has only weakly occurred. Although a middle class of peasants has emerged in the Gezira and elsewhere, they are involved in commodity production: agricultural labor further serving capital accumulation.

Ethnicity

The largest country in Africa and the Middle East, Sudan is among the most ethnically and linguistically heterogeneous.[54] The manner in which this diversity has been described in the literature reveals the politics of ethnographic classification, in part a legacy of colonial administration. Sudan's ethnographic complexity follows logically from artificial political boundaries drawn under the Anglo-Egyptian Condominium. Part of Sudan's sometimes acrimonious and brutal interethnic relationships are a result of the separate colonial administration of the "north" and "south," the latter constituting one third of the country and approximately 25 percent of the population.

The sociological, administrative, and popular literature on ethnicity in the north conventionally lists diverse groups under "Arab." Placing that term in quotes is not to imply that there are not Arab *tribes*.[55] But the people themselves rarely use the ethnic categories bestowed on them by historians and anthropologists, referring to themselves instead by extended family, clan, tribal, or regional names. The general and inclusive term "Nubian," for example, has not always had meaning for the people themselves and has only recently come into common use. Nubians have an array of ethnic/linguistic/regional self-identifications. From an "insider's" (northern Sudanese) point of view, the north is as much an ethnic conglomeration as the south. Many northerners consider Islam the major culturally unifying force.

In contrast, outsider (anthropologists) classifications of people in the south have been elaborate and segmental. Groups such as Nilotic, Nilo-Hamitic, and Sudanic are not only divided into "tribes"—e.g., Dinka, Shilluk, Bari, and Azande—but are further divided until maximal lineages appear as ethnic units. Because the British colonial regime was ruling the south directly, following government anthropologists' fragmentary classifications of southern peoples made sense; that is, it was a useful rationale for governing a congeries of very diverse people as if there were no unifying culture or politics.

The politics of census-taking played a major role in Sudanese politics, from the British to the current regime. In the only census where ethnicity was surveyed, some 39 percent of Sudanese claimed to be Arab and more than 50 percent to speak Arabic.[56] Estimates of how many in the north are Muslim and how many in the south, Christian, remain but estimates. The reason we cannot correlate ethnicity and religious affiliation accurately is because no question about religion—not even the broad classifications

"Muslim" and "Christian"—has ever been asked on the census. We are, therefore, reliant on questionable estimates by religious officials, individual ethnographers, and other self-interested people. For example, one southern Sudanese writer published a very low estimate of the proportion of Muslims in the north: 70 percent.[57] I have heard estimates as high as 90 percent by government officials and university intellectuals, but these usually excluded refugees (e.g., southerners, Eritreans, etc.), many now permanent residents and not Muslims. A 1956 document reported 23,000 Muslims in the south; Protestants totaled only 30,000, whereas Roman Catholics numbered 200,000, the total of all these religions amounting to only 9 percent of the indigenous southern population.[58] Another source estimated the Christians to be only 4 percent of the entire Sudanese population, raising questions about how/why the civil war was presented as Christian resistance to Islamic domination.[59]

Giving low population estimates for Christians is not to dismiss the importance of the longtime presence of a powerful middle-to-upper-class Christian population of various ethnicities and denominations in the northern towns—especially in Greater Khartoum. This group, now much diminished, consists primarily of people of Egyptian, Lebanese, Syrian, Armenian, Greek, Cypriot, and Italian descent. This mainly commercial and professional elite set itself apart through occupation, dress, schooling, and social facilities, rarely intermarrying with other Sudanese, and frequently in the past not identifying as such, even though many who disdained the national label may have been citizens. Sometimes I would hear them set themselves apart from what they called "the Sudanese" in much the same way as those indigenous groups would refer to themselves as "the real Sudanese." The Egyptians, Lebanese, and Syrians refer to themselves as "Arab" (only in that sense considering themselves *northern* Sudanese) and interact socially and economically with the riverain Sudanese elite (discussed below).

These northern Christians have been greatly constrained in recent years, their power elite broken by President Jaafar Nimieri's nationalization policies of the early 1970s. Many, taking their money not already stashed in European or Lebanese banks, emigrated. Although Nimieri soon reconsidered, apologized, and beckoned their return, restoring land and properties in the process, many never returned, their fortunes secure in foreign banks. Others continued to have a financial grip on Sudan, but maintained their domiciles outside the country.[60] Some Christians held bureaucratic (civil service) positions of some importance during British rule, but following independence (1956) they rarely held political office or gained prominence in the military. Like the urban Nubian elite (Muslims), who were also patronized by the British, "foreign" Christian groups (e.g., Greeks) have been deeply resented by those who consider themselves the "real Sudanese," namely, the Muslim Arab groups of the north-central riverain area.

It is of some note that the Christian groups produced ostensibly socially emancipated women, although their reputations were based almost solely on the fact that they held jobs in the formal, public work-force, could mix with men more freely in various settings, and usually did not wear tobes. For complex reasons, however, they often did not par-ticipate in national politics, were rarely feminists, and were often not taken very seriously. It is possible that the general political conservatism of these elite women was influenced or reinforced by the patriarchal ide-ology of the Christian British colonizer. The women who eventually assumed leadership roles in Sudan were Muslims. Still, one should not overlook the fact that a small number of Christian women were among early role models in the professions, e.g., as physicians.[61]

Arabs and Nubians: The Core of Northern Sudan's Patriarchy. Together Nubians and Arabs form the north-central riverain culture, the dominant core culture of Sudan.[62] An understanding of this culture is useful to my analysis of gender arrangements. The past interactions of Arabs and Nubians are old and constant enough biologically and cultur-ally to obscure their individual ethnographic development. Numerous controversies over origins, directions of migrations, genealogies, linguis-tic classifications, and patterns of assimilation are in the literature. Who assimilated to whom continues unresolved, reflected in expressions like "Arabized Nubians," and "Nubianized Arabs,"[63] to refer to the popula-tion of the north-central riverain area. Both expressions, of course reflect-ing the ideological and epistemological stances of the scholars, well indicate the bidirectional nature of the assimilation process. My field experience with Nubians confirms that "the local population has become to some extent formally affiliated, by fictitious agnatic descent, to Arabs and Turks, and at the same time Turks, Arabs and other immigrants have become culturally and linguistically Nubianized."[64]

In the north-central riverain towns, Arab and Nubian identities have frequently become fused. For example, in describing a suburb of Khar-toum, one anthropologist, unable to differentiate the customs of Arabs and Nubians, conflates them: "all those [Nubians] living in Burri al Lamab are *indistinguishable* culturally from the Arab tribes."[65] This fusing of cultural patterns in public urban arenas can be seen in residence pat-terns, life-cycle ceremonies, religion, education, use of the same official language (Arabic), governmental and legal institutions, occupational structure, urban neighborhood structure, and public recreation.

From the Nubian standpoint, much of the fusing is a conscious pro-cess, but reflects only public behavior. That is, for centuries Nubian men (famous for their tradition of urban migration) have been moving in and out of dominant Arab culture, accommodating and assimilating—"passing"—as it benefited them. So long as Nubian culture was maintained in the hands of the women in the home villages, Nubian men could be "Nubian" in some contexts and "Arab" in others, as it served them. Men were free to embrace the dominant urban culture and rise to the top of Sudanese society, which they did. Nubian men referred to Nubian women as "keepers of the culture," and acknowledged that the positioning of women as repositories of the culture enabled the men's cultural flexibility. They could still be "good Nubians" or "pure Nubians." This bicultural male process took on even greater importance when the building of the High Dam at Aswan in the 1960s forced both Nubian men and women into diaspora.

During three years of fieldwork in the 1970s I explored what happened to Nubian women's culture and autonomy after the mid-1960s, when Nubians were evacuated from the northern villages to the towns of Sudan or to the relocation area of Khashm el-Girba, southeast of Khartoum. I learned that women were taking the place of the homeland, with all its mysticism and romance; they became a physical representation of the homeland in the minds of men—a point to return to. Women as reproducers of Nubian-ness offered the stability and continuity that allowed the men to change. Women, without the veiling or mandated seclusion that we see in some other societies, were set apart, seemingly "invisible" in a private world that had become increasingly devalued in favor of the material world of incipient capitalist development. Therefore, the contradiction emerged that, while relying on their woman-maintained private-world-in-reserve and exalting it for its cultural purity, Nubian men scorned women's interpretation of the culture as quaint, embarrassing, even "backward."

The Nubian example is not very different from the process of the cultural positioning of women that we see in other northern Sudanese groups. However, ethnic identity and shifts in the gender hierarchy were more highlighted during the 1960s' and 1970s' crisis of relocation. In Arab and Nubian groups we can observe other situations where the women reproduce the "traditional" culture, allowing men to move in and out of, say, village and urban society. Men often pretend not to understand "women's world," mystifying and exalting it in the same process. What happens is that women, who are now the central agricultural workers in most of Sudan, are not seen as the material providers that they are, but instead as keepers of the mystical/ritual realm. The effect is to diminish the power of women by dislocating them from the material base.[66]

The amalgam of Arab/Nubian culture is most pronounced in Greater Khartoum, and patriarchal customs still prevail. However, there have been alterations in village culture resulting from the urbanization process. For example, there is now a tendency towards neolocal or virilocal residence. Still, a wife often spends considerable time in her father's house during pregnancies and deliveries. The exact kinship alignment is often re-arranged to accord with the proximity of extended family members. Marriage preferences are broadened, often allowing home locality to outweigh blood ties.

The urban wedding ceremony itself, a symbol of the marriage contract, is often an amalgamation of traditional Arab and non-Arab customs adjusted to urban conditions. The "Omdurman wedding" (as these urban amalgams began to be called in the 1960s), generally lasts from three to seven days and is ornamented and orchestrated according to local variations. Its rituals symbolize such themes as the submission of women, men's strength and dominance, female sexual purity, special sexual attributes (e.g., the woman's sensuousness and cleverness), fertility and sexual prowess, future abundance (e.g., children and economic status), familial solidarity and alliance, safeguards against danger and pollution, generosity (e.g., bride price, bridal gifts, payments to nuptial functionaries, and lavish food and drink displays), and familial economic or political status.

Therefore, even though many changes have occurred such as considerable mixing among ethnic groups and alterations in the material environment and mode of production (e.g., urbanization and relocation), patriarchal gender arrangements prevail.

Even if we accept the arguable notion that women had more power in matrilineal societies, we can speculate that the small degree of power they could glean from matrilineal groups (such as the pre-Islamic Nubians) was subverted, in part, through the above process.

Although we cannot attribute all things patriarchal to Arabs, the powerful impact of Arab penetration on indigenous Sudanese groups cannot be denied. For one thing, the migration of Arabs into Sudan, although generally considered to have been peaceful, lasted a long time—from the seventh to the fourteenth centuries. That is a very long time to alter indigenous social structures that may arguably be described as gender egalitarian. It would take many books to compare gender relations in every Arab and non-Arab group in Sudan, associating or dissociating various customs, behaviors, legal institutions, and the like. We cannot even neatly disaggregate the groups themselves, let alone be sure of the significance to gender arrangements. Nonetheless, we can infer gender hierarchies from histories and studies of Sudanese groups and related groups in other areas of the Middle East. More significantly, we can use the testimonies of contemporary women. What does it mean to northern Sudanese women that they are descended from Arabs or a mixture of Nubians and Arabs?

In chapters 6 and 7 I discuss "Arab" identity and its meaning to the women activists of the National Islamic Front (NIF), suggesting that, because of some of the repressive and oppressive customs and attitudes within Arab patriarchy (as symbolized, for example, by some of the wedding rituals, one of which is described below), some Islamist women are abandoning Arab identity in their pursuit of what they see as the "ideal" Muslim life: nontribal and nonpatriarchal.

The Social Forces of Urban Sudan

Most of the subjects, processes, and events I deal with in this book are either present in Greater Khartoum or experienced there in their more intensified forms. Sudan is, however, not a highly urbanized country, which makes Greater Khartoum all the more prominent. Towns of 20,000 or more had 13.4 percent of the total population in the 1970s, and 20.2 percent in the 1980s. Urban areas contained, respectively, 19.2 and 21.1 percent of the total female and male populations,[67] more than half whom live in the seven largest towns.[68] Even in the 1950s, Khartoum province, essentially the metropolitan area of Greater Khartoum, was the most highly urbanized province, with 59 percent of its population living in towns.[69] By 1973 this reached 72 percent,[70] and every source points to even higher figures in the 1990s, due partially to the influx of thousands of refugees from civil wars—Sudan's and neighboring countries' (e.g., Eritrea/Ethiopia). We see only estimates of the population of the Three Towns, primarily from nongovernmental sources.[71] It would be dangerous for the government to acknowledge the demographics in print, as the numbers in the burgeoning shantytowns would then require a reassessment of services needed. Counting the fringes might also necessitate recognizing the decline of Arab/Nubian numerical domination.

Concentrated in Greater Khartoum are the country's most skilled and formally educated people, as well as a large proportion of its wealth. In the 1970s the Three Towns accounted for only 6 percent of the country's population, but had 85 percent of its commercial companies, 80 percent of its banking, 75 percent of all industrial labor, and 73 percent of all industrial establishments.[72] Most industrial development still takes place here despite some efforts to decentralize and though the area possesses few natural resources. The transportation net converging on the Niles' confluence, though inadequate to national needs, facilitates economic concentration.

In the political and administrative spheres, too, one finds extreme centralization. Greater Khartoum seats the central government, the judiciary, the headquarters of most political parties (when they are legal), and is the repository of the majority of people conscious of and active in national, ethnic, religious sectarian, and gender politics. Governmental facilities are so extremely centralized that hardly any effective administrative branches exist elsewhere.

In the realm of social services, Greater Khartoum is supreme in the urban hierarchy. The most important educational center, the conurbation has over 100,000 students, some 11 percent of the national enrollment, a disproportionate share of secondary schools and specialized institutes, and five colleges and universities. Similarly, there is a marked concentration of medical services and highly specialized doctors. About 20 percent of all Sudan's hospitals beds, more than 50 percent of its doctors, and 70 percent of its private clinics are situated in Greater Khartoum.[73]

The townspeople in the formal workforce obtain their living essentially in one of three places: government, commerce, or industry. The resultant occupational structure is more diverse than elsewhere, with more categories requiring considerable knowledge and skills.[74] Expectably, the income of the Greater Khartoum labor force exceeds that of any other place. In 1972 figures showed an approximate per capita income of $245 for the Three Towns, compared with $85 for the whole country.[75]

Such a profile points as much to a hierarchical class structure as to an enlightened center. Greater Khartoum's burgeoning subaltern population is among the poorest in the world. These urban slum-dwellers and foragers, who in any way possible eke out (rather than are "paid") an income, have become some of the most resourceful people I have ever encountered. Yet, the poverty is staggering and the social consequences are great.

> There is a group of small children in the suburb of Zagalona (meaning "we have been cheated") ... there are ... Approximately 100,000 children ... homeless in Khartoum. The *shamasa*, as they are called, wash cars, beg, steal ... What is known about how they live indicates that many have formed gangs with tightly knit hierarchies and rules.[76]

Khartoum is a city in trouble. The residents have learned to depend on the state, yet know that they can*not* depend on it. Basic utilities and social services cannot even be supplied the middle and upper classes, who spend increasingly less time in the country. Wealth can get a family a generator for when the electricity cuts off sometimes for days or weeks, but no amount of wealth can keep that generator working under the strain of constant use. And these are the fortunate people.

This Sudanese city's dire condition reflects the health of the nation. Both give the impression of falling apart, precisely what some of the older residents are worried about. They see displaced populations taking over. "Many ... bemoan the massive westernization of their culture, the disembodying signs of illicit sex, drugs, and alcohol" (166). They see a fragmenting culture and careful British/Sudanese urban planning gone awry.

Anything, they argue, would be better than this. Some young intellectuals and new middle class point to Islam as a possible solution: Doesn't the Islamic movement also speak to the dispossessed? Wouldn't it answer wayward dreams?

> Sudan is frequently cited as an example of political intractability—a nation that has foolishly squandered good will and relative prosperity for unreasonable dreams. From thinking it could be the breadbasket of the Arab world or the pioneer of a new form of Islamic governance, Sudan is an absurdly conceived country encompassing a seemingly irreconcilable excess of diversity, be it linguistic, ethnic, or religious. It lives uneasily with the extremes of its past—it once defeated an Anglo-Egyptian army to set up a revolutionary state; it once had the strongest trade union movement on the continent; it once had the most talented corps of civil servants and foreign diplomats. The singularity of these legacies may be in dispute, but they are the mythologies the Sudanese live with (165).

Before we write off the city as hopelessly lost, it might be useful for us momentarily to replace our abstract theorizing, or for the Islamists to suspend their abstract idealism (such as their arguments about cultural authenticity) to learn from the subaltern. Timothy Simone reminds us that "for millions of people with few resources and opportunities, what they do with their imaginations in order to stay afloat is hardly a lame imitation of Western style. They may foolishly play on the wrong side of the economic odds, but a very strange and resilient city is being built in the meantime" (166).

Loose urban networks are forming (e.g., illicit distribution systems, illicit services, non-Islamic ritual practices) that neither the Islamists nor the Sudanese Communist Party choose to notice; when they do, it is usually to attempt to eradicate them.

Women form some of these loosely knit networks, hold many of the illicit jobs (e.g., prostitutes, brewers), and participate in a number of non-Islamic practices (e.g., the zar). They are ingenious planners and everyday visionaries. Sudanese feminists and Islamists often rely on the financial and political agendas of their party or the state for their feminist and womanist projects. But most women of Khartoum do not, and cannot, rely on or look to these for their survival as women, or for their religious expression.

The State, Gender, Religion, and the Military: The Dynamics of Post-Independence Politics

Questions about the relationship of the state to gender and religion must consider not only internal dynamics, but also external forces in the form of international capital. The particular forms that class politics have taken are not only related to international capitalism, but to the socioeconomic forms of various colonial regimes. In this section and more elaborately in following chapters I attempt to isolate the mechanisms that the state and/or party employ for achieving political and cultural hegemony.[77] In Sudan this has meant examining identity and class politics that may be reactions to these hegemonic processes.

As discussed above, Sudan's economic situation and political forms have been adversely affected by waves of colonialism in the past and by the influx of large numbers of international corporations and agencies in the present.[78] State capitalism has transformed and shored up its mainly agricultural economy in the twentieth century. Since independence in 1956 the military has been in power much of the time. For most of the postindependence years the country has also been divided by civil war.

Outsiders often present modern Sudanese politics as the imposition of two "alien creeds" (parliamentary politics and Communism) seen as antithetical to traditional sectarian politics.[79] That seems myopic in the sense that one can locate indigenous "democratic" forms not unlike parliament in its ideal form, and a kind of primitive communalism not unlike communism in its ideal form. This is not to say that there is nothing new under the sun or to reiterate the cliché of old wine in new caskets (or vice versa), but really to say that in Sudanese politics, at least these last two centuries, nothing is completely new—or totally traditional (or authentic or indigenous).

Sectarian Politics and Sufism

The basis of much of twentieth-century Sudanese politics has been sectarian, so an ambiguous boundary has persisted between politics and religion. Two Sufi-inspired parties have dominated: the Umma ("nation") Party, the political wing of the Ansar (followers of the Mahdi, whose hybrid of Sufism and Sunni fundamentalism defies facile classification); and the People's Democratic Party (PDP, after 1968 forming the Democratic Unionist Party in coalition with the National Unionist Party), the political wing of the Khatmiyya (or Mirghaniyya) sect.[80] In the 1980s and 1990s, however, various internal and external factors converged to create a seemingly different Islamic polity: first a civil government's "New Islamic Trend," and now a military government's "National Salvation Revolution." I leave a discussion of these developments for chapter 6.

One of the central "themes from northern Sudan"[81] (at least by the number of sources on the subject) is sectarian (namely, Sufi) politics. Practically everyone who writes on Sudanese history, politics, geography, anthropology, or religion pays homage to this ambiguous boundary between religion and politics. For example:

Sudan's Islamic political heritage has deep roots: the Funj Islamic state, the formal Islamic policy of Muhammad 'Ali during Ottoman Egyptian rule, and the Mahdist Islamic state ... the spread of Islam in the Sudan was due primarily to the activities of merchants, itinerant preachers, and, in particular, Sufi (mystic) brotherhoods or orders *(tariqas)* ... The significance of Sufism for Sudanese politics and society cannot be over-estimated. *The Sudanese Islam is Sufi Islam.*[82]

Another scholar extolled Sudanese political leadership as having been

a unique Messianism, ranging from the savagery of the Mahdi's fundamentalist *ansar* via the sophistication of [Muslim Brotherhood and now National Islamic Front leader] Al-Turabi's modernizing Islamists to the intellectualism of Mahmud M. Taha's pacifist "Republicans" and the Third World Revolutionism of [southern Sudanese guerrilla leader] John Garang's Marxist [Sudan People's Liberation Army (the military wing of the political movement)].[83]

All but Garang are religious figures.

If one accepts el-Shahi's argument, politics and Sufism are one, and leaders to followers is a patron-client relationship within the Sufi orders.[84] He saw Sufism as Sudan's "orthodoxy," adding that the crucial difference between Sufism and orthodox Islam concerns the position of saints.[85] The heads of Sufi orders (sheikhs) claim to be able to perform miracles, a power deemed hereditary, thus forming holy families. Also, "Because Islam was primarily introduced to Sudanese by Sufis, the disagreement between the orthodox learned men, *'ulama*, and the Sufis ... is not a feature of Islam in Sudan" (25).

El-Shahi places virtually everyone as a Sufi and under a Sufi: "Sufi orders ... came to be organized gradually with the purpose of linking the followers in various parts of the country with the spiritual authority" (26). "[M]en of religion such as *'ulama*, *shaikhs*, and *fakis* [teachers in a Quranic school or healers] are invariably either followers of Sufi orders or in alliance with these orders" (26).[86] These sheikhs have always played major roles in politics: the Mahdi "used religion as a pretext for political protest and action" (24); twentieth-century sheikhs have played definite roles in electoral politics (27). According to el-Shahi, "Even members of the growing educated class, who advocate the secularity of politics, are either followers of Sufi orders or have allied themselves with these orders" (23).

Esposito follows el-Shahi in looking to Islam as the major source of local and national leadership, adding that Islam has inspired many interest groups, organizations, and parties, and claiming that even secular-oriented nationalists have had to acknowledge Sudan's Islamic past as the "origin of Sudanese nationalism."[87]

Undoubtedly, then, politics and religion are linked. But how does this relate to gender? It never ceases to amaze me how much emphasis is placed on the turuq and the politics they spawned without any mention of the fact that women figured hardly at all in their history and development. Technically not members, except as extensions of male relatives, and certainly not leaders, when women became active in the nationalist movement, it was usually as "Greek chorus" supporters of the orders their male relatives belonged to. Only in very recent history were women even encouraged by men to form auxiliaries, and these were usually mutual-aid or charitable societies; i.e., not strictly political.

There is much emphasis in the literature on the Mahdiyya (i.e., the Ansar) and the Khatmiyya (based on *khatim el-turuq* or "seal of all orders"), numerically and historically the two most powerful orders. As discussed above, the former movement was derived from the nineteenth-century messianic figure, Mohamed Ahmed; the latter, from a powerful religious leader, Ali el-Mirghani. Both movements have been as political as religious and, except for the military, have virtually dominated twentieth-century Sudanese politics and have virtually excluded women in their religiopolitical ranks.

The symbiosis of colonial powers and orders is the story of contemporary politics. During the Turco-Egyptian reign, ethnic groups from the north and east, especially the Shaygiyya (Khatmiyya supporters), were used as tax collectors and military irregulars. Some Sudanese scholars have maintained that Mahdist resentment toward the Khatmis and Shaygis developed, contributing to the rise of the Mahdi, whose goal was to topple the Ottoman reign. According to el-Shahi the Khatmis did not join the Mahdists against the Turco-Egyptians because they believed Mahdiyya success meant an end to their privileged status. When the Mahdists won without Khatmi support, the Khatmis went into exile in Egypt, consequently forming a close union with Egypt. That affinity produced a Khatmiyya nationalist rallying cry for Nile unity—i.e., with Egypt.[88]

Following the British reconquest, the patron-client relationship of the Khatmis and Ottomans (Egyptians) at first served the Khatmis well. "While the Mahdiyya was suppressed by the authorities, the Khatmiyya, in view of its opposition to the Mahdiyya and its pro-Egyptian stance, was favored. But the position was later reversed" (28–29), as the British began to patronize the posthumous son of the Mahdi, whose views were more aligned, and to suppress the Khatmiyya, whose unionist stance was inconducive to Britain's plans for Sudan.

Northern sectarian-party formation, contemporary history, and ideological differences have been well-documented:[89] the Ansar forming the Umma Party in 1945; the Khatmis establishing, in coalition with non-Khatmis, the Ashigga ("brothers") Party in 1943, which became the National Unionist Party (NUP), then the Peoples' Democratic Party (PDP) in 1956, and finally the Democratic Unionist Party (DUP) in 1968.

The Muslim Brotherhood, the National Islamic Front, and the Republicans

If Sufist politics is to be our norm, then one must add that four primarily northern-based, influential political parties or interest groups are opposed to Sufism: the Muslim Brotherhood (*el-ikhwan el-Muslimun* or *Ikhwan*); its offshoot the National Islamic Front (NIF); the Republicans (formerly Republican Brothers, *el-ikhwan el-jumhuriyun*); and the Sudanese Communist Party (SCP).

Just as the Ansar (or at least the Mahdi and his descendants) can only arguably be classified as Sufi, the Muslim Brotherhood has a complicated relationship to Sufism (rejecting, for example, the concept of union with god because such an idea was not preached in the early period of Islam).[90] Descending from the fundamentalist movement in Egypt and often referred to carelessly as "fundamentalist," the Muslim Brotherhood has more modernist tendencies than its critics acknowledge. (The NIF, the focus of chapter 6, is even more the case.)[91]

Moscow-oriented and "secular," the SCP has had an ambivalent relationship with its Sufi heritage, freeing its members to engage in private religious practice and choosing, as a party, not to confront many oppressive aspects of Islam, e.g., family status laws. The party's relationships to gender, culture, and religion are the focuses of chapters 5 and 7.

One of the more compelling religious/political movements in contemporary Sudan is the Republican movement, which was originally led by the late Mahmoud Mohamed Taha. The movement is small, mainly urban, and highly intellectual. Its reformist attitude toward Islam, especially sharia, is as refreshing as its attempt to build a nonsexist, nonracist, nonchauvinist community within an Islamic framework. Taha proposed to create a modern version of sharia through a shift in the foundation of Islamic law from one class of religious texts to another. The goal was to usher in a new egalitarian era of Islamic jurisprudence. Although highly respected by moderate, liberal, and progressive Sudanese, especially intellectuals, the movement was too small and powerless to be highly effective when most needed.

This is a test period for the Republicans. President Jaafar Nimieri executed Taha for heresy in 1985, effectively beheading an already small and nonhierarchical organization. After Taha's execution, Abdullahi Ahmed

An-Na'im, one of Sudan's most brilliant scholars, became active in disseminating the teachings of the late leader. He described part of the philosophy in this way:

> Ustadh [revered teacher] Mahmoud ... tried to establish a community which applied ... the main tenets of his vision of Islam. As a small community within Sudanese society, the Republicans were unable to implement the full scope of their beliefs in the organization of the Sudanese state, but they strove to lead their personal lives and organize their own community in accordance with those beliefs. In particular, the community largely succeeded in applying the principles of equality between men and women ... Women members participated fully in all the group's activities, and they were often leaders of activist groups on university campuses and in public parks and street corners—a highly controversial practice in ... patriarchal society.[92]

According to An-Na'im, the movement attempted to revolutionize marriage practices within the framework of sharia without offending prevailing custom. Marriage institutions of north-central Sudan are very oppressive to women, if not technically in the law, at least in practice in the courts.

> Although the Hanafi school of Islamic jurisprudence applied by the Shari'a Family Law Courts of the Sudan permitted a husband to give his wife the right to divorce herself unilaterally, no use was made of this provision in actual practice. Further, the Qur'anic principle of arbitration *(tahkim)* to settle family disputes ... was not used. Instead, marital differences were routinely submitted to the formal courts, which were unsuitable for settling such delicate and personal issues with the sensitivity and candor of private arbitration (6).

The Republicans, putting words into practice in their own lives and using themselves as role models, negotiated bride-price *(mahr)*, the cost of weddings, and divorce within each union in a way that was less extravagant and more egalitarian (6–7).

When I first became aware of the Republicans in the 1970s, I was surprised at the extent to which women participated in the movement. Other scholars had the same reaction. For example:

> In the mid-seventies Mahmud M. Taha's followers set up their own women's organization, the "Republican Sisters" *(al-akhawat al-jumhuriyat)* ... Egged on by ... Taha himself ... [they] assumed more and more responsibility within the ever growing organizational framework of the movement as well as in the public representation of their group. At first, such exposure of females in public debates and street discussions was pro-

vocative to a traditional society ... *At times it appeared as if the "Republican Sisters" were the spearhead of the movement.*[93]

The Republican influence with regard to women's emancipation likely affected many other political groups, even the Muslim Brotherhood, whose leader, Hasan el-Turabi, declared that Islam favored coeducation, and later as NIF leader encouraged the political activism of women. Even the women of the Umma Party became more publicly visible, evidenced by the political activism of Sara el-Fadl, wife of the most recent civilian ex-prime minister, Saddig el-Mahdi.

But the Republicans were as poor as the Ikhwan and NIF are wealthy. With their founder and leader dead and the current regime repressing all political and religious dissent, the movement's development will be problematic.

Nimieri, the Military, and Contemporary Politics

Every Sudanese party or political/religious interest group has had to contend with significant social and economic issues: the civil war, the drought, the chronically bad and worsening economic situation, the interference of international capital, and the restless and ambitious military.

Sudan began the postindependence (1956) era as a parliamentary democracy. The military was invited into power by the civilian regime in 1958 and stayed in power until a civilian overthrow in 1964. But jostling parties—old sectarian, progressive (e.g., the SCP), and conservative (e.g., the Muslim Brotherhood)—created a confusion of alignments and realignments, stalemating the new democracy. From 1969 until 1985 the military, under Gen. Jaafar Nimieri, resumed control.

From its 1969–71 communist-influenced period (the coup d'état was carried out by the Free Officers),[94] through a vaguely pan-Arabist, one-party system (the Sudan Socialist Union) that became increasingly repressive; through a period of "National Reconciliation" when some of the old sectarian groups were returned to power and the Muslim Brotherhood was invited to join (1977); to an Islamist period (especially intensified by 1983)—Nimieri's military regime is very difficult to characterize.

After a civilian coalition of professional unions, students, southerners, trade unionists, and intellectuals overthrew the Nimieri regime in the 1985 Intifada (Uprising), the government elected the next year was initially dominated by the Ansar sect—led by Saddig el-Mahdi, head of the Umma Party—but evolved into an "Islamic Trend" government inspired by Ikhwan elements, the NIF. In June 1989 another military coup—a "National Salvation Revolution" led by Lt. Gen. Omer el-Bashir—replaced the civilian government and installed, in essence, an NIF government.[95]

Arguably, one can say Sudan has carried out one of the most successful of contemporary Islamic revolutions. But that statement is somewhat
misleading. As we have seen, the reign of political Islam, even radical
Islam, is more a continuity with Sudan's Islamic past than it is a diver-
gence.

In 1988, during my most recent field trip, Sudanese were still permitted by the state to debate strategies for democratic change. Intellectual
and political excitement generated by the 1985 Intifada still prevailed,
and debate over the advantages and disadvantages of an Islamic state
and accompanying sharia was intense. Dozens of newspapers were
active, as were radio and television; unions, professional associations,
political parties and interest groups assembled frequently. Two women
were elected to the People's Assembly, and the long-dormant Sudanese
Women's Union was active again. Heady times: not dissimilar to the
immediate postindependence atmosphere, or to the 1964 democratic era
following the overthrow of the Abboud military regime. But the atmosphere changed abruptly with the demise of democratic processes in 1989
and the establishment of the National Salvation Revolution, a right-wing
Islamic military government.

The nature of debate within the brief (1985–89) democratic era remains
of considerable significance, not just for Sudan, but for other settings
where Islam is or may become a factor in the political process. Statements
about the curtailment of democratic processes with the rise of political
Islam may not have the same meaning to those who are not aware of
Sudan's postcolonial record of democratic institutions and grassroots
populism, even when the military was in control: a twentieth-century
story of strong and independent trade unions and professional associations. Sudan had one of the largest and most revered communist parties
in Africa or the Middle East, as well as a powerful Women's Union. When
I first arrived in 1961, Euroamerican expatriates in Khartoum praised
Sudanese for their "relaxed attitude" toward religion. The progress of
women's rights, though gradual, was upward, with women's suffrage
won in 1965, accompanied by a number of other rights and legal protections. Non- or minimal violence had marked Sudan's nationalist period
and the achievement of independence from the British in 1956. And
Sudan's postindependence politics have twice been punctuated by a civilian coalition overthrowing a military regime in nearly bloodless encoun-
ters, the last occurring in 1985. The NIF was an integral political force
during that period, which culminated in an Islamist regime.

The right-wing Islamist military government has held power since
1989. It immediately dissolved Parliament (a democratically elected People's Assembly; Hasan el-Turabi refers to the existence of an appointed
parliament),[96] suspended the Permanent Constitution, and outlawed all

political parties, unions, and professional associations—even the venerable Sudan Bar Association and Doctors' Union. Sharia and governance were imposed even on non-Muslims (nearly one third of the country). Rights of due process were suspended or ignored; hundreds languished in jails, some still there after years; executions were common; and torture and disappearances were reported by Amnesty International (e.g., May 1992) and other watch groups. Middle-class civil servants, including large numbers of university faculty, were sacked. In general, opposition elements were eliminated.

Women's freedom of movement and association were sharply curtailed and the agenda for women co-opted by the Islamic revolution. In November 1991 "The Islamic Fundamentalist military junta decreed ... that henceforth all Sudanese women will wear long black dresses to their ankles and a black veil covering their head and face ... those who disobey to be instantly punished by whipping."[97] Hasan el-Turabi, virtually in charge of the Islamic revolution, claimed in a May 18, 1992 lecture at the University of Southern California that the dress code is not enforced except by "peer pressure," but fear is that it can be imposed anytime by administrative fiat.

As mentioned above, the country is in economic disarray. The capital is overextended in social services and has become poverty-ridden, unhealthy, and dangerous. Migrants—especially southerners and westerners—pour into Greater Khartoum only to have their shantytowns demolished by the government and themselves driven out into the desert. As local militias carry out genocidal attacks, thousands of southern and western Sudanese starve. A May 1992 report by Amnesty International informed us that around the country more and more dissidents were being arrested, imprisoned, and executed, especially members and supporters of the Sudan People's Liberation Movement (SPLM).[98]

Turabi has increasingly been viewed as one of the most important Islamic leaders in the world and has attracted a great deal of controversy and commentary,[99] not limited to those opposed to Islamism but extending to those within Islamism who see Turabi as too liberal or "quasi-liberal." For example,

> Much has been said about al-Turabi's innovative creativity in the interpretation of Islam and about his *quasi-liberal* ideas on democracy, the status and role of women, the rights of non-Muslims, especially their right to hold public office including that of the head of state. Such innovative interpretations have even led to schism within the Ikhwans' ranks. The ideological purists, led by al-Sadiq Abdallah and al-Hibr Nur al-Daim (who now call themselves the Muslim Brothers) regard such departures from orthodoxy as opportunism.[100]

Turabi has spoken a great deal about "democracy," the emancipation of women, and human rights within Islam.[101] About women, for example, Turabi stated:

> With respect to the status of women generally in society, we don't have any more problems ... the issue of women in the Sudan is no longer a topical issue ... we don't bother ourselves a lot about it anymore in the Sudan ... In the Islamic movement, I would say that women have played a more important role of late than men (46–47).

As for the democratic nature of Islamism in Sudan, Turabi claimed: "But people, either deliberately or mistakenly, call them [the Islamic movements] antidemocratic. But these movements are essentially grassroots movements; they are populist movements. And if you scrutinize the model of the movement itself, it's highly democratic" (18). But critics have contended that

> Even if one concedes ... that al-Turabi's views on women democracy, and human rights are relatively liberal, such liberality has not been reflected in the policies of the present government ... The prohibition of free travel for women except in the company of a male *mahram* ... the segregation of public transport on gender lines; the imposition of an Islamic dress on women; and the massive dismissals of women from public service seem not to reflect the quasi-liberal views of al-Turabi on encouraging women to "escape social oppression and discrimination and to play a full part in [the] building of a new society."[102]

It is difficult to know what a "quasi-liberal" view of the role of women in Sudanese society will mean for women. Turabi has been consistent in his argument that a pure Islam that is a pan-national movement can have the effect of emancipating women. To what degree women accept that argument, and to what degree they might be hoodwinked by their culture, remains to be seen. Certainly, oppositional organization is made more difficult in that discontent is at least momentarily defused.

Although chapter 6 briefly chronicles the rise of Islamism in Sudan, it is important here to underscore that in Sudan's religious history, there has always been political Islam or an Islam intertwined with politics. This is true for the colonial intruders, the Sudanese responses, the postindependence democratic party politics, the religious framework of the Republicans, and even the "strange bedfellows" coalitions that the SCP formed with various sectarian groups and its strategy of coexistence with Islam (discussed in chapters 5 and 7).[103]

Despite my emphasis on sectarian and Sufi politics in this chapter, one should not underestimate the military as the force to contend with. Very little has been published about the Sudanese military's composition—class, ethnicity, religion—but we are led to believe that it crosses class and ethnicity. Duran observed, however, that "There is a preponderance of 'black' soldiers in the Sudanese army (some estimates mentioned 75 percent), mainly because of the high proportion of Westerners (from Darfur) [non-Arab Muslims, some of whom are from West Africa] with their military tradition."[104] Other sources say the army consists of many southerners, but these do not make up the officer ranks; still others talk of the military dominance of the Shaygiyya. Turabi says of the composition of the military, "If you pick a random sample from the army, most of them would be Islamists."[105] The sources are in fact weak, and not much is known about the composition of the military except the obvious: the poor join the lower ranks, the elite become officers, women play virtually no role.

Like militaries elsewhere, Sudanese regimes have seen politics as dirty, politicians as corrupt, and sectarianism as divisive. Military institutions see themselves as possessing a purity, a simplicity, an independence from confusing arrays of political choices of civilian administrations, as representing a national unity through a secular rationality. Many civilians have agreed.

In contemporary Sudanese politics the state used to be controlled fairly directly by the bourgeoisie, but recently that control has been eroded and the society has become increasingly militarized. That military and the militias it has spawned have taken on not only a "tribal" identity (e.g., the local militias), but a religious one as well (i.e., the military in support of the NIF). This has amounted to a resurgence of the warrior tradition and a remasculinization of the society.[106] This remasculinization is parallel, but perhaps contradictory, to the (re)positioning of women as bulwarks for the (re)building of "authentic" culture.

Such are the tensions of gender politics in Sudan, a society where a weak state has been buffeted by competing oppositional groups and where the processes of state feminism have been discontinuous. In chapter 5 I analyze the gender politics of one oppositional group, the SCP; in chapter 6, of another, the NIF, which was to become, in essence, the state.

Notes

1. The "Three Towns" refers to Khartoum, Khartoum North, and Omdurman—three separate cities at the confluence of the Blue and White Niles. Khartoum is technically the capital. The 1983 census estimated their populations (respectively, 473,597; 340,857; and 526,192) at 1,340,646. These figures are from United Nations, Department of Economic and Social Development, Statistical Department, *Demographic Yearbook, 1991* (New York: United Nations, 1992), 226.

There is every reason to believe that this is a low count, the government reluctantly enumerating the surrounding shantytowns. See below for further comment on the low population estimates of the Three Towns.

2. These figures are taken, respectively, from Magda M. el-Sanousi and Nafissa Ahmed el-Amin, "Sudan," in *Women and Politics Worldwide*, ed. Barbara J. Nelson and Najma Chowdhury (New Haven: Yale University Press, 1994), 674 (box); and Nahid Toubia, ed. with Amira Bahyeldin, Nadia Hijab, and Heba Abdel Latif, *Arab Women: A Profile of Diversity and Change* (Cairo: Population Council, 1994), 14. The former uses figures from the Sudan Government, Population Census Office, Department of Statistics *National Census* (preliminary report) (Khartoum, 1989); Toubia et al. use 1994 UNICEF figures.

3. El-Sanousi and el-Amin, "Sudan," 674, taken from the 1989 census material cited above.

4. This is a common phrase in the literature on Sudan to describe an area along the Nile River, which runs south-north through more than two thirds of the middle of the country. It is an area of mainly Nubians and Arabs, who have intermingled for centuries and culturally dominate the country. For this reason I refer below to the culture of this area as the "core culture."

5. This is *not* to deny political, economic, and cultural activity in other important regional and urban centers. Religious movements, labor movements, ethnic-revival politics, and the like have taken place outside central riverain culture. Besides, centers of cultural and political power and energy have shifted spatially and temporally.

6. Questions of Nubian origins and ethnicity have puzzled scholars and lay people alike, but whatever the uncertainties, a great many hypotheses have been proposed. At one extreme of the spectrum, influential scholars like Batrawi and Seligman bestowed upon Nubians the high status of "Hamite." In its most common form, the idea is that everything of value in Africa at the time of European imperial contact was brought by Caucasoid Hamites. See, e.g., A. Batrawi, "The Racial History of Egypt and Nubia," *Journal of the Royal Anthropological Institute* 75 (1945): 76, 81–101, 131–56; and C.G. Seligman, *Races of Africa*, 3d ed. (London: Oxford University Press, 1957), 8. The culture of Nubians was too advanced and the history too honorable for early scholars and travelers to attribute to "Negroid" origins. Nubians for some time, along with the ancient Egyptians, were assigned "Caucasian" racial characteristics, the highest distinction white scholars could think of to award an African people.

That Kush/Meroe was Christian for a very long time drops out of many sources, including this one. Moreover, we have virtually no sources on gender relations in the early Christian Kingdoms. This note acknowledges the absence of this topic.

7. Respectively, the sources for these expressions are Bashir Muhammad Sa'id, *The Sudan: Crossroads of Africa* (London: Bodley Head, 1965); William Y. Adams, *Nubia: Corridor to Africa* (Princeton: Princeton University Press, 1977); and L.P. Kirwan, "Nubia—an African Frontier Zone," *The Advancement of Science* 19, no. 80 (1962), 330–37.

8. John Sommer, "The Sudan: A Geographical Investigation of the Historical and Social Roots of Political Dissension" (Ph.D. diss., Boston University, 1968). Italics mine.

9. J.S. Trimingham, *Islam in the Sudan* (New York: Barnes and Noble, 1965 [1949]), 18.

10. A recent human rights report has chronicled the brutality on both sides. Human Rights Watch/Africa, *Civilian Devastation: Abuses by All Parties in the War in Southern Sudan* (New York: Human Rights Watch, 1994).

11. Yusuf Fadl Hasan, *The Arabs and the Sudan* (Edinburgh: Edinburgh University Press, 1967). In this background summary I have not returned us to Pharaonic Egypt, nor to the early Christian kingdoms of Kush and Meroe.

12. For a sociopolitical and economic historical interpretation of the Funj state, see Jay Spaulding, *The Heroic Age in Sinnar* (East Lansing: Michigan State University Press, 1985).

13. The Mamluks were an elite military force of white slaves in Egypt whom Mohamed Ali nearly exterminated in 1811. Many subsequently fled to Sudan, where they remained, melting into the population. See V. Lutsky, *Modern History of the Arabs in the Sudan*, 2 vols. (Cambridge: Cambridge University Press, 1969), 48–53.

14. The information in this section comes from Lutsky, ibid.

15. Sudan, *Report of the Commission of Enquiry into the Southern Sudan Disturbances during August, 1955* (Khartoum: Sudan Government, 1956). This is a highly respected report.

16. Richard Hill, *Egypt in the Sudan, 1820–1881* (London: Oxford University Press, 1959), 129.

17. Sudan, *Report of the Commission of Enquiry*. The Danagla, from Dongola in the north, are one of the Nubian groups.

18. Colonialists of the "Turkiyya" were the descendants of Mohamed Ali, who was not a "Turk," but an Ottoman. Although it is technically incorrect to use the terms "Turkiyya" and "Mahdiyya" as time periods rather than as adjectives, it is a convention widely accepted by historians of Sudan.

19. Samir Amin, "Underdevelopment and Dependence in Black Africa: Historical Origin" (revised version of working paper prepared for United Nations African Institute for Economic Development and Planning, Dakar, Senegal, 1971).

20. Many historical materials have been condensed here; for example, P.M. Holt, *The Mahdist State in the Sudan, 1881–1898* (Oxford: Clarendon Press, 1958); Hill, *Egypt in the Sudan*; Richard Gray, *A History of Southern Sudan, 1839–1889* (London: Oxford University Press, 1961), and his "Some Obstacles to Economic Development in the Southern Sudan, 1839–1965," in *Nations by Design*, ed. Arnold Rivkin (New York: Doubleday, 1968), 121–34; Lutsky, *Modern History of the Arabs*; and Spaulding, *The Heroic Age in Sinnar*. For interpretations of the rise of capitalism, however, I have used Carole Collins, "Sudan: Colonialism and Class Struggle," *Middle East Research and Information Project* (MERIP), no. 46 (1976): 3–17, 20; Fatma Babiker Mahmoud, *The Sudanese Bourgeoisie: Vanguard of Development?* (London: Zed, 1984); and, especially Amin, ibid.

21. The interpretation is based mainly on Amin, but the extrapolations regarding gender are mine. Amin, "Underdevelopment and Dependence in Black Africa," like most of the sources, does not deal with gender relations.

22. As to southern interethnic relations, some mixing occurred with exchanges of captives and intermarriages. Exchanges and intermarriages across "north-south" ethnic boundaries (e.g., among the Kreish and Baggara) and trading alliances (e.g., between the Turco-Egyptians and the Shilluk) were also effected. However, natural barriers, economic self-sufficiency, and ideological coherence militated against any extensive ethnic interaction. So, when pressures and tensions intruded from the outside, the prevalent social divisions were easily exploited. Gray, *A History of Southern Sudan*, 11.

23. Lutsky, *Modern History of the Arabs*.

24. Holt, *The Mahdist State*, 20–21.

25. J.S. Trimingham explained that "The whole Egyptian administration was rotten to the core ... [The Mahdi began a] *jihad* [holy war] against the infidel Turk 'to purify the world from wantonness and corruption.'" *Islam in the Sudan*, 93–94. Although this is true, the Mahdi did not emerge from an international vacuum to purify the world. The British had invaded Egypt; there was a complex relationship between Egypt and Sudan, with the Egyptians, then, having enough to manage. The international bungling and mismanagement of the "Gordon affair" was also a major factor in the Mahdi's rise and success.

26. Holt, *The Mahdist State*, 17.

27. The term, *el-mahdi* means "the guided one," possessing divine guidance. The *mahdi* is also head of an Islamic community. Holt has differentiated the Sudanese Sunni form of mahdism from the Shiite form in which the mahdi is the hidden Imam, returned to rule the community. Eventually followers of the Mahdi became known as "Ansari," which they are still called today. Trimingham, *Islam in the Sudan*, 21–22. Whether or not we can still consider the Mahdi a Sufi, and the Ansar Sufists, is a matter of some debate, and is discussed later.

28. Hill, *Egypt in the Sudan*, 117–18.

29. Using the "north-south" dichotomy at this point in Sudanese history is anachronistic; it was only with the coming of British administration that these two regions were treated as separate entities.

30. Collins, "Sudan: Colonialism and Class Struggle," 17.

31. El-Hag Hamad Mohammed Kheir, "Women and Politics in Medieval Sudanese History," in *The Sudanese Woman*, ed. Susan Kenyon (Khartoum: University of Khartoum, 1987), 24. Kheir also has coauthored a paper with Maymouna Mirghani Hamza, "A Case Study of Mahdist Historiography" (Conference on Mahdist Studies, Khartoum, 1981). Nawar Mahgoub, a member of the Mahdi family, has carried out research since the 1980s on women during the Mahdiyya period.

32. Marjorie Hall and Bakhita Amin Ismail, *Sisters under the Sun: The Story of Sudanese Women* (London: Longman, 1981), 40.

33. Ibid., 40–41.

34. It is always dubious, if not entirely false, to refer to anyone as being condemned "to a state of ignorance," as having "no concept of a wider horizon," and as offering "little existence." We do not yet know what women in this period

accepted or resisted. As for the description sounding familiar, I suspect the authors imposed a superficial view of 1970s Sudan on the past.

35. Zeinab Bashir el-Bakri, Fahima Zahir (el-Sadaty), Belghis Badri, Tamadur Ahmed Khalid, and Madiha el-Sanusi, "Sudanese Sub-Project: Women in Sudan in the Twentieth Century," in *Women's Movements and Organizations in Historical Perspective*, ed. Saskia Wieringa (The Hague: Institute of Social Studies, Women and Development Programme, [post-1987?]), 176.

36. Zeinab Bashir el-Bakri and el-Haj Hamad M. Khier, "Sudanese Women in History and Historiography: A Proposed Strategy for Curriculum Change" (Workshop on Women's Studies in Sudan, Khartoum, Sudan Family Planning Association, National Council for Research, 7–9 February 1989), 6.

37. Ibid., 16.

38. The concept of "patriarchy" has achieved renewed respectability in Middle East scholarship; see, e.g., Mervat Hatem, "Class and Patriarchy as Competing Paradigms for the Study of Middle Eastern Women," *Comparative Studies in Society and History* 29, no. 4 (1987), 811–18; and Hisham Sharabi, *Neopatriarchy: A Theory of Distorted Change in Arab Society* (New York: Oxford University Press, 1988).

39. The technical name for the colonial regime. According to the Anglo-Egyptian Conventions of 1899 (the Condominium Agreement) Sudan was to have separate status from Egypt (which was already under British rule) and would be ruled jointly by Egypt and Britain. The de facto rule, however, was British.

40. For one example of the process and results of that co-option see my "Elite Nubians of Greater Khartoum: A Study of Changing Ethnic Alignments," in *Economy and Class in Sudan*, ed. Norman O'Neill and Jay O'Brien (Aldershot: Avebury, 1988), 277–90.

41. Karen Sacks notes this as a familiar African colonial pattern in "An Overview of Women and Power in Africa," in *Perspectives on Power: Women in Africa, Asia, and Latin America*, ed. Jean F. O'Barr (Durham: Duke University, Center for International Studies, 1982), 1–10. She points out that when the kinship system was patrilineal, it was preserved, but when it was matrilineal, it was changed in the name of "progress." One can observe the same pattern for northern and southern Sudan, the latter area containing more matrilineal societies.

42. El-Bakri et al., "Sudanese Sub-Project," 177.

43. Arriving in Sudan as early as 1961 gave me the advantage of seeing clear vestiges of colonialism. Many British were still in their posts, their positions not yet having been "Sudanized." I found that many of the British men who still influenced the country were far more conservative about the role of northern Sudanese women than were many Sudanese men. Or, if they pretended not to approve of the asymmetry in gender relations, they would ordinarily dismiss it as the "natural order of things"—i.e., in Sudan. Certainly gender relations in the "expatriate" community were asymmetrical. That there were few British women in paid employment, that they mainly managed the households, and that they were but shadows of their husbands was usually rationalized as appropriate behavior in the Sudanese context—i.e., as if it were the "fault" of the Sudanese that British colonial wives were subordinate to their husbands.

44. For a study of Nuer (southern) women, see Ellen Gruenbaum, "Nuer Women in Southern Sudan: Health, Reproduction, and Work," working paper no.

215, Michigan State University, East Lansing, Mich., 1990). Considering the high level of heterogeneity of both the north and south, these statements must be read as generalizations.

45. This can be recognized as a hypothesis, one that will not be "tested" in this work. However, Zeinab B. el-Bakri and el-Wathig M. Kameir agree in "Women and Development Policies in Sudan: A Critical Outlook" (paper no. 46, presented at the 2d OSSREA Congress, Nairobi, 28–31 July 1986), 3.

46. Ibid., 3.

47. Mahmoud, *The Sudanese Bourgeoisie*, 2, uses the analysis of Samir Amin, *Unequal Development* (Brighton: Harvester, 1977), 333: "He traces the pre-mercantilist period back to the era of the Sultanate, when long-distance trade existed with Egypt and to the East. According to Amin, the Sudan was integrated in the capitalist market during the Turko-Egyptian colonial period, when Sudanese nomads participated in trade by acting as middlemen for Turkish, Syrian and European merchants. They then moved to agriculture on lands given to them by the Turko-Egyptian system. These agricultural undertakings were largely commercial. At this stage, although new farming methods were introduced, the relations of production were still based on the use of serfs and slaves. Wage labour was not known."

48. Mahmoud, *The Sudanese Bourgeoisie*, 13–14.

49. Tony Barnett, "The Gezira Scheme: Production of Cotton and the Reproduction of Underdevelopment," in *Beyond the Sociology of Development: Economy and Society of Latin America and Africa*, ed. I. Oxaal, T. Barnett, and D. Booth (London: Routledge and Kegan Paul, 1975), 203.

50. This particular statement is taken from Collins, "Sudan: Colonialism and Class Struggle," 10. Useful sources on the Gezira that I have integrated into my analysis are Barnett, "The Gezira Scheme," ibid., 186–207; Tim Niblock, *Class and Power in Sudan: The Dynamics of Sudanese Politics, 1898–1985* (Albany: State University of New York, 1987); and Norman O'Neill, "Class and Politics in the Modern History of Sudan," in O'Neill and O'Brien, *Economy and Class in Sudan*, 25–59.

51. Peter McLoughlin, "Economic Development and the Heritage of Slavery in the Sudan Republic," *Africa* 23 (1962): 377.

52. For an argument about the role this capitalist class plays in Sudanese politics, see Mahmoud, *The Sudanese Bourgeoisie*. She argues that because of its alliance with colonialism the Sudanese bourgeoisie has no progressive role to play in the development of Sudan.

53. David Roden, "Regional Inequality and Rebellion in the Sudan," *Geographical Review* 64, no. 2 (1974): 498.

54. The first Sudan census stated that there are 572 "tribes" and many more "subtribes." There are, perhaps, as many as 110 separate languages. Sudan, Ministry for Social Affairs, Population Census Office, 21 *Facts about the Sudanese: First Population Census of Sudan, 1955/56*, prepared by Karol Jozef Krotki (Khartoum: Sudan Government, 1958), 23.

55. I use the term "tribe" advisedly. For an exhaustive account of Arab tribal history and genealogy, see H.A. MacMichael, *A History of the Arabs in the Sudan* (Cambridge: Cambridge University Press, 1922). For a Sudanese account, Yusuf Fadl Hasan, *The Arabs and the Sudan* (Edinburgh: Edinburgh University Press,

1967). P.M. Holt, the early British dean of Sudan historians, is more general in his *A Modern History of the Sudan* (London: Weidenfeld and Nicolson, 1961). A very different perspective is V. Lutsky's *Modern History of the Arabs in the Sudan*, 2 vols. (Cambridge: Cambridge University Press, 1969).

56. Sudan, *21 Facts about the Sudanese*, 26.

57. Cecil Eprile, *War and Peace in the Sudan, 1955–1972* (London: David and Charles, 1974), 27.

58. Sudan, *Report of the Commission of Enquiry.*

59. Eprile, *War and Peace in the Sudan*, 27. A recent newspaper article, citing a work by Norman A. Horner (*A Guide to Christian Churches in the Middle East* [Elkhard, Indiana: Mission Focus, n.d.]), estimated the number of Christians in Sudan at 71,950 or 3.69 percent. This is a statement by Christian officials, so it is difficult to refute them as low: It is unlikely that church officials would underestimate Christians. Nick B. Williams, Jr., "In Mideast, a Christian Exodus," *Los Angeles Times* (10 August 1991), A16. One of the most reliable works written on the north-south conflict is Mohamed Omer Beshir, *The Southern Sudan: Background to Conflict* (London: C. Hurst, 1968).

60. There is a poor Coptic minority clustered mainly in the northern towns. These are primarily "Nagadiyya," turn-of-the-century migrants from Upper Egypt. Originally they specialized in dyeing the traditional blue cloth worn by women. In Khartoum they are now small merchants or petty craftspeople such as ivory carvers. A few extended families have achieved wealth, but continue to live in modest circumstances and are held in low esteem by other northern Christians. Only in recent years have some successful Nagadiyya been accepted as marriage partners by other Copts.

61. Some women of the Lebanese Shashati family and the Catholic Syrian Kronfli family became doctors as early as the 1950s.

62. Because of the numerical dominance in the north of people claiming Arab identity, the first-order categorization of ethnic groups is commonly into "Arab" and "non-Arab." Even if used only heuristically, such a binary grouping of opposites can obscure the fact that these broad categories contain groups of people whose linguistic, social, religious, economic, and ecological characteristics cut across the categorical boundary separating them. Moreover, these broad categories are not geographically exclusive. We are as yet unable, by means of blood-typing or any other physiological device, to define clearly the physical differences between "Arabs" and "non-Arabs."

Whatever our scholarly deficiencies or reservations, the folk ideologies of Arab descent stress somatic differences. So, despite the impossibility of isolating "pure Arabs" or "pure Africans," Sudanese claims to Arab affiliation remain the salient ethnographic fiction, accepted as fact and acted upon. In my ethnographic fieldwork I accepted claims to Arab genealogy if a person so self-identified. However, in regard to the question of genealogy, this can be problematic:

> In theory, direct descent in Moslem society means, of course, exclusively patrilineal descent. However, most of the peoples of North Africa reckoned descent through the mother in pre-Islamic times, and the tradition, though unacknowledged, has by no means died out ... in the case of the Nubians, this has facilitated a claim of Arab

or Turkish ancestry on either side of the family. In the course of time the prestigious ancestor is surreptitiously transferred into the male line, perhaps by omitting from the genealogy the generation in which the female link occurred or by substituting the mother's brother for the biological father. The unreliability of "Arab" pedigrees is not limited to distortions of this kind. A study of a large number of *nisba* [genealogy] collected in the Republic of the Sudan has shown that they usually contain wholly spurious or "dummy" ancestors in the earlier generations. (William Y. Adams, "Ethnohistory and Islamic Tradition in Africa," *Ethnohistory* 16, no. 4 (1969): 282.)

I have written on the subject of ethnic complexity in the central riverain area in *Nubians: A Study in Ethnic Identity* (Khartoum: Institute of African and Asian Studies, University of Khartoum, 1971); "Nubians in the Urban Milieu: Greater Khartoum," *Sudan Notes and Records* 54 (1973): 57–65; "The Ethnic Identity of Sudanese Nubians," *Meroitica* 5 (1979): 165–72; and "The Changing Ethnic Identity of Nubians in an Urban Milieu: Khartoum, Sudan" (Ph.D. diss., University of California, 1979).

63. Harold Barclay used the former, "Process in the Arab Sudan," *Human Organization* 24 (1965): 43–48; Hasan used the latter term in The Arabs and the Sudan, 1967.

64. Andreas and Waltraud Kronenberg, "Preliminary Report on Anthropological Field-Work 1961–62 in Sudanese Nubia," *Kush* 12 (1964): 284.

65. Harold Barclay, *Buurri al Lamaab: A Suburban Village in the Sudan* (Ithaca, New York: Cornell University Press, 1964), 94–95. Italics mine.

66. My fieldwork on urban Nubians was carried out 1971–72 and 1973–75. These were among my major themes of my "Changing Ethnic Identity of Nubians," and were articulated most recently in "The Impact of Immigration on Women: The Sudanese Nubian Case," in *Across Cultures: The Spectrum of Women's Lives*, ed. Emily K. Abel and Marjorie L. Pearson (New York: Gordon and Breach, 1989), 53–56.

67. El-Sanousi and el-Amin, "Sudan," 674 (box).

68. International Labour Organisation, *Growth, Employment and Equity: A Comprehensive Strategy for the Sudan* (Geneva: International Labour Office, 1976), 364; el-Sanousi and el-Amin, "Sudan," 674 (box).

69. Sudan, 21 *Facts about the Sudanese*, 36.

70. The 1973 census was only partially released and difficult to obtain. I am using figures taken in note form from a provisional form of that census. This census and others monitored different categories, thereby diminishing their comparability. This is especially important with regards to ethnicity, since only the 1955/56 census recorded ethnic information. See ibid.; Sudan, Department of Statistics, *First Population Census of Sudan 1955/56: Town Planners Supplement* 1, prepared by D.G. Climenhaga (Khartoum: Sudan Government, 1960); *First Population Census of Sudan 1955/56. Final Report*, 3 vols. (Khartoum: Sudan Government, 1962); and *Population and Housing Survey 1964/65: Khartoum* (Khartoum: Sudan Government, 1965).

71. See note 1 above.

72. El-Sayed el-Bushra, "Sudan's Triple Capital: Morphology and Functions," *Ekistics* 39, no. 233 (1975): 250.

73. Ibid., 250.

74. Information for these statements is from el-Sayed el-Bushra, "Occupational Classification of Sudanese Towns," *Sudan Notes and Records* 50 (1969): 78; and *Sudan, Department of Statistics, First Population Census of Sudan 1955/56,* 68–85, table 9.12.

75. Salih el-Arifi, "Urbanization and Economic Development in the Sudan," in *Urbanization in the Sudan,* ed. el-Sayed el-Bushra (Khartoum: Philosophical Society of the Sudan, 1972), 63.

76. Timothy Maliqalim Simone, "Metropolitan Africans: Reading Incapacity, the Incapacity of Reading," *Cultural Anthropology* 5, no. 2 (1990): 170.

77. See note 1, chapter 1, for the Gramscian writings that have guided the framework on the state. Ideas on women and the state were stimulated by Carole Pateman's *The Sexual Contract* (Stanford: Stanford University Press, 1988), and her *The Disorder of Women* (Stanford: Stanford University Press, 1989). Ideas about the state in the Middle East were stimulated by Lisa Anderson, "The State in the Middle East and North Africa," *Comparative Politics* 20, no. 1 (1987): 1–18. Although she is using a modified Weberian approach, Anderson presents some interesting ideas, e.g., about the distinctions between European and Middle Eastern states, the latter marked more by the participation of "corporate, lineage, and tribal groups in exercising political authority ... within centralized bureaucratic administrations" (14). I have had to take into account Timothy Mitchell's critique of recent writing (Mitchell and Roger Owen, "Defining the State in the Middle East," *Middle East Studies Association Bulletin* 24 [1990]: 179–83) in which the Middle Eastern state is presented as either a freestanding object located outside society or as a structure. His interest in the "effect" of the modern state provokes analyzing the state as presenting itself "both as part of society and yet apart from society at the same time" (180). Fatima Babiker Mahmoud (*The Sudanese Bourgeoisie*) and John Waterbury ("Twilight of the State Bourgeoisie?" *International Journal of Middle East Studies* 23 [1991]: 1–17) have both stimulated my analysis of the class nature of Sudan's society and state. Beyond Mahmoud, O'Neill and O'Brien are correct in their introduction to *Economy and Class in Sudan* that "in most studies of the political economy of Sudan ... two subjects remain conspicuous by their absence: class formation, and the class structure of this post-colonial state" (1). The authors noted Mahmoud and Carole Collins ("Colonialism and Class Struggle in Sudan") as exceptions. Some of the framework for the Sudanese state is from Niblock, *Class and Power in Sudan,* and Peter Woodward, *Sudan, 1898–1989: The Unstable State* (Boulder: Lynne Rienner, 1990). Analyses of gender and the state in the Middle East are lacking. A most outstanding exception is Deniz Kandiyoti, ed., *Women, Islam and the State* (Philadelphia: Temple University Press, 1991). As to the relationship of gender to the state in Sudan, there is virtually nothing. Sources refer to the women's movements and women's rights, but not to gender ideology as it emanates from the media, the educational system, or is reflected by political interest groups.

78. The most useful discussion of this penetration by multinational corporations and international capital can be found in Mahmoud's discussion of Nimieri's "open door" policy of the mid-1970s. Most of these projects focused on rural development; e.g., the Kennana Sugar Scheme (partnership of the Sudanese government, Kuwait, Lonrho, the Arab Investment Company, a Japanese company,

and Gulf International Corporation). The effect, Mahmoud notes, was not only to weaken the state and increase the dependency of the bourgeoisie on the metropolitan centers, but "increased outflow of profits from Sudan and thus continued underdevelopment and further dependency." Mahmoud, *The Sudanese Bourgeoisie*, 70–72.

79. See, e.g., Gabriel Warburg, *Islam, Nationalism and Communism in a Traditional Society: The Case of Sudan* (London: Frank Cass, 1978), 93.

80. For historical background on Islam in Sudan and religious sects, see Trimingham, *Islam in the Sudan*; for politics in the modern period, see Warburg, *Islam, Nationalism and Communism*; Niblock, Class and Power in Sudan; and Woodward, *Sudan, 1898–1989*, among others. Afaf Abdel Majid Abu Hasabu is especially helpful in sorting out the factionalism in Sudanese politics in *Factional Conflict in the Sudanese Nationalist Movement, 1918–1948* (Graduate College Publications No. 12, University of Khartoum, Khartoum, 1985).

81. To borrow the title of Ahmed el-Shahi's *Themes from Northern Sudan* (London: Ithaca, 1986).

82. John L. Esposito, "Sudan," in *The Politics of Islamic Revivalism*, ed. Shireen T. Hunter (Bloomington: University of Indiana Press, 1988), 187. Italics mine.

83. Khalid Duran, "The Centrifugal Forces of Religion in Sudanese Politics," *Orient* 26, no. 4 (1985): 597.

84. Most of the religious orders (turuq; see chapter 2, note 4) in Sudan are Sufi (mystical) orders. Among them are Mahdiyya (Ansar, or followers of the Mahdi), Khatmiyya, Shadhiliyya, Qadiriyya, Sammaniyya, Tiganiyya, Majdhubiyya, Ahmadiyya, Idrisiyya, Hindiyya, Ismailiyya, and Rashidiyya. Trimingham's *Islam in Sudan* chronicles these orders and others. More contemporary sources (e.g., J. Abu-Nasr, *The Tijaniyya* [London: Oxford University Press, 1965]; John O. Voll, "A History of the Khatmiyya Tariqa in the Sudan" [Ph.D. diss., Harvard University, 1969]; and Idris Salim el-Hassan, "On Ideology: The Case of Religion in Northern Sudan" [Ph.D. diss., University of Connecticut, 1980]) have researched individual orders. "But the Sufism which became popular in the Sudan was at variance with that of the early mystics," partially as an accommodation to local conditions. "To the true mystic or Sufi there is a need to satisfy the deeper longings of the soul which seeks a perfect communion with God and ultimately an identification with Him, the Divine Oneness." El-Shahi, "Sufism in Modern Sudan," in *Themes from Northern Sudan*, 24. This would have been considered heresy by non-Sufis, so instead they stressed devotion and ascetic discipline, adhering to a hierarchy. El-Hassan, above, observed that the distinction between orthodox Islam and Sufism "is the way knowledge and truth are thought to be obtained. For the *sufi, marifa* (divine knowledge) can only be achieved through spiritual experience and its final goal is absolute truth" ("On Ideology," 72). He related that for the *ulama* (religious scholars) knowledge is gained through study of formal texts (73).

85. El-Shahi, "Sufism in Modern Sudan," 24.

86. A sheikh may also simply refer to a man of religion, or to a village headman. For a woman it is *sheikha*, but this often has different connotations—e.g., a zar functionary may be referred to as sheikha.

87. John Esposito, "Supplement: The Sudan and Lebanon," in *Islam and Politics*, ed. John Esposito (Syracuse: Syracuse University Press, 1987), 283.

88. El-Shahi, "Sufism in Modern Sudan," 28.

89. See, e.g., Woodward, *Sudan, 1898–1989*, 112; see also Muddathir Abd el-Rahim, *Imperialism and Nationalism in the Sudan* (Oxford: Clarendon Press, 1969); Abu Hasabu, *Factional Conflict*; and Niblock, *Class and Power in Sudan*.

90. El-Shahi, "Sufism in Modern Sudan," 33. In my interviews there was much debate about whether or not the Mahdists are Sufis, a debate that is touched on in a later chapter.

91. See Gabriel Warburg, "Mahdism and Islamism in Sudan," *International Journal of Middle East Studies* 27 (1995): 219–36, for a discussion of the relationship of Hasan el-Turabi (NIF and Ikhwan) and Saddig el-Mahdi (Umma Party, historical figure within Sufism) and their ideological and political differences.

92. Abdullahi Ahmed An-Na'im, translator's introduction to *The Second Message of Islam*, by Mahmoud Mohamed Taha (Syracuse: Syracuse University Press, 1987), 5–6.

93. Duran, "Religion in Sudanese Politics," 598. Italics mine.

94. Woodward describes the Free Officers as a radical movement spawned during the Nasser years in Egypt by left-oriented military officers. "After a minor group had been nipped in the bud in 1957 [in Sudan], a more substantial movement developed in the 1960s, with a variety of radical themes ... A number of the Free Officers had links with the SCP" (*Sudan, 1898–1989*, 37).

95. For an account of the relationship between Nimieri, Turabi, and Saddig el-Mahdi, see Warburg, "Mahdism and Islamism in Sudan."

96. Turabi, in response to a question about the lack of elected democratic institutions in his regime, rationalized that parliaments are not representative anyway, and that *consensus* is the goal. He said, "a parliament was nominated [appointed] to develop procedures of consensus." Arthur L. Lowrie, ed., *Islam, Democracy, and the State and the West: A Round Table with Dr. Hasan Turabi* (Tampa: The World and Islam Studies Enterprise, 1993), 27.

97. Reported in the *Sudan Democratic Gazette*, no. 19 (December, 1991): 8. This report on current conditions in Sudan has been gleaned from personal letters, colleagues' firsthand reports, a number of U.S. and European newspapers, *Africa Watch*, and *The Nation*.

98. For an update on some of the recent difficulties of the Sudan People's Liberation Army, see Gill Lusk, "Democracy and Liberation Movements: The Case of the SPLA," *MERIP* 22, no. 1 (1992): 30–31.

99. See, e.g., Abdelwahab el-Affendi, *Turabi's Revolution: Islam and Power in Sudan* (London: Grey Seal, 1991); Peter Nyot Kok, "Hasan Abdallah al-Turabi," *Orient* 33 (1992): 185–92; Tim Niblock, "Islamic Movements and Sudan's Political Coherence," in *Sudan*, ed. Herve Bleuchot, Christian Delmet, and Derek Hopwood (Exeter: Ithaca, 1991), 253–68; Khalid Mubarak, "The Fundamentalists: Theory and Praxis," *el-Hayat* (30 June 1992); Alex de Waal, "Turabi's Muslim Brothers: Theocracy in Sudan," *CovertAction*, no. 49 (1994): 13–18, 60–61; and Haidar Ibrahim Ali, *Azmat el-Islam el-Siyyasi fi Sudan* (The Crisis of Political Islam in the Sudan) (Cairo: Centre of Sudanese Studies, 1991), 99–216.

100. Kok, "Hasan Abdallah al-Turabi," 187. Italics mine.

101. E.g., Lowrie, *Islam, Democracy, and the State and the West*.

102. Kok, "Hasan Abdallah al-Turabi," 189, quoting Turabi from the NIF electoral manifesto of 1986.

103. One of the best contemporary collections of articles about post-1989 politics is a special issue on Sudan in *The Middle East Journal* 44, no. 4 (1990). Gabriel Warburg, for example ("The *Sharia* in Sudan: Implementation and Repercussions, 1983–1989," *The Middle East Journal* 44, no. 4 [1990], 624–37), examined the development of "the Islamic Path," as policy under Nimieri, and the importance of the Muslim Brotherhood in this period. Another collection is in "Sudan: Finding Common Ground," *MERIP Middle East Report* 21, no. 5 (1991).

104. Duran, "The Centrifugal Forces of Religion in Sudanese Politics," 592.

105. Lowrie, *Islam, Democracy, and the State and the West,* 22.

106. For a discussion of state-sponsored tribal militias, see M.A. Mohamed Salih, "'New Wine in Old Bottles': Tribal Militias and the Sudanese State," *Review of African Political Economy,* no. 45/46 (1989), 168–74.

4

Women in Contemporary Northern Sudan

Introduction

In this chapter I discuss state gender ideology and gender as they intersect health, economics, labor, education, and law. Like the book itself, this chapter is as much about different modes of representation as it is about everyday life. Here I examine various representations and self-representations of contemporary northern Sudanese women. Although I refer to non-Sudanese-authored data and demographics (e.g., from the United Nations), to enrich my arguments I privilege the debates among Sudanese about the conditions and future of women's lives.

Some of the figures from Sudanese sources may seem outdated, but they are indicative of the statistical constructs developed in the years represented and the ways that demographic ideology has been shaped. While recognizing that all demographic models are social constructs, I have presented an overview of the situation for women, using insider/outsider sets of statistics.[1]

This chapter differs in approach from the ones that follow, for although here I make passing reference to my 1981 interviews with urban women workers, these interviews are used only as supplements to the summary sketch that initiates a general discussion of health, economics, labor, education, and law. In chapters 5–7 Sudanese women's voices, representing themselves, resound through the interview data.

State Gender Ideology—Gender, Labor, and Class

In chapter 2 I proposed that, in Sudan in the 1980s and 1990s, state-sponsored Islamism in the form of the military elite/political party has attempted to maneuver religious ideology toward a more "legitimate" and "authentic" culture.[2] In this regard Islamists see "women's culture" and its representation as central to this project, try to nullify and redirect recent changes in the gender division of labor, and attempt to purge "women's culture" of particularly "negative customs."[3]

At least two types of women's movements, emanating from secularists and Islamists, coexist in contemporary northern Sudan and contest its social terrain. Their platforms are similar in the sense of positioning women at the center of an authentic culture and claiming the elevation of women as a goal. Part of the similarity derives from the fact that both of these politics of authenticity are class-interested.

Here, and extending into the following chapters, I intersect economic patterns, sectarian and secular politics, gender arrangements (especially in education, labor, and law), and the state. Since 1899, with the establishment of the British colonial regime, the state in Sudan has been active and expanding, initiating and controlling (at least nominally) almost all development and investment. The state likewise has controlled nearly all social and political institutions: foreign affairs, education, media, communications, utilities, recreational facilities, social clubs and associations, housing and planning, the police and military, oftentimes the judiciary, many formal religious institutions, and most legal political-interest groups and parties. That is not to say that it has always been a strong state or even a stable one, or that it has had profound meaning in every citizen's daily life (quite the contrary). Nor should these statements imply that the state has always been the same—not in its various colonial guises, and certainly not in its post-independence forms.

In the years just after independence (1956) the state disseminated gender ideology primarily through state radio and (by the mid-1960s) state television, usually expressing the message that a developing Sudan needed emancipated women—or at least women who had equality with men in developing the new country. At that time, with the expressed need to build up the urban workforce, the term "emancipated" was thought of as synonymous with "literate, educated (i.e., secondary school or higher) wage-earner" in the bourgeois-liberal parlance (as well as in the Marxist and some of the nationalist vocabularies of postcolonial Sudan). Government media and other state apparatuses (e.g., civil-service recruitment and school curriculum) urged gender partnership as a necessity in developing Sudan. Media images (billboards, posters, illustrations in government pamphlets, and the like) presented the new Sudanese woman as sophisticated consumer or respectable civil servant (earlier as nurse or teacher and later sometimes as doctor). By the early 1960s the state could point proudly to the first government-educated, "truly Sudanese" women doctors.[4]

Whether or not prior to the Islamist state there had always been a clearly defined gender ideology, or *any* gender ideology, emanating from the state, is arguable. Much of it has been implicit (for example, embedded in the religious framework of the sectarian parties). However, some aspects have been explicit, such as the spelled-out, singled-out rights of women in the various provisional constitutions; the gender rights-and-obligations provisions in the codified or uncodified personal status laws within *urf* (customary) and sharia (Islamic) law; and, in general, through various state- and/or party-sponsored feminisms (e.g., the Union of Sudanese Women, the Sudan Socialist Union's organization,[5] an official, state-sanctioned women's association that functioned from 1972 to 1985). Since 1983 through various political-interest groups and parties, and now through the Islamic state, gender ideology has been stated more explicitly.[6] These developments are the meat of the next two chapters.

What is the situation for northern Sudanese women? What is the relationship between state/party gender ideology and the status of women?

In relation to conventional studies of "the status of women" (the indexes of which have always been arguable),[7] Sudanese women present a number of contradictions. For example, on the one hand, most Sudanese women undergo circumcision, a practice viewed by many international scholars, activists, and Sudanese as evidence of the singular subordination of Sudanese women. Northern Sudan has one of the highest concentrations of the custom in the world, and some of the most severe forms of genital surgeries are carried out there. Toubia, a Sudanese activist medical doctor, calculated the prevalence of what she terms "female genital mutilation" at 89 percent, or 9,220,400, and noted the high prevalence of infibulation, the most severe type. She also noted "a small overall decline in the 1980s" and a "shift from infibulation to clitoridectomy."[8] It is too soon to tell what impact the Islamist regime will have on the slightly declining practice.

On the other hand, the number of Sudanese women doctors (the most prestigious profession) is among the most in the Third World; a high proportion of lawyers and other professionals are women; and there is a history of strong women's organizations and politicians. Labor rights for women included equality before the law, equal pay for equal work, and supportive work laws that protected women as workers and mothers.[9] This would seem to support a claim that Sudanese women have a great deal of autonomy.

Critics of that claim point to the fact that Sudanese women are veiled, i.e., they wear a lengthy body wraparound (tobe) in public, and often in the 1980s and 1990s, the hejab (modest Islamic dress). A Sudanese counterargument is that, for some decades, when women wore tobes, they could go nearly anywhere in public and carry out any number of activities, including political activism. Many observers and Sudanese claim that the tobe has reached the status of national dress and is worn as such.

Some add that dress is not an index of women's status.[10] I have argued elsewhere that we need to look at the reasons why women are wearing the tobe, that individual motivations are important, as is whether or not women have options or feel coerced.[11]

Those convinced of northern Sudanese women's low status point to repressive family or personal status laws based on sharia and urf. In rebuttal, others underscore family status laws that are protective (patronizing) of women, as well as the various safeguards in abrogated constitutions.[12]

Now, with the rise of Islamism and Islamic sentiment, many outside and indigenous observers expect there to be greater subordination of women (an expectation Lazreg has criticized as the assumption of oppression when outsiders view Muslim societies);[13] and indeed it is difficult to ignore inevitable commentaries on the quality of life, e.g., the appalling health statistics for Sudanese women (see below). But at the same time, Sudanese women are as politically active as at any time in history—or even more so.

Hence, I am exploring the paradoxical forces in postcolonial Sudan that have produced, on the one hand, an apparent secularization of the societal institutions and a concomitant, perhaps surficial, public/visible rise in the status of women; and on the other, the rise of Islamism, with its active, woman-oriented component. Both secularists and Islamists work to develop a gender ideology wherein women are central in socializing the nation. We see these agendas manifested through the gender division of labor. Partly because Islamic doctrines, including sharia, are so rich in proscribed and prescribed gender behavior, Islamists have a richer field than, say, Marxists and liberals, from which to develop a gender ideology. As a consequence, much of the liberal and left rhetoric on "the woman" has been co-opted and undermined in the 1990s by a subversive Islamism, the product of an urban middle class that is trying to answer the continuing crisis of Sudan's economy by impressing international capitalists with some liberal window-dressing (a "modern" look) without being culturally imperialized. Women and the family unit are essential in these stratagems. Analytically illuminating in investigating these processes are: women's domestic and wage labor; the form, field and quality of education for women; the gender components of the legal structure; and political participation.

Clearly, at least for particular classes of women, a crisis has been developing in Sudan. In recent decades, capital-intensive economic schemes, the appearance of multinational corporations and agencies, uneven regional development, labor migration, ethnic power realignments, and developments in cultural imperialism have all preceded sociopolitical and economic crises, which in turn have profoundly impacted gender arrangements.[14]

Possibly the most significant postcolonial crisis for many middle-class and professional women is the rise in the 1970s of the "Islamic Trend"—the intensification of Islamism—whose ideological expressions are often essentialist, promoting a romantic image of women that effectively fulfills the gender ideology of the middle-class Islamist movement. This essentialist representation requires the redomestication of women, the reconstruction of the moral fabric of society, and the assignment of women as agents of that reconstruction. Furthermore, the romanticizing of reproduction can pressure some categories of women out of the labor force or maneuver them into appropriate jobs. If these trends develop further, they could effect a major setback for non-Islamist middle-class and professional women. Yet the problem is attenuated by the fact that the National Islamic Front (NIF) also uses the claim of "equal participation" for women. (The NIF, heir to the Muslim Brotherhood, came to power through the military in 1989 and remains the de facto ruling party.)

Early in the century attitudes in Sudan towards women's "emancipation" (defined then as reform in marriage and family structure, and equal access to education and jobs) took two forms, each associated with a social class and a nationalist ideology. On the one hand, liberal and moderate nationalists of the upper and upper middle classes viewed social reform along liberal Western lines as prerequisites for independence. The emancipation of women was viewed as essential to reform.[15]

On the other hand, more "radical" nationalists of the lower middle classes were demanding an end to British rule, and as a part of that struggle, they romanticized "indigenous" values to foster cultural nationalism. These cultural nationalists generally opposed women's emancipation in the Western sense, arguing that it was an imitation that would weaken the nation's basic Islamic unit, the family. They also romanticized women's domestic role, essentializing women as the embodiment of the culture. In chapter 6 I describe a reversal in class standpoints on women's emancipation that Sudanese are experiencing, whereby the newly educated urban middle class, in the form of the NIF, is now espousing cultural nationalism, attaching profound importance to the family, and emphasizing women's roles in resisting and/or abrogating Western culture.

Explaining this ideological reversal is as complicated as explaining the rise of Islamism and the NIF. Certainly the forces that brought the NIF to power had been building up for some time. However, some recent phenomena associated with international capital intensified the buildup. In the 1970s, for example, the unemployment rate rose and salaries did not keep up with inflation, enormously increasing male labor out-migration.

At first, gender arrangements did not tilt in such a way as to threaten the prevailing gender ideology, because the out-migration was of working class or minor civil servants. But soon it was intellectuals and middle-to-senior-level personnel, and although the brain drain coincided with World Bank and International Monetary Fund pressure to prune the over-burdened civil service, the labor force also felt the impact. A report from UNESCO confirmed:

> Experienced professionals and the most qualified graduates are attracted towards the neighbouring high-wage countries. Although to some extent the emigration of highly educated people helps the country's balance of payment situation through remittances, loss of much needed skilled work-ers, technicians and professionals create bottlenecks for economic devel-opment. It is observed that the experienced and the better qualified constitute a significant proportion of the emigrants.[16]

When women began to move into some of these better jobs formerly held by men and perceived to be "men's jobs," the effect was to tilt the gender ideology.[17]

Before 1983–89, when the Islamist ideology was crystallizing, the state had effectively disseminated the liberal ideology of capitalism through-out urban Sudanese society. A woman with a wage was seen as an impor-tant progressive element in the society. Many women I interviewed over the years looked upon wage-earning as a panacea. I began to use the slogan "Wages are the opiate of women" because the interviewees all looked upon women working outside the home as one of the positive trends in an increasingly liberal environment. Any contrary suggestion on my part was received with surprise; they considered the United States a prime example of liberated women in the workforce. Although their descriptions of alienating, impersonal bureaucratic jobs contrasted with their descriptions of non-alienating, personal, direct-reward domestic labor, they still described themselves as "happy" to be wage-earners outside the home. This was the case even when they earned 30 Sudanese pounds (£S) monthly, had a dull, repetitive, unskilled job, and traveled long distances on public transport to work. That their economic fortunes were admittedly declining as a concomitant of Sudan's deteriorating economy did not mitigate their positive attitudes toward their jobs. Their self-representation did not involve describing themselves as marginal in any sense, at home or in the economy. They often expressed to me high self-esteem about their job performance and the importance of their work, rarely any thoughts about what I interpreted as their increasing marginalization under capitalism. I observed the reality of their material lives to be that they carry the society on their backs in terms of production and reproduction and that they hold down two full-time jobs. If they held these same ideas, it did not dampen or alter their optimism about their condition. Instead of seeing their material conditions worsening in relation to men, they saw relative success in comparison to the precolonial past, to their mothers' lives, and to earlier periods of their own.

Observing particular points in the histories of Western industrialized societies, it is clear that women are sometimes led to believe (through media and schooling) that the cause of their alienation from domestic labor is their public labor. In other words, when it serves the state or a segment of society, women are socialized into thinking that they are neglectful mothers, poor housekeepers, and undutiful wives and daughters as a result of working outside the home. At a profound subjective level, this is what Sudanese women workers were going through and, I maintain, accounted for their 1981 statements to me that they wanted to return to the partially abandoned domestic roles in that ideal future when their money would no longer be needed. Domestic labor, in a cash economy with the wage as a central organizing principle, becomes devalued. The contradiction is that while women's domestic labor is not what *counts*, it is still counted *on*, making it possible for men to work for wages outside the home. Further, while the status of the domestic laborer under capitalism is undermined, the domestic sphere simultaneously becomes mystified and romanticized: "Motherhood," for example, is seen and treated as a glorified category or state of being instead of being materially rewarded for reproducing the society. Biological reproduction ceases to be seen as contributing to material life.

With the deeper penetration of capitalism in the postindependence period, women's options diminished, while seeming to increase.[18] Their domestic labor (especially in an urban milieu) lost value as their work in the formal sector became more necessary. Another perspective, however—that of Sudanese women workers themselves—emerges in the section below. At the end of the section, labor is presented within a framework of developing gender ideology, thus bridging these two perspectives. First, however, a demographic sketch of Sudanese women.

General Profile: State of "Well-Being"

Although we have few widely accepted models for assessing "well-being" or the material and social conditions of people's lives, we can still develop a heuristic model that takes into account health, economics, labor, education, and law. Using these intersecting variables, in this study I construct a general view of the social environment for Sudanese women. The implicit question is, What is their state of well-being? I do not pretend this is "objectively" derived.

In terms of political rights, law, education and labor, Sudan's record on women is inconsistent. Health indexes are clearer, if not conclusive, in assessing well-being. For example, although 51 percent of the population has access to health services, in general the health profile is not good.[19] Life expectancy is low: 51.0 for women and 48.6 for men.[20]

As previously stated, Sudanese have a very high birth rate. Maternal, infant, and child mortalities are also very high.[21] Women's obstetrical health problems, e.g., complications from female circumcision in a country where a high percentage of women have some form of genital surgeries, are also significant.[22] (Some of the possible health hazards in Sudan of giving birth, such as the prevalence of anemia, are offset by (1) the legality of abortion to save a mother's life, and even the possibility of a judicial ruling in the cases of rape or incest;[23] and (2) the high percentage of births attended by trained health providers. Sudan ranks among the low-income countries within the Arab world, but within that group, it "has reached an attended-birth coverage of 69% despite its low GNP. Sudan has a well-established program of community-level midwife training, which began in the 1950s" [24].)

Other negative birth factors are the social and psychological pressures to give birth to a boy. Sudan ranks quite high in the index of son preference: "expressed by the ratio of the number of mothers who prefer that the next child be male to the number of mothers who prefer that the next child be female" (20), there is a one and one-half times greater preference for boys. Sudan is ranked low in terms of an effective family planning program and the availability of modern birth control methods (25). Positive factors surrounding birth are the progressive laws governing maternity protection, e.g., legally mandated eight weeks' maternity leave with 100 percent pay (about average for Arab countries),[24] and the right for women to leave work to nurse their children at home (in effect while I was in Sudan in 1988). Contributing to the poor quality of life for women and complicating births is the fact that, although the mean age for marriage is 18.7,[25] in Sudan the legal age is at puberty, and may be as young as eleven years old. In fact, "A girl could be married at 10 years if her guardian convinces the court that there is a benefit to her."[26]

Regarding political participation, in 1953 women graduates of secondary school or above were granted the right to vote; in 1965 this right was extended to all women, as was the right to stand for election.[27] In the following election that same year, Fatma Ahmed Ibrahim, longtime leader of the left-oriented Sudanese Women's Union (WU), became the first woman elected to parliament. In 1988 two other women were elected. Political power and participation are elaborated upon later.

As for social issues, the average household size is 5.1 persons; the mean age at first marriage is 25.8 for men and, as I stated above, 18.7 for women, both relatively late by African and Middle Eastern standards.[28] Although this may seem a high average-age-at-marriage statistic, the fact is that with the backing of the law, there is the potential for very young marriage.[29] As in many Arab and other Muslim societies, polygamy is not the norm, in Sudan hardly occurring anymore.[30]

The girl/woman does not have the right to sign the marriage contract; only her father or guardian can do so. In other words, women/girls do not have definitive choices in the matter, which can proceed without the court being consulted. However, the court can intervene if there is a dispute.[31] The right to divorce, as in all societies, is complicated in Sudan. The husband has repudiation right, with some exceptions. The wife also has the right to divorce, technically even the right to initiate it, although in observing such cases I conclude that success for the woman is very difficult. Likewise, a mother's custody rights are limited; a father can claim custody of daughters at nine years old; of sons, at seven. The time may be extended (with a court order) to marriage for girls and puberty for boys (60).

As for legal rights, under civil law Sudanese women had equality. But this statement, like most of the data above, refers mostly to the quarter-century prior to the Islamist coup in 1989 and the Muslim Act in 1991. Under the Transitional Constitution of 1985 and its predecessors, Sudanese women were assured unconditional equality with men and the right to live without discrimination. Women also had the right to enter into contracts and to own money and property. Islamic law also gives women such rights, as well as the right to enter into business transactions without the consent of their husbands. Toubia points out some problems:

> Sudan never passed a permanent constitution. The last Transitional Constitution was drafted in 1985 and repealed after the coup in 1989. Currently, only *Constitutional Decrees* are passed by the government. The first such Decree acknowledges all international and regional treaties to which Sudan is party. No other rights are explicitly mentioned (61, n.6).

It is complicated to interpret women's rights in the absence of a constitution. Nonetheless, we get some idea of the state of flux in laws protecting women by the fact that with the passage of the notorious "September Laws" during the Nimieri regime in 1983, the law against infibulation was dropped. Toubia again:

> Infibulation was illegal in Sudan under British rule, but the "milder" form of female circumcision, clitoridectomy, was not mentioned in that law. The law remained on the books until 1983, when it was dropped with the passage of the first Islamic Penal code and no mention of the practice was made. Very few cases were ever brought to court over the years. Since the

law was dropped, it has remained unclear whether infibulation can be prosecuted under the general section of the Penal Code covering physical injury.[32]

Legal protections and constitutional rights are discussed again later in this chapter.

I will now outline girls'/women's rights to education and what the figures indicate. Sudan ranks low in the Arab world in female literacy and in school enrollments for girls. Over 88 percent of the women are nonliterate, compared to 57.3 percent of the men.[33] Girls constitute only 30 percent of combined primary and secondary school enrollment (in contrast, the figures for Bahrain, Jordan and Qatar are all over 90 percent).[34] As for male/female educational ratios in Sudan, in 1970 the primary school ratio was 61 girls to 100 boys; in 1985/87, 68 to 100. The secondary school numbers rise dramatically, starting in 1970 with 39 and moving in 1985/87 to 73 girls to 100 boys. The post-secondary ratio for 1985/87 is 68 to 100.[35] University enrollment in 1980 was 27 percent women and in 1990, 41 percent,[36] another dramatic increase that includes 43 percent women students in the field of medical science.[37]

With reference to labor, Sudanese are mainly rural dwellers and agricultural workers. Of a 24–25 million total estimated population, 20.2 percent is urban; 19.2 percent of all women live in urban areas, almost equivalent to the percentage of men. Of the economically active population, 22.7 percent are women. In agriculture, which engages 66.4 percent of the labor force, 24.1 percent are women.[38] The United Nations estimated that in 1990 women officially constituted 29 percent of the Sudanese labor force, ranking highest in the Arab world.[39] Women 15 and over number 1,668,000; i.e., 24 percent of the population considered economically active.[40] Women's labor may be one of the most significant variables investigated in this study, as women's participation in the workforce is salient among development theorists, feminist researchers, liberals, and Marxists alike.

Women's increased participation in the urban workforce and in the labor force in general prompted my 1981 Khartoum pilot study,[41] based on case histories of sixteen women wage-earners and interviews with fellow researchers and officials. The data offered provocative suggestions about women and work in Sudan, and challenged my conventionally held theoretical-political-economic notions about "public" and "private" labor in a "developing" area. *Listening* to the women workers forced me to confront what participation in the urban workforce meant to them in their *everyday lives*.

Beginning the research, I had a basic assumption that the very areas of the "Third World" where "development" has been most capital-intensive and where a liberal ideology partially accruing from colonialism and cap-italism had brought more women out into the official labor force may be, paradoxically, where women are most alienated from their labor. In sub-sequent studies of new industry in developing areas, Sacks and others hypothesized that women participating in wage economies are far from liberated.[42]

Contrasting the public and private spheres of women's labor forced me to alter some of my preconceptions. My early data suggested that women workers, even when relatively successful in the formal workforce, were often frustrated in the private sphere. Many saw themselves as still relegated to "traditional" tasks and roles they felt they had outgrown.[43] I investigated what I had perceived as the growing gap between the private and the public and analyzed what that gap did to the material conditions of women's lives and to societal attitudes about women's con-tribution to social production and domestic labor.

My aim was to examine and challenge orthodox sources (e.g., Engels) with field data and fresher theoretical approaches (e.g., *Beyond the Frag-ments*).[44] Evaluating whether or not urban women workers held their public jobs in high esteem—and if so, what this did to their implicit or explicit views of their own domestic labor (which continued unaltered and unmitigated regardless of the demands of their wage-earning occu-pations)—I was dealing with changing consciousness about one's labor, as well as the emotional components of that consciousness. The self-devaluation of domestic labor and the concomitant societal devaluation of "women's work" guided my research.

By exploring the personal aspects of women's lack of autonomy in both the public and private spheres in a "developing" society, I intended to understand something of the subjectivity of oppression, ultimately to make connections between the emotional components of consciousness and the material base. That meant asking whether or not Sudanese women have gained in social, political, or economic autonomy by moving into the paid labor force in greater numbers. That question is unresolved: The patterns are fragmented and the statistics that exist unreliable. None-theless, we can look at the patterns that do emerge.

For example, "Sudan remains one of the world's least developed countries, in terms of such criteria as GNP per capita and its rate of growth, the level of industrialisation, the level of literacy, etc."[45] The Inter-national Labour Organisation (ILO) estimated at the time of my 1981 study that only some 25 percent of the country's population lived in urban areas. About half of the urban workforce was concentrated in Greater Khartoum and Port Sudan, and close to half was female (141).To women workers, what meaning does a poor urban setting have in evalu-ating the significance of being in the workforce?

Sudan's pre-Islamic-state labor legislation mandated a minimum wage for public-sector and government employees (raised in 1983 to £S40 monthly plus £S15 for transport (191), but greatly inflated since then) and equal pay for women for equal work. However, the reality was, and is, a consistent differential between the pay men and women in similar occupations receive. In most cases women receive lower wages than men. Women are indeed concentrated in the lower pay echelons, regardless of the law. The ILO flatly stated:

> in urban Sudan many jobs are sex specific ... [also] female workers are concentrated in the lower wage brackets to a far greater extent than male workers. In white collar occupations they are generally engaged in secretarial or clerical tasks, while in unskilled work they are more likely to be found in assembly line jobs or activities such as spinning (168, 170).

In the medical category, men had a mean annual salary of £S2,709, compared to £S1,560 for women. Clerks, government employees, and secretaries, in terms of mean annual salary, were as follows: male government employees £S1,644, females £S1,144; male secretaries £S1,428, females £S1,768; male clerks £S1,349, females £S837 (141).[46]

The bulk of Sudan's women wage-earners were in Greater Khartoum, site of more than 75 percent of all socioeconomic investments. As stated earlier, for all the capital-intensive investment centralized there, Sudan as a whole is relatively poorer than in centuries past.[47] Sudan is experiencing a particular form of increasing underdevelopment that combines constraints reinforced by cultural conventions (patriarchal, Arab, Muslim, Christian) with the inherent inequalities of capitalism and multicorporate neocolonialism—or the "internationalization" of capital. Workers—male and female—are increasingly marginalized by these factors. However, men's economic options are often widened through geographical mobility and other factors, giving them greater personal autonomy, whereas women become increasingly restricted to "appropriate" jobs (often after abandoning their "rural" skills) and are deprived of higher-paying/ higher-status positions.[48]

Many women workers in Greater Khartoum have been channeled into dull, repetitive jobs with low pay;[49] concomitantly their personal lives reflect a rigid division of labor in that domestic work is still "women's work." The arenas wherein women might achieve some power or have their role valued more highly have often been assumed by other agencies, or have lost their importance. For example, in recent decades there has been a decline of homemade crafts, often produced by women, in favor of imports. Furthermore, some of the socialization of children had begun to be assumed by men (in households where women earn wages outside), or more commonly in the middle class, by the schools, media, or child-care centers. The inference is that, ironically, Sudanese women have begun to have less control over their social reproduction, a result of the liberal gender ideology whereby there is more sharing with men in intimate family matters, e.g., marriage choices for children, formerly the primary domain of women.[50] Such an observation problematizes the conventional capitalist/liberal approach that a woman's increased potential for decision-making is correlated to her earning outside income, and makes it even more difficult to measure autonomy. The following statement by el-Nagar, considered the expert on urban women's employment in Sudan, embodies some of the contradictions:

> Among working class employed women, single women are taking [a] role in budget decision[s] for their high income although other factors are also involved. In some case[s] of middle class women predominance in budget decision[s] is related to education and changing attitudes of the family enhanced by the economic contribution the women make. The data shows [a] high rate of *non-participation in budget decision[s]* indicating *no great impact of employment* ... Among upper classes the tendency is for women to decide on items related to their concern ... As to division of labour at home employment has no effect as women are still responsible for all domestic activities.[51]

Another factor in the decline of women's power and autonomy is that urban women are more isolated from each other, even from their own extended families—in effect reducing their potential for raised consciousness, solidarity, and empowerment.

In my attempt to assess if and how urban women are alienated from their domestic and wage-earning labor, I interviewed in depth sixteen women, ages 24–44, who had been in the labor force 2–10 years, whose salaries ranged from £S27 to £S400 monthly, whose education levels ranged from intermediate school to university graduate, who were married, unmarried, and divorced, and who had 0–2 children. All but two were "white collar" (e.g., clerical or civil-service) workers, a category I selected because it is the largest urban occupational category for women and probably will be for some time. Because assembly-line work is the most common "unskilled" occupation for women, I included two plant workers.

I was interested in self-esteem about work, power in the family (or lack of it), gender division of labor within the household, and sociopolitical attitudes. Attempting to observe something most of the interviewees had already thought about at some length—intergenerational change—I asked them to compare their lives with their mothers', none of whom were formally educated and only one of whom earned money outside the home.

Like el-Nagar, I found many contradictions. For example, all the women said they liked working outside the home for money, although many wanted a "better job," usually defined as better paying. All the white-collar workers save two expressed respect for their public-sector jobs, but most thought of their positions as easy or "not difficult." Only one thought her job challenging; she and two others saw themselves as contributing to society. All the white-collars but one were disdainful of domestic labor (an attitude not shared by the assembly-liners). To my surprise, however, 12 of the white collars expressed a desire to "return to the home" at some point, i.e., quit their jobs (and join the leisure class?). In contrast, the assembly-liners refused to imagine returning to the domestic sphere, having struggled so to be free of their particular families' restrictions on work outside the home. One said she would rather be dead.

The women stated that they worked because they wanted independence, and not just economic; they wanted to get out of the house. They never said they were "working for fun" or "to pass the time"; nor did they say they absolutely needed the money, though in most cases this was obvious to me. They tried to give me the impression that their salaries were "supplemental." Often no cash flowed from the woman worker to the other members of her family. Instead, she usually bought household goods that she (and other members of her family) labeled "nonessential" or "luxury items." Most of these items (e.g., bed linens and dishes) would be considered relatively essential, especially in middle-class families. The women described the men of the family as the central providers, i.e., as the ones who usually paid for food and basic shelter. I would have thought this was a culture-specific response (i.e., family pride in the men being the "breadwinners" and not wanting to divulge otherwise to me), were it not also such a common attitude among women in the United States.

Although this book focuses on urban women, especially of the middle class, the forces of colonialism and neocolonialism, technology and development have had a negative impact on all women. In the following section I focus on the urban and rural poor and the dispossessed.

Technology and "Development": Neocolonialism and Gender Ideology

In this section emerge familiar Marxist feminist themes of the last couple of decades: that women have fared less well than men under colonialism, and even worse under neocolonialism; that Western neocolonialist ideology has had a negative impact on women through its technology;

and that Western ideology has appeared in the Third World in the exaggerated patriarchal forms we have come to associate with capitalism.[52] I also include familiar approaches to women and development of a number of international agencies, scholars, and indigenous Third World governments. I implicitly critique these approaches, which have usually called for funding projects that entail getting women into the wage-earning workforce, involving them in other income-generating projects (especially commodity production), and/or "teaching" them "appropriate technologies."

Sudan data encourage particularly powerful challenges to a number of the above approaches, a consequence of the especially rich and varied sociocultural, political, and economic histories of the area. The region now known as Sudan has experienced many colonialisms, each serving ruling groups and/or international capitalism well; has experienced waves of migration and invasions, many sets of missionaries from various religious sects, the establishment of theocracies, periods of intense assimilation, one group to another; episodes of civil war and genocide, constant situations of land alienation and dislocation, forced labor and forced relocation, the development of major irrigation or agricultural schemes ranging from plantation-type production relations (with slaves or corvée labor) to tenant farming; and has experienced the imposition of various military regimes and economic visitations (at first by communities of foreign traders, then by international agencies, and ultimately by contemporary multinationals). The effects of the above have often adversely affected women, which is not to say that women have been passive victims acted upon by historical processes. Colonized women have always resisted colonialism and other forms of victimization, and Sudanese women have been as adaptable and resilient as other women who have lived under adverse conditions. To see the resilience in people's everyday lives, one only need visit the shantytowns ringing Greater Khartoum—populated primarily by people displaced by civil war, drought, and famine.

Currently there are millions of displaced people all over Sudan, fleeing war, drought, and famine in the south and west. They are primarily agriculturalists who can no longer farm or eat. Their numbers are estimated at some 3.5 million southerners and 2.5 million westerners, mainly women and children.[53] El-Sanousi and el-Amin remark:

the physical circumstances in which the displaced people live are wholly inadequate. Permanent shelters and privacy are lacking. Water is often nearly a half-mile away … In many ways displaced women are the ultimate objects of policies and forces far removed from their everyday lives. Their responses to profound upheaval constitute the politics of their everyday lives (684).

Such situations devastate the social fabric, and the additional burden on women to hold things together appears intolerable. In Darfur and Kordofan in western Sudan women run both the farms and household production, producing a variety of handicrafts for domestic use and for the local market. A severe drought in 1984 damaged crops and annihilated livestock, forcing thousands to flee to Greater Khartoum where many still use cardboard boxes *(cartona)* as shelters, and where women, formerly agriculturalists and craftspeople, forage on the margins of society.[54]

If these forces were not enough to test human endurance, flexibility, ingenuity, and resilience, Sudanese have begun to feel the effects of another force that is partially a culmination of previous processes: the deterioration of the environment. One concomitant is the devastation of women's material world, which one environmentalist has referred to as the "downward spiral" for women.[55]

Agriculture in Sudan is the primary form of economic activity. Repeating some statistics from previous pages: 85 percent of the labor force is engaged in agriculture, contributing 40 percent to the gross national product, 90 percent of the country's hard currency, and 90 percent of its exports.[56] Approximately 87 percent of women classified as in the labor force are involved in agriculture in some form. From that population some 78–90 percent are engaged in the "traditional" subsistence sector and only some 10 percent in the "modern" sector.[57]

As mentioned in chapter 3, there was capitalist penetration of Sudan before British colonialism; this twentieth-century penetration, however, has been the most marked phase. Through the processes of supplying cash crops and raw materials for British industries (e.g., oilseeds and cotton) and serving as a market for mainly European or European-controlled manufactured goods, Sudan underwent both economic and sociopolitical transformations. The British clearly limited the growth of industry in Sudan (including even handicrafts) to ensure the importation of foreign goods. Subsistence production was slowly integrated into the money economy, and small-scale agriculture and pastoral production were linked to the export market by growing numbers of traders, small brokers, and wholesalers—i.e., the bourgeois and petit-bourgeois classes.[58] Since decolonization the Sudanese capitalist classes have continued these processes, resulting in further land alienation, the increasing marginalization of great numbers of subsistence producers, the dislocation of household economies, and extensive rural-urban migration. By the late 1970s, a very high percentage of the labor power in the urban economy was absorbed by petty-commodity production. The Sudanese state called upon international development agencies to contain the production of the so-called "informal sector" (to transform, for example, handicraft production into "industries").[59] The entrepreneurial dynamism of the informal sector began to be seen as a frontier for development.

We have scant data on women's participation in petty-commodity production, but my own field observations point to the predominance of women in this form of production, especially in the urban areas. El-Nagar (one of the few sources we have on women's nonagricultural activities in Greater Khartoum) found that self-employed women were mainly petty traders with small capital. They frequently deal with women's consumer goods and "are predominant in the sale of foods, liquor and sex. Besides, they are greatly involved in domestic services, and to a limited extent in tailoring."[60] We know that, historically, in generating household income for subsistence and commodity exchange women have performed significant economic functions, namely, handicraft and food production.

El-Nagar maintains that women seek employment mainly to help their families financially, that the decisions to seek employment or work for money "are greatly influenced by the women's family conditions," and that "few work for self-fulfillment."[61] Although I find this conclusion contrary to some of my own research findings about women's attitudes towards their jobs,[62] it is certainly true that the dislocation of many household economies has compelled women increasingly to engage in petty commerce and related activities. In chapter 7 and elsewhere I present an example of this petty commerce, the *suq el-Niswan* (women's market), a separate section women control in the large marketplace of Omdurman.[63] Since the end of the nineteenth century, women here have moved goods and services they produced within the household into an arena for community consumption. Capitalist integration and monetization of the economy, exacerbating the dislocation of household economies, have forced women to "diversify" and expand their commodity production, especially for exchange.

Following the policy of incorporating informal-sector enterprises, most development projects, even most community-development programs, encourage women's participation in "income-generating" projects. These are usually attempts to mobilize women in petty-commodity production. Hall and Ismail remarked that in the 1970s, using the rationale of eradicating illiteracy among rural women and elevating the standard of living of their families, community-development projects also taught "home economics." Women were encouraged to develop (redevelop) their skills through such formerly "domestic" production as pottery, weaving, reed products, leather products, needlework, and dressmaking.[64]

While researching Sudanese art, I observed that arts preservation, or revival, was initiated under the Ministry of Culture and Information. Sudanese artists and designers "retaught" women to make art objects (formerly associated with home economies) for commodity exchange, usually tourist items sold or exhibited at bazaars. Anthropologists collected "folk objects," recorded regional folk dances, which were either exhibited, performed in a theater, or "sold," becoming commodities in the name of preserving native cultures.

The state furnished the raw materials and "appropriate technology" for women's cooperatives, sometimes organized by the SSU's Union of Sudanese Women;[65] women were expected to produce for the market through catering, bazaars, and workshops. With these economic activities, both household and petty commodity production are integrated in a subordinate way into the capitalist sector, which exploits them.

International agencies and the Sudanese state, through various development projects, had also attempted to contain and limit women's reproduction: Household skills in the form of healing, health, sanitation, nutrition, socialization, and the like have been "retaught" to the rural and urban poor. One task of these projects is to determine the social values women are to reproduce for the capitalist economy.

Some of the patronizing attitudes in support of income-generating and acquisition-of-"appropriate technology" projects are contained in this statement by Fahima Zahir (el-Sadaty), sometime head of the Department of Social Anthropology, University of Khartoum, and a progressive feminist:

> To release women from their misery is to provide them with *appropriate* and simple *technology* for food production, to extend health training and health measures, to initiate *income-generating* activities, to provide *sanitary* housing and shelter; thereby saving time and energy and thus restoring human dignity. It may yet be argued that there are numerous *international agencies*, state departments [Sudanese government], the university, the National Council for Research and other research bodies and organizations which are developing new techniques, tools, equipment to ameliorate women's environmental disabilities.[66]

With such stances women become a charity group for which we all put our heads together in our attempts to teach them an "appropriate technology" that will bring them into the market economy and generate income for them. Women and their productive and reproductive labor are placed at the service of the state and international capital. Zahir also states:

> as long as women's time and labour power is consumed in the use of outmoded and inappropriate techniques in producing and preparing and storing food, constructing houses, collecting fuel, giving birth and providing care for children and traditionally dealing with disease and illness, they have little time to innovate, let alone undertake the formidable task of realizing that all her disabilities and difficulties are connected with what

we call economic planning, the state institutions and the state responsibilities.[67]

In addition to their positive approach to "income-generating" projects, other authors in the same work[68] insist that women are key to water technology projects because they (with their children) are the primary water collectors and handlers.[69] Women are also the primary teachers of other women and children about water treatment and hygiene.[70]

These ideas are challenged by others, who, for example, contend:

> ... the *modernization of technology* [in agriculture] *will eliminate women's contribution to agriculture* altogether. For, as manual work is replaced by machinery, women's role will diminish, and, if the non-agricultural market cannot absorb these displaced workers, they will return to the home and the man will become the sole family supporter. In many cases, the family income will be reduced and women will be denied the option of working outside the home.[71]

And,

> ... the improvement of water supply, while bringing greater benefit to the community as a whole, tends to *widen the gap in income between men and women* because the latter cannot utilise the monetary benefits which come from improved water supply applied to cash crops. Also, the improved water supplies in distant places mean that the men are away from their villages for longer periods and a further burden falls on the women while the men are deriving larger incomes from their increased herds. Thus, as customary law gives few property rights to women and gives her no independent decision-making power, she will not be able to derive any fundamental benefits from improved water supplies.[72]

In her introduction to the essays quoted above, Baxter outlines the dismal situation for women and the environment in Sudan, diagramming what she refers to as the "spiral of neglect" of women and the environment.[73] The environment is becoming imbalanced and natural resources are being reduced or eliminated. In such a situation women's work increases in nearly every way. In a country where most people are cultivators and nomads, the economy is highly vulnerable to changes in social fertility, water supplies, and pasture availability. The economic activities of agriculture and pastoralism, however, are creating a disaster for Sudan in the form of desertification. The effects are less-productive lands, slow agricultural production, and less land for grazing. "While the major environmental problems are generated largely by men's activities—live-stock herding, charcoal production and mechanised farming—it is the women who cope with the consequences on a day-to-day basis" (5).

Various students of the political economy of Sudan point to the ironic fact that development efforts aimed at alleviating the effects of such problems—afforestation projects, gum arabic plantations, cash-crop projects, and range management schemes—aim at improving income. But there is little concern about how a development project might impact the *distribution* of income within and among families.[74] Projects often increase employment for men, which may result in women/wives no longer being expected to work. In the urban areas, especially, this may amount to a return to at least partial seclusion, limiting women's economic options.

Here is a basic portrait of women and technology under a neocolonial situation of increasing impoverishment and expanding international capital. Rural women in Sudan are much more economically active than urban women; 90 percent of them work in agriculture.[75] Most of their time is spent in family subsistence food production, which produces very little income. When women work on agricultural schemes, it is usually as poorly paid and highly exploited seasonal laborers. Ironically, when new technology is introduced, they may be out of a job. The Gezira Scheme is a case in point. When this largest of Sudan's agricultural schemes was established in 1925, women worked to clear the land, sow, weed, harvest—the very tasks that eventually became mechanized, and women ultimately dropped out of agricultural wage labor. The money and efforts of subsequent investments concentrated on improvements that expedited men's work, rather than on less costly technologies such as improved hand tools, animal-drawn equipment, solar cookers, methane stoves, storage cribs for crops, and mills for grinding flour, which might have expedited women's.[76]

Capitalism is penetrating and pervasive. In Sudan, increasing sectors of the economy are being brought under international capital. Most rural families now, by necessity, are expected to produce for the cash economy. Consequently, women and children are forced into heavy, more capital-intensive agricultural activities—at the expense of domestic crops. Aping the West, development planners assume men to be heads of household and the central breadwinners. Improvements are aimed at men: improved seed, credit and marketing facilities, and agricultural extension services (10). At the same time, with male labor out-migration rates growing, women and wives are increasingly becoming single heads of households, managing and supporting the family: caught between their continuing roles as family food-producers and domestic reproducers and the pressures on them to engage fully in the market economy. No amount of science or technology, as we currently understand them, will resolve this dilemma. And substituting Islamic versions of capitalism may be just that—substituting.

The Conditions of Women's Lives—Sudanese Perspectives on Demographics, Education, and Labor—A Commentary

In this section I lay out how Sudanese themselves—mainly women—explain the conditions of Sudanese women's lives.

In 1987 Sudan's Population Council formed a Task Force of leading women's studies scholars, who produced a lengthy paper about the conditions of Sudanese women's lives. The authors are five women whose views I know to range from somewhat conservative to somewhat radical, and thus it is difficult to categorize the paper. It is clear that sections were written by different people, but the end effect (probably the result of final compromises) was to state a liberal-to-moderate position within the universe of northern intellectual, professional, politically active women. Because these scholars are influential in Sudan and reflect fairly common points of view, I quote them several times, referring to them as "Ahmed et al." In some cases I offer contrasting views. The Task Force report begins with a summary of the "current status" of Sudanese women:

> (1) low status tied closely to high fertility for women; (2) lagging opportunities for educational enrollment; (3) a lack of vocational education; (4) non-coordinated gender education; (5) limited literacy programmes; (6) limited participation in the labour force; (7) lack of a data base for measuring female's productive activities; (8) low-paid jobs in urban centres; (10) bad working conditions (i.e., industries); (11) equality with men by law but non-awareness about it; (12) custom overruling law in personal issues; (13) discrimination in the functioning of the law.[77]

Rejecting what they refer to as a call for change by "radical structuralists" Zeinab el-Bakri and el-Wathig Kameir, the Task Force advocates a moderate course.[78] They make a clear attempt to exempt religion as a cause of women's subordination: "the emphasis on the reproductive capacity of women in Sudan is largely a by-product of multidimensional constraints created by customs and traditions—*more than by religion*—on women."[79] And, "It is only through the increased awareness of women about their own rights both in *Sharia* (Islamic) and civil laws that a *revival of these rights* can be highlighted and incorporated into attempts for legal reform."[80]

Ahmed et al., using demographics, subtly blamed women for their situation.[81] For example: "women are more suppressed when attempting to increase their participation outside the domestic domain" (10); and *"women are led to manipulate men* through high fertility to keep them [the men] bound to the family and away from divorce and polygamy" (9, italics mine).

Using projections from the Sudan census, Ahmed et al. estimated the 1987 total population at 21,593,000–10,629,000 of them women.[82] Following are some of the figures that contribute to Sudanese (and others') ideas about population dynamics as causal of women's subordination.

Ahmed et al. point to high fertility as a cause of women's subordination: "Increasing the number of children becomes and is one of the means by which women may increase their status within the family as they have no viable alternatives to their family role. Childbearing augments female status within the household and acts as insurance against repudiation."[83] Sudan has one of the highest fertility rates in the world. Women of reproductive age (15–49) numbered some 5,004,000; the average number of children per woman in 1983 was 6.89,[84] which is fairly constant, regardless of region or milieu.[85] Expectably in such a poor country, the mortality rate (said to be declining) is also quite high. The death rate is 17 per 1000 annually, while the birth rate is 48 per 1000, resulting in a population-growth rate of 3.1 percent per year at the time of the Task Force report.[86] Atif Saghayroun, perhaps Sudanese women's studies' leading demographer in the 1980s, uses Ministry of Health estimates, World Health Organization figures, and some of his own survey material to inform us that the infant mortality rate is 600 deaths per 100,000 live births. A government source (Department of Social Welfare), cited below as Hassan et al., calls this "one of the highest in the world."[87] Maternal mortality rates range (by year and by region) from 541 to 2,270 per 100,000 live births, a 665 national average.[88]

To further account for what the authors refer to as women's low status, Ahmed et al. point to the "predominance of arranged and enforced [forced] marriages" that "keep women dependent on their families."[89] Constraints in marriage and against divorce are used as other indicators of low status, as is polygamy (9). Hassan et al. give us a very different ideological approach to the family: "The Sudanese society takes the family as the basis of its construction and works for its solidarity and to preserve and protect its organisation against factors of weakness and disintegration."[90] Unlike Ahmed et al.'s liberal-to-moderate position, the moderate-to-conservative government position of Hassan et al. does not take a negative position toward elements of "women's culture," although a veiled statement against circumcision appears on the last page under "disability," warning that there needs to be an "enlightenment of women about the dangers of customs such as circumcision of girls" (15). Ahmed et al. more openly criticize circumcision, the zar, and other customs: "Another set of constraints on women is the predominance of traditionally oppressive practices against them such as female circumcision, *Zar rituals* and marriage rituals. All of these reinforce subordination of women, though this is not yet *perceived so by them.*"[91] The indictment of the zar is fairly common to this class of women professionals, although many of them participate in zar activities. It is also typical for them to see less-educated, working-class, or peasant women as having false consciousness.

One common solution to subordination offered by government officials and intellectuals/professionals is to educate women. The kind of education women need, however, evokes sharp differences in opinion— i.e., what are they being prepared for? In chapter 6 I present some of the ideological foundations of Sudanese society as they relate to cultural policy and school curricula. I include the debate about appropriate kinds of education for women and men. Below I offer a brief overview of gender differentials in literacy and education.

Not everyone points to education as a panacea. Even the moderate-to-conservative Hassan et al. admit: "Development of women cannot be attained merely by abolishing the veils or gaining women political rights and acknowledgement of [their] right in education."[92] Acknowledging that Sudan's nonliteracy rate "seems to be of the highest rate in the world" (that is, men 76 percent, women 85 percent),[93] they give a higher overall rate for women than do some other sources. Compare Ahmed et al: men 55 percent, women 82 percent; in urban areas, men 35 percent, women 60 percent.[94] The central fact is that nonliteracy for women is very high, even in the urban areas. This not only affects the jobs women are able to attain, but also the strategies that change-oriented groups must use for organizing.

For many reasons education is significant in a discussion of the condition of Sudanese women's lives. The educational system in the north has been state controlled and, except for the highest levels, gender segregated. Also relevant to women's status are the kinds of institutions girls/women are allowed or encouraged to attend and their numbers relative to boys/men; the fields into which they are socialized or coerced; how high they are expected to go; and what they are taught in terms of the gender, class, race, and religious ideologies embedded and encoded in the curriculum. Ahmed et al. claim that during the early years of colonial British rule "none of the fairly large number of policy declarations even mentioned the education of women" (12). Until 1920 there were only five girls' schools, all in the north. The south was left to missionaries and to languish in isolation. In the north, "The content in programmes for girls' schools were different from those for boys and were of a lower academic standard and included substantial instructions in home crafts, needlework, etc"[95] El-Bakri and Kameir's article shows that none of the various development plans (e.g., the Five-Year Plan of Economic and Social Development [1970–75] and the Six-Year Plan [1977–83]) specifically included women.[96]

Most of the liberal-to-moderate commentators point to girls' equal (or even slightly higher) enrollment relative to boys' at the elementary level, especially in the urban areas, as evidence that girls are catching up, and attribute the disparity at the higher levels to a residual of past inequities.[97] Alternate explanations for the poor female-retention rate are early marriage, the need for girls to help with domestic labor, and girls' generally lower work, career, and intellectual/academic expectations.[98]

Isolating this last factor, a 1987 study surveyed 827 male and female secondary-school students.[99] Considering higher-education expectations (58–61), field-of-study preferences (13), and the desire to study abroad as indexes of life aspirations, the study claims that the women's goals were lower than the men's. Further, the authors suggest other causes for women's lower expectations; e.g., women were less likely than men to be counseled by their teachers to pursue higher education (58). The greatest gender disparity is in aspirations to attend higher technical institutions (60), reflecting the fact that although technical training offers the best hope in Sudan for a promising career, the jobs themselves are, for women, nontraditional, and thus too daunting for most even to consider.

The Ahmed et al. report uses a number of government sources to illustrate that since 1977 (1) more schools have been built for boys and (2) although the female-to-male ratio has increased at the institutions of higher education, boys still greatly outnumber girls.[100] However, another government report, issued by the Department of Labour and authored by Nur el-Tayib Abdel Gadir, contends that from 1970 to 1980 the numbers of girls' higher secondary schools in relation to boys' increased considerably.[101] In 1970/71 there were 44 schools for boys and 16 for girls; in 1979/80 those numbers rose to 87 and 45, respectively.[102] Further, Amna Badri points to both absolute and relative increases in female enrollments at all three levels of education[103] between 1977 and 1982/83. For example, the enrollment of female students in secondary schools grew 168.9 percent, while the number of male students increased 109.7 percent.[104]

Abdel Gadir, using Ministry of Education data from 1984, shows that, statistically, male and female student populations remained fairly constant over time, with girls gaining slightly in a number of categories. For example, girls' 1978/79 primary-school enrollment was 68 percent of boys', and in higher secondary/academic, 52 percent. Two years later, girls' primary enrollments were 75 percent of boys'; in higher secondary/academic, 58 percent—not much change. But from 1978/79 to 1980/81, female higher-secondary/technical enrollment increased from only 2 percent of males' to 78 percent.[105]

These figures alone are not a convincing picture of the state's attempt to channel women into less-academic education. After all, one would have to ask about the drop in male enrollments in the technical sphere. In terms of the rise of technical education for women, Table 4.1, based on Abdel Gadir, presents even more dramatic data. Two new schools were built in only seven years, with a 118 percent increase in courses offered and a more than tenfold student increase. To make a more certain statement about state intent and shifts in gender ideology, we would have to know if this was a new school population of women—i.e., women who would not have been able to go on with an academic education—or women who might have aspired to an academic education but were instead tracked into a technical one. From the comments on aspirations, it would seem that females had misgivings about technical education, but were tracked into it anyway. In 1988 Islamists and government officials actively attempted to track women into technical education, with only a limp attempt to conceal their intent to free more university slots for males.

In 1985 el-Nagar presented a useful portrait of women in "specialized institutes." Her table, slightly modified (see Table 4.2) gives a historical picture and indicates the range of technical training. The 1973/74 period el-Nagar deals with (one I observed firsthand) was when the move to give women more technical education began. The process of curtailing their academic education did not occur until the 1980s, with the economic crisis and the concomitant rise of Islamism.

Certain patterns are familiar in Table 4.2. Women were funneled into nursing, hygiene, secretarial/clerical studies, fine arts (only the middle and upper classes), laboratory technology, and certain teaching fields. These generally do not lead to higher paying jobs, but the movement of women into these jobs subverts the traditional and stereotyped job struc-

TABLE 4.1   Technical Education for Women

Year	No. of Schools	No. of Courses	No. of Students
1971/72	1	2	87
1972/73	1	4	100
1973/74	1	6	267
1974/75	1	9	417
1975/76	1	9	417
1976/77	3	14	717
1977/78	3	17	941

Note: Adapted from Abdel Gadir, *el-Mara el-Amila,*18, table 9.

ture. Within technical training the better jobs are in the surveying, forestry, and electrical/mechanical fields. The high enrollment of women at Ahfad College (now Ahfad University for Women) a private institution, is partly because it is gender-segregated. Ahfad pioneered in vocational and "practical"/applied education for women, and is the first to offer women's studies.

The Ministry of Education has been active in attempting to eradicate nonliteracy, which as noted is especially high among women. Literacy campaigns—what Ahmed et al. used as an example of "non-formal education"—have often been used as temporary substitutes for formal education, which is besieged with problems.[106] Another state campaign that targeted women heavily was sponsored by the Higher Council for Youth and Sports. The project involved the teaching of vocational skills for particular jobs and was designed to reach dropouts or those who never attended school (23).

Changes in the postsecondary-education fields women entered were rather dramatic from the mid-1970s to the mid-1980s. For reasons that are not clear and are more complicated than we can deal with here, women were performing better than in the past and better than men on the Sudan School Certificate Examinations (SCEs)[107] and were, therefore, entering universities and colleges in greater numbers, and into some of the more prestigious faculties at the elite Khartoum branch of the main state university. Fields of study at the University of Khartoum from which women had initially been barred, then discouraged from entering were now where they were placed. The complicated "boxing" system whereby students are ushered into particular faculties according to the courses they took and the scores they received on the SCEs was resulting in women being sent into such fields as agriculture. (To repeat: Sudan's economy is primarily agricultural, and most investment is geared towards agricultural development; therefore, education toward agricultural jobs is closely monitored.) However, we have no indication that women *wanted* to enter agriculture. State-sponsored feminism in those years pushed women toward such fields, in many cases regardless of where women's consciousnesses may have been at that time. Thus, women were often sent in nontraditional directions by a state educational system committed to gender equity in certain arenas.

Not just agriculture was being invaded by women students. Table 4.3 illustrates two themes: women entering universities and colleges in much greater numbers in the mid-1980s than in the mid-1970s, and entering nontraditional fields. Many more women took up religious law (sharia) at the University of Khartoum, and women graduates from Omdurman Islamic University went from zero in 1973/74 to 33 in 1975/76 to 95 in 1981/82.[108] At Omdurman Islamic University, Cairo University, and the

TABLE 4.2 Women in Higher Specialized Institutes, 1973/74

Institution or College	Pop. Women	Total Pop.	% Women
College of Fine and Applied Arts	23	155	14.8
Institute of Textile/Weaving Technology	3	64	4.7
Shambat Institute of Agriculture	31	350	8.9
Higher Institute for Surveying	–	103	–
Institute for Survey Technicians	–	57	–
Forest Rangers College	–	29	–
Institute for Lab Technicians	10	39	25.6
Khartoum Nursing College	71	71	100.0
School of Hygiene	3	40	7.5
College of Business Studies	22	228	9.6
Institute of Secretariat	48	76	63.1
Higher Technology Teachers Training	12	115	10.4
Higher Teacher Training Institute	92	511	18.1
Civil Engineering and Architectural Technology Institute	13	76	17.1
Khartoum Institute of Mechanical and Electrical Engineering Technology	10	93	10.8
Ahfad College	125	125	100.0
Higher Teachers Physical Education Institute	25	102	24.5
Total	493	2,438	20.2

Note: Adapted from el-Nagar, "Patterns of Women," 518, table 6.

University of Khartoum in 1972, 842 women studied sharia, 52 medicine, and 31 agriculture.[109]

The increased presence of women in these fields of study at the University of Khartoum can also be underscored by looking not only at agriculture (where the population of women students quadrupled, from 4.8 to 18.7 percent, in six years [1973–79]), but at medicine (where it tripled from 7.9 to 21.8 percent those same years) and science (where it more than doubled).[110]

State-sponsored feminist advances and/or the "brain drain" (i.e., out-migration of male labor, leaving jobs for women) may partially explain, for example, the well-documented movement of women away from their traditional bastion—arts (including humanities). In 1976, 16 percent of women's enrollments were in arts; in 1982, 12 percent. Feminist messages that women, too, could be/should be doctors and lawyers, and not just teachers and nurses, were succeeding. However, the same sociopolitical trends do not explain the movement of women into another of their traditional enclaves—education (8 percent in 1976; 15 percent in 1982).[111]

By the early 1980s, however, with Nimieri's desperate manipulation of religious ideology culminating in the 1983 imposition of sharia and general repression of secular, "Western," and non-Islamic modes of behavior and thinking (discussed in chapter 6), we see women's entrance into fields such as agriculture sharply declining. Table 4.4, which lists the numbers of women students at the University of Khartoum over a decade, manifests the precipitous drop in women's enrollments in agriculture, where they had been steadily climbing. That only 10 women were admitted in 1980/81 suggests a policy change. The national debate surrounding that change is discussed in chapter 6.

The sharp decline in women entering biology is unexplained except as a policy change about appropriate fields for women and the growing chilly climate in fields either deemed inappropriate for them or seen as needing to be preserved for men. In medicine there had been a steady increase, from virtually no enrollment in 1971, to 48 in 1981. In 1988 interviews women informed me that by 1983 the numbers had risen even more, precipitating the debate mentioned above.

Increased enrollment for women at all levels of education (certainly including the technical/vocational level), culminating in a 41 percent increase at the University of Khartoum in ten years, is striking and appears to fortify an argument that the status of women had improved. Yet the declines in particular fields indicate a shift in gender ideology and the state's activity in this process.

While the liberal-to-moderate argument is that education is the key to equality for women, I argue that much more is involved. Under the current Islamist regime, for example, we may very well see continued increase in technical- and academic-education enrollments for women. But it is the form and, especially, *content* of that education that is of interest here. Even the Ministry of Social Welfare report (Hassan et al.), which espouses a moderate-to-conservative position, makes this point:

> The girls education sector in the Sudan accomplished great achievements during the last two decades ... However, qualitatively speaking, the woman has inherited wrong beliefs in the community as related to her

TABLE 4.3   Enrollments of Women in Institutions of Higher Education in Sudan (in percent)

University or College	1977	1985
University of Khartoum, College of		
Medicine	21	42
Pharmacy	18	39
Engineering	8	13
Agriculture	16	40
Veterinary Medicine	11	35
Arts	16	38
Economics	12	31
Education	26	49
Science	21	41
Law	15	58
Gezira University (in Wad Medani)	74	4
Juba University (Southern Sudan)	4	27
College of Fine Arts	8	10
College of Secretarial Studies	50	96
College of Commercial Studies	3	6
College of Nursing	100	100
Ahfad University College	100	100
Institute of Music and Drama	10	19
Institute of Land Survey	0	2
Omdurman Islamic University	25	25

Note: This table is adapted from Ahmed et al., "Population Problems," 22, table 9. Their figures are from Sudan, Ministry of Education, National Council for Higher Education (Khartoum: Sudan Government, 1986). Gezira and Juba Universities are relatively new branches of the main state institution of higher education, the University of Khartoum. Ahfad University for Women is gender-segregated. One new institution emerged since these figures were available: Omdurman Ahlia University, which has a large number of women students and an emphasis on such fields as computer science.

TABLE 4.4 Number of Women Students in Various Faculties, University of Khartoum

Faculty	'71/'72	'72/'73	'73/'74	'74/'75	'75/'76	'76/'77	'77/'78	'78/'79	'79/'80	'80/'81
Agriculture	–	–	–	–	–	56	52	71	81	10
Art	49	26	20	42	46	36	42	45	59	47
Economics	23	21	16	10	23	18	33	47	47	35
Engineering	–	–	–	–	–	6	8	7	11	9
Civil Engineering	6	4	3	2	3	6	6	7	5	5
Biology	82	109	122	142	124	43	39	44	63	47
Math	7	11	10	13	11	3	4	4	15	9
Medical	–	–	–	–	–	42	41	59	44	48
Dental	–	–	–	–	–	–	6	12	8	9
Pharmacy	–	–	–	–	–	9	7	18	13	12
Law	–	–	9	12	15	13	13	10	11	13
Veterinary	–	–	–	–	–	8	11	19	26	29
Fine Arts	–	–	–	6	2	4	13	14	10	5
Life Science	–	–	–	14	11	12	29	24	38	29
Math	–	–	–	–	–	3	2	4	4	9
Home Economics	–	–	–	–	–	–	27	18	16	28
Total	167	171	180	247	226	261	330	400	454	400

Note: Adapted from Abdel Gadir, *el-Mara el-Amila*, 24, table 11. Some of the blanks are due to the field (e.g., home economics and fine arts) being new, not to the absence of women students. In some cases statistics on women were simply not kept, as perhaps there were too few of them or it was seen as unimportant. In the areas of agriculture, engineering, civil engineering, and math, however, we can be fairly sure there were either few or no women in the time periods indicated.

nature position and duty where she is considered less than man mentally and physically and that she is more emotional and agitated, has less ability and capacity for sciences and mathematics with tendency to literature and arts and that her right place is the house as a wife and mother. And even if she goes to work she must be confined to teaching, secretariat, home-economics and social services.[112]

There is more agreement among Sudanese scholars and government officials on the necessity of education for women, the moderate success of the last few years, and the potential for women's equality or liberation, than there is on labor-force issues. But even there, general agreement exists as to certain facts: that women are more economically active than any census has indicated; that rural women are especially active; that urban women lag behind urban men in workforce participation; that women's participation increases as job status declines; that better-paying industrial jobs tend to be male-intensive and lesser-paying service activities, female-intensive; that women still do all the domestic labor whether or not they are in paid employment; and that even though women are equal under the law, in practice they do not receive equal pay for equal work or have an equal chance for job opportunities. There is also agreement on the fact that women recognize their situation and, as a consequence, have lower aspirations.

Comparing 1973 to 1983, the ratio of women to men in some occupational categories is what we might expect, with many more male production workers; more men, in proportion to their overall participation, in technical and professional jobs; and a rise in the percentage of women in clerical positions. The numbers have remained fairly constant, except for the rise in the female clerical force (from 9 to 20 percent), especially in urban areas where the civil service bureaucracy had expanded.[113]

According to Alawiya Salih, in 1980 women were 12 percent of the Greater Khartoum workforce: 23 percent of sales; 17 percent of service; and 18 percent of trade.[114] Table 4.5 shows the general picture of women's economic activity in Greater Khartoum.[115]

The category "inadequately defined" is inadequate for any analysis. It assumably includes a large number of women in the "informal" sector— e.g., those engaged in service occupations that are illegal or disreputable, and itinerant traders (not mutually exclusive categories.)

The state is one of the largest employers in Sudan (in fact the largest in the urban areas), and in hiring and promotion, gender, ethnic, and religious "neutrality" is its reigning ethic. Within the state employment structure, employees are promoted in degrees/scales.[116] Amna Badri's study illustrates that in 1984 women held few top-scale jobs, e.g., government minister, deputy minister, judge.[117]

TABLE 4.5 Women's Economic Activity in Greater Khartoum (Women as 12 Percent of Total Workforce)

Occupational Category	Women as Percent of Category
Professionals	20
Clerks	17
Sales	23
Service	15
Farmers/Fishers	0
Production	4
Inadequately Defined	40

Note: Adapted from Salih, "Women in Trade," 7.

In general, women's participation decreases the higher the scale of the job. Giving these jobs a name makes the picture clearer, so I have used the findings of Abdel Gadir on the distribution, according to gender and degree/scale, of civil-service jobholders in 1983.[118] Once again, in government-classified first-to-seventh degree jobs, women were employed in greater numbers in occupations seen either as extensions of their domestic labor (such as nurses, veterinarians, and even doctors) or as related to their past economic activities (e.g., agricultural workers). They were not as well-represented in jobs seen as requiring decision-making skills, reason, and scientific knowledge. In Sudan as a whole, the number of women in degree 1–7 positions (e.g., pharmacist, judge, researcher) was only 16 percent that of men, compared with 30 percent in degree 10–15 positions (from clerk to storekeeper), a considerable discrepancy.[119]

In the Greater Khartoum public sector, women still do not do as well as men in degree and type of employment. Their numbers, compared with men's, are, in technical jobs, 23.9 percent; in administrative, 14 percent; clerical, 36.7 percent; sales, 1.9 percent; services, 15 percent; agriculture, 2.8 percent; textiles (factory), 1.6 percent; and production, 1.2 percent; for a total of 13 percent.[120]

When we consider nursing, clerical, service, and petty trading—jobs where women are most prominent—it is obvious that these are not lucrative and the working conditions are often poor. Ahmed et al. address the problems of nurses: "[M]any women avoid nursing because salaries are low and the conditions of work are not satisfactory, in addition to a social stigma associated with the job."[121] They say the same about service activities. Jobs that are unlicensed and unregulated, such as petty trader, are very popular with urban women, especially migrants. Not only is the woman trader liberated from job discrimination, but the hours and conditions are flexible. Ahmed et al. represent the blame-the-victim position of liberal-to-moderate observers, especially when regarding rural, nonformally educated women:

> The absence of such services as food and refreshment centres in the highly congested parts of the cities opens avenues for unemployed, uneducated women to participate in the labour force. Migrant women from rural areas enter into such jobs to generate income for their survival in the urban centres. The repercussions of this are reflected in larger numbers of settled migrant families in the shanty towns of the cities. The outcome is the overburdening of the infrastructure of the urban centres, the scarcity of consumer goods, and other related deterioration in health services, transportation, etc.[122]

In the conclusion of her thesis, which I paraphrase here, el-Nagar sums up the situation of women workers in Greater Khartoum: Women's participation in nonagricultural activities in Greater Khartoum has been increasing since independence and women have been entering nontraditional occupations, but there are still severe limitations on them, and their participation is much lower than men's. They are concentrated in the traditionally gender-specific, lower-paying jobs (secretaries, nurses, typists, and the like) and are rarely found in engineering and technology. Therefore, the majority of women are concentrated in unskilled occupations and their numbers decrease the more skill the occupation requires. Women are considerably underrepresented in top positions in government, industry, and other professions. When self-employed, mainly as petty traders with small capital, women sell liquor and sex and other personal services. These mostly disreputable jobs, which service men, have historically been left to women and have thus become gender-specific.[123]

While my 1981 pilot study suggested that many urban women work for self-fulfillment (including the feeling of freedom), not financial necessity, el-Nagar, whose fieldwork was much more extensive, maintains that women work mainly to help their families and that although some middle- and upper-class women work because their economic conditions secure them chances of specialization in highly prestigious professions, few work for self-fulfillment. She insists:

> Female employment is not necessarily an indication of changing idealogies [sic] and attitudes of the family or kinship unit. It is rather a response to changing costs and opportunities on the part of families with no change as concerning the stereotypic perception about women. That is why the decision to work and the education and kind of job a woman takes, are greatly influenced by the woman's family conditions (470).

Moreover, women's horizons are greatly limited because of conservative attitudes that prevail in the family. El-Nagar reports that if a crisis arises or a time conflict in the family, the husband's job is always given priority and that the woman worker has very heavy kin-keeping and kin-caring responsibilities. Their energy is also severely affected by having to perform most of the domestic work even when they have a paying job outside the home (471).

Although Badri's findings bear some similarity to el-Nagar's, her points are more often congruent with my 1981 findings. For example, Badri finds self-fulfillment to be an important element: "The women are highly committed to their careers. The majority indicated they would choose their careers over social demands."[124] Badri's findings differ from mine in the women's acknowledgment of income as a necessity. States Badri: "About 75 percent of the women reported that their income was vital to the economic well being of their families."[125]

To return to the problem of the burden of all domestic labor falling on women, employers see women workers as less valuable, often indicating that they lost a lot of work hours because of family responsibilities.[126] Abdel Gadir comments on the mental and physical suffering that accrue from discrimination against women as a result of "double-day expectations." She contends that women's low productivity and absenteeism are also a result of lack of modern domestic technology.[127]

El-Nagar, one of the progressive feminist voices in Sudanese women's studies, addressing the issue of more job opportunities for women as a corollary of the expansion of capitalism, maintains that capitalist expansion is also limiting to women. For example, women experience more unemployment than men.[128] Moreover, as we have seen, women are funneled into particular jobs, often dull and repetitive or physically or psychologically taxing. Low salaries are part of these negative job conditions. Ahmed et al. summarized their section on urban labor:

> women in the urban areas are concentrated in low paid jobs with the exception of a few educated elite. Women face difficulties of transportation, promotion and bad working conditions, especially in industries. They find difficulties in the coordination between their domestic and extra-domestic roles especially with absence of supporting service sectors such as kindergartens, nurseries and other public services. Many women retreat to their traditional domestic roles as wives and mothers since the public service sector does not provide them with sufficient services.[129]

Positions taken by the women scholars and government officials cited above most certainly do not support the idea that women who work for a wage are emancipated. Yet by 1965 Sudanese women, in terms of their legal and political status, were ahead of many women in the world, including the United States. And that leads to the question of how much equality and emancipation can be achieved through the law. In the next section I discuss law and politics, the last of the variables selected for the two sections on the conditions of women's lives.

The Conditions of Women's Lives—
Sudanese Perspectives on Legal and Political Status—
A Commentary

A great deal has been written about Sudan's plural legal system—customary (urf), civil (based on British common law), and sharia—and it is not the goal of this book to describe or analyze this pluralism. My interest is in the evolution of the dominance of Islamic law as it relates to women.

After the British gained control of Sudan in 1899, two sets of courts functioned: secular courts for all civil matters and for personal matters of non-Muslims and consenting Muslims; and sharia courts for personal matters of Muslims and consenting non-Muslims. Sharia courts were indisputably secondary to secular courts, but after independence in 1956, with a growing movement toward Islamization of the legal system, this began to change. Eventually the transitional constitution was amended and the Sharia Courts Act of 1967 passed. Dina Shiekh el-Din Osman marks this act as the end of the subordination of sharia courts.[130]

By the 1970s, following Osman, there was a growing tendency toward the Islamization of the legal system. Nimieri's movement toward conservatism gained momentum after the abortive leftist coup in 1971, and was reflected in the legal system. For example, the Judicial Authority Act of 1972 merged secular (civil) and sharia courts; the Organization of Laws Act in 1973 restored the supremacy of common law, paving the way for the dominance of local customs and religious ideals; and article 9 of the Permanent Constitution of 1973 mandated Islamic law and custom the main sources of legislation. In 1983, after alienating or repressing most of his supporters, Nimieri, in a bold move to hold onto power, abruptly announced major changes that would force the legal system to conform to sharia. The Judicial Decisions Sources Act of 1983 mandates the court to decide in accordance with the Quran and *Sunna* or principles of *Ijtihad* (legal interpretation of these holy sources). The Evidence Act of 1983 applies conservative laws of evidence to women and non-Muslims. For example, two women witnesses are needed to offset the testimony of one man. An Islamized Civil Code (1984) followed.[131]

Women were being given contradictory messages. They achieved universal suffrage in 1965 during the brief leftist interlude after the fall of the Abboud military regime; they earned equal pay for equal work in 1968;

and in 1975 they attained the right to pensions. Public Service Regulations also gave them special benefits such as paid maternity leaves. Moreover, the same Permanent Constitution of 1973 that raised the spectrum of a more Islamized Sudan, provided equality for women in a number of areas. Osman indicates that in part 3 of the constitution, which deals with human rights and duties, there is no gender distinction (i.e., women are not excluded).[132] Article 38 provides: "The Sudanese have equal rights and duties irrespective of origin, race, locality, *sex*, language or religion."[133] Article 56 is a workforce antidiscrimination clause that covers gender: Women are given rights to equal education, to hold public office, to freedom of association and unionization, and to freedom of speech and movement. Osman points out that Article 55 even accords women and children *special* protection by the state (126).

Osman was writing in the mid-1980s, when little doubt was in the minds of most moderates and liberals that the rules of civil and criminal law, procedure and evidence, discriminated against women. Nonetheless, most moderate-to-liberal Sudanese sources also agree that, before the 1989 Islamist military regime suspended most civil laws and the Transitional Constitution of 1985, women had a number of rights and protections under the law. Ahmed et al. summarize the issue: "In terms of work laws, political rights, educational and civil rights, Sudanese women have an equal status to men ... In terms of religious and customary laws we find that some are protective to women and others are not."[134]

A partial list (after Ahmed et al.) of labor and personal status laws or sections thereof, passed in the 1970s and 1980s—i.e., prior to the 1989 coup—that have influenced some women's working conditions and personal well-being is as follows:

1. Equality in civil service hiring and promotion based on merit (art. 16, part 6, Civil Service Act, 1973).
2. Equality in payment for equal work (art. 9, Public Service Act, 1973).
3. Equality of pensions and gratitudes (art. 80, Social Insurance Act, 1974).
4. Equal right for training (art. 6, National Training Act, 1976).
5. Equality in obtaining annual and education leave (Transitional Constitution, arts. 31, 17, and 12).
6. Maternity leave for eight weeks (art. 25 (1), Individual Labor Relations Act, 1981).
7. Leave for mourning period following the death of husband for six weeks (art. 94 (1), Public Service Regulations, 1975).
8. Leave of at least one hour from work for the purpose of lactation (art. 30, Public Service Regulations, 1975).
9. Right to apply for four years of unpaid leave for accompanying husband in travel for purposes of education or work (art. 89, Public Service Regulations, 1975).

10. Right to apply for one year of unpaid leave for lactation purposes (Public Service Regulations, 1975).
11. "No woman shall be allowed to work between 10 PM and 6 AM with the exception of those working in social, health services as in administration, professional and technical work" (The Industrial Safety Act of 1976 states).
12. No woman should be employed in ways dangerous to her health (Industrial Safety Act of 1976).
13. The age of pension for women is 55 and for men 60 (Social Insurance Act, 1974).[135]

Ahmed et al., certainly not idealists, point to the discrepancy between the law and practice. They relate a 1987 situation where 500 of 900 candidates for judiciary posts were qualified women, but only twelve appeared on the short list of forty-two. In response to charges of gender discrimination, the Public Service and Recruitment and Selection Board acknowledged the discrimination, indicating that it was based on women's refusal to serve in the "remote provinces"—a policy requirement for every graduate (36).

Ahmed et al. and other sources point to the discrepancy between the protections and rights for women in the personal status laws of sharia, and the patriarchal traditions of the society. For example: "A girl has the right of consent to a marriage suitor and can get married by court if her guardian did not give his consent; in such case the judge acts as a male-guardian. Yet it is considered an *act of shame* for a girl to resort to court."[136] A legal foundation for change may now have been completely swept away in the Islamization process and the passing of the Muslim Act in 1991.[137]

Conclusion

The contemporary situation for Sudanese women is complicated, somewhat contradictory, and dynamic. Their legal and political status is changing as I write. The conditions of women's lives, for the most part, looked good on paper. In practice, however, many of the laws are/were not upheld but were generally subordinated to what was usually, if not always, patriarchal custom.

This is not to say that women were the passive recipients of oppressive customs and/or did not mobilize against traditions they saw as antithetical to their well-being. On the contrary, many women's organizations have addressed significant women's issues since the 1940s, and although perhaps we cannot yet speak of a unified "women's movement," still we can point to considerable political activism by women, and men, on behalf of women. In the next chapter I analyze the gender relationships of the Sudanese Communist Party (SCP) and its affiliate, the Women's Union (WU), in the course of their activism on behalf of women; and in chapter 6, gender relations and activism within the National Islamic Front.

But in the final analysis we may want to raise the critical questions of whether women's *everyday* lives have ever been profoundly affected by party- and state-sponsored feminism, and whether women's own political organizations have had any personal impact. For as a number of women asked me rhetorically in 1988: "What have *any* of the parties ever done for us?" My experience of living in Khartoum tells me that women have, especially in crises, relied on themselves, their families, their neighborhoods, and their communities for concrete changes, or simply for maintenance and survival, in their everyday lives.[138]

Notes

1. Sudanese demographers and other social scientists are, of course, influenced by outside constructs.

2. I do not attempt to define "authentic." Sudanese used the word to refer to a culture that emanates from "true Islam." I grew to realize that "true Islam" was as much an invention of culture as a return to something (as is connoted by "fundamentalism" and denoted by "atavism" [see chaps. 6–7]).

3. Interviewees in both the SCP and the NIF used this expression in reference to the zar (see chap. 1, note 9). In fact, the zar was *always* singled out. When I inquired about other "negative customs," respondents only rarely added "female circumcision." My guess is that many were unwilling to add particular customs surrounding childbearing.

4. "Truly Sudanese" is my translated term, parallel to the common expression "real Sudanese" mentioned earlier. These are, with few exceptions, central riverain self-identified Arabs who are *not* Egyptians, "Levantines," Greeks, or "Others."

5. This is a co-opted name, causing many to confuse the SCP's Women's Union with the SSU's.

6. Gender rights-and-obligations provisions in Islamic law include detailed instructions to Muslims regarding marriage, divorce, support and custody of children, transference of wealth and property, and other rites of passage and people's everyday lives. See Carolyn Fluehr-Lobban, *Islamic Law and Society in the Sudan* (London: Frank Cass, 1987).

7. Some possible indexes for assessing the "status of women": participation in the job market and the level of jobs; participation in educational institutions and in public life; legal/political rights; and the newly devised Human Development Index (HDI), measuring education, health, and purchasing power. In 1993 the United Nations Development Program introduced a separate female index in its Human Development Report (*Los Angeles Times* "World Report" section [29 June 1993]). A number of articles in a recent work on women and development (Irene

Tinker, ed., *Persistent Inequalities: Women and World Development* [New York: Oxford University Press, 1990]) discuss various indexes.

8. Nahid Toubia, *Female Genital Mutilation: A Call for Global Action* (New York: Women, Ink., 1993), 25.

9. I shift here to the past tense because the current regime is in the process of subverting and/or diluting these rights.

10. See Elizabeth Fernea's documentary, *A Veiled Revolution* (New York: First Run/Icarus Film, 1982).

11. Sondra Hale, "The Politics of Gender in the Middle East," in *Gender and Anthropology: Critical Reviews for Research and Teaching*, ed. Sandra Morgen (Washington, D.C.: American Anthropological Association, 1989), 246–67. See also my arguments about "veiling" and the tobe in chapter 2.

12. Nahid Toubia, ed. with Amira Bahyeldin, Nadia Hijab, and Heba Abdel Latif, *Arab Women: A Profile of Diversity and Change* (Cairo: Population Council, 1994).

13. Marnia Lazreg, *The Eloquence of Silence: Algerian Women in Question* (New York: Routledge, 1994).

14. For a useful analysis of Sudan's crisis, see Tony Barnett, "Introduction: The Sudanese Crisis and the Future," in *Sudan: State, Capital, and Transformation*, ed. Tony Barnett and Abbas Abdelkarim (London: Croom Helm, 1988), 1–17; and Norman O'Neill and Jay O'Brien, eds., *Economy and Class in Sudan* (Avebury, London: Gower Publishing Company, 1988), especially their introduction and first chapter.

15. The gender hierarchy and class structure of Sudan has some historical similarity to Egypt's. For many of the following ideas I am indebted to Judith Gran, "Impact of the World Market on Egyptian Women," *MERIP Reports* no. 58 (1977): 3–7; and Judith Tucker, *Women in Nineteenth-Century Egypt* (Cambridge: Cambridge University Press, 1985).

16. B.C. Sanyal, L. Yaici, and I. Mallasi, *From College to Work: The Case of the Sudan* (Paris: UNESCO, International Institute of Educational Planning, 1987), 8. A table follows the quote. See also Mohamed el-Awad Galaleldin, *Some Aspects of Sudanese Migration to the Oil-Producing Arab Countries During the 1970's* (Khartoum: Development Studies and Research Centre, University of Khartoum, 1985), 1–52.

17. See Nur el-Tayib Abdel Gadir, *el-Amila fi el-Sudan* (The Working Woman in Sudan) (Khartoum: Department of Labour and Social Security, Division of Research, Information, and Media, 1984); and Samia el-Nagar, "Patterns of Women Participation in the Labour Force in Khartoum" (Ph.D. diss., University of Khartoum, 1985). The latter is one of the few extensive sources on the subject of women and the urban labor force. She distributed questionnaires to 650 women workers, interviewed eighty of them in depth, and carried out 180 interviews with self-employed women in Khartoum (13–14). Information also based on summer 1988 interviews with Afaf Abu Hasabu, Programme Officer, United Nations Development Programmes; Nahid Toubia, medical doctor; and Fawzia Hammour, Women's Studies and Bibliographer, Development Studies and Research Centre, University of Khartoum.

18. A number of Sudanese sources (e.g., Zeinab el-Bakri and el-Wathig M. Kameir, "Women and Development Policies in Sudan: A Critical Outlook" [paper

no. 46, presented at the 2d OSSREA Congress, Nairobi, 28–31 July 1986]) confirm this position. One of the three limited options open to women is the consequence of migration to urban areas "where women have resorted overwhelmingly to begging and prostitution [the other two options]" (16).

19. Toubia et al., *Arab Women*, 31

20. Magda M. el-Sanousi and Nafissa Ahmed el-Amin, "Sudan," in *Women and Politics Worldwide*, ed. Barbara Nelson and Najma Chowdhury (New Haven: Yale University Press, 1994), 674, box.

21. The birthrate is 45 per 1,000; maternal mortality is 660 per 100,000 live births; infant mortality is 107 per 1,000 live births; and the mortality rate for children under five years old is 181 per 1,000 live births. From el-Sanousi and el-Amin, "Sudan," 674, box.

22. Regardless of "a small overall decline" in infibulations, 90 percent of those who undergo some form of genital surgery are infibulated. Toubia et al., *Arab Women*, 27.

23. Ibid., 55. The same work also explained that, although Sudan has one of the strictest criminal laws against abortion, "Senior Islamic scholars in Sudan, including the grand mufti in 1976, held the view that abortion should be permissible, though disliked, to preserve the mothers [*sic*] health and well being provided that the pregnancy is under 4 months" (54).

24. Nadia Hijab, *Women and Work*, A Special MERIP Publication on women in the Middle East, *MERIP Middle East Report* no. 3 (1994): 7, table 3.

25. El-Sanousi and el-Amin, "Sudan," 674, box.

26. Toubia et al., *Arab Women*, 56.

27. "In Sudan the right to vote and nominate oneself for election is legally granted to women. This right may be rendered ineffective by other laws that require women to obtain permission from their husbands or guardians to take part in political activities. If the guardian does not grant permission or grants it and then withdraws it at a later date, the woman's position could be severely compromised." Nahid Toubia et al., *Arab Women*, 51.

28. El-Sanousi and el-Amin, "Sudan," 674, box.

29. Toubia et al., *Arab Women*, 56. According to Toubia et al., some 41 percent of women under the age of 20 are married (25).

30. Magda M. el-Sanousi and Nafissa Ahmed el-Amin, "The Women's Movement, Displaced Women, and Rural Women in Sudan," in *Women and Politics Worldwide*, ed. Barbara Nelson and Najma Chowdhury (New Haven: Yale University Press, 1994), 676. I do not take the position that polygamy automatically negatively determines any aspect of a woman's status, but a potential negative impact is with regard to legal consent, i.e., the fact that in Sudan polygamy is permitted freely, not prohibited by law, and not, as is the case in some other Middle Eastern countries, permitted only in court (Toubia et al., *Arab Women*, 60).

31. Toubia et al., *Arab Women*, 57.

32. Ibid., 54. Also see Asma M. Abdel Haleem, "Claiming Our Bodies and Our Rights: Exploring Female Circumcision as an Act of Violence," in *Freedom from Violence: Women's Strategies Around the World*, ed. Margaret Schuler (New York: United Nations Development Fund for Women, 1992), 141–56.

33. Toubia et al., *Arab Women*, 38.

34. Hijab, *Women and Work*, 4, table 2. Hijab has taken her figures from a 1989 United Nations World Survey on the Role of Women in Development.

35. Ramla Khalidi and Judith Tucker, *Women's Rights in the Arab World*, A Special MERIP Publication no. 1 (1994): 4–5, table 3. The authors use a 1990 United Nations report. The figures are slightly higher than Hijab's (ibid.).

36. Toubia et al., *Arab Women*, 39.

37. Ibid., 41.

38. El-Sanousi and el-Amin, "Sudan," 674, box.

39. The first set of figures is from el-Sanousi and el-Amin, ibid. The 29 percent figure is from Hijab, *Women and Work*, 2, table 1. Hijab is using United Nations Development Programme, *Human Development Report* (London: Oxford University Press, 1993). The 1991 population was estimated at 25.9 million; the labor force, at 35 percent of the population.

40. Toubia et al., *Arab Women*, 47.

41. Sondra Hale, "'Private' and 'Public' Labour: The Sudanese Woman Worker in the 1980's —A Pilot Study," *The Ahfad Journal: Women and Change* 2, no. 2 (1985): 36–40.

42. For example, Karen Sacks, "A Two-Way Street: Gendering International Studies and Internationalizing Women's Studies," working paper no. 24, Southwest Institute for Research on Women, Tucson, 1987.

43. El-Nagar elaborated: "As to division of labour at home, employment has no effect as women are still responsible for all domestic activities" ("Patterns of Women," 467).

44. Friedrich Engels, *The Origin of the Family, Private Property and the State* (New York: International, 1972); Sheila Rowbotham, Lynne Segal, and Hilary Wainwright, *Beyond the Fragments: Feminism and the Making of Socialism* (London: Merlin Press, 1979).

45. International Labour Organisation, United Nations High Commissioner for Refugees, *Labour Markets in the Sudan* (Geneva: International Labour Office, 1984), 2.

46. The ILO was using 1973 Sudan census data projections made in 1976.

47. Several sources make this point. See, e.g., David Roden, "Regional Inequality and Rebellion in the Sudan," *Geographical Review* 64, no. 2 (1974): 498–516.

48. Dorothy Remy, "Underdevelopment and the Experience of Women: A Nigerian Case Study," in *Toward an Anthropology of Women*, ed. Rayna Reiter (New York: Monthly Review Press, 1975), 370.

49. See el-Nagar, "Patterns of Women," 469.

50. Women's decisions about mate selection are limited, however, by the needs of men to use marriage to form political and economic alliances.

51. "Patterns of Women," 466–67. Italics mine.

52. See, e.g., Tinker, *Persistent Inequalities*.

53. El-Sanousi and el-Amin, "The Women's Movement," 683, citing the figures of the Council of the Displaced.

54. El-Sanousi and el-Amin (ibid., 683–85) presented powerful descriptions and case studies of displaced women.

55. Diana Baxter, "Introduction—Women and Environment: A Downward Spiral," in *Women and the Environment in the Sudan*, ed. Diana Baxter (Environmental

Research Paper Series No. 2, Institute of Environmental Studies, University of Khartoum, Khartoum, 1981), 1.

56. Taisier Mohamed Ali, "Towards the Political Economy of Agricultural Development in the Sudan 1956–1964" (Ph.D. diss., University of Toronto, 1983), 9–10.

57. Amna Farah, "Enhancing Women's Participation in Agriculture and Rural Development" (paper presented at the Conference on the Contributions of Women to Development, Development Studies and Research Centre, University of Khartoum, Khartoum, 11–14 April 1984), 11.

58. See Fatma Babiker Mahmoud, *The Sudanese Bourgeoisie: Vanguard of Development?* (London: Zed; Khartoum: Khartoum University Press, 1984), for an outline of these political-economic processes.

59. David Lee, "Space Levels of a Sudanese Villager," *The Professional Geographer*, 29, no. 2 (1977): 160–65.

60. El-Nagar, "Patterns of Women," 469.

61. Ibid., 470.

62. Even if self-fulfillment may not have been the stated motivation of my interviewees for *entering* the workforce, it was mentioned as one of their reasons for staying.

63. Sondra Hale, "The Wing of the Patriarch: Sudanese Women and Revolutionary Parties," *MERIP Middle East Report* 16, no. 1 (1986): 25–30.

64. Marjorie Hall and Bakhita Amin Ismail, *Sisters under the Sun: The Story of Sudanese Women* (London: Longman, 1981), e.g., 34.

65. When the WU was legal and allowed by the state to function, it often organized collectives, which it continued to do even when banned. However, in the period under discussion, such activity was carried out by the SSU's women's organization, under the aegis of the state.

66. Fahima Zahir el-Sadaty, "Women and Their Environment: An Overview," in Baxter, *Women and the Environment*, 18. Italics mine.

67. Ibid.

68. See, e.g., Amna el-Sadik Badri, Mariam Khalf Alla Shabo, Elhan el-Nujumi, Maarwa Ahmed el-Obeid, and Majda Mustafa Hassan, "Income Generating Projects for Women," in Baxter, *Women and the Environment*, 30–35.

69. Yagoub Abdalla Mohamed, "An Overview of the Water Situation in the Sudan," in Baxter, *Women and the Environment*, 48.

70. Samia el-Azharia Jahn, "Traditional Methods of Water Purification of Sudanese Women," in Baxter, *Women and the Environment*, 56.

71. Kamil Ibrahim Hassan, "Women's Contribution to the Economy," in Baxter, *Women and the Environment*, 110. Italics mine.

72. Asha Mustafa, "Women and Water in Western Kordofan," in Baxter, *Women and the Environment*, 69. Italics mine. See also Mustafa's "Role of Women in the Traditional Food Systems of Drought-Affected Environments: A Study of Kordofan Region—Sudan," Research Report (Khartoum: Women in Development Programme, Development Studies and Research Centre, University of Khartoum, [1985–88?]). A paper that assesses various approaches to development is el-Bakri and Kameir, "Women and Development Policies in Sudan." The most comprehensive in-country study of women and agricultural development is Food and Agri-

culture Organization of the United Nations, *National Conference on the Role of Women in Agriculture and Rural Development in the Sudan: Interim Report* (Shambat, Khartoum North: College of Agricultural Studies, Khartoum Polytechnic and FAO-Project GCP/SUD/030 [FIN], 18–22 January 1987).

73. Baxter, "Introduction—Women and Environment," 1. These investments were at first mainly British and European, then multinational by the 1970s, and now often Arab and Iranian.

74. Samira Amin Ahmed carried out a survey of 440 families among Sudanese migrants living in Riyadh, Saudi Arabia. In 232 cases the wives had independent incomes that were significant to the family income. Yet in most cases, especially the professional or clerical jobs, such a contribution did not contribute to the woman's autonomy; whereas among *kisra* (thin bread) sellers and other petty traders, there was more economic autonomy. "The Impact of Migration on Conjugal Relationships: A Study of Sudanese Migrants in Riyadh (Saudi Arabia)" (Ph.D. diss., 1986).

75. International Labour Organisation, *Growth, Employment and Equity: A Comprehensive Strategy for the Sudan* (Geneva: International Labour Office, 1976).

76. Baxter, "Introduction—Women and Environment," 6.

77. Samira Amin Ahmed, Inaam A. Elmahdi, Belgis Y. Bedri, Samya el-Hadi el-Nagar, and Amna Badri, "Population Problems, Status of Women and Development" (paper presented at the Third National Population Conference, University of Khartoum, Khartoum, 10–14 October 1987), i–iii, 1–53. The quote is from page i.

78. I am guessing that Ahmed et al. were referring to el-Bakri and Kameir, "Women and Development Policies in Sudan," in which the latter stated that only "truly radical policies towards women can ... succeed radical changes in the balance of socioeconomic forces in Sudanese society" (18). Or they may have been referring to the same authors' "Aspects of Women's Political Participation in Sudan," *International Social Science Journal* 35, no. 4 (1983): 605–23.

79. Ahmed et al., "Population Problems," 6. Italics mine.

80. The preceding passage states: "It is clear that religious matrimonial laws of Islam, for instance, have been distorted to suit the *man's love of dominance*, especially in matters relating to polygamy and divorce. This distortion has given rise to the impression that Islam allows wives to be treated capriciously by husbands which is not true." Ibid., 9–10. Italics mine.

81. The demographic argument is complex, made more perplexing by the lack of availability and general unreliability of the statistics. According to the Sudan, Department of Statistics, *National Census 1983* (Khartoum: Sudan Government, 1988), Sudan's population was 20,598,000, women numbering some 10,083,000. The Ahmed et al. study focuses on some 3,390,688 women from the northern, central, and Khartoum regions.

82. Ahmed et al., "Population Problems," 4.

83. Ibid., 8.

84. Ibid., 4–5.

85. See also Atif A. Saghayroun, "Women in Demographic Trends" (paper presented at the Workshop on Women's Studies in Sudan, National Council for Research and Sudan Family Planning Association, University of Khartoum, Khartoum, 7–9 February 1989), 10–14.

86. Ahmed et al., "Population Problems," 8. A more recent source (1994) was cited in chapter 3, note 3. El-Sanousi and el-Amin ("Sudan," 674, box) claim the birthrate is 45.

87. Amna Abdel Rahman Hassan, Sakina Mohamed el-Hassan, Nawal Ahmed Adam, Afaf Ali Rehiman, Shahowa el-Gizouli, Mahasin Khider (el-Sayed), Ehsan Hussein, Asha Abdulla, and Ibrahim Ahmed Osman, "Woman Strategy for the Year 2000: Submitted to the Arab League in December, 1986" (Khartoum: Sudan, Ministry of Social Welfare and Elzakat, Department of Social Welfare, 1986), 8.

88. Saghayroun, "Women in Demographic Trends," 17, using figures from the Sudan Government, Population Census Office, Department of Statistics, *Second and Third Population Census, 1973 and 1983* (Khartoum: Sudan Department of Statistics, 1979 and 1987); the World Health Organization (1985); and the Arab Medical Bulletin (1983).

89. Ahmed et al., "Population Problems," 8–9.

90. Hassan et al., "Woman Strategy," 9.

91. Ahmed et al., "Population Problems," 10. Italics mine.

92. Hassan et al., "Woman Strategy," 13.

93. Ibid., 11–12.

94. Ahmed et al., "Population Problems," 12.

95. Ibid.

96. El-Bakri and Kameir, "Women and Development Policies in Sudan," 17.

97. Ahmed et al., "Population Problems," 13 and 14, are an example.

98. Other data show that girls are continuing in school at levels close to that of boys; see, e.g., Nafisa Salman Bedri and Lee G. Burchinal, "Educational Attainment as an Indicator of the Status of Women in the Sudan," *The Ahfad Journal* 2, no. 1 (1985): 30–38. In my own informal surveys, males always answered with more certainty about their higher education goals and future occupations.

99. Sanyal et al., *From College to Work*, 60.

100. Using the Department of Statistics, 1962; Ministry of Education, 1984; and National Council for Higher Education, Khartoum, 1986—Ahmed et al. compiled nine tables that are very revealing. "Population Problems," 16–22.

101. By 1984 the Ministry of Education had divided schools into primary, secondary, and higher secondary levels, more or less equivalent to the North American elementary, junior high, and high schools. Higher secondary was subdivided into academic and technical (vocational).

102. Abdel Gadir, *el-Mara el-Amila*, 15, table 6.

103. See note 98 above.

104. Amna el-Sadik Badri, "Women in Management and Public Administration in Sudan" (paper presented at the Conference of Business and Administrative Sciences Education in the Sudan, School of Business and Administrative Sciences, University of Khartoum, Khartoum, 15–18 November 1987), 5, table 1.

105. Abdel Gadir, *el-Mara el-Amila*, 15, table 7.

106. Ahmed et al., "Population Problems." The authors claim that formal education "is strangled by problems of insecurity, male [out]-migration and environmental degradation" (23).

107. These exams are equivalent to the Scholastic Aptitude Tests (SATs) in the United States.

108. Abdel Gadir, *el-Mara el-Amila*, 25, table 17.

109. Ibid., 18, table 14.

110. El-Nagar, "Patterns of Women," 516–17, tables 4 and 5. She uses statistics issued by the Ministry of Education (1974) and the National Council for Higher Education.

111. Sanyal et al., *From College to Work*, 42–43, tables 10 and 11. For the more recent years, the authors are using figures from Sudan's National Council for Higher Education.

112. Hassan et al., "Woman Strategy," 12.

113. Some of these ideas have been gleaned from Badri, "Women in Management," 6, table 2.

114. Alawiya Osman M. Salih, "Women in Trade (The Case of the Sudan)" (paper presented at the Workshop on the Conceptualization and Means of Measuring Female Labour Force Participation, Khartoum, March 1985), 6.

115. Ibid., 7. Salih uses Sudan, Department of Statistics, *Household Income and Expenditure Survey, 1978–80* (Khartoum: Sudan Government, 1981), table 2.6.

116. The civil service job scale is divided into fifteen degrees, fifteen being the lowest, and one, the highest.

117. Badri, "Women in Management," 8, table 4.

118. Abdel Gadir, *el-Mara el-Amila*, 42, table 22A. Ellen Gruenbaum has challenged this table, indicating that there are a number of male nurses that do not appear in the figures and that the figures for women nurses are too low. Letter to author, 6 October 1992.

119. Abdel Gadir, *el-Mara el-Amila*, 42, tables 22 A and B.

120. Ibid., 38, table 19.

121. Ahmed et al., "Population Problems," 29–30.

122. Ibid., 31. When read carefully, it sounds as if women who sell food in the urban centers are responsible for the deterioration of the quality of life.

123. El-Nagar, "Patterns of Women," 468–69.

124. Badri, "Women in Management," 9. She is using a report on all regions of Sudan (my study was Khartoum only) by Munira Ahmad Abdel Azim et al., *Women in Public Administration and Management: Upward Mobility and Career Advancement* (Omdurman: School of Organizational Management, Ahfad University, 1984).

125. Badri, "Women in Management," 9, using Azim et al., *Women in Public Administration and Management*.

126. Among others, reported by Badri, "Women in Management."

127. Abdel Gadir, *el-Mara el-Amila*, 55.

128. El-Nagar, "Patterns of Women," 470.

129. Ahmed et al., "Population Problems," 32.

130. Dina Shiekh el-Din Osman, "The Legal Status of Muslim Women in the Sudan," *Journal of Eastern African Research and Development* 15 (1985): 125. Because this is a section on Sudanese perspectives, I have not included material from Carolyn Fluehr-Lobban's impressive, if not definitive, *Islamic Law and Society in the Sudan*, much of which is devoted to personal status laws (e.g., chapter 4 is "The Status of Women in Islamic Law"). See also Fluehr-Lobban's more recent "Islam-

ization in Sudan: A Critical Assessment," *The Middle East Journal* 44, no. 4 (1990): 610–23.

131. Osman, "Legal Status of Muslim Women," 126.

132. Ibid., 126.

133. Ibid., 126. Osman's italics.

134. Ahmed et al., "Population Problems," 34.

135. Ibid., 34–35. This is neither a quote nor a verbatim list, but a reconstruction.

136. Ibid., 38. Italics mine.

137. As mentioned above, Sudan never passed a permanent constitution, the transitional one of 1985 being repealed when Islamists came to power in 1989. Now the country is guided by "Constitutional Decrees," but no human or civil rights have been spelled out. See Abdullahi Ahmed An-Na'im, "The Elusive Islamic Constitution: The Sudanese Experience," *Orient* 26, no. 3 (1985): 329–40.

138. Although lacking in a theoretical or conceptual framework, and dealing only with "middle-class housewives," perhaps Ellen Ismail comes the closest to the heart of everyday life in Khartoum. See her *Social Environment and Daily Routine of Sudanese Women: A Case Study of Urban Middle Class Housewives* (Berlin: Dietrich Reimer, Kolner ethnologische Studien, Band 6, 1982).

PART THREE

Two Case Studies

5

The Wing of the Patriarch: The Sudanese Communist Party and the Women's Union

Introduction

This chapter is a critical interpretation of gender interests and relations associated with a Third World communist party, the Sudanese Communist Party (hereafter the SCP or the Party). More specifically it is a critical interpretation of one male-dominated organization and its sister traveler, the Sudanese Women's Union (hereafter the WU or the Union). I draw upon interviews with women members of both organizations, numerous conversations and interviews with other progressive Sudanese variously positioned along the leftist continuum, and a fairly extensive literature, which includes some of the sparse documentation issued by these organizations. This study derives from my interest in how the gender ideologies and practices of Marxist organizations worldwide manifest themselves organizationally and strategically. It also stems from my concerns as a Sudanist with gender ideology and relations that infuse Sudanese civil society and the state. My goal is to shed light upon how men within the SCP position women within culture and politics to serve their movement's ends.

On the Margins of the Story

I lived in Sudan during the 1960s and 1970s, still the heydays of the SCP and the WU, and have been back for extensive stays since. I have

This chapter is dedicated to Abdel Khaliq Mahjub, executed Secretary General of the Sudanese Communist Party, and to Fatma Ahmed Ibrahim, longtime leader of the Sudanese Women's Union.

witnessed the waxings and wanings of these organizations' influence on Sudanese politics and society. I have argued with cadres and rank-and-file alike about the comparative effectiveness of Leninist and Maoist strategies for change in an agrarian society like Sudan's. Sometimes a lengthy dialogue with a colleague about women's issues would be interrupted by his/her arrest or my departure from Sudan, and picked up again years later. I like to think that I am a small part of the story, even if only intermittently (often at a distance), but always on the margins of the struggles of progressive Sudanese women and men to bring about meaningful changes in society and in their own lives.

This chapter has been informed by my association with the Sudanese left, which has spanned some thirty-five years, and I have been greatly influenced by close communist and socialist friends, by scores of professional colleagues, and by a body of progressive political and academic literature and artistic production. In particular I want to acknowledge the late Abdel Khaliq Mahjub, Secretary-General of the SCP, with whom I had two lengthy conversations, some of his close associates, and various communist, socialist, and WU activists, with whom I had many exchanges and numerous formal and informal interviews.

On Theorizing Women and Progressive Social Movements in the Periphery—the Sudanese Communist Party and the National Islamic Front

This chapter and the next are case studies of the Sudanese Communist Party (SCP) and the National Islamic Front (NIF), two social movements/political parties seemingly poles apart on the Sudanese political spectrum and in their relationships with women. The SCP is commonly characterized as leftist, progressive, secular, and modernist; the NIF, as rightist, conservative, Islamist, and traditionalist. Both representative of nationalist and internationalist movements occurring throughout the world. In these chapters I challenge the frequent dichotomizing of the Sudanese left and right in such ascriptive terms by many analysts of social movements/political parties. I question, for example, just how "secular" the SCP has been and how strong its commitment to transforming the social position of women may be, and the extent to which the NIF is a "traditional religious" movement opposing changes in the position of women in Muslim society. Further, I dispute whether either movement/party could, based on its stated positions, produce a truly liberating transformation in the position of women in Sudan that would sufficiently empower women's lives and culture.

My selection of the SCP and NIF for major treatment in separate chapters stems from their successes, and failures, as visible oppositional (to the state) movements/parties that have forwarded gender-interested agendas. I did not choose them as exemplars of binary oppositions in some secular versus Islamist model. My investigations of them have given me the opportunity to demonstrate that the cultural positioning of women by men to serve the aims of their movement(s) is not confined to either end of the Sudanese political spectrum.

On Theorizing Women and Progressive Social Movements in the Periphery—Relating Women's Emancipation to Liberation Movements or Parties

The association of women's emancipation with liberation movements or parties raises questions in international feminist debates that are pertinent to this study of the SCP and the WU. Foremost among these questions is the issue of whether or not a generalized struggle against society-wide oppression dissolves more specific differences and their associated discriminations, exploitations, and suppressions. Some students of revolutionary struggles have maintained that actors with specific grievances based on class, ethnic identity, race, or gender have lost their specificity as they have become subordinate to the hegemonic aims and rubric of a wider revolutionary movement.

Molyneux disagrees. In analyzing the Nicaraguan struggle, she asserts: "the universalization of the *goals* of revolutionary subjects does not necessarily entail a loss of their specific *identities*."[1] Women in particular do not lose their gender identities, she argues. "Rather, representatives of women acquired new connotations, ones that *politicized* the social roles with which women are conventionally associated, but not dissolve them" (228). Circumstances and situations may exist, even if momentarily, in which revolutionary women can press their own gender-specific concerns and attempt to carve out social spaces for them.

But what identifies "women as women" remains problematic. For instance, what interests do women have in common? How might these have to be constituted and constructed? Molyneux contends that "there is no theoretically adequate and universally applicable causal explanation of women's subordination from which a general account of women's interests can be derived" (231). However that may be, we still have to find ways to differentiate among women's variegated interests, as well as a language with which to describe these interests. In this regard I think it useful to distinguish, as does Molyneux, between *women's interests* and *gender interests*. The former refer to those interests that seem at variance with men's, perhaps a problematic theoretical distinction but one that may oftentimes be programmatically useful. The latter are interests that develop by virtue of women's social positioning based on their gender attributes.

Molyneux distinguishes yet further between *strategic gender interests* and *practical gender interests*. The first are associated with feminist concerns: abolition of the gender division of labor, alleviation of burdens of child care, the attainment of political equality, measures against male violence and control over women, reproductive freedom, and the like. The second refers to domestic provision (such as the livelihood of families) and public welfare. This is a serviceable distinction because we can deduce the former from an analysis of women's subordination and infer the latter from concrete conditions in women's lives.[2]

In a related matter I, like many internationalist feminists who work within a Marxian framework, have not given up on the "promissory note," that implicit contract between women and socialist movements (which all conceive of women's liberation as integral to the revolution).[3] Yet like many students of Marxism, I am also critical of the fact that socialist theory in application has too often meant that, categorically, women have had little opportunity to contribute to the building of emancipatory practice, structure, or theory. Awareness of such socialist practices has led us to examine twentieth-century liberation movements, especially in the periphery, for evidence that they are seriously concerned with women's interests, to see what their experience, theory, and practices may be, and to find out which ones are addressing *women as women*.

We are asking whether women participating in liberation movements in the periphery are able to revolutionize their specific conditions of oppression: If so, to what extent and how? If not, would it be better, as some of us suggest, if women initiated the process themselves? Further, do women's indigenous structures (which are sometimes prefigurative political forms[4]) give us clues to effective gender strategies? In short, are women, whether identifying as progressive or not, making transformations in their own names? Or are they still being handed their revolution by "another revolution"?[5] What is the role of women in making the revolution?

How sweeping and profound can women-generated transformations be? Some scholars have presumed that women in the periphery, because they suffer manifold oppressions (e.g., race, gender, class, colonization), can change their society's entire structure of exploitation when they move to alter their negative social circumstances.[6] Such a presumption has serious implications for the revolutionary strategies of women in struggle, as well as for socialist movements in the periphery. It seems to challenge the more conventional structural relationships of women's organizations—especially in regard to their relative autonomy—to mixed-gender, but male-dominated, vanguard and "mass" national organizations.

Such a presumption also privileges women's interests, if not their strategic gender interests. Privileging women's interests is not an accepted maxim of most Marxist revolutionary movements: The goal of most twentieth-century vanguard parties has been to liberate societies from class-based oppression and imperialist domination, and then to protect what has been won. Consequently, while struggling to attain power, vanguard parties have mostly muted or marginalized women's strategic and practical gender interests; after seizing control of the state other priorities and tasks commonly prevail.

But at some point—sometimes during the struggle to power, sometimes afterwards—it becomes politically useful, even necessary, for the vanguard party to acknowledge the *help* of women, occasionally stating that the revolution is, or was, not possible without that help. In some instances, women may be asked to help achieve specific revolutionary ends in ways that manipulate them. Massell offers us an example, involving women in the highly traditional Muslim societies of Soviet Central Asia (1919–29). The Soviet goal, according to Massell, was to undermine the traditional social order to create a mass revolutionary ideology. This meant destroying traditional family structures and values as well as breaking down the kinship system. Since Communist Party cadres perceived Central Asian women as being segregated, exploited, degraded, and constrained, and imagined them as "structural weakpoints" in a traditional social order, it was thought that they could be mobilized for social change. Once they were mobilized, then the entire exploitative structure could be altered. This approach became a kind of "new orthodoxy" for Soviet-style revolutionary parties and associated movements and organizations, and endured well into the last decades of the twentieth century. Official postrevolutionary Soviet policy allowed women, through carefully orchestrated administrative assault and revolutionary legalism, to be used as a "surrogate proletariat."[7] I find this to be a clear case of the Communist Party positioning women to serve the revolution.

However, effective local resistance thwarted the policy, making it apparent that "a revolution in social relations and cultural patterns evidently could not be managed concurrently with large-scale political, organizational, and economic change."[8] Overlooked by the Soviets was the fact that although these were strategies carried out in the name of women, they were not strategies developed by women for themselves.

These questions about the centrality of women and women's interests and about who makes the revolution for women, although raised in the context of a study of the SCP and its policies towards women, obviously have wider application. My concern is to identify what might be an effective strategy for women's emancipation and gender egalitarianism not only within the remaining Marxist-Leninist parties in the Third World, but within other progressive movements, there and elsewhere.

Recently, international feminists have accorded some progressive Third World movements, and their women leaders and cadres, a great deal of credit because they are reputed to have played major roles in liber-ation struggles. In some rare cases, women have even had their goals incorporated into revolutions during the course of the struggles, not simply as an afterthought.[9] Given the many failures of the Western left to come to terms with women's interests, numerous Marxist feminists have turned for inspiration, perhaps a bit romantically, to the experiences of these Third World movements, parties, and women.

I would be among the first to acknowledge that we Western feminists can learn a great deal from them.[10] Nonetheless, I suggest that we set aside any myth-making and use our critical faculties. We should, I urge, heed the admonishments of *Promissory Notes* editors Sonia Kruks, Rayna Rapp, and Marilyn Young about socialist states and social movements, whether in Asia, Africa, Europe, or Latin America, still espousing, in min-imally altered forms, nineteenth-century scientific socialism:

> The model has been applied whether a given country's social relations were taken to be feudal, tribal, or protocapitalist, whether the country had been fully colonized or not, whether the state in question had been unified or had remained fragmented. Nor did differences in the form of kinship and marriage impede application of the nineteenth-century view that located women's subordination in private property relations, whether family forms were monogamous or polygamous, involved dowry or brideprice.[11]

As men and women engaged in them have attested, these liberation struggles, with few exceptions, have failed to end most patriarchal forms of gender domination, to reintegrate the public and private domains, to emancipate the self through sexuality, and to mobilize the networks of everyday life. It is distressing to acknowledge that, except for their *public* roles in the wage-labor pool, in women's organizations (often serving as fronts), in agrarian cooperatives, or, in some cases, in the military, most Third World women have far less autonomy than men.

The inadequate efforts of progressives to transform gender ideology in public spheres are unsurpassed in the private domain. Domestic labor re-mains unchanged: women still have little autonomy in this major material area of their lives. In the personal, subjective realms of their everyday lives, the same holds true.[12]

Directing their comparative perspectives on socialist movements and landscapes, some international feminists have noted:

> What is striking, across this vast geographic, social, and historical landscape [Cuba, Nicaragua, Mozambique, Yemen, Vietnam, West Bengal, and post-Maoist China], is the extent to which the analysis used and the

policies developed are similar. Thus in each place, the very same problems remain unresolved and the very same questions are left unaddressed.[13]

Sudanese Muslim Arab culture bears a great deal of resemblance to the above societies and offers some of the same challenges to Marxist strategists. But Sudan's problems, as I have argued in chapter 2 and elsewhere,[14] are exacerbated by the politicization of gender, of Islam, and of their relationship to each other.

I turn now to the SCP, which for years has tried to bring about social and socialist change in a peripheral country dominated by conservative Arab and Muslim identities, patriarchies, and politics. In many ways its experiences, history, and politics in the areas of women's issues typify leftist parties of its kind throughout the Third World. However, in other ways these variables are particularly Sudanese.

The Sudanese Communist Party and the Women's Union

As Sudan's main leftist party, the SCP seems no more threatening than any other party in the country, or than most leftist parties anywhere. Yet its very existence has been challenged, it has been driven underground and into exile, and it has been beheaded. The Party has fought for social revolution via paths mostly eschewing armed struggle, the failed 1971 coup d'état being one of the exceptions. The SCP's experience and history differ from those leftist movements that took up arms and fought to achieve either national independence or socialist revolution. Also, since full-scale revolutionary process in the Marxist sense has not occurred in Sudan—in fact has seen a severe setback—now may be the time to assess the meaning and ramifications of any such process for women.

For some years I have been investigating just how revolutionary the SCP has been, or could be, in bringing about any serious transformation of gender alignments in Sudan.[15] My work has led me to propose that the patriarchal ideology and structure of the Marxist-Leninist SCP and the gender strategies it has followed have greatly diminished its effectiveness as an agency of any genuine socialist transformation that takes women seriously.

From my observations of, and discussions with, Party members, it is apparent that the cadres have not adequately understood "the subjectivity of oppression, of the connections between personal relations and public political organization, or of the emotional components of consciousness."[16] Nor have they understood issues of sexuality, let alone directly addressed them. These deficiencies are not unique to SCP members, or to the Sudanese left. As is well known, open discourse across gender lines about sexuality remains taboo virtually everywhere, not just within Islamic and other Third World societies.[17]

I conclude that, even if the SCP had succeeded in its various attempts to initiate social change, to advance the secularization of social and cultural behavior, values, and institutions, and to gain power, it probably could not have done more than just politicize the conventional roles of Sudanese women. While it would be wrong to say the Party did not consider the role of women in building the revolution or did not imagine the place of women in a liberated Sudan, it did not advocate or engage in, even within its own organization, transformative practices aimed at dissolving the conventional gender roles. The leadership anticipated such a strategy would encounter political difficulties; it would be perceived as anti-Islamic. So the Party made the choice—not an unusual one for the times—to direct its energies and resources to other, more significant tasks. In so doing, it enhanced the likelihood of failure in the socially necessary tasks of, among others, reconstituting private and public social spaces, modifying gendered behaviors in these renewed spaces, and emancipating women. SCP support for the establishment of the WU could not overcome such a strategy, considering its limited allocation of energies and resources. Neither the Party nor the WU could decisively reconstruct the contemporary gender division of labor; even less could they radically alter the oppression in women's personal lives.

So, what has the SCP attempted, what has it achieved, where has it been silent, and where has it failed? What could it have done differently?

A Significant Party in an Unlikely Place?[18]

That a strong communist party emerged in Sudan is surprising. That it emerged in northern Sudan—a predominantly rural region whose mostly localized tribes, villages, and ethnic groups hold intransigent allegiances to "holy families"—is even more surprising. Although segments of its large peasant and nomadic populations had played militant roles in internecine struggles and against the Turco-Egyptian and British colonial regimes, they were conservative and religious in outlook and culture and, with few exceptions, hardly class-conscious. But, if the Party could form anywhere, the slightly urbanized areas of the North, where a small working class and intelligentsia existed, provided the likeliest places where it could happen. Furthermore, if places existed in Sudan where progressive people could imagine a future in which women's lives, along with those of Sudanese workers, would be better through education, emancipatory reforms, and social structural changes, then the towns of the North had to be those places.

Although Sudan in the late 1940s and early 1950s, when the SCP emerged, was still seeking to shake itself free of imperialism, the economic and social geographies of the day provided only highly localized economic and social conditions for the founding of a communist party. Most of the large rural population of nonliterate cultivators and pastoralists were barely implicated in Sudan's as yet weakly developed market and wage-labor economy; workers on the large-scale Gezira cotton-growing scheme were the chief exceptions. The minuscule urban working class clustered in the few northeastern and central towns and along the modern but skeletal transportation and communications networks. Also clustered in places such as these was Sudan's small intelligentsia, including its British- and Egyptian-trained officer corps, who struggled with questions of the country's future as they were subjected to surveillance and manipulation by the colonial state apparatus.

Since well-established orthodox and popular Islamic institutions, practices, and traditions permeated the cultural, social, and political landscapes of the north, any party committed to a secular modernist agenda, let alone a socialist one, would have to struggle mightily to create political and social space for itself, even in the towns. So even though the emerging SCP succeeded in positioning itself as anti-imperialist and nationalist in the politics of an emerging independence movement, and as radical in championing trade unionism and workers rights, it still had to contend with widespread hostility from within the Muslim community and with direct challenges to its ideological legitimacy, its secularism, and its perceived atheism. In addition, the Party had to position itself in relation to antagonisms existing among various popular Islamic turuq, to theological cleavages between them and the ulama (orthodox clergy) and/or qadis (Islamic judges), and to strong patron-client relations and other crosscutting ties that shaped familial and communal loyalties and politics. Building such a class-based party then, meant having to face opposition from much of society at large and withstanding an implacable animosity from zealous sectarian parties on moral, philosophical, and political grounds.

Yet the post-World War II years were a time of growing unrest and rising national consciousness. More and more, changes in economic, social, and political conditions involved the development of a large public sector, active trade-union organizing within it, the expansion of public education, and growing multifaceted radicalism in the modern sectors of society. In such a swirling and uncertain political terrain the various national movements, the sectarian and nonsectarian political parties, the movements for cultural reassertions, and the communists variously wound up both competing with one another and at times having to cooperate in the overall anti-imperial effort.

Because the Party was particularly effective in its anti-imperialist stance, making its rhetoric and strategy concrete through demonstrations and strikes, its influence and membership grew, especially within the trade union movement, among the Gezira tenants, and among students and professionals. In response, the authorities were ever alert in the towns and other presumed places of communist activity and engaged in a virulent propaganda campaign, charging the Party with a foreign subversive ideology and links to the Soviet Union and Egyptian communists. The colonial regime's adamant, open hostility to the SCP, however, lent additional credence to the Party's agenda and its growing reputation for militancy and effective action. The state suppressed the Party and its activities wherever and whenever it could.

It is generally agreed that one could not easily have predicted in the mid-1940s that a not-yet-begotten SCP was going to become among the largest, strongest, best organized, and most promising of all communist parties in the Middle East and Africa. However, by 1971, at the very moment of its beheading and precipitous decline, the Party was reputed to hold such status.[19]

How could this have happened? If we follow Marx, the extant objective conditions were not sufficient for the successful establishment of a communist party. Yet some favorable social conditions must have existed to nurture the incipient Party through its vulnerable early stages and to foster its rise to prominence, if not to social revolution.

Gresh identifies as well as anyone the main social and political factors accounting for the SCP's rise. He posits that it developed at the same time as other Sudanese nationalist parties and shared some of their legitimacy. The sectarianism of the two major religious parties repelled many of the intelligentsia and undermined expected support from the scant Sudanese bourgeoisie. Significant elements of the urban elite recognized the SCP's high quality of leadership (especially Abdel Khaliq Mahjub's) and gave it substantial political, if not much financial, support. Gresh attributes a high political value to the close, carefully cultivated relationship between the SCP and the Sudanese labor movement.

Gresh maintains that the proximity of the Egyptian Communist Party meant that its experiences and support could be drawn upon. But he implies that its purported influence should not be overemphasized: the Egyptian Communist Party suffered identity, leadership, and membership crises domestically in consequence of its substantial foreign and minority leadership and membership, whereas the SCP could boast of indigenous, nonminority cadres and leaders. This, of course, conveyed "the party's genuinely national character [one that] could not be seriously challenged."[20] Finally, the SCP's late founding came at an historical moment when communism had a great deal of prestige among Arabs, colonized peoples in general, and antifascists.

Although the founding of the SCP is conventionally put at 1946, occasional communist and/or communist-influenced activities date from earlier in the century. Egyptian sources aroused these earlier activities and inspired the later,[21] but the British too, however unintentionally, introduced various socialist, Marxist, and even Leninist influences in the decades before independence. Some came directly in the persons of teachers, soldiers, clerks, and the like from all over the British Empire; others were introduced indirectly via literature, including leftist book-club publications, newspapers, and magazines.

The Sudanese themselves formed literary discussion circles as early as the 1920s and 1930s in places like Omdurman, Khartoum, and various provincial towns. Only a few of these groups were socialist and egalitarian in perspective, but even these, along with most of the others, were elitist in their presumption that well-educated graduates should take the lead in shaping the Sudanese future. The Graduates Congress, graduates' clubs, workers' clubs and like institutions served as incubators of progressive ideas coming from Britain, Egypt, and elsewhere. Communist ideas also diffused through the state educational system. The secondary schools, Gordon Memorial College (which became the University of Khartoum in 1956), and the Khartoum branch of Cairo University all functioned as loci wherein a growing body of students, and teachers, attempted to discuss the issues of the day and organize to take subversive action.[22]

It was after World War II that communism in Sudan emerged in any unified way. The first organization that we could term "communist" was the Sudanese Movement for National Liberation (hereafter, SMNL), formed in 1946 amidst a vortex of political activity and discussion. During the next decade or so, the SCP organized into its "modern structures," with base units (called "combat units"), regional offices, a central committee elected at the Party Congress, and a political bureau. Such a structural form—not dissimilar to the Soviet model, but with significant small differences[23]—allowed the SCP to function above and below ground as circumstances dictated.

The activities and organizations that breathed life into the fledgling communist movement were overwhelmingly male-dominated. Labor organizing activities commenced in the early years of the Condominium, with sporadic strikes breaking out in the expected places: among workers employed by Sudan Railways, Port Sudan harbor, government departments, and the cotton-ginning factories. In the 1920s militant nationalists sought to organize workers in the political struggle against the British but were beaten down. The minimal written evidence suggests that women were, at best, marginal to these activities.

Saad ed-Din Fawzi tells us that the Sudanese trade union movement, a locus of communist strength, really didn't begin until 1946 with the Workers' Affairs Association, the first voice of the railway workers. That organization in 1950 merged into the Sudan Workers' Trade Union Federation. Centered in Atbara to the north of Khartoum, the railway workers constituted some 90 percent of the town's workforce and came to form, with their dependents, a considerable bastion of organized political strength.[24] These workers were in a strong position because Sudan Railways was the transportation lifeline of the modern sector of the economy: Sudan's chief hard currency earner, cotton, moved almost exclusively over its rails to Port Sudan and the world market. The militant union was highly successful in organization and action, forcing many concessions from the government. The union became core and catalyst of the working-class-based SCP. The importance of this relationship was never more apparent than when, in the 1964 elections to the governing council of the Sudan Workers' Trade Union Federation (SWTUF), communists won 45 of the 60 contested seats.[25] The railway workers specifically, and the trade unions in general, have remained a core constituency of the SCP. When the trade unions are allowed to express themselves relatively freely, those enduring ties manifest themselves.

But for women, the railway union story—in fact the trade union story—was different. While it is true that family members benefited from the gains made by the railway workers, and that some were even drawn into the Party and/or its auxiliary organizations, women were virtually unrepresented in the railway workers' union (most directly because Sudan Railways employed men) or any other trade union. But even in the 1960s and 1970s this situation did not change much. It is true that an attempt was made before independence to organize nurses along trade union lines, but the authorities frustrated it. Later on, more working-class Sudanese women found limited low-wage employment in the growing number of factories and workshops, but few of them were ever organized.

A second bastion of communist activism, organization, and support lay in some of the rural tenants' associations. The largest and most powerful of these, the Gezira Tenants' Union (GTU), was the only one substantial enough to play a political role beyond defending tenants' interests in negotiations with agricultural scheme management. Its roots also went back to 1946, to a dispute over the allocation of cotton profits by management and to the subsequently successful outcome of organized strike actions, which revealed to tenants what could be achieved through collective pressure on Scheme management. Outside political support came from the Graduates Congress and newly formed nationalist movements, including the SMNL. In the years that followed, GTU members steadily perceived their problems in the context of issues facing Sudanese nationalism. The radical leadership of the GTU attempted to open the organization up to the nontenant rural labor force, but the Condominium authorities would not tolerate it.

The SMNL (and later the SCP) was never committed to organizing peasants outside the modern sector, seeming to feel them lost to sectarian tradition and leadership. In fact, even within the modern sector, although influential for some time in the GTU, the SCP never felt as confident of the support of the Gezira tenants as it did of the support of the railway workers. Even the close ties between the GTU and the SWTUF (which, as indicated earlier, had a strong communist presence)[26] did not stem the waning SCP influence in the GTU, especially after 1965. The SCP's peasant base continued to decline.

Through it all, women were not prominent in the GTU or any other tenants' syndicates. Despite their numbers and long hours spent in the fields, Gezira village women, from tenant and nontenant households alike, were perceived essentially by a culturally conservative and religious community as mothers and housewives. Few likely ever participated in the syndicates themselves; most would only offer support as family members for spouses and male relatives involved in political activities, or would serve in some mutual aid or social welfare role. Of course, women might benefit along with other Gezira residents whenever concessions were gained, e.g., expanding educational opportunities or public health services. The SCP did not target women or women's issues in the Gezira for organizing roles beyond those involved with women's education and the like. The Party was unwilling to take what it saw as a risk: by organizing women it might lose what it had gained among a culturally and socially conservative peasantry whose support it considered tenuous.

After 1956 the SCP began building a third core constituency—among the educated elite; that is, among the growing numbers of students, administrators, teachers, and other professionals. During the late 1940s and early 1950s each of these groups agitated over wages and working conditions, and for union with Egypt or independence. They debated, organized, made demands, and took actions. Moreover, they interacted and sometimes collaborated with one another. Wherever sizable concentrations of these groups could be found, mostly in urban locations within the Nile valley, the SCP seems to have committed sizable organizational resources to the tasks of building organizations, of shaping issues, policies, and strategies, and of taking action.

The SCP was very successful, as attested by the resilience of its political strength among these groups throughout the late 1950s, 1960s, 1970s, and 1980s—despite various strategic and tactical mistakes, lengthy periods of state oppression; death, jail, and/or exile for many of its leaders, defections from its ranks, and severe challenges especially from the radical right in the form of the Ikhwan and NIF.

But these areas of intellectual (and political) and professional life were, as usual, male-dominated. The Graduates Congress, for example, formed in 1938 to give greater voice to the Sudanese intelligentsia, had no women members[27] despite the fact that starting in the late 1940s small numbers of women gained access to modern education, with some becoming graduates.

The growth of a graduates' constituency as an increasingly important player in the drive towards independence resulted in the early 1950s in a small set of nongeographically based seats in the assembly, and later in parliament, being reserved for the educated professional class. Through the 1950s no women members were ever elected.[28] But by 1965 social attitudes in general had changed. Many more women had passed through secondary school, some had become teachers, administrators, doctors, and other professionals, and they finally had the vote. When the SCP won eleven of the fifteen Graduate constituencies in that year's national elections, Fatma Ahmed Ibrahim became the first woman member of parliament, one of the very few, ever.

After 1946, the numbers of students and professionals grew apace. They formed organizations to represent their own, and what they saw as national, interests. The ever-expanding student movement was particularly important since over the years its politicized members (high school-educated young Sudanese) went on to university, technical schools, or directly into the governmental employment sector. Upon entering the professions and the public sector labor force, they formed professional organizations that became highly influential in the capital and in national politics. Among these politicized graduates were secularized activists who went on to become SCP leaders, cadres, or followers. Some students who studied in Egypt came back politicized as well.

In the early years the numbers of women students and professionals were few, the latter mostly teachers and trained nurses. As women's education expanded in the decades following World War II, the numbers of women doctors, lawyers, and state bureaucrats became substantial. It was difficult for middle-class women professionals to move into positions of influence and leadership in professional organizations, even if and when the organizations were communist-led. But as early as the late 1940s and early 1950s some of these women were instrumental in the formation of women's professional organizations (e.g., nurses and teachers associations), political class- or mass-based organizations (e.g., the WU), and various women's associations (e.g., charitable and religious groups).

Finally we come to the Sudanese military, the most powerful force in Sudanese politics for much of the postindependence period. The extent to which the SCP had influence within the military is a question. We know that some sort of "left" was present in the Free Officers' movement of the early 1950s. SCP opposition to the Ibrahim Abboud military regime (1958–64) established a link to the Free Officers that contributed significantly to the coming to power of the Nimieri regime in 1969, as well as to the challenge to Nimieri in 1971.[29] As Woodward argues:

> It would have been surprising if the Nasser years [in Egypt] had *not* spawned a Free Officers' movement in Sudan, as elsewhere in the Arab world ... After a minor group had been nipped in the bud in 1957, a more substantial movement developed in the 1960s, with a variety of radical themes reflecting ideologically derived criticisms of the Abboud regime and the civilians who replaced it ... A number of the Free Officers had links with the SCP.[30]

There have been powerful communist officers in the military, including Hashim el-Ata, Babiker el-Nur, and Farouk Hamdallah, but this still does not tell us the extent of SCP influence there. The military is an area where, once again, women have exerted little or no influence.[31]

The Relationship of the Sudanese Communist Party and the Women's Union

The links between the SCP, the trade unions (the backbone of the SCP), and the WU are perhaps personified by Fatma Ahmed Ibrahim and el-Shafi Ahmed el-Shaykh. The former, for some decades one of Sudan's most progressive voices, is a communist and the longtime head of the WU. The latter was a member of the SCP central committee and a renowned Sudanese trade union leader who became a significant force in the international trade union movement, serving as a high-ranking officer in the World Federation of Trade Unions. From 1966 until el-Shaykh's execution in 1971 following the abortive coup against Nimieri, the two were married to each other.

The partnership of the SCP and WU was more long-standing. In the preceding sections I discussed the size, power, and importance of the SCP, the primary progressive organization in Sudan. The Party's very dominance, in combination with its patriarchal structure and ideology, make it a powerful case study for examining the relationship of a mixed-gender mass party to a women's front organization. At one time the WU itself was very large and dominant (among women's organizations). The 15,000-member WU was one of the largest women's organizations on the continent.[32]

For some decades the hope for a progressive society in Sudan seemed to rest with the SCP and its strong affiliates: the women's organization and the highly organized labor unions (especially the railway workers).[33] But the potential for revolutionary transformation may have been lost.

In the 1950s and 1960s the SCP exhibited effective strategies for instigating mass mobilization, demonstrated by, among other things, its success in organizing women. Yet the conditions the Party addressed on behalf of women are today worse than ever, and the strategies for addressing them remain basically unaltered. As discussed in chapter 4, despite greater numbers of women in the official workforce, work conditions are worse than before independence. Although we cannot entirely attribute these conditions to failures of the SCP, we can be critical of some of its stated policies and strategies. The gender division of labor, in both the wage-earning (formal and informal) and domestic spheres, is more pronounced today than in the past. One cause is the tight control of women's participation in the labor force, including using women as a labor reserve, one of the more sophisticated mechanisms and institutions of oppression that have grown out of twentieth-century colonialism and capitalism.

Why were the progressive organizations, beyond encouraging more women to enter the increasingly capital-intensive public sector and working on reforms within that context, reluctant or unable to address such issues as the growing rigidification of the gender division of labor? Why, by the time of the 1985 coup d'état that overthrew the Nimieri military dictatorship and reinstalled a "democratic" multiparty system that again legalized the SCP and WU, were there only vestiges of the once-powerful Union?[34]

It is important to acknowledge that the SCP was the first political party in Sudan to open its membership to women and to establish women's emancipation as one of its goals. The same year the SCP officially emerged, 1946, Rabitat el-Nisa el-Sudaniyyat (League of Sudanese Women [the League]) was organized by women Party members, among them Dr. Khalda Zahir, the first president (and Sudan's first woman doctor), and Fatma Talib, the organization's first secretary. Founded in Omdurman by mainly urban, educated, middle-class women, the League aimed generally at improving the quality of life of Sudanese women. "Improvement" meant establishing a night school—with associated nursery—to teach literacy, sewing, home economics, health issues, and the like. The nursery later became a primary school, underscoring the early emphasis on education as a strategy for women's emancipation.

During the nationalist period of the late 1940s and early 1950s—the last decade of the colonial regime—a number of women's organizations and unions rose and fell. Each of them representing a particular class interest and political sect, their leadership struggles and factional disputes followed the national political pattern. Some of the leaders and members of the League left the organization and joined Jamiyat Taruiyat el-Mara (Society for the Prosperity of Women), founded in Omdurman in 1947, representing the class interests of some of the feudal land-owning aristocrats (the Mahdists).[35]

Open only to educated women, and literacy among women probably being below five percent at that time, the League remained small. El-Sanousi and el-Amin refer to women's activism in such organizations as "elite women's political engagement."[36] El-Bakri and Khier amplify:

> The basis of these [elite] organizations lay largely in the urban middle classes, which meant a general lack of understanding of the real needs of rural women or even, of poor urban women, let alone women in remote parts of the country such as the south. They were relatively isolated also from other political groups, such as trade unions, which represented different interests from those of traditional political associations, and which did have specific tactics for change. By the 1950s and with the intensification of the nationalist movement a need was once again felt for a new organization for women which would raise their standard and promote their participation.[37]

In 1952, in response to the SCP's call for broader recruitment, including among women, a handful of women, most of them communists and some who had helped form the League, founded Itihad el-Nisai (the Women's Union [WU]), which was, again, a group of educated women, mainly teachers, government officials, students, nurses, and the like. And again, literacy was a condition of membership. However, once it became clear that such a requisite for membership would greatly inhibit mass recruitment, the condition was dropped.[38]

The WU, which began with five hundred middle-class women, expanded into a large mass organization with branches throughout the country. It campaigned for equal pay for equal work, longer maternity leave, and tried to resolve other problems faced by urban women workers. By 1955 the WU was publishing *Sawt el-Mara* (The Woman's Voice), one of the most progressive publications in Sudan's history. It was a relatively free forum for debating such issues as female circumcision and ethnic facial scarification. Fatma Ahmed Ibrahim, one of the founders of the journal, estimated the circulation by the late 1950s at 17,000, a healthy figure for any publication anywhere.[39] Ibrahim has always been a regular contributor.[40] Although a communist with close ties to the SCP and its leadership, she also sees herself as an independent thinker and as having struggled for what little autonomy the WU had.[41]

Such a visible international figure is Ibrahim—recently, for example, receiving a United Nations Human Rights Award—one is tempted to count only her voice when tracing the history of the WU. Many other activists have indeed made major contributions to the existence and ideology of the WU, but because Ibrahim has headed the WU intermittently for nearly four decades, I often cite her for historical perspective alone. Here I compare Ibrahim's 1952 and 1954 versions of WU blueprints. She remarked:

> [W]e do not consider men our enemies. *We do not consider Islam our opponent.* We refuse to accept the Western model of liberation as our blueprint, nor do we recommend copying men's behavior as a means of reaching emancipation and equality. We expressed [in the journal] our respect for the positive traditions of our culture. We demanded political, economic, and social rights for women, equal opportunities for employment, and an equal role for women within the family. We conveyed our belief that *women's rights must be seen within the context of the welfare of the family* and the community and must be sought on the basis of our sociocultural roots. We held that *feminism is indigenous to our culture,* and full equality can be reached on the basis of our own *religious and cultural precepts.* We knew we must reassure our people that *we did not mean to change the basic tenets of our traditions.*[42]

The tone is very different two years later:

> We emphasized that it was necessary to change the traditional role of men and women in the family if we were to have full participation for women in the work force. We demanded, among others, accessible and dependable childcare facilities, the right to divorce, increase in the minimum age of marriage, and limitation of polygyny. *But our main concern was to achieve political participation in order to give women the power of their votes* (198; italics mine).

By 1954, according to Ibrahim, WU members began to reject confining themselves to reformist activities such as charity work and literacy classes, and began to work for "substantial changes in the condition of women," i.e., "to change the political infrastructure" (198). However, in my mind this is a reconstruction of the past based on wishful hindsight. As late as 1988 Ibrahim was highlighting literacy classes and sewing cooperatives as the activities of the WU, with political education presented in the margins.[43]

Although I have implied that the WU is a front organization for the SCP, the relationship is far more complicated and dynamic. How independent we might see the WU depends on the source of our information. Not all of its members, or leaders, were communists or members of the SCP, and there was much struggle between communists and noncommunists over control of the WU and over its relationship to the Party. The state always managed to exert more control over the WU than over the

SCP and more easily has infiltrated the WU with state supporters, trying to influence or force the WU away from the SCP. The closeness of the SCP and WU tie changed historically, oftentimes depending on who was elected Union president. In general, however, WU leaders, even if closely tied to the SCP, tried, for a number of reasons, among them group survival, to discount notions that the WU was a SCP "front." Fatma Ahmed Ibrahim, claiming no differences between the SCP and the WU on women's issues, told me, "The Communist Party gives us its full support in every detail of women's rights. This is why people think we are a part of them, and we are not."[44]

Membership numbers were so impressive, and during public demonstrations the cadres so robust, no one seemed to realize how vulnerable to state repression the WU was or how easily the demise of the organization could occur. That vulnerability exemplifies the problems of any women's organization surviving for very long in an androcentric society. Apart from these general problems, the WU experienced difficulties particular to its relationship with the SCP, most importantly a gender ideology that did not spell out women's interests beyond calling for women's active workforce participation and "equal" this and "equal" that. Particularly troubling was the SCP's position on "traditional" culture (dealt with at some length in the concluding chapter).

The structure of the SCP and the connections between the SCP and WU (a consequence of the Party's gender ideology) were problems. Even though the SCP, unlike many Middle Eastern communist parties, had a truly national character in its leadership, the Party and its auxiliary organizations followed the structural pattern of most Marxist-Leninist communist parties. What that meant was that the Party was not considered an autonomous unit, but rather a branch of the main (Soviet) party. Its structure reflected that relationship. As I mentioned above, the Party was organized into base units, local and regional offices, a central committee, and a Political Bureau. The WU was organized on the same general hierarchical principles: a central committee, local and regional cells, and it also had little autonomy. Initially even the leadership of the WU was chosen (either formally or informally) by the SCP central committee.

Although WU recruitment appeared to be effective in terms of numbers, the nature of the recruitment pool remained problematic. At first the Union relied on the SCP for most of its members, a large proportion of whom were the spouses, relatives, and friends of male SCP members, a weak base for any organization. Such heavy reliance on the SCP for recruitment meant that few nonorthodox socialist ideas about gender arrangements filtered in. Women remained tied to the class of their male associates, and their loyalty was as much to the Party as to the Union. The Union gained strength when on its own it began to recruit from the population at large, forming regional branches among fresh recruits. Membership, however, still reflected mainly low-level and some middle-level professional women (primarily elementary and intermediate school teachers) who had some ties to the mainly urban male membership.[45] Fatma Ahmed Ibrahim explained to me the SCP and WU relationship:

> Some members of the Party do not understand that to mix Party work with the Union is very dangerous. We have had many problems. We have even fought against our colleagues ... [We are keen] to keep the women's organization independent ... From the beginning it was very clear from the communist girls that the Union should be independent and not affiliated with the Party. [The women of the Union] were keen to turn it into a mass organization ... If it is affiliated with the Communist Party, it will not be [one]. That is why the SCP wrote in its Constitution that these organizations—women's, youth, students—should all be independent.

The Party's contributions and achievements, however, should not be discounted. Certainly no supporter of the SCP, Warburg, who attempted to minimize the Party's potential at every turn, paid this tribute:

> while communism never succeeded in becoming a major force in the Sudan, its impact on Sudanese politics was nonetheless considerable, especially during periods of crisis. This was due to three main reasons: Firstly, the penetration of the SCP into the most important sectors of Sudanese society: the cotton growers, the railway workers and the intelligentsia, enabled the party to become an effective pressure group despite its relatively small numbers. Secondly, the SCP provided the only consistent alternative to the sectarian and factional divisions which harassed Sudanese politics ever since independence ... Lastly, the leadership of the SCP, since 'Abd al-Khaliq Mahjub became secretary-general, was probably the most capable leadership of any communist party in the region. Its flexible attitude towards religion, nationalism, Arab unity, etc. enabled the party to retain its freedom of action ... and was the only political force which advocated regional autonomy for the South ever since independence.[46]

Warburg has written more extensively on the SCP than any non-Sudanese, but he ignores the SCP's contribution to the women's movement. The fact is, the SCP was the first party to open its doors to women, to "teach" them the Marxist-Leninist concept of organization, and to politicize them in the male-dominated public domain. Besides encouraging women to enter the public arena, the Party offered educated women an outlet for some of their enlightened views and opened its membership to a broad cross-section of the female population, creating a more socially heterogeneous environment for educated and class-bound women who were often isolated from the rest of the female population. But none of this related to women's private lives, to their increasingly undervalued domestic labor, to their lack of control over their reproductive resources, to their repression under the type of Islam that had developed under colonialism and capitalism, to domestic violence, or to such practices as female circumcision.

The involvement of women in *public* political activities was an integral part of the SCP program. There was, of course, a long socialist tradition for this. But the "woman question" was secondary in the overall ideological development of the Party, and as an appended form, the main function of the WU, as seen by the SCP, was to recruit members for the Party in order to have a second line to call upon in crises (the "women-as-Greek-chorus" syndrome).[47] In other areas of the world, this same process can be seen in the way in which women are recruited into the military or paramilitary. Women were assigned to be the terrorists and saboteurs of the Algerian revolution of the 1960s, but only seemingly as *substitutes* for the dead, imprisoned, exiled, or circumscribed male revolutionaries.[48]

Among women members of the SCP and WU there was very little consciousness-raising about their oppression as women or their special problems as workers. The individual trade unions grappled with these issues much more effectively. In 1952, for example, the Union of Women Teachers sent a letter to the (then British) Director of Education, requesting "equality of men and women teachers as regards scales, increments, stipends, and pensions."[49] More along the lines of *gender interests* in a conservative context, they requested that during transfers, "in keeping with Sudanese customs and traditions each woman teacher be provided with a chaperon from her family, and that chaperons be authorized to travel in the same class as their protegees." Further, they requested, "Since married women teachers have heavy commitments in carrying out their official duties and also acting as wives and housekeepers ... a distinction be made between them and their unmarried colleagues, namely that they be not transferred to locations far from where their husbands live." Another request, also seeming somewhat conservative while serving *women's interests*, was that "a woman teacher in a boarding school who performs additional duties should be paid an allowance for such duties." Although these "women's duties" were not spelled out and we can assume that male teachers in boarding schools also performed additional duties, it is nonetheless clear that the letter was referring to the uncompensated nurturing and domestic-labor skills of women. Basically, the teachers' union was requesting "wages for housework."

The issues WU members were encouraged to confront were usually not *strategic gender* (i.e., *feminist)* interests. When the WU did deal with what were viewed as women's "problems," the activities carried out often reinforced traditional roles instead of *building* onto extant formations within women's culture and communities that could be mobilized. The SCP and WU leaderships held conventional ideas about structures (for the most part limited to unions, student groups and other formalized structures) that could be mobilized.

When women of the Party or Union addressed personal, private issues such as the division of labor within the domestic unit or violence in the household, they told me for years that they were either ignored or were accused of "bourgeois feminism" or "bourgeois individualism." There were always more "important" issues at hand, such as the goal of subverting or overthrowing the current regime, and women were sung the familiar refrain: wait until *after* the revolution. Fatma Ahmed Ibrahim, from exile in England, concurred:

> My work with women used to be the most energizing part of my day at home [in Sudan], but here [in England], even though I am engaged in the work of the [International Democratic] Federation [of Women], it is less fulfilling, because I feel my ideas and opinions are different from most of the others [from other countries]. *They want to concentrate on rape and violence and sexual choice.* I am concerned with these issues, but *I am much more aware of the problems of simple survival. What priority can sexual choice have to a woman whose child is dying of hunger in her arms?* [50]

After the aborted leftist coup in 1971, all political parties were banned except the government organ, the Sudan Socialist Union (SSU). The SCP and WU went underground. Like many communist parties elsewhere, Sudan's had always thrived underground and in crises. This was not to prove true of the WU. It was very awkward for women from "respectable" families (Muslim or Christian) to go to clandestine meetings— usually held late at night and in dubious neighborhoods. Muslim Sudanese women cannot easily go underground, and the Party, because of its androcentric ideology, had not paved the way for women of the SCP and WU to be impervious to moral sanctions. But even when women members chose to brave these social problems, they were told by the male membership that their unusual presence in such locations aroused suspicion. For the most part, after the failed coup, women were asked to stay away from crucial strategy and survival meetings. They were, nonetheless, called upon for individual acts of nurturing (e.g., medical assistance to male members underground).

The ban on and subsequent underground movement of political groups after 1971 exposed profound problems in the WU, most of which were a result of the relationship between the SCP and WU. I attribute the near demise of the once-powerful WU to its lack of politicization about socialism, splits among older, socially conservative women and younger, socially progressive women, general social and political repression, and damage to its morale and structure caused by a number of its second-rung leaders and many members leaving to join the women's wing of the SSU, taking with them organizational know-how as well as internal information about the SCP and the WU. Many of these women, because of their lack of training about ideology, their few chances for leadership, and the short shrift women's interests were always given, had little commitment to the SCP, and consequently, to the WU.

The report of the September-November 1971 session of the SCP central committee, commenting on these defections, reflected fairly typical male-biased and unself-critical attitudes by "blaming the victim," i.e., the WU, for its weaknesses:

> The [Women's Union] has been exposed to open subversion and corruption. And despite the facilities rendered by the state, yet the official women's organisation still depends mainly on the cheap propaganda provided by the official mass media and is capitalising on the *weaknesses* of the democratic women [*sic*] movement.[51]

From 1971 until the 1985 Intifada, the SSU established its own women's branch and persuaded many of the WU's secondary leaders to join. The ease with which the WU's role was co-opted, the quality of the women leaders who agreed to collaborate, and the respectable organization that grew out of these events greatly affected the future of the WU. Leftist critics have been harsh towards these SSU women, some of whom, like Nafissa Ahmed el-Amin, are among Sudan's most prominent and talented women. Until the Intifada, these women formed the "vanguard" of the Union of Sudanese Women (SSU), co-opting the WU's name and forming a large bourgeois women's organization with branches throughout the country. However, this organization was haunted by the same problems of existing in an androcentric society as the WU. By 1981, articles referring to the "inadequacy" of the Union of Sudanese Women were appearing in the press.[52]

For some time after the decline of the WU, recriminations from the SCP and self-recriminations from the WU dominated the communist left. Over the last few years, however, some members have begun to realize that the "weaknesses" of the WU may not all have been of their own making, but were, in part, an inevitable consequence of the structure and ideology of the SCP: androcentric dogma that neglected women's interests as women defined them, ideological rigidity, inequality in the Party hierarchy, and a puritanism that had not even kept abreast of the tone in the society at large.

To a large extent, puritanism in the SCP, which was foisted upon the WU (some SCP members claim it was vice versa), was a result of the policy of coexisting with traditional culture—both in the realm of patriarchal customs and the patriarchal aspects of Islam.

These patriarchal attitudes, an aspect of the gender ideology of the SCP, could be seen in the way that potential SCP members, especially women, were screened for moral behavior. Having members of ill-repute would reflect negatively on a Party struggling within an Islamic framework. In short, women of the SCP and WU, to appease conservative male Muslims (and Christians) in the society at large, must have acceptable social reputations. With the population acutely sensitive to the rise in conservative Islamic sentiments, this attention to "morals" and appropriate social behavior has become keen. Khartoum feminists and younger WU and SCP members complained to me in 1988 that Fatma Ahmed Ibrahim insisted on pulling her tobe over her head and face when she appeared on television, and that such conservative practices from a major left-feminist role model were hurting their cause (i.e., women's emancipation). Speaking from political asylum in England, Ibrahim stressed repeatedly that she was conscious of her moral reputation. "I had chosen to uphold an image of myself as a traditional, respectable, family-oriented Muslim woman in my private life. This image gained me the credibility that allowed me to be radical and outspoken in my public life."[53] She described some of her circumspect behavior:

> I also made sure that my reputation was well protected, because it was important in my work ... I never rode in a car alone with a colleague, nor attended a meeting in a house where no woman was present. I made sure to come home from any activity in the early evening ... I didn't want rumors and innuendo (203).

The coexistence with "traditional" culture was the critique I heard most often from a new generation of Sudanese feminists. From exile, Ibrahim critiqued international socialism: "I have concluded for myself that socialism failed in many parts of the world because it was not interpreted and implemented correctly. Another *grave mistake was denial of God and religion*, which is the mainstay of many people's moral and spiritual existence" (206; italics mine). I have been told that Ibrahim is seen as too conservative to lead the WU anymore, but that challenging her leadership has been impossible: she has become an international human-rights icon. Some members are willing to criticize Ibrahim and the WU, but off the record. One Sudanese feminist, a communist but not a Party member, who asked not to be identified, remarked:

We have begun to analyze our relationship to Islam, to *sharia*, to family conventions, and in general to the gender roles and ideology that the state and party expect of us—in fact, have constructed for us. We need to challenge domestic violence, the division of labor, and in general, as radicals, this role of "companion" we are expected to play—whether as companion political organization to the SCP—or as wives, girlfriends, and relatives of SCP members. The SCP and the WU have been too conservative undertake these tasks.[54]

One of the sharp critics of the WU is Suad Ibrahim Ahmed, longtime activist on the left and a feminist. She holds a Ph.D. in education and has taught for some time. In one of our interviews she stated that there were two points of view on the subjects of moralism, religion, and Party/Union strategies:

One point of view is that progressives should use Islam to defeat the fanatic Islamicists. This is Fatma's view. The other view is that we should face them with secular ideas. This is my view. I believe that working within an Islamic framework limits progressives to using the framework of their adversaries. Progressives should reject this approach.[55]

Ahmed agreed that the conservatism of the WU was a problem, but denied that blame for that can be placed directly at the feet of the SCP. She related the events of a series of meetings of individual women, women's organizations, and other mass organizations held in the Three Towns in 1987. Although the agenda was open, attendees discussed women's activities and the development of strategies for the political and social struggle against those Ahmed referred to as "Islamic fundamentalists." Ahmed recalled:

After being underground for sixteen years one is surprised at how many people you don't know. It was the first time I had seen 18- to 30-year-olds with whom I had had no contact during the repressive years [of the Nimieri regime]. I was surprised at the clarity of vision, the openness of criticism [of the SCP and WU], and their readiness to fight. And they know what the cost is. There is a new generation that does not accept anything without questioning ... They think that the WU, as it stands, tended to be *conservative*, that it was not *facing Muslim Brothers*, that they are giving in too much. [These young people] think that using an Islamic approach itself is defeatist because it limits us. And although it is important to talk about traditional women's roles in the family and reproduction, the real arena for this struggle is not the home but the work place.[56]

There was a major split within the WU, Ahmed continued; this "new generation" represented "a volatile and vocal group within the WU that has priorities other than the ones that were set by the traditional leadership … including Fatma herself." Ahmed related that these younger members did not want to hive off from the WU and were very respectful toward Ibrahim, but "there's no question that they have other interests. And they do not accept the idea that people [women] in pants with short hair are not revolutionaries!"[57] The younger women were making reference to the Union's puritanical attitudes toward personal choices in hair and dress styles.

To my observations that the SCP was too moralistic and the WU might have needed more autonomy, Ahmed responded sharply:[58] "Lack of autonomy? Oh, the problem is too much autonomy! The problem is that this relative independence was used to the utmost. The fact that the WU has among its membership communists and non-communists gave its leadership the right to say that they are not a communist party branch." About moralism:

> In fact, the WU is the one that is moralistic. One of the areas of friction between the Party and the WU was the fact that the WU in its own consti-tution said that a member has to be of moral virtue … it could exclude … anyone who has Afro hair and jeans. And this alienates young people, for example, people in the performing arts, are they moral or immoral? Some people believe that to sing in public is immoral, or dance, or play basket-ball.

Ahmed maintained that the WU strategy of not confronting conservative elements in society has only made women internalize anti-feminism and male chauvinism, and that the SCP made a mistake in not criticizing the WU openly. "That is why, as a Party, we have to carry the burden [take the blame] for any conservative stance [the WU] may have taken in the past." She said SCP members were aware of problems in the WU, but kept postponing their criticism. By the 1980s, everyone was so oppressed under the military regime that they were preoccupied with surviving. Members saw more need to support than to criticize each other. Besides, women of the WU were very useful to the SCP at this time, as women were less suspicious to the regime than men and could move about more freely—at least during the day—without being stopped by the secret police. They were also less frequently arrested, so, if needed, they could carry on the struggle in a limited way.

With a dismissive tone, Ahmed claimed, "I am not involved in the WU anymore and haven't been for twenty years now." Her attitude toward the WU was similar to another major left figure's. Khadiga Safwat was one of Sudan's leading women intellectuals before she left the country in the late 1970s. A communist, she was well connected to SCP leadership.

Considered by most to be a feminist, her feminist views are tempered by her more rigid Marxism. Safwat was outright disdainful of the WU and of feminism either in its "Western" form or as played out in Sudan. Once, during our many conversations in Khartoum in the 1970s,[59] a comment I made that assumed that she, as a woman communist, would automatically have been a member of the WU, provoked the responses, "I don't know what those women are doing these days; I really don't pay any attention to them"; and, "They don't seem to have a profound understanding of the class struggle."

Fatima Babiker Mahmoud is another leading voice of the Sudanese feminist left. She self-identifies as a "womanist within the class struggle," but adds, "I don't want the class struggle to deny me the right [to have] my feminism."[60] Her position is that the SCP cannot claim to be the ones to fight for women:

> Nobody [but women] can fight on behalf of women for women ... we [women] cannot ... wait for the revolution to come and socialism to be established and then say 'listen, now that the revolution has come let us stay on the bed and look into the woman situation.' That cannot be ... We [men and women] have to go together (85).

In a rather scathing critique of male attitudes towards women in the SCP, Mahmoud said:

> [SCP men] tell me "we believe in women's liberation," "you are equal" and so on. I don't want that. I don't want what I see in the party, like when a woman is talking in a communist party meeting, men would rather read the newspaper than listen to her. They don't take her seriously, and then they go home and they wait for the woman to serve them. They do not implement what they say in practice (85–86).

Mahmoud, limiting her critique of SCP male cadres to their practice, insisted:

> the moment when we can talk about the liberation of the African woman will come when the progressive movement of so-called communists and socialists has this unity of what is in their heads [theory], in practice ... There is *no contradiction between the women's movement and the revolutionary movement unless the revolutionary movement does not address itself to the question of women* (86; italics mine).

Other left feminists, some of them fallen-away or disenchanted with either the SCP, the WU, or both, criticized the organizations and their leadership for not addressing issues of sexuality in its broadest sense, or reproductive freedom. These were often doctors concerned with health issues. When I repeated to some of them Fatma Ahmed Ibrahim's comment to me that no one dies of circumcision but that people die of hunger and difficult births and that babies die at a high rate, that approach was dismissed as not being concerned with the "quality of life," only with death. What these professional women saw as the "excessive moralism" of the SCP and WU seemed a prevalent critique among women under the age of forty. Said one,

> The men of the Party need to support women when they are being criti-
> cized for their social behavior or dress, not join in the criticism. Men often
> do not have the courage to stand up against these social attitudes. It is
> deeply ingrained in them that their honor is at stake when the women
> with whom they are associated, whether family or not, are questioned.[61]

Another commented to me that she believed people should abide by the rules of their culture, not try to live outside it. But she maintained that there is a double standard for men and women, and that is what she objects to.

Conclusion

It is clear to me, after years of talking with hundreds of leftist Sudanese women and men, that even SCP men try to position women within the culture to serve men's best interests. Both the SCP and the WU try to position women to be the guardians of the morality and of the standards of the Party and society. To communists, women reflect on the Party and its work. People spoke dramatically as if women carried within their bodies the purity of the cause. One male SCP intellectual told me that you can discern "how hard people work to achieve their aims, how noble the cause is and the people who work on its behalf by looking at the women who belong to the organization." Another, in a discussion following my lecture at the University of Khartoum on rising Islamism in Sudan, commented that he regretted that the communists had not moved forward in "cleaning out all the prostitutes" before the Islamists did it. As if there was a contest for the cleansing of "dirty" women!

In the 1980s, especially during the brief period following the 1985 Intifada, a new generation of left feminists began to challenge what they saw as narrow moralism. The rising tide of Islamism, however, has made it nearly impossible now to confront issues of puritanism.

Aspects of the various critiques above are applicable to the WU during most of its history. Whether in terms of *strategic* gender interests, which Fatma Ahmed Ibrahim rejected above as not being a central priority in Sudan, or *practical* gender interests, which Ibrahim claimed she embraced, the potential for a mass movement generated by women themselves, as a response to their own oppression *as women*, has not been considered by the Party or the Union. The Party's institutions and practices do not reflect a vision of a new society—a race-, class-, and gender-egalitarian postrevolutionary society—one that could have been in process *before* the revolution. A progressive party or a more independent WU might have built on extant socioeconomic, consciousness-raising, self-help, experiential, occupational, and neighborhood networks—i.e., the networks of everyday life. A more autonomous WU might have chosen to deal more critically with aspects of "traditional" culture (patriarchal customs and patriarchal aspects of Islam) and with the new phenomenon: radical, political Islam—Islamism—discussed in the concluding chapter.

Notes

1. Maxine Molyneux, "Mobilization without Emancipation? Women's Interests, the State, and Revolution in Nicaragua," *Feminist Studies* 11, no. 2 (1985): 228.

2. Ibid., 232–33. Molyneux has too quickly concluded that we cannot say that women have interests in common. Deduced or not, unequally aligned gender arrangements may also be measured concretely and take similar, though not identical, forms cross-culturally.

3. I took the term "promissory notes" from the title of a provocative work that was published as I started this book. The authors assess the relationship between women's emancipation and socialism. *Promissory Notes: Women in Transition to Socialism*, ed. Sonia Kruks, Rayna Rapp, and Marilyn Young (New York: Monthly Review, 1989).

4. See chapter 1, note 9, and chapter 7, note 21.

5. Judith Stacey, "When Patriarchy Kowtows: The Significance of the Chinese Family Revolution for Feminist Theory," in *Capitalist Patriarchy and the Case for Socialist Feminism*, ed. Zillah Eisenstein (New York: Monthly Review Press, 1979), 338.

6. This is paraphrased from Eleanor Leacock, "Women, Development, and Anthropological Facts and Fictions," *Latin American Perspectives* (special double issue on women and class struggle) 4, nos. 12/13 (1977): 9.

7. Gregory Massell, *The Surrogate Proletariat: Moslem Women and Revolutionary Strategies in Soviet Central Asia, 1919–1929* (Princeton: Princeton University Press, 1974), xxii–xxiii.

8. Ibid., 408.

9. See, e.g., Stephanie Urdang, *Fighting Two Colonialisms: Women in Guinea-Bissau* (New York: Monthly Review Press, 1979).

10. I am certainly not attempting to detract from women's contributions to the movements in Guinea-Bissau, Algeria, Palestine, Angola, Mozambique, Eritrea, Nicaragua, Ethiopia, Vietnam, Guatemala, and El Salvador. And Cuban women are now making major contributions (see note 12 below).

11. Kruks et al., *Promissory Notes*, 9.

12. Cubans, for example, developed a Family Code after the fact, and are, therefore, having great difficulty implementing changes in the sphere of domestic labor and social reproduction. Students of Cuban society are somewhat justified in maintaining that Cuban revolutionaries did not have the benefit of a long period in which a vanguard party was developing a vision of a new society, nor much of an opportunity for women to be integrated into the armed struggle.

13. Kruks et al., *Promissory Notes*, 12.

14. Sondra Hale, "The Politics of Gender in the Middle East," in *Gender and Anthropology: Critical Reviews for Research and Teaching*, ed. Sandra Morgen (Washington, D.C.: American Anthropological Association, 1989), 246–67.

15. My links with the Sudanese left are ideological, personal, long, and profound. I hold the SCP in high regard as oftentimes the only progressive voice in Sudan. The following critique, then, is offered in good faith. My information is based on many conversations and interviews with Party members and fellow travelers, many of whom, because of Sudan's current political climate, I cannot name.

16. Sheila Rowbotham, Lynne Segal, and Hilary Wainwright, *Beyond the Fragments: Feminism and the Making of Socialism* (London: Merlin Press, 1979), 7.

17. Kruks et al., in their essays on a number of movement case studies from all over the world, comment on the general absence of discussions of sex and sexuality. *Promissory Notes*, 11.

18. Although I am uncomfortable with some of the terminology, one scholar typified the approach to the development of the SCP: "there is a paradox that needs clarification; it is that one of the most 'backward' countries of the Arab world should have given birth to one of the most powerful communist parties in the Middle East—one of the very few that has been in the running for power." Alain Gresh, "The Free Officers and the Comrades: The Sudanese Communist Party and Nimeiri Face-to-Face," *International Journal of Middle Eastern Studies* 21 (1989): 393–409. The quote is on 394–95.

19. Many sources comment on the strength and influence of the SCP; among them are Gabriel Warburg, *Islam, Nationalism, and Communism in a Traditional Society: The Case of Sudan* (London: Frank Cass, 1978). Warburg writes: "The accurate number of SCP members is not known. According to The World Today, London January 1965, there were 10,000 party members at that time" (234). Fatima Babiker Mahmoud remarks: "the Communist Party of the Sudan (CPS) is the most influential revolutionary organization in the country and one of the leading Communist Parties in Africa and the Middle East" (*The Sudanese Bourgeoisie: Vanguard of Development?* [London: Zed; Khartoum: Khartoum University Press, 1984], 130). For descriptions of the SCP or leftist politics in Sudan in general, consult J.M.A. Bakheit, *Communist Activities in the Middle East Between 1919–1927, with Special Reference to Egypt and the Sudan* (Khartoum: Sudan Research Unit, University of Khartoum, 1968); Salah el-Din el-Zein el-Tayeb, *The Student Movement in Sudan, 1940–1970* (Khartoum: Khartoum University Press, 1971); Saad ed-Din Fawzi, *The Labour Movement in the Sudan, 1946–1955* (London: Oxford, 1957); Carole Collins, "Sudan: Colonialism and Class Struggle in Sudan," *Middle East Research and Infor-*

mation Project (MERIP), no. 46 (1976): 3–17, 20; Gresh, ibid.; sections of Mansour Khalid's, *Nimeiri and the Revolution of Dis-May* (London: KPI, 1985), and of Tim Niblock's *Class and Power in Sudan: The Dynamics of Sudanese Politics, 1898–1985* (Albany: State University of New York Press, 1987); and various communist sources, e.g., *The African Communist* (London); Mohamed Sulaiman, *Ten Years of the Sudanese Left* (in Arabic) (Wad Medani: Alfagr Books, 1971); SCP publications, *Thawrat Shaab* (A People's Revolution; in Arabic) (Khartoum: Socialist Publishing House, 1967); *Marxism and Problems of the Sudanese Revolution* (in Arabic) (Khartoum: Socialist Publishing House, 1968); Abdel Khaliq Mahjub, *Lamahat min tarikh el-hizb el-Shuyui el-Sudani* (Dar el-fikr el-ishtiraki, 1960); and the SCP organ, *el-Midan*.

20. Gresh, "The Free Officers," 395.

21. In particular, see Bakheit, *Communist Activities in the Middle East.*

22. The most useful source on communism and the student movement is el-Tayeb, *The Student Movement in the Sudan.*

23. Gresh, "The Free Officers and the Comrades," 395.

24. Fawzi, *The Labour Movement in the Sudan*, 36–37.

25. Warburg, *Islam, Nationalism and Communism*, 114–115.

26. In 1964, for example, a prominent communist served as GTU president.

27. Magda M. el-Sanousi and Nafissa Ahmed el-Amin, "The Women's Movement, Displaced Women, and Rural Women in Sudan," in *Women and Politics Worldwide*, ed. Barbara Nelson and Najma Chowdhury (New Haven: Yale University Press, 1994), 677.

28. Niblock, *Class and Power in Sudan*, 62–81.

29. Gresh, "The Free Officers and the Comrades."

30. Peter Woodward, *Sudan, 1898–1989: The Unstable State* (Boulder: Lynne Rienner, 1990), 137.

31. It remains to be seen if this will change under the current NIF-military regime. Large numbers of women are being recruited into militias referred to as the Popular Defense Forces.

32. We cannot know the exact figures; this is the estimate usually taken from Arabic or Sudanese sources and the one I was most frequently given during my interviews in the 1960s. A written source I have used is Carolyn Fluehr-Lobban, "Women and Social Liberation: The Sudan Experience," in *Three Studies on National Integration in the Arab World* (information paper no. 12, Association of Arab-American University Graduates, North Dartmouth, Mass., 1974). She was reliant on the major source in English in the 1970s of our knowledge of the Sudanese women's movement, Fatma Babiker Mahmoud, "The Role of the Sudanese Women's Union in Sudanese Politics" (M.A. thesis, University of Khartoum, 1971), and on a booklet by Nafissa Ahmed el-Amin, *The Sudanese Woman throughout the History of Her Struggle* (Khartoum: Government Press, 1972). We now have a number of other sources (see note 35 below).

33. The most useful history and analysis of the trade union movement in Sudan is ed-Din Fawzi, *The Labour Movement in the Sudan.*

34. See "Sudan's Revolutionary Spring," *MERIP Reports'* special issue on the 1985 Intifada. As for the WU, in that issue, in his article by the same title, Eric

Rouleau reported that the Sudanese "Pasionaria," Fatima Ibrahim Ahmed, was ubiquitous during the uprising as an activist on behalf of women and that she addressed the first public meeting of the WU in fourteen years on 21 April 1985. "Sudan's Revolutionary Spring," *MERIP Reports* 15, no. 7 (1985): 4.

35. For historical details on Sudanese women's organizations I have relied on a number of sources, e.g., Mahmoud, "The Role of the Sudanese Women's Union"; El-Amin, *The Sudanese Woman*; and summaries of these works by Fluehr-Lobban, *Three Studies on National Integration*; also works by Fatma Ahmed Ibrahim, e.g., *Tariqnu ila el-Tuhasur* (Our Road to Emancipation) (Khartoum: n.p., n.d.); *el-Mara el-Arabiyya wal Taghyir el-Ijtimai* (The Arab Woman and Social Change) (Khartoum: el-Markaz el-Tibai, 1986); and a series of her publications in *Sawt el-Mara* (The Woman's Voice) (Khartoum: n.p., appearing sporadically from 1955 to the present). Additionally, consult Hagga Kashif-Badri, *el-Haraka el-nisaiyya fi-el-Sudan* (The Women's Movement in the Sudan) (Khartoum: University Publishing House, University of Khartoum, 1980); and in English, Kashif-Badri's "The History, Development, Organization and Position of Women's Studies in the Sudan," *Social Science Research and Women in the Arab World* (Paris: UNESCO, 1984), 94–112. Two other recent sources in English are Zeinab Bashir el-Bakri and el-Wathig M. Kameir, "Aspects of Women's Political Participation in Sudan," *International Social Science Journal* 35, no. 4 (1983): 605–23; and el-Sanousi and el-Amin, "The Women's Movement." El-Bakri has a number of works in progress and in press, e.g., "On the Crisis in the Sudanese Women's Movement" (The Hague: ISIS, in press). See also el-Bakri and el-Haj Hamad M. Khier, "Sudanese Women in History and Historiography: A Proposed Strategy for Curriculum Change" (paper presented at the Workshop on Women's Studies in Sudan, National Council for Research, Sudan Family Planning Association, Khartoum, 7–9 February 1989). My interpretation and synthesis of the development of women's organizations, especially the WU, was first published as "The Wing of the Patriarch: Sudanese Women and Revolutionary Parties," *MERIP Middle East Report* 16, no. 1 (1986): 25–30.

36. El-Sanousi and el-Amin, "The Women's Movement," 676.

37. El-Bakri and Khier, "Sudanese Women in History and Historiography," 619.

38. During the civilian regime in 1965 women were given the right to vote, but once again literacy was a requirement, a condition the WU supported, according to Fatma Ahmed Ibrahim. (Interview with Ibrahim at her home in Omdurman, Sudan, 12 July 1988. Unless otherwise indicated, quotes and ideas attributed to her are from that interview.)

39. Fatma Ahmed Ibrahim, "Arrow at Rest," in *Women in Exile*, comp. Mahnaz Afkhami (n.p., University Press of Virginia, 1994), 199.

40. Some of the information for this section is based on my 12 July 1988 interview with Fatma Ahmed Ibrahim, in Omdurman, Sudan, but also on two interviews with Suad Ibrahim Ahmed, leading woman communist, Khartoum, Sudan, 25 and 26 July 1988.

41. In the interview she oscillated between presenting her role as struggling to maintain what little autonomy the WU had in relation to the SCP and insisting that the two organizations had always been separate.

42. Ibrahim, "Arrow at Rest," 197–98. Italics mine.

43. Omdurman interview, 12 July 1988.

44. Ibid.

45. This critical information is from a number of confidential interviews with women communists and/or sister travelers.

46. Warburg, *Islam, Nationalism and Communism*, 166.

47. Sondra Hale, "Transforming Culture or Fostering Second-Hand Consciousness? Women's Front Organizations and Revolutionary Parties—The Sudan Case," in *Arab Women: Old Boundaries, New Frontiers*, ed. Judith Tucker (Bloomington: Indiana University Press, 1993), 159.

48. Juliette Minces, "Women in Algeria," in *Women in the Muslim World*, ed. Lois Beck and Nikki Keddie (Cambridge: Harvard University Press, 1978), 159–71. Marnia Lazreg, *The Eloquence of Silence: Algerian Women in Question* (New York: Routledge, 1994), offsets some of Minces argument and challenges conventional interpretations of women in the Algerian revolution.

49. This letter is reproduced in Kashif-Badri, *el-Haraka el-nisaiyya*, 106–09. Quotes below are from the same source until otherwise indicated.

50. Ibrahim, "Arrow at Rest," 207. Italics mine.

51. Warburg, *Islam, Nationalism and Communism*, 211. Italics mine.

52. "The Sudan Women's Union [a co-opted name; I have used Union of Sudanese Women in the text] has recently been the target of massive criticism. Most women complain that the SWU does not reach enough of Sudan's female population, and that its achievements have been, at best, minimal." The writer, Awatif Sidahmed, was interviewing Nafissa Ahmed el-Amin, one of the former WU members and then Secretary General of the Union of Sudanese Women and Political Bureau member of the SSU, who stated, "[W]e do not deny the fact that the SWU [Union of Sudanese Women] was inadequate for a long time." *Sudanow* (January 1981), 41–42.

53. Ibrahim, "Arrow at Rest," 199.

54. Interview, Khartoum, 18 July 1988. Name withheld by request.

55. The first of two interviews with Suad Ibrahim Ahmed was at her home in Khartoum Number Two, a suburb of Khartoum, 25 July 1988.

56. Ahmed, second interview, Khartoum Number Two, 26 July 1988.

57. Ibid.

58. The following quotes are from Ahmed, second interview, Khartoum Number Two, 26 July 1988.

59. In 1971–72, while carrying out my dissertation fieldwork, I lived for some weeks with Safwat and her family in the New Extension (Khartoum), and afterwards was treated to weekly dinners and political and literary discussions. I was just coming into my feminist consciousness, and she, while living the life of a very emancipated woman, could not have been more disdainful of feminism.

60. Fatima Babiker Mahmoud, "Capitalism, Racism, Patriarchy and the Woman Question," *Africa's Crisis* (London: Institute for African Alternatives, 1987), 85.

61. Informal interview, Khartoum North, 16 July 1988. Name withheld by request.

6

Islamism and the Women Activists of the National Islamic Front

Introduction

In this chapter I examine identity politics as a strategy of the military-supported state (and in this case, party) hegemonic processes. I critique the modernist Islamist (political Islam) movement of the National Islamic Front (NIF), analyze its manipulation and re-creation of religious ideology toward a more "authentic" culture, and explore the centrality of Muslim women and the Muslim family in creating an Islamic state and a Muslim *umma* (nation). Islamist women are both organizers within the NIF and socializers within the family. In the latter role, women in general are seen by Islamist men as the potential instrument to lay the foundation of an authentic culture, one that, although based on an Islamic past, is not atavistic or fundamentalist.[1]

Islamist men—using law, education, and media—position women within the culture to serve the movement. This approach creates a new trend in the gender division of labor whereby women are active in the workforce, but only under conditions that fulfill the requirements of the party/state and of the umma. Islamist women, at least the activists, are complicit in this process.

I examine the potential impact of Islamism on the gender division of labor and other gender arrangements, such as those prescribed in the personal status laws.[2] I do that by analyzing the NIF, a revisionist offshoot of the Ikhwan, referred to by some as a modernist reform movement within an Islamic framework.[3] I have selected the NIF because it has been the most effective political machine in Sudan in the 1980s and 1990s and, arguably, in the twentieth century.[4]

Because the membership of the NIF is middle-class, educated, and heavily urban, we can expect the authentic-culture campaign to be class-interested—that is, to invent a culture and develop an economy to serve that class. In fact, Brenner and others have hypothesized that the Islamists are a counter-elite "produced by the same processes and interests which produced the secularists."[5] In the face of international interlopers (mainly Westerners), nationalist tendencies in the service of those class interests can also be expected. This authentic-culture framework verges on essentialism,[6] especially regarding women and the family. Women's behavior is circumscribed by male-controlled religiopolitical institutions in order to mold the "ideal" woman as the moral center of the "ideal" family.

Overprivileging Islam?

Like Deniz Kandiyoti, I maintain that "analyses of gender relations and ideologies in Muslim societies have been dominated by a persistent preoccupation concerning the role of Islam."[7] Therefore, since one of my goals is to avoid overprivileging culture and ideology—especially Islam— I am here regarding Sudan's Islamic movement as no more than politics-as-usual instead of as an Islamic "revival." However, Sudan's Islamic past is crucial to an analysis of the relationship of gender to the state.

As frequently as it is overprivileged by scholars of Middle Eastern studies and in popular writings on the region, Islam is essentialized and ahistoricized. No less frequently have women been essentialized and gender arrangements ahistoricized. I have stated elsewhere that in analyzing the relationship of gender and religion we need to avoid (1) treating Islam as a superstructural monolith; (2) oversimplifying Islam's impact on women—as if women are a passive, undifferentiated mass and not actors in their own story—and overlooking the strategies of resistance, adaptation, or accommodation that women everywhere employ in situations of oppression and subordination; and (3) overlooking people's everyday lives by privileging theory.[8]

Islam does not and cannot explain the condition of women. In each culture, gender and religion intersect differently. Women embrace, resist, and subvert Islam and other institutions—i.e., have agency in their own lives. However, despite criticism since 1979, most sources on Muslim women have privileged Islam in explaining women's "role" or the conditions of their lives.[9] Other scholars, especially within anthropology, have tried to avoid overgeneralizing Islam's impact on women by producing more culturally *specific* women-centered studies in which Islam is seen as only one variable.[10] But moving away from universalistic (e.g., patriarchal) approaches toward theoretically and ideologically safer ones does not help us address major concerns of Marxist feminism, still arguably the most vibrant paradigm for the interpretation of gender/class/race relationships.

The aim, it seems to me—and Kandiyoti has advanced this most clearly—is to avoid automatically conflating patriarchal gender relations and religiously sanctioned patriarchal codes. Kandiyoti likewise warns against the conflation of Islam and cultural nationalism.[11] Are there forms of patriarchal gender ideologies and arrangements that have become embedded in Islam—i.e., been given Islamic trappings—that can be extracted and analyzed separately? How would a separation of patriarchal customs and Islamic institutions and doctrines alter the Sudanese discourse about cultural authenticity? In the Sudan context, is it analytically useful to differentiate between "Arab" and "Muslim," another common conflation?[12]

In a wider context, are there qualities in some religions that lend themselves to co-option and manipulation by power seekers? Much has been written on the concept of the "religion of the oppressed," which refers to people's propensity, during periods of extreme oppression, to embrace religion, to accept a religious regime, and to ignore leadership motivation.

Using the religion-of-the-oppressed approach suggests that there are no special qualities in Islam (or any other specific religion) that made it an effective instrument in the hands of Nimieri, i.e., that he might have been able to use any national indigenous religion to arouse the masses in a time of economic crisis. But are there elements in the Judeo-Christian-Islamic tradition that give these religions political instrumentality during economic and political crises? Do these religions reinforce or reassert social processes that allow a society to realign itself when there are disruptive elements present? (Are there elements that can easily be operationalized?) Does Islam lend itself more easily than other religions to a resolution of conflict? Are there fewer contradictions in Islam than in other religions? Many religions have succeeded in co-opting secular themes; that is not unique to Islam. And, although Brenner is referring specifically to Islam, his comments below remind us that there is a particular set of links that may often lead to the growth of political consciousness and institutional development in any religion:

> There is a relationship between the emergence of modernized, mass education (whether secular or religious), the founding by educated persons of voluntary associations to represent and protect their own interests, and efforts by political leaders to co-opt religion as a "political resource."[13]

Although Islam is our best example, other religions may also be said to encompass a cultural-social-political-economic worldview in which the religious doctrines have something to say about public and personal life and the world around. I suggest that, without privileging Islam in the sense of presenting it as an unstoppable hegemonic force that acts on the masses, it is possible to extract a special set of qualities that, when linked to other societal processes, privilege Islam at particular times in a society's history. I concur with Brenner that "when Islam becomes 'rationalized' and politicized, it becomes susceptible to the same forces which mould any social and political ideology, and can in turn act in order to affect these forces. And Islam is certainly one of the most powerful ideologies functioning on the African continent today." [14]

In the last chapter I raised the question of why such a strong Communist party emerged in Sudan, seemingly an "unlikely place." In the following section on Nimieri and the rise of Islamism during his regime, I raise the question of why one of the strongest Islamist movements in the world also emerged there.

Background: Nimieri's State, Islam, and the Rise of Islamism

An examination of the rise of "Islamism" in Muslim northern Sudan since 1971, and in particular of its gender dimension, is instructive theoretically and comparatively. In chapter 3 I discussed the importance of Sufism and other forms of Islam in Sudanese history and contemporary politics. Gabriel Warburg comments that "the Sudanese are first and foremost a religious society."[15] Many Sudanese scholars, Islamic apologists and not, agree with Ahmed el-Shahi's statement that "Sufist religious orders have a strong and real claim to represent Islam in the country."[16] Comments such as Warburg's are very common and are part of the general patronizing European attitude toward Sudanese. British ex-colonials remarked to me in the 1960s that the Sudanese were "sweet," "innocent," and "tolerant." Other condescending attitudes painted Sudanese as not being concerned enough with religion to be doctrinaire. Given this picture, then, could a hard-line Islamic revolution in Sudan have been predicted? Yes, Sudanese society was and is religious, but it was not seen as fanatical—this in the face of the only successful revolution based on a messianic figure, the Mahdi, on the continent. What is now happening is not a resurgence of sectarian politics or the reawakening of Sufism: The contemporary, politically powerful religious sentiment is of a new order, referred to by many adherents as the "New Movement." And it is strongly anti-Sufist.[17]

In chapter 3 I presented some sociohistorical processes and conditions to account for the nature of the present Islamist regime. Like many societies, Sudan is steeped in indigenous and oftentimes conflicting traditions. For example: Sufi-Sunni interaction has been highly complex, and the sectarian ethnic-identity politics emanating from this religious history remain active. Islamic patriarchal institutions and customs have intersected Arab/Nubian/African male-authoritarian customs, and all, in turn, have been reinforced by the intersections of sharia, civil law, and customary law. Within the last two decades these conflicts have been aggravated by Sudan's economic "crisis."[18]

One concomitant of the crisis was the silent alteration of the gender division of labor in the workforce and in the home. A shift in gender labor arrangements ensued as hundreds of thousands of male workers and professionals were forced into labor migration, thereby vacating jobs that women began to fill.[19] A major cause of both the shift and the crisis was the pronounced influx of multinational corporations, nongovernmental organizations, and foreign aid projects (Arab, European, and American) that dominated Sudan's economy from 1972 to 1989, impacting both the class and the gender structures. Many Sudanese see these developments as challenging their entire culture.

The reaction to these conditions by the NIF-military junta that gained control of the state in 1989 was to impose another Islamic hegemony, those of the past—Sufism and Mahdism (also a form of Sufism)—seen as having failed.[20]

In the past, despite internecine feuds that resulted from sectarian politics, and aside from the north's attempt to suppress other religions in the south, northern Sudanese had been relatively relaxed about Islam, displaying tolerance for diversity.[21] Sharia was part of the legal system prior to 1983, but civil and customary legal codes were dominant.[22] Although northern Sudanese women wore tobes (which some might see as a conservative mode of dress)[23] and underwent genital surgeries (both clitoridectomy and infibulation), observers considered them among the "emancipated" women of the Muslim world (see chapter 4), especially after 1965, when women earned universal suffrage, and 1973, when the Permanent Constitution offered both women and men a number of civil rights and freedoms and singled out women for specific gender-related protections.[24]

This changed drastically in September 1983 when Nimieri declared Sudan an Islamic republic and ordered strict adherence to sharia and attempted to enforce some of its harshest aspects, e.g., amputations for theft and public flogging for moral trespassing. Although factional struggles had been characteristic of Sudanese politics for some time (see chapter 3), these unpopular "September Laws" were the catalyst that intensified the struggle between (1) secular groups, e.g., liberals and socialists, who saw the non-Muslim southern Sudan and women as potentially disenfranchised, (2) religious groups, e.g., the Republicans, opposed to sharia in its harsh form and to the formation of a theocracy, and (3) Islamists who saw the wisdom of organizing under the banner of a "pure" and authentic Islam and presenting it as Sudan's only defense and cultural salvation against an invading West and the only answer to Sudan's dismal economic situation.

Nimieri's relationship to Islam and to Islamic authorities (e.g., the ulama), his struggle with Islamists such as Turabi, the Islamists' relationship to the state, and Sufi and anti-Sufi sentiments were complicated, a continuation of the dynamic tension in the history of Sudan's religion and state relationship. These tensions, however, had not been the salient feature of 1970s state politics under Nimieri. In fact, questions of the separation of religion and state might have remained sublimated in the 1980s and 1990s had Nimieri not forced the issue.

Bearing in mind that Nimieri's one-party state (the Sudan Socialist Union [SSU]) and its apparatuses were technically secular, it may seem both contradictory and facile to attribute the rise of Islamism to Nimieri's regime (1969–85). Yet Nimieri's acts in 1983 signaled the onslaught of radical Islam and were among his major mechanisms for developing an Islamic state. He also invited Islamists into his government, e.g., Hasan el-Turabi, then leading figure in the Ikhwan, who soon after founded the NIF. For the first time in its history, the Ikhwan achieved a visible and recognized state political power base, ending its marginality as a fanatic group and legitimizing the organization in terms of mainstream politics.[25]

Scholars and political leaders have pondered why Nimieri launched an intensified Islamization process when he did. His military regime originated in 1969 as a leftist military coup. However, once in power, Nimieri began to shed the more extreme left influence, and his regime became steadily conservative. He moved more pronouncedly to the right after an abortive 1971 coup by leftist members of the military, the Federation of Trade Unions, and the SCP. Following a spate of executions, including that of Secretary-General of the SCP Abdel Khaliq Mahjub, Nimieri continued to distance himself from liberals and socialists and for the next twelve years brutally suppressed all opposition, isolating himself in the process.

By 1983 the regime was in difficulty. The spiraling national debt, the pressure the World Bank and the International Monetary Fund were putting on the state to prune the civil service and raise food prices (which had already caused riots in 1979 and 1982), an increasingly successful insurrection in the south, the formation and development of the National Front (a coalition of political opposition groups), a three-month long judges' strike in 1983, and the doctors' strike in early 1984—all led to various desperate moves on the part of the dictator. Judges and doctors were powerful professional groups, the Doctors' Union being one of the most prestigious organizations in the country. The strikes led to the declaration of a state of emergency.[26] In suppressing these rebellions, Nimieri resorted to increasingly harsh measures. Most of my interviewees attested that by 1983 Nimieri had run out of supporters.

The move to Islamize, then, made a lot of sense for Nimieri at a political level. But there is more to the explanation than troubles in his regime. Some hypothesize that Nimieri's reasons may have been as much personal as political,[27] that moving toward an Islamic state was consistent with what was happening to him in terms of his life- and leadership styles.[28] People reported to me that the dictator had begun to make public displays of his religious devotion. Portraying himself as religious in his personal life and carrying out political acts to Islamize gave Nimieri some continuity with the Islamic character of Sudanese politics and social culture. Even secular-oriented nationalists have had to acknowledge Sudan's Islamic past as the "origin of Sudanese nationalism."[29] Esposito, however, accuses Nimieri of "opportunistic Islamization," pointing to Sudan's reliance on oil-rich Arab states (primarily Saudi Arabia) and the advantage of co-opting some of the NIF's Islamic themes.[30] But Islamization also paved the way for the NIF to gain political ascendance at the same time that most of its members were gaining ascendance as part of a new middle class.

Mansour Khalid, liberal intellectual and longtime political figure, was even less charitable in his explanation of Nimieri's turn to Islam. It was to

1. Tak[e] the wind out of the sails of all the Sudanese Islamic movements (the Muslim Brothers, Mirghani and Sadiq el Mahdi). [Nimieri] knew that Islam was gaining momentum inside and outside the Sudan.

2. Skirt[] the haunting internal problems and turn[] people's attention from government mismanagement, soaring inflation etc. The Sudanese were being asked to exercise self-discipline and accept their lot in this world; they were to think of the life to come and store up treasures in heaven. The role of the leader is no longer to rule and deliver the promised goods, but to impregnate people with faith through the drone of oratory, this time from pulpits.

3. Turn[] people's attention away from government corruption, mainly palace corruption. People should no longer talk about Nimeiri's cronies but about friends, relatives and neighbours of theirs who have been accused of and tried for alcoholism, adultery and other heinous acts. These trials are broadcast daily as major news items to give a new staple for gossip.[31]

In the year or so after the enactment of the September Laws, Sudanese saw the establishment of "decisive justice courts," the application of *hudud* (Islamic criminal punishments such as amputations), the replacement of income tax by *zakat* (an alms tax), and an attempt to Islamize all the banks, with the aim of outlawing such practices as charging interest.

In the streets women were harassed about their conduct or dress by self-appointed male moral guards; Nimieri himself carried out endless ceremonial "Islamic acts" (e.g., pouring alcohol into the Nile) as "expressions of his appropriation of Islamic leadership and legitimacy to justify authoritarian rule."[32]

Mainly poor women bore the brunt of the moral guards. The regime harassed, arrested, flogged, and occasionally executed prostitutes, those seen as the "same as prostitutes," and vendors of local brew. Many middle-class and professional women were also accosted by the same moral guards and questioned about their presence in public and their relationships to the men in their company.

This treatment hinted ominously at things to come, such as the national debates held by authorities to determine if too many women were being trained in certain professions. The administration of the University of Khartoum, for example, considered quotas for women in particular fields.[33]

During this time Nimieri's treatment of the Ikhwan was typically Macchiavellian. Although he was the first head of state to embrace and openly invite them into his government, he simultaneously undermined them, a familiar Nimieri strategy of appropriating opposition groups and then repudiating them. Near the end of his regime Nimieri arrested Hasan el-Turabi and hundreds of his followers, scapegoating them for the failures of his administration. However, his decision to martyr Mahmoud Mohamed Taha, leader of the Islamic reformist Republicans (see chapter 3), on charges of apostasy backfired and led, some believe, to Nimieri's eventual downfall in 1985.

Under Nimieri, state leaders courted the Ikhwan and the NIF but sometimes sought to disavow or distance themselves from "fundamentalism." This dynamic changed after Nimieri's overthrow and the return to high office of Prime Minister Saddig el-Mahdi. Saddig, like his brother-in-law Turabi, was from a Sufi family. Previously considered a "moderate," Saddig carried out political acts and made coalitions that confounded political observers. He formed the "Government of Consensus" in the summer of 1988 and, as part of that process, invited the NIF into the official ranks of government.

If one views Saddig's conciliatory stance toward the same Islamists that he had always opposed as accommodation, one can say that accommodation has worked both ways. In its attempt to gain power, the NIF adopted a "modern" look. Saddig and the NIF referred to their alliance as an "Islamic Trend" government, "trend" suggesting forward-looking, keeping abreast of contemporary behavior.[34] The NIF's attempt to appear "modern" has meant establishing institutions (banks and insurance companies) and embracing behavior (using modern technology) generally considered secular, under an Islamic umbrella. The NIF is one of the first organizations in Sudan to use television effectively for missionary work and recruitment. One of the most striking modernist approaches of the NIF is the open recruitment of women—in Islamic dress only—for political organizing. The Republicans and the SCP are the only other political organizations that have so effectively recruited women.

The NIF's movement into commerce was no surprise, but the organization's business and political acumen astonished some secularists I interviewed. For example, the NIF effectively recruited government employees, who used their influence to obtain building permits for mosques and passed on information about tax breaks for businesses built above mosques.

The NIF attempted to run social-service industries (schools, literacy programs, health clinics, social centers, welfare programs, regional and neighborhood voluntary associations, and programs for women) on "Islamic principles." Organizing strategies focused on the poor (e.g., in the shantytowns) were sometimes not original (e.g., giving them food), but the NIF's acts of paying for group weddings in the football stadium and giving the newlyweds essential furniture were strokes of organizing genius.

In the next sections I offer some explanations for what has been happening in contemporary Sudanese society and the world that is, using an expression often repeated to me by Sudanese, breaking down the social fabric. A full explanation, which requires economic/historical contextualization and positioning within the world capitalist system, cannot be offered here. But I can offer some clues about the gender component of Sudan's social crisis.

Women, Labor, Education, and Personal Status Laws—The Public Debates

Before the consolidation of Islamist power in 1989, formal and informal national and local debates were taking place about gender, law, and labor, spheres in which the interests of Islamist men and non-Islamist women, in particular, sometimes conflict.

Women's participation in the formal workforce had increased at a regular, if somewhat slow pace in the three decades after independence. Initially women's participation was encouraged by the state. Jobs were available; the state wanted to appear "modern" to the outside world, so government propagandized women's education and work participation—the basic ingredients of a liberal society and also in line with the kind of Marxism we see operationalized in some of the poorer countries. The legal and constitutional apparatuses seemed to support the idea of women being active in the workforce (see chapter 4).

But economic conditions were changing, and what had seemed the voluntary nature of women entering the workforce became less a matter of volition. Whether or not acknowledged publicly or by the state, in Sudan's depressed economy many women are compelled to work for wages outside the home. Since the Islamization process became more formalized, however, very subtle legal means have been used to discourage women from some areas of work.

By the early 1980s religion was being brought to bear on the creation of the woman citizen—even, as we shall see below, in the documents of the Union of Sudanese Women (of the SSU). Although this organization with its co-opted name was an arm of the state, it had many progressive and feminist members and was the main women's organization during a time when the Sudanese Women's Union (WU) was banned. A 1980s summary of its working plans articulates the proper role of women and moral checks on their behavior.[35] In the area of planning and research, the *Summary* declares the organization's agenda: "*scientific* research on certain topics which should be published in the woman's magazine ... : women and *Islam; Islamic laws* for women" (13; italics mine).

The Law

Islamization did not occur just during Nimieri's regime. It was a gradual, sometimes imperceptible process within postindependence Sudanese society's education, arts, media, medical and legal systems, military, and other state apparatuses. Islamization was a force that rivaled secularization. During the last part of Nimieri's regime, however, Islamization intensified while the forces of secularization were being discredited. Islamization was far from complete when the Uprising (Intifada) of April 1985 overthrew Nimieri. However, because an Umma Party member and Ansari (Saddig el-Mahdi) was elected to office not long after, the politicization of Islam would continue. After all, the Mahdists represented the land-owning and commercial ruling class and had their class interests to protect by remaining in power. And power in this era of Sudanese politics was clearly with the Islamists. Besides, the Ansari were devoted to a special Sudanese combination of Sufism and "fundamentalism," which fit neatly into an accommodationist strategy. As mentioned above, Saddig had become more conservative and more accommodating to the NIF, ultimately denying the Sufist tendencies in Mahdism.

During the brief "democratic" era (1985–89), sharia's future legal and societal roles stirred a great public debate. Many voices raised significant issues such as the ongoing relationship of sharia and customary law and the problematical application of sharia to non-Muslims and in parts of the country where non-Muslims were not numerically dominant. More to the point of this study were the contentious issues around the continuance of sharia personal status jurisprudence imposed under Nimieri, and its possible extension, as Islamists desired. Of further concern to secularists and other non-Islamists was the future of various civil rights and protections for women established in the 1973 constitution and implemented under civil law.

How such questions would be answered was of grave concern to moderate to progressive women because they had already experienced or seen societal subversion of each protection under the law. Among the major voices in the debate were the five Sudanese women scholars and professionals I presented in chapter 4, Ahmed et al. They outlined some of the personal status laws' strongest points for women. But for each protection, they point to a societal subversion of the law. The following is a paraphrase:

1. Sudanese personal status laws demand that the age of marriage should not be less than 14 years for girls. But no publicity of the law is made and many educated *women do not know about it.*

2. The law of recognizing marriage as de jure was passed to secure women's rights in inheritance, support, etc., when a husband deserts her. Marriage certificate is supposed to be done by the *mazoon,* a man who draws marriage contracts, but *custom overrules* and certificates are rarely kept, especially in rural remote areas.

3. A girl has the right of consent to a marriage suitor and can get married by the court if her guardian does not give his consent; in such cases the judge acts as a male-guardian. Yet it is *considered an act of shame* for a girl to resort to court.

4. In Islamic law, a woman at the time of the marriage contract has the right to ask the spouse to give her the right to divorce herself (i.e., to be the one to initiate the divorce). Despite the effectiveness of this law in reducing divorce claims in courts and releasing women from compensation problems, women do not ask for this right because *it is not customary.*

5. Another forsaken legal right is that a woman can, at the time of marriage contract, ask for certain stipulations which will be binding if the husband accepts them—e.g., the right to work, to seek education after marriage, to own household property, to agree on the amount of bride wealth, etc. Yet *it is not customary to put these down on paper.*

6. Divorced women have the right of *nafaqa,* or support, from the husband for four months and ten days if they have no children. If they have children, nafaqa is till children become independent. This is enforceable by the court, but *divorced women do not customarily take advantage of this,* since their families take the responsibility of protecting them.[36]

Women's Labor and the New Middle-Class Islamists

The relationship in Sudan of Islam, commercialism, consumerism, and urban-middle-class occupations has its roots in the nineteenth century. According to Jay Spaulding, commercial capitalism began to replace feudalism in the Nile valley about 1800 and accelerated after the Turco-Egyptian conquest of 1821. Aristocracy gave way to a new middle class consisting mainly of merchants who needed a more sophisticated legal and commercial code, which turned out to be Islam, an urban and commercial religion with a codified legal system.[37]

This relationship between Islam, the middle class, and capitalist activity is on the rise today. That is, Islamism as an ideology reflects class interests. Islamic "fundamentalism," at least in the form of the Ikhwan in Sudan, and now including the Islamism of the NIF, mainly recruits from the urban professional middle class. The NIF is developing a sophisticated rationalization and articulation of Islam and commerce. Women are definitely important in the building of the infrastructure of the new Islamist middle class, but not as important, and not in the ways that professional and middle-class women had been in a more secular environment. Now their labor was being highly scrutinized and manipulated.

In the hands of the young, recently urbanized middle class, Islamism has emerged as a capitalist enterprise. Perceived threats to its hegemony have caused this class, which has only recently moved into power, to operationalize certain aspects of Islamic ideology in the family and in everyday life (including work). In this section I discuss the Islamists' ideological prescriptions about women's labor.

Fatima Mernissi claims that we can observe a contemporary socioeconomic phenomenon in much of the Islamic world: economic and political competition between young men of newly urbanized middle- and lower-middle-class backgrounds and women from predominantly middle-class urban backgrounds who have some autonomy in their lives. Mernissi claims that these two groups are in conflict over scarce resources and over the construction of a moral framework. These conflicts have a great deal to do with changing processes in the world economy and two material processes on a more local level: the exercise of political power and consumerism.[38] The use of Islam by the state to accommodate these young followers (and at the same time to manipulate them) "makes sense," claims Mernissi, "because Islam speaks about power and self-empowerment" or "worldly self-enhancement" (9). Such benefits are attractive to societies reluctantly confronting "the inescapability of renegotiating new sexual, political, economic, and cultural boundaries, thresholds and limits. [They have seen] invasion of physical territory ... invasion of national television by 'Dallas' ... invasion ... by Coca-Cola (9)."

One of many perceived challenges to Muslim men is the upheaval in gender arrangements (e.g., women working outside the home, dressing and acting in particular ways that may challenge authority figures, and holding positions of power), a perceived dislocation that challenges what Mernissi refers to as "authority thresholds" (10). Since independence, women have had access to jobs, education, benefits, and political participation. Conservative men see public women as a threat to social order and to the status quo.

Certainly Mernissi's argument has merit in the Sudan case. State feminism is often disturbing to men, who may view women as receiving preferential treatment. Early in Nimieri's regime his state apparatuses very actively supported the rise of women—as can be seen from changes in the law. For some time Nimieri had a good reputation with liberal feminists. In fact, Hall and Ismail refer to him as a "dedicated feminist"![39] As I discussed in chapters 3 and 4, Sudan's economic situation had reached crisis proportions by the 1980s. The government was extracting surplus, and inflation was increasing; only the upper middle classes were doing more than surviving. The unemployment rate rose and salaries could not match inflation.[40] Another factor affecting male workers was the pressure that international lending agencies were applying on the Sudanese government to reduce Sudan's overdeveloped civil service. This resulted in even fewer jobs. Men left to find jobs and earn more money. Hall and Ismail remark: "The dearth of trained personnel, especially with the emigration of many Sudanese [men] to the oil-rich Arab States, acts in women's favour and enables them to rise rapidly ... to positions of *great authority.*"[41]

It took awhile for the population to realize that women were taking over jobs vacated by the absent men. At first the gender arrangements were not affected in ways that threatened the prevailing gender ideology, because the out-migration of male labor was of working-class or minor civil-service personnel. But soon the exodus was of intellectuals and middle- to senior-level personnel who left behind jobs, perceived by Islamists and others to be the preserves of men, which were being filled by women.[42]

Islamists interpreted this demographic upheaval as a threat to their class interests and began to agitate. An example of this agitation, which also reveals the NIF's gender ideology and strategy, was the national debate, called by a bloc of conservatives including NIF supporters, about whether too many women were being allowed to study medicine (tables 3 and 4 [see chapter 4] show the dramatic increase in women entering the Faculty of Medicine at the University of Khartoum). But the fact remained that over 80 percent of male medical graduates were leaving for more lucrative positions in the Gulf States. Faced with that reality, political conservatives, underpinned by Ikhwan and later NIF ideology, mainly took the position that women doctors were needed, but should be directed into *appropriate* fields of medicine. The fields deemed inappropriate for women, surgery and obstetrics, were seen as too strenuous for them. Obstetrics, besides, was thought inappropriate for women, as they might be called away from their family duties at any time, day or night. Leaving their homes for work late at night is not considered respectable or safe for women, no matter what the work. Despite objections, women began to invade these two fields—not incidentally the most lucrative in Sudanese medicine. As one woman obstetrician remarked: "They expect us to believe their logic about why these particular fields were singled out as inappropriate for women when we know the underlying question is who will have economic power! They must think we are fools!"[43]

A cause for alarm among middle-class professional women was the number of well-known, impeccably credentialed women doctors deprived of senior positions in certain areas of medicine. The Ministry of Health attempted to channel women into mother-and child-health clinics, into public-health positions (public health is not a powerful, policy-making arena in Sudan), and more significantly, into the least prestigious field, general medicine.[44] NIF women doctors, who have been organizing and recruiting extensively within the field of general medicine, act as apologists for this discriminatory policy.

Also debated in the popular media was the increased numbers of women entering the University of Khartoum's Faculty of Agriculture, long exclusively male. Sudan's system of "boxing" (placement) admits students to faculties based on their performance in the Sudan School Certificate Examinations, which means women were often registered in agriculture whether they requested it or not. Since Sudan is a basically agricultural society, agricultural policy making is probably the most significant in its economy. Allowing women into the field means power sharing. Women, of course, perform a high percentage of agricultural labor but have not held high government positions in agricultural development planning and economics.[45]

Islamists have been clever in their strategies, attempting to offset outside or inside impressions that there has been a wholesale demotion of women from more prestigious jobs. For example, Islamist women professionals have tried to allay the fears of non-Islamist women by presenting themselves as active and successful, not suffering any losses due to the formation of the Islamic state. Furthermore, women in lucrative positions are being replaced in small, nearly imperceptible increments intended to extend over a long time. However, even though women may not have been directly fired from their posts, the Islamist ethos concerning their usefulness has been changing. Women with lucrative jobs are no longer seen by state and individual male Islamists as making a major contribution to society, but are seen as competitors. One Islamist man explained it to me very carefully:

> It is not that we forbid women to work. If she must work, then perhaps it is to the husband or to other male members of her family where we should look for any criticism. We only blame her if she goes to work as a frivolous act and does not behave appropriately in the workplace. For example, she must dress according to the respect she wants. We *want* to respect her.[46]

This is the NIF's modernist approach. Islam and sharia contain provisions for women to work outside the home, but such provisions are conditional: Women should work only if they have no children and if their income is needed by the family. The latter means, of course, that women from working-class families need to work. Islam and sharia make allowances for them. But women's jobs should not threaten the power structure and should be "appropriate"—that is, should be extensions of women's domestic labor and reflect the essence of woman, i.e., should uphold the special qualities of the Muslim woman. Ironically, middle-class and professionally trained women who can afford to have their children properly cared for, or who have women relatives at home to perform child-care duties, are the ones most suited to enter the workforce. These women, who threaten the power structure, are the very ones most under assault. Simone comments on the post-1989 women-and-work issue: "Women have increasingly entered the work force as clerks and secretaries in order to boost household income. After the 1989 coup, many were 'retrenched' for 'religious' reasons, but they have mainly been allowed back as long as they dress in proper Islamic attire."[47] As for professional women, he adds: "[After the 1989 coup] women were removed from many public positions, including the renowned judge Aminah Awad. Certainly the movement contained many contradictory opinions about the role of women in public life."[48]

Conversely, the state can tolerate having in the workforce unskilled and noneducated women (i.e., those who do not threaten the power structure), but these workers, although needing to work, generally cannot afford to have their children cared for.

In a study of Iranian women in the postrevolutionary workforce, Moghadam examined the effectiveness of the initial state rhetoric discouraging women's employment and imposing an ideology of domesticity and found a "discrepancy between ideological prescriptions and economic imperatives."[49] Similar discrepancies appear in the NIF's ideological prescriptions and the society's economic imperatives. Above I presented examples from medicine and agriculture, fields where women are needed by the society but where their behavior is being circumscribed. There is another set of discrepancies. Jobs in the informal economic sector held by low-income women (e.g., vendors of local brew, prostitutes, and some entertainers) are under attack as affronts to Islam.[50] Neighborhoods where prostitutes work have been swept and brothels and beer halls closed. But the jobs themselves have not been eliminated. Does that tell us that the jobs are *needed by society?* These jobs are basically held only by women, yet women are being told by the Islamists that they cannot hold them. Necessary but not appropriate is the labor message given a large number of Sudanese women workers; appropriate but not necessary is a companion message.

Questions about appropriate work for women are at the heart of the movement to authenticate the Islamic revolution. For most of this century nationalists of the mainly rural lower middle classes romanticized "indigenous" values, which included the exaltation of women's domestic role. In the 1990s we can still see these attitudes, focused on now by the urban middle class and clothed very differently. The NIF makes claims about the equality of women and denies discriminatory policies and practices. Gender shifts in the workforce are rationalized as part of the movement to reinvent an authentic Islamic culture. Islamist activists, both men and women, point to the active political role of women in the movement. Even though women are central to the movement in many ways, I still question how emancipatory an NIF regime can be for them. Cultural nationalists, from which most of our contemporary Islamists have sprung, have historically opposed women's emancipation in the Western sense, arguing that it was an imitation of the West that would weaken the basic Islamic unit, the family.

The newly educated urban middle class is now placing Islam at the apex of Sudanese culture, attaching profound importance to the family, and romanticizing women's primary role in the rejection of Western culture. By being positioned within Sudanese culture to represent rejection of Western culture, women become the embodiment of oppositional culture. Women and the family are at the core.

Socialization and the New Family

Sudanese strategies for shaking off the influences of Western education have been taking shape for some time. It is, of course, not enough to "shake off" an influence; something must take its place. Suad Ibrahim Ahmed commented to me that the mechanisms for the creation of an Islamic family and ideal Islamic woman were activated in the 1950s—primarily in the school curriculum. Since independence in 1956, and certainly throughout the 1980s, schools, media, and other apparatuses of state hegemonic processes have been building the spiritual infrastructure.[51]

Ikhwan and NIF involvement in subverting the secular, British-oriented educational system has been considerable. The method for abrogating Western educational influence was to infuse the school system with Ikhwan ideology. The Ikhwan, and later the NIF, concentrated much of their organizing in schools throughout the country—not only in elementary through secondary and vocational schools, but also in nursery schools, some of which were built onto mosques as part of a general plan. Elementary and nursery-school teachers are mostly women, meaning that women have been the primary educators toward an Islamic ethos.

Not surprisingly, the NIF has been very active at the university level as well; incorporating universities into its program was a primary goal. After all, the NIF is an urban-middle-class movement, and university education is important to this class. For some two decades the Ikhwan and then the NIF dominated the student unions of various institutions. According to Abbas, the NIF controlled "student bodies, especially the Khartoum University Student Union, for much of the 1978–84 period."[52] Nimieri "gave the NIF a free hand in higher secondary schools in exchange for a task that the NIF was more than willing to perform: keeping campuses quiet."[53] The NIF regime appointed high-ranking NIF officials to top administrative positions in education, instituted a new requirement that students accepted to the university first serve in the militia of the Popular Defense Forces, and discharged progressive or oppositional university faculty. Further, in line with the cultural hegemony that the NIF was imposing, a government decree mandated Arabic the language of university instruction.[54] While secular universities were being brought under control, Omdurman Islamic University, given full university status in 1975, was being expanded and was receiving more funds.[55]

Changes in the ideology of education were reflected in the writings of professional educationalists even before the NIF came to power. An example is "Education and Family," a 1981 article by liberal feminist Nafissa Ahmed el-Amin, a longtime activist on behalf of women.[56] El-

Amin critiques the "dualism" (Islamic/Western) of the Sudanese school system (a British colonial holdover), explaining that Islamic and Western systems are incongruent and that there is a need for Sudanese to discover "the cultural identity of the community" (89). She argues for *naturalizing* the Sudanese education system and offers ways to do it.

El-Amin points out that family laws are often the only visible sign that a country is Islamic, and that these laws rest on the notion that men and women are the progeny of one soul and are equal and subject to the same moral code. El-Amin asserts that men and women have different roles, and that the woman's role is superior:

> That function is not restricted to the rearing of children or looking after the house, but goes beyond that to encompass all social life in the house and outside. Man, who is commanded to exert his physical energy and earn a living, is not made a master by so doing; he is a servant to woman who is *performing the real work of building the social structure* ... society must pay woman for the great work she performs (92).

The fact that this article was published by a feminist just two years before Nimieri imposed the September Laws (1983) is disturbing because it signals a broad base of support for Islamization, even among liberals. El-Amin, former head of the Union of Sudanese Women (SSU) but not an NIF supporter, was expounding on an idea that was continued and developed by the NIF.

Even earlier, a document published by the Union of Sudanese Women (SSU) outlined strategies for action, a large number of them involving training and education toward an Islamic family and society. Stated strategies were for women and men "to tell women about the values of the religion," to use the media in this work, to deliver talks on Islam and women, to "educate [women] with the values and beliefs of the religion," to use kindergartens so that "children should be brought up in an Islamic way," and to carry out research on such topics as women and Islam and Islamic laws for women. Clearly, educating very young children and *adults* was of prime significance.[57]

By the 1980s the media had begun to play an active role in resocializing the populace toward the creation of a truly Islamic family. A great deal of the popular press material of the mid-1980s declared among the functions of the September Laws to protect the family and to educate toward an Islamic family system.[58] Certainly other media were also working to produce a cultural model of an Islamic family as the core of the new Islamic society.

Omdurman television, the only broadcaster, dates from the 1960s and is owned and run by the state. Television writers and commentators in the immediate postindependence era sought to cultivate the image of the "modern" woman in a new society (see chapter 4), only one of many state propaganda uses of the medium since its inception. During the Nimieri era, disseminating state ideology and educating the public through television came of age. By the mid-1970s and early 1980s, the state intensified its invention of an Islamic Sudanese identity. Watching Sudanese television on my various research visits between 1966 and 1988, I noted an accelerated increase in religious programming, as well as a distinct family-engineering agenda, after 1981.

In my interview with southern Sudanese (Dinka) judge John Wuol Makec, a Christian, the subjects included sharia, religious tolerance, and the media. Justice Makec maintained that Sudan is very diverse, that the ethnic and religious boundaries between groups had always fluctuated, and that the government increasingly stifled that cultural diversity in the media, especially television.

> One could never tell from the media that there are cultures in Sudan other than Muslim and Arab. These other cultures are not reflected on public radio or television. What does this mean? If we just consider religion, for example, other groups also have religious activities. These cultures should also have access to television. Instead, one religion [Islam] dominates television from morning until evening—throughout the day—day after day. This has always been the case, but not to the same extent as we see it today [1988]. In the past we could at least see limited aspects of other cultures. Now it is all closed. Such a situation reflects the attitude of the legal [political] system itself. There is no tolerance in this.[59]

Television in 1988 showed mainly religious imagery. Programming began and ended each day with reading from the Quran. My two research assistants observed television for five hours over two days, Sunday and Monday, noting the subject and content of the programming and how the women were dressed. This was not a "scientific" survey, but it gives one a general idea of the content of Sudanese television programming less than a year before the NIF came to power. Since then, by all reports, religious programming is the norm.

Sunday:

6:00 P.M.   An Iraqi woman was narrating a documentary/travelogue on Baghdad. It was mainly historical, emphasizing religious sites.

6:30   Time for prayer was announced by a woman (dressed in hejab), but a man led the prayers.

6:35 The "Evening News"—a daily program. A boy and girl sang a very famous song from the nationalist period, "Ana Omdurman" ["I Am Omdurman"]. The news was delivered by a man, in Arabic.

7:00 The news in English was usually delivered by three people: two women, one a southerner; the other a mixed Indian-Sudanese. The women were not wearing a tobe or *tarha* (head covering).

7:30 In the interim a woman announced a new program for the next six months. One of the new programs is on "Studies of the Muslim Woman." The woman wore a fashionable sheer tobe and had salon-styled hair.

8:00 An Egyptian soap opera was announced by a woman wearing a fashionable tobe.

The soap opera was an hour long, and no women appeared after 9:00 P.M. The news was presented by men, in Arabic, followed by a session on the Ministry of Commerce, and that program followed by a feature film. My assistants' report on Monday was less complete. The news on Mondays is usually given in French for one-half hour, sometimes by a tobe-wearing woman.

Monday:

5:00 P.M. Programming began, as always, with the reading of the Quran by a man. Reading of the Quran was often a part of a religious program.

6:00 The "Evening News," emphasizing international developments, was alternately presented by a man and a woman (tobe-wearing). Men and women were not shown on the screen at the same time.

6:35 "Studies on the Islamic Woman" was announced by a woman (tobe-wearing). The woman who narrated the program was in a hejab. She talked with two women, one of whom was wearing the hejab; the other in a tobe wrapped "severely." The program discussed how the Islamic Organization helped them with social services in regional migration to Khartoum.[60]

Considering the limited hours—5:00 P.M.–12:00 A.M. daily (except Friday, the holy day, when, to allow a number of prayer programs throughout the day, programming starts at 10:00 A.M.)—religion and the role and responsibility of women within the religion are referred to, directly and indirectly, a great deal.

Cultural hegemonic processes include what is removed as well as what is presented. Media and arts censorship became very common. While I was in Khartoum in 1988, the new Islamist Minister of Information and Culture dismissed five liberal television directors. The television advertising for a popular musical I had attended, *Bit el-Mina Mawsoud*, was removed because the women in the play appeared on stage without tobes. The script and lyrics had already been censored in order to remove words such as "wine."[61]

Public Debates on the Social Construction of Woman—Commentaries on the Islamists, Sharia, and Everyday Life

In the summer of 1988, through formal and informal interviews and by studying the popular press (very active at the time, with over forty newspapers in existence, each representing a particular political position) and attending open meetings of various associations, e.g., the Sudanese Bar Association, I was exposed to the active public debate on the potential impact on various groups if Hasan el-Turabi and Saddig el-Mahdi, under the "Islamic Trend" banner, succeeded in remandating sharia for everyone. The question seldom addressed in the press or among intellectuals was what the formation of an Islamic state with sharia as the legal framework would mean to women in their everyday lives.

Earlier I suggested that examining the meaning of Islam and some of its institutions in women's daily lives was one way to avoid regarding Islam as an omnipotent, monolithic force acting upon an undifferentiated and passive mass of women.

In my 1988 interviews I asked men and women—across religion, class, and political bent—what changes they anticipated in their daily lives should sharia be remandated. Some were experts in their fields, e.g., two judges (one of sharia, the other a Christian southerner), several lawyers, doctors, and religious figures, and a number of educators. I also interviewed noneducated (in the formal sense), nonliterate, and working-class women whose lives had been disrupted by the 1983 September Laws, as well as women who described themselves as "ordinary" (e.g., middle-class "housewives" and government clerks).

Excepting the NIF women elite, activists, and sister travelers, none of the women I talked with who self-identified as religious saw themselves as the embodiment of the culture or as the nexus for legitimizing an authentic culture, or saw Islam as the deus ex machina that would save

Sudan in its time of "crisis." Nor did they speak of sharia in any way that revealed an interest in the intricacies of its jurisprudence or about the formation of the Islamic state. For many of them, Islam was private, personal, and simple. I asked a woman from the Nuba Mountains about her reaction to the imposition of sharia and about her own religious views.[62] She said, "I am just a Muslim. I pray, but I am not as fanatic as the Muslim Brothers ... I'm not a fanatic, but I am religious ... I'm religious because I pray and that's all."[63]

Although most men make a public spectacle of the act, I rarely saw women pray. Except for the NIF women elite, activists and sister travelers, I seldom heard any missionary statements or anything that suggested a desire for jihad. Most women seemed disinterested in the political aspects of religion; some even disapproved of Islam being used for political purposes.

Non-Islamist women's low level of interest and participation in religious "orthodoxy" or the more formal or doctrinal aspects of the religion and in organized religiopolitical activity can be attributed to three factors: (1) women's historical marginality in the orthodox religion; (2) their lack of time and resources to participate; and (3) their indirect (distant) relationship to the state, including state religion.

As in many societies, the everyday religion of women is generally not "orthodox." "Orthodox" in the Sudan setting usually has meant Sufism and membership in a tariqa (see chapter 3), to which women have only been connected through their male relatives. Women engage instead in less organized "heterodox" practices such as tomb visitation, saint worship, river rituals based on Nile superstitions, and other customs associated with women's culture.[64] Like women everywhere, Sudanese confirm their membership in a community by tending the rituals of birth, circumcision, marriage, and death. These rituals take on a "religious" quality, as do most of the superstitions involved in life-cycle ceremonies, and women speak about these customs and rituals as if they were part of the religion.

In addition to historical distance from the heart of orthodox religious practice—symbolized by, though not limited to, attendance at the mosque—women's marginality is the result of lack of time and resources to participate. For one thing, they have to spend a great deal of time managing the "crisis." For some time Greater Khartoum has been in economic disarray (see chapter 3). At no time in Sudanese history have we seen women's economic networks (e.g., rotating credit rings and cooperatives) so important and active. Women of all classes have become urban foragers. Shortages, the black market, the ongoing search for scarce commodities, locating commodity substitutions—all must be dealt with, leaving little time for organized religion or politics.

The relationship of most women to the state (or even to state-sponsored feminism) has been very indirect and distant and usually mediated by brotherhoods or parties, which have attempted to control women's morality without giving them a voice in religious affairs. Islamist women, in contrast, are interested and do take an active role in organized religio-political activities such as missionary work and propaganda, moving to the forefront as the most activist women in Sudan and co-opting the role of the secularist WU as the major voice in debates about women. By the brief (1985–89) "democratic" era, for complex reasons (see chapter 5) the WU had lost a great deal of influence. In its stead, activist voices of the Islamists and conservative wings of old sectarian parties co-opted the debate on women's rights. Organizations such as el-Jabna el-Nisaiyya el-Wataniyya (the National Women's Front, hereafter NWF), the women's wing of the Ikhwan/NIF, and the women's wing of the Umma Party (led by Sara el-Fadl, Saddig el-Mahdi's spouse)—some new, some re-emergent—had one thing in common: they claimed to speak for and to carry out work on behalf of women.

Founded by two disaffected members of the WU as a protest against the WU's decision to demand political rights for women, the NWF has been active since 1964, when political parties and associations again became legal after the fall of the Abboud military dictatorship. Co-opting the liberal, left, and feminist discourses, NWF members claim they are helping working women, fighting sex discrimination in employment, extending maternity leave, offering free transportation for women workers, organizing women in the informal sector. Despite modernist language, the main goal was, as one of my interviewees expressed it in familiar essentialist language, to build an image of the "Ideal Muslim Woman."

In the 1980s an older organization that had previously played but a charity role in women's communities had a political resurgence. Jumaya Raidat el-Nahda, an Ikhwan women's organization, had transformed into a more political female youth wing. El-Bakri et al. describe the organization:

> [It] claims to present a programme using Islamic interpretations of women's status as a basis to improve it. Its activities are largely of a charitable nature, and unlimited financial resources allow it to spend lavishly on these activities. Among its aims is also the support of Muslim Brothers; thus it is widely involved in producing propaganda about other organizations, which it views as atheist, communist, etc.[65]

Much of the work of the Union of Sudanese Women (SSU) in the waning years of Nimieri's regime was clearly directed toward designing

the ideal Islamic woman and family. *A Summary of Working Plans* issued
by the SSU's women's affiliate outlined various "fields" for women's
activism—e.g., family and legal affairs, education, media, health, and
"thought and training." Goals were to educate women about Islam and
"make them aware of their rights according to the Quran and Sunni." So
that "children should be brought up in an Islamic way," kindergartens
were established.[66]

"Islamic welfare work" was a dominant function listed for the
women's organizations registered under the Ministry of Social Welfare.[67]
Virtually all the organizations (about twenty) intended to create nurseries, to work on child-rearing, health and nutrition, to build awareness,
and to "eradicate bad customs." The Association of Sudanese Women
Believers stated their objectives: to develop "the whole of Sudan together
in one group as God wishes; [to] teach correct childrearing, Islamic Studies, and patriotism [and to] make people aware of Islam."[68] The Charity
Union of Worshippers of God purposed "to give importance to Muslim
women [and] encourage Islamic instructions" (5). The Charity Association of Imam el-Mahdi for Women (Ansar tariqa) aimed "[t]o encourage a
modern Islamic society and make a link between individual behavior and
the behavior of a person in Islam and to encourage Mahdist culture under
Islamic culture" (4).

Among the more active moral welfare groups was the Association of
Leading Reformers, which resolved

> to make a family aware of how important family unity is; to direct female
> students in a direction which will make them acceptable in society;
> eradicate evil customs; to discourage women from doing anything
> dubious in public (going around in cars, smoking, etc.); to encourage good
> values and to see that they are practiced by women (4).

This group campaigned against illicit unions by performing *zowag el-
kora* (translated loosely it means "putting all the people in a bowl and
marrying them")—free mass wedding ceremonies for the poor in the
football stadium. Because marriage and wedding expenses had become
prohibitive for most of the poor, this Jumaya Raidat el-Nahda organizing
strategy was effective and spread to other Islamic political parties such as
the Umma Party.[69]

Even Islamic economic institutions have been active in shaping the
ideal Islamic woman and family. The Development Cooperative Islamic
Bank was established in 1983 "to enable women who have training in
home economics to purchase their work requirements; the bank strives to
establish family production societies."[70] Simone summed up the Islamist
work on behalf of women:

Some of the most viable productive units currently in operation are religious communities organized around a Quranic learning center, where up to several hundred men and women are housed and work large plots of communal land ... There are emphases in the current Islamic movement that have significant social potential, such as a focus on group marriages, which defray the exorbitant and often prohibitive costs of dowry, and the provision of short-term free housing, which provides couples time to get to know each other without having to reside with one of their parents. Women are being encouraged to open businesses and produce for the market by the provision of credit schemes ... women were well on their way to outnumbering men at the universities—in large part due to the work of the Islamic movement itself.[71]

At the end of Nimieri's regime, proper social conduct was being monitored not only in the streets, but in various government institutions. Nafissa Ahmed el-Amin, chair of the Union of Sudanese Women (SSU), was barred from chairing a session in Khartoum on "Women's Rights under Islam" at the First International Islamic Conference on the Implementation of Sharia. The Saudi delegation protested that it was not Islamic to permit a woman to chair a meeting where men were present.[72]

The fundamentalist spirit embodied by the NIF is not a rejection of social progress but emanates from an understanding that social progress is all too necessary. Women are viewed as essential players in national development and must involve themselves in politics. Still, *the involvement of women in the movement must be handled with care*. They are expected to spend long hours away from home, to attend meetings at night. Potential conflicts with the family are avoided by presenting the movement in terms they can understand. Who can deny a daughter leaving the house at night ... [for] a meeting ... that will *restore Islamic law to the land?*[73]

Resistance Right and Left

Attempts to remold Sudanese women to fit a Muslim ideal were not totally accepted by either the right or the left. NIF ideology, as interpreted by Hasan el-Turabi, was considered too liberal by many ultraconservatives. In fact, the NIF derives from a moderate foundation. Sayyid Mohamed Rashid Rida, one of the theoreticians who laid the foundation for the Ikhwan, not only supported, but called for the active participation of women in all of society—with notable exceptions.[74]

Fundamentalist groups such as the Ansar el-Sunna are repelled by what they interpret as the NIF's "liberalism." To this group a woman's voice is the same as her breasts showing![75] They and other ultraconservative Muslims rejected many of the NIF's modernist ideas, especially the notion that women, under limited and controlled circumstances, might participate in the workforce and contribute to the building of the umma. One Sudanese man, contemptuous of the idea of women in political and economic life, wrote in *el-Sahafa*, a leading newspaper:

> Those who noisily applauded women's political triumphs and the entry of women into the sanctum of law-making should have been behaving as pall-bearers and mourning the fall of women ... For a woman is the lady of a house, the cradle of a family, the seat of the noblest emotions. [Yet] women are abandoning the most sacred mission known in life to gain an independent personality [and use it] to compete with men in the domains in which men work ... Equality is not necessarily a matter of women doing men's work. She must know that men and women are both one thing that cannot be divided into pieces. Nature has endowed one sex with characteristics that are not found in the other ... For a woman to do a man's work will create a contradiction ... and will ... mark her with the stamp of coarseness ... This threatens our life with collapse.[76]

Extremist Islamist rhetoric was very common in Khartoum when I was there in 1988 and was fiercely different from anything I had heard or read in earlier decades. I was often shocked at the violent nature of the vocabulary and the extreme statements such as removing anyone from the country who was not Muslim or killing all the prostitutes.

Secular and non-Islamist women were very active in the public debates: writing in the newspapers, making public speeches, and generally speaking out. Women of the SCP and WU verbally campaigned against the Islamic Trend. I heard outcries against the formulaic imposition of sharia even from very religious Muslim working-class women, such as one very old Arab who said she would "take to the streets again" if sharia were remandated. The woman from the Nuba Mountains said,

> I greet men with my bare hands [Islamist men and women do not shake hands] ... What they say about the equality of men and women in sharia is false. [Women] are not equal in the eyes of sharia—even if they do the same job their wages are not equal; the way they are viewed is not equal. There is discrimination ... I want absolute equality with men ... I'm doing the same job, so why not? I am doing my job better than any man and I think that, in general, in Sudan women do their jobs better than men.[77]

In the post-Intifada democratic period (1985–89) such talk was deemed safe. It was only talk, after all, in a time when freedom of speech was being protected. Now, however, opposition to the military government, even talk, is considered very dangerous.[78] The regime, very repressive from the start, chilled the free speech that characterized the democratic period. It banned the People's Assembly, trade unions, all political parties and associations, women's organizations, and all non-governmental media. While organized resistance and public oppositional speeches and writings are rare, individual acts of resistance to the cultural hegemony being imposed on women and men alike have been constant.

Some people I spoke to in 1988 expressed doubt (this from SCP supporters as much as from any other group) that anything would change in their everyday lives because of the implementation of sharia. This sentiment was strongly rebuffed in other discourses, e.g., by nurses and workers from Abu Anja Hospital in Omdurman, who expressed defiance against attempts to shape their lives through sharia. A young male doctor at that hospital said the strict application of sharia would negatively alter women's lives, with mandated women's dress at school and work, fewer openings for women in higher education, and different admissions requirements for men and women at various institutions. He was most concerned about interference in private lives. A senior-level male doctor at another hospital, an activist in the banned Doctors' Union, criticized impending segregated schooling, maintaining it would result in inferior resources for women and less effective medical care for women patients. He, along with other male doctors, was concerned that women, just as they were advancing, would be removed from top medical posts.[79]

To lawyer Taha Ibrahim, a leading oppositional voice, enforced sharia would adversely affect the lives of everyone, especially women and non-Muslims. Ibrahim denounced the religious manipulation by Nimieri, Saddig, and Turabi as motivated to save the Islamic banks (a common sentiment expressed throughout my interviews), and his portrayal of women's lack of capacity and legitimacy as legal entities under sharia (echoed by a number of women interviewees) was bleak:

> In sharia there are theoretical and practical rules related to women. Theoretically, *all* the rules concerning women derive from the slavery system ... a man can buy a woman with his money [dower], and she becomes a thing, not a human. With his money he can do anything with this thing. Islam knows two sorts of male/female relationships (1) buying her—as a slave—and he can do anything with her he likes—violate her in any way ... he also owns his own children and can sell them ... and (2) marriage: in Islam the relationship is based solely on buying and selling ... he owns her ... he owns her sexual parts ... to such an extent that, if she is ill and cannot give him what he wants at any time he wants, she cannot collect alimony. So, with the dower *(mahr)* he buys her sexuality.[80]

Republican activist Batoul Mukhtar Mohamed Taha, niece of executed Republican leader Mahmoud Mohamed Taha, in a series of provocative newspaper and magazine articles challenged the right of two NIF women representatives in the People's Assembly to speak for all women. Society needed to value women as human beings, "not as a mere type, the 'Female'"—Taha argued—and the two NIF women accepted traditionalist assumptions that men were the custodians of women, subscribed to the marriage of four women to one man, to the woman's "house of obedience," and to the beating of women, and conceded the exclusive and unilateral right of divorce to men.[81]

A number of other non-Islamist women I interviewed were less confident about their political stances in the Islamic era and seemed to be reassessing themselves in relation to society. These women, clearly affected by the activism of the Islamist women, expressed uncertainties. One liberal married to a communist told me: "There are elements in society—mainly women—who are creating a revolution—and because it is coming from women considered conservative or 'traditional,' it is very confusing to women like me—educated, liberal women."[82]

By 1988 NIF ideology had permeated middle-class urban society. I conducted a group interview with five students at the University of Khartoum; none identified as NIF members or supporters. They or their families were members or supporters of the Democratic Unionist Party (DUP), Umma Party (Ansar), and the secularist Baathist Party.[83] Nonetheless, they expressed views close to the NIF's. One hejab-wearing woman, whose family is DUP, asserted: "I still do believe that woman's place is in the home. She has something more important to do at home—looking after the children, teaching them properly—their norms, their values."[84] A woman student from an Umma family, not wearing a hejab or tobe, commented that women got equal pay in Sudan, but have a problem being hired, mainly because of their poor work record: "My father owns a factory and he has no women at all in the factory. Even when I graduate he is not going to give me a job because ... Women don't work at all [i.e., do not perform well]. The problem is with our sex [i.e., with women]."
A male student, a self-described Sufist from a DUP family, extolled the traditional role of woman: "She has babies and she deals with the three stages of the human being. She has a wide experience. This job cannot be done by a man. It is the most important job, more so than engineers or architects." All five students felt it was the man's *responsibility* to work outside the home, but the woman's *duty* to be at home.

Some Islamist Women

The most visible Islamist woman activist in 1988 was Suad el-Fatih el-Badawi, one of two women representatives in the People's Assembly, both NIF members. She took great effort in her press statements to be forwarding-looking and open, stating, for example, "We [NIF] are not opposed to corrections and changes [in the current sharia laws] so long as [they do not] take us back to the English laws." Moreover,

> I do not believe in separatist roles [for men and women] in the construction of the nation. Men and women complete and perfect each other ... It is an obligation for women [to make] the representation of women *authentic* and *real* ... Those women who have attained a high level of consciousness which is *progressive* and *untainted* by blind imitation of both the East and the West must not be stingy with their intellectual effort ... This era is marked by issues of development which the *enlightened vanguard* must struggle to solve in a fundamental way.[85]

Reading this passage I was struck by the juxtaposition of language from the discourses of both the left and the right. Using terms such as "enlightened," "vanguard," and "progressive" is a co-optation of leftist discourse, whereas "authentic" and "real" women who are "untainted by blind imitation of both the East and the West" is part of the discourse of the right.

Three well-educated, professional, and upper-middle-to-upper-class Islamist women I interviewed more than once, in a group and individually, gave me the fullest explanation of the Ideal Muslim Woman. Nagwa Kamal Farid, who dissociates herself from public politics, was Sudan's first woman sharia judge; Wisel el-Mahdi, wife of Hasan el-Turabi and sister of Saddig el-Mahdi, is a lawyer and an NIF activist; and Hikmat SidAhmed is an Arabic teacher and was the other NIF representative in the government with Suad el-Fatih el-Badawi.

SidAhmed, echoing el-Badawi, stressed the idea that the Muslim woman is responsible for the education of the new generations. In an *el-Sahafa* article and in our interview she referred to a "correct model" for teaching, which should be the same for home, school, and work, but she seemed unable to define it. She expressed concern for women who are gainfully employed. Although she paid lip-service to their role as "partners" in the construction of the nation, she also was patronizing toward them, expressing concern for their moral reputations, for their becoming coarse from hard work, and for whether they would have to neglect their children due to unsatisfactory child care. She asserted that women should be home producing some of the local raw materials to substitute for foreign imports, and that technical training was needed.[86]

SidAhmed[87] believes that only women who *have* to work should work, and only if they have "appropriate" child care (preferably a close relative). When I pressed the issue of what was meant by "appropriate" child care and wondered aloud at its affordability, she told me that intense missionary work was being carried out by NIF women in existing nurseries, and that Islamic child-care institutions would be constructed for working-class women whose abilities to raise their children in an "Islamic way" were seen by the NIF as limited. The state, then, would provide Islamic teachings.

In a one-on-one interview, Judge Nagwa Kamal Farid enumerated women's many rights in sharia. She proclaimed the equality of men and women—save for the "differences in small detail" in their everyday lives. Of going to the mosque she said:

> Men get 27% more benefit from praying at the mosque. Going in a group gives more benefit than if you pray alone ... it is better for women to pray at home and not go to the mosque at all. She has duties at home. But if she prays at home, she has the same benefits as men. Men are compelled to go [i.e., for women it is voluntary].

About polygamy:

> The reason for this [men being allowed to have four wives] is that for some men one wife is not enough. Instead of playing around with other women, he should get married. He should be a good Muslim. This acts as discipline ... some men have a wife at home, but they run around and play with other women. Our culture, Islamic, hates that. If the first wife does not have kids, this gives him a better excuse. But even if there is no excuse, he has the right for another wife—just because we want him to be a good Muslim ... Maybe the first wife was not one he wanted ... maybe his first wife got old, and men do not get old as quickly as women, so he thinks of having another wife. Why not? It is better than having him look around outside of marriage.

As to inheritance inequities, Judge Farid asserted that sharia protects women so that they never have to support themselves:

> If sharia were implemented here in Sudan, life would be very different and people would be much happier. No woman would be needing anything ... People keep asking why in sharia women get less [inheritance] than men. But the situation is that she is not supposed to support herself; that burden falls on men, so they need more inheritance.

In the group interview Judge Farid was even more adamant about women's equality under sharia, their responsibility to be "respectable" at all times, and the reasons for them to remain at home with family duties unless more compelling reasons (e.g., financial need) forced them to enter the workforce.

Sharia permits a woman to go out to work, the group agreed, but Judge Farid added,

> [t]here is one condition in Islam … It says that the first … message for the woman … is to raise her children and take care of her house. So, if she wants to go to work she should be well-dressed, not too much perfume so as not to attract attention … She has to go out respectably … to cover her hair, all of her face and hands should be inside, not too colorful … When a man stands beside her, he should remember work and nothing else.

Some women workers, she continued, set very bad examples—lack of punctuality, too many sick days—"She's there; her effect is there, but she's not there working."

On the subject of work, Wisel el-Mahdi claimed, "There is no program as such of the NIF to take women out of the workforce." Hikmat SidAhmed added that Sudan and the NIF needed women to work. All agreed that conditions must be appropriate and that women need to raise their children first, and should not leave them in the care of "servants."

El-Mahdi maintained that women have a "broad range of options" under Islam and sharia. (Vague, elusive statements such as this were characteristic of many Islamists.) If differences are spelled out in the law, el-Mahdi continued, "It is because women are different by nature." And they should want it that way: "We are *women* after all … I am *not* like a man." She went on to say that a woman can be or do anything.

All three interviewees commented on the *nature of woman* and the inherent differences between men and women, especially respecting sharia's dictate that two women witnesses are required to offset the testimony of one man in criminal proceedings. Hikmat SidAhmed explained:

> We know that women are different from men … women, by their *nature*, sometimes forget. Sometimes they sympathize with somebody. Perhaps he may be a criminal … when one of them [woman witness] forgets, the other will remind her, and if one of them sympathized with the criminal, the other could correct her … I don't think it is a problem for women to find themselves treated differently in the court … because it is *natural* … the entire principle [in sharia] is in accord with the way women are *created*, since women are *naturally empathetic*. (Italics mine.)

Wisel el-Mahdi used a murder trial as an example:

> in a situation of somebody taking a … knife and stabbing another, a woman would be so *excited* that she would not recognize exactly what happened, because after all, a *woman is weaker than a man* and all her

nervous system is made different [from a man's] ... so she may say
something that she believes ... happened, not what she saw happen ...
women are more *sentimental*, because they are the mothers who breed
children ... That is why, in sharia law we guard against the sentimentality
[*aatifiyya*: 'empathy,' 'compassion,' 'sympathy'] of *womankind*. (Italics
mine.)

She clarified: "This does not mean that a woman is less than a man, or
that her *mental capacity* is less than a man. It means that her *disposition* is
different than [a man's]. We are equal in all rights in Islam. (Italics mine.)"

Significantly, the three women attempted to place blame for the
oppression of women on Arab culture, not Islam. They implied that the
oppression of women would end if Arab Sudan were truly Islamic, i.e., an
Islamic state with a legal code fully in place.

The three women contended that men oppress women, that Arabs
have a low opinion of women, and that Arab men try to give a false idea
to women about their rights in sharia. To Judge Farid, "Sudan is still a
man's society ... the man is the boss." Wisel el-Mahdi, remarking on the
ultraconservative Ansar el-Sunna, which opposes any public activity by
women, said, "They are against women ... They think a woman's voice is
like women's breasts showing." She restated it in Arabic, "*Sawt el-mara
awra*—a woman's voice is a private part that must be concealed."

El-Mahdi's comments against male oppression of women, sometimes
"radical feminist" in style and content, were the most defiant of any
Islamist I spoke to.

[Arab men] are against women, and that is why *we are much against them.*
We know our rights; we have learned the Quran and sharia; we know
what sharia gives us ... we think that *women are better human beings* than
they think ... And ... *we are standing up for our sex.* We are working in the
NIF *to praise women* and to make women have a better status and to tell the
world that we are as equal as men and are as efficient as men and we are as
educated as men and we are as good as men and as great as men. (Italics
mine.)

According to el-Mahdi, women in all of the other political parties
"have the same feeling." She exclaimed that, "We are Muslims *by nature*,"
and that the NIF is merely emphasizing the Islamic nature of society
more. She saw no distinction between politics and religion or between
public and private life. Women are active in the NIF because the NIF supports sharia, which grants women equal rights. But even more,

[w]e want Islam to judge [rule] our cases; we want Islam to judge our economical activities; we want Islam to judge our foreign relations. We want

Islam to be practiced in everyday life, not just inside the house ... we don't want it to be only in a corner of the life of the family. We want it to be the *core* of life ... [for] the whole society and the whole Sudan and the whole Muslim world. That is the only difference between the NIF and the [rest of] Sudanese society as it has existed since independence. (Italics mine.)

The comments of SidAhmed, Farid, and el-Mahdi together conveyed an internalized view of women as weak, emotional, and sentimental, their primary duties domestic. Nonetheless, these women are defiant and actively seeking to change the status of women despite male hostility. That they seek this change in an Islamist framework is why I see at least one of them, Wisel el-Mahdi, not as a "feminist," but as a "gender activist."[88]

The three women's devotion and commitment to the ideas of the NIF were striking, as were the militancy and defiance of Wisel el-Mahdi, Suad el-Fatih el-Badawi, and others with whom I spoke. But that is not to overlook the fact that these women are among the elite and, thus, also class-interested.

Women are the nexus of the NIF in a number of ways.[89] They are among the most active and *visible* organizers. The party's strong appeal to women is manifest in the fact that, from my observations of University of Khartoum students in 1981, I estimate that only some 10 percent of women students wore dress approximating the hejab; in 1988, over 50 percent of women university students were so attired.[90]

Women are relied on to socialize the young with Islamic values and to carry out this job at locations such as the nursery schools the NIF has been establishing for a number of years in mosques all over Sudan. This socialization duty is also carried out in the schools, a sphere where the NIF has been effectively organizing since the 1950s and where there are many women teachers. The NIF pointed to this *public* activity of NIF women as its answer to the clichéd charge that should the party come to power it would send women back into the home.

Critics of Islamism claimed that under an NIF regime the NIF's essentialized view of women would relegate women to tasks that were but extensions of their domestic roles. In answer to this criticism, NIF supporters pointed out that the only two women elected to the People's Assembly during the 1985–89 "democratic" era were NIF candidates.[91] Suad el-Fatih el-Badawi and Hikmat SidAhmed, the two politicians, had high public visibility.

The wives of NIF politicians describe themselves as active behind the scenes as well as in public. An activist in her own right, Wisel el-Mahdi—although she has never practiced the legal profession for which she was trained, adheres to the hejab, maintains a house that is segregated into women's and men's quarters, and follows a lifestyle in which she observes strict Islamic dictates about men's and women's roles—considers herself a powerful force "behind" Sudan's most powerful figure, her husband.

Conclusion

Religions, because of their fundamentally moralist, normative, and prescriptive core regarding sexuality, reproduction, the gender division of labor, and the family,[92] are useful to people in power in protecting class interests and in obscuring secular/economic interests. Thus I expect the Ideal Muslim Woman as the representation of the ideal Sudanese woman to saturate the media and the school curricula. However, the program of most religious states is not so straightforward on the issue of women's labor. So far there are indications that the various Islamic groups in Sudan—and at this point the NIF is the most influential and powerful—will *not* affect the numbers of women in working-class or traditional occupations, but will selectively control women's access to private and public power and privilege.

Notes

1. Debates within Middle Eastern studies about the language we use to describe Islamic movements have resulted in the questioning of the terms "fundamentalism" and "sectarianism." Some scholars even see "Islamism" as totalizing and essentializing. My Sudanese interviewees often used the term "New Movement" to steer observers away from fundamentalist assumptions. "Islamism," however, is the term of choice by most interpreters of the new Islamic movements, and is defined here as "political Islam." This generalizing terminology is not to deny the particularism of some of the movements (i.e., it does matter where the movement is taking place), nor is it intended to deny the nationalist, cultural nationalist, and pan-nationalist/pan-Islamic elements within them.

2. Carolyn Fluehr-Lobban comments, "In most Muslim countries ... Islamic law has been relegated to the status of personal law governing family relations and personal affairs between Muslims ... The status of women ... is intimately connected with the Shari'a law of personal status involving ... marriage, divorce, maintenance of women and children, guardianship and custody of children and the inheritance law." *Islamic Law and Society in the Sudan* (London: Frank Cass, 1987), 86. See also John L. Esposito, *Women in Muslim Family Law* (Syracuse: Syracuse University Press, 1982).

3. It should not go unmentioned that the Republicans (formerly the Republican Brothers) are also referred to and refer to themselves as a modernist reform movement within an Islamic framework. Interview with Abdullahi An-Na'im, Faculty of Law, University of Khartoum, 30 July 1988.

4. I argue in the preceding chapter that the SCP was highly effective in its organizing techniques, especially during the 1946–71 period.

5. Louis Brenner, ed., *Muslim Identity and Social Change in Sub-Saharan Africa* (Bloomington: Indiana University Press, 1993), 3.

6. See chapter 1, note 10.

7. Deniz Kandiyoti, "Women, Islam and the State: A Comparative Approach," in *Comparing Muslim Societies: Knowledge and the State in a World Civilization*, ed. Juan R. Cole (Ann Arbor: University of Michigan, 1992), 237; and Sondra Hale, "The Politics of Gender in the Middle East," in *Gender and Anthropology: Critical Reviews for Research and Teaching*, ed. Sandra Morgen (Washington, D.C.: American Anthropological Association, 1989), 247.

8. Sondra Hale, "Gender, Islam, and Politics in Sudan," working paper no. 10, The G.E. von Grunebaum Center for Near Eastern Studies, University of California, Los Angeles, Los Angeles, Cal., 1992, 4.

9. Among those who have critiqued the 1970s' and 1980s' gender-and-Islam scholarship for ahistoricism and a lack of a class perspective are Nikki Keddie, "Problems in the Study of Middle Eastern Women," *International Journal of Middle East Studies* 10 (1979): 225–40; Judith Tucker, "Problems in the Historiography of Women in the Middle East: The Case of Nineteenth Century Egypt," *International Journal of Middle East Studies* 15 (1983): 321–36; and Reza Hammami and Martina Rieker, "Feminist Orientalism and Orientalist Marxism," *New Left Review* 170 (1988): 93–106. The last source calls for the privileging of subaltern voices.

10. I analyze this process in chapter 2 and have written about it as the "New Ethnography" in "The Politics of Gender in the Middle East." A similar reaction in the scholarly literature to the overuse of the concept of "patriarchy" to explain all gender asymmetry caused the perhaps too-hasty abandonment of that concept. The term itself all but dropped out of usage in the early 1980s, but by the late 1980s was revived. See, e.g., Mervat Hatem, "Class and Patriarchy as Competing Paradigms for the Study of Middle Eastern Women," *Comparative Studies in Society and History* 29, no. 4 (1987): 811–18; Hisham Sharabi, *Neopatriarchy: A Theory of Distorted Change in Arab Society* (New York: Oxford University Press, 1988); and Kandiyoti, "Women, Islam and the State."

11. Kandiyoti, "Women, Islam and the State," 238, 243; see also Aziz el-Azmah, "Arab Nationalism and Islamism," *Review of Middle East Studies* 4 (1988): 33–51.

12. In a critique of a paper on the subject of this chapter that I delivered at the University of Khartoum in June 1988, anthropologist Belghis Badri suggested that I would improve my analysis by not necessarily mixing Arab patriarchy with Islam. This suggestion presaged the anti-Arab-male statements made by Islamist women mentioned later in this chapter. Dr. Badri reiterated this distinction between Arab patriarchal customs and Islamic ideas in my 5 July 1988 interview with her at the University of Khartoum.

13. Louis Brenner, "Introduction: Muslim Representations of Unity and Difference in the African Discourse," in Brenner, *Muslim Identity and Social Change in Sub-Saharan Africa*, 8.

14. Ibid., 20. However, I question the use of the term "rationalized," even placed in quotes as Brenner has done.

15. Gabriel Warburg, *Islam, Nationalism and Communism in a Traditional Society: The Case of Sudan* (London: Frank Cass, 1978), 147.

16. Ahmed el-Shahi, *Themes from Northern Sudan* (London: Ithaca, 1986), 33.

17. For a discussion of anti-Sufism in Africa see Brenner, *Muslim Identity and Social Change*. In addition to Brenner's "Muslim Representations," two essays on Sudan (R.S. O'Fahey, "Islamic Hegemonies in the Sudan: Sufism, Mahdism, and Islamism," 21–35; and Awad el-Sid el-Karsani, "Beyond Sufism: The Case of Millennial Islam in Sudan," 135–53) chronicle and analyze the rise of the new anti-Sufi sentiment and activism that culminated in the current Islamist regime.

18. Even the most optimistic observers and experts have become discouraged. The word "crisis" appears in print regularly (e.g., Abdel Ghaffar M. Ahmed and Gunnar M. Sorbo, *Management of the Crisis in the Sudan: Proceedings of the Bergen Forum, 23–24 February, 1989* [Bergen: Centre for Development Studies, University of Bergen, 1989]).

19. This idea is still hypothetical. A number of sources document the "brain drain," but only by my interviewees were the phenomena of labor out-migration and shifts in the gender division of labor linked. Interviews in Khartoum with Dr. Afaf Abu Hasabu, Programme Officer, United Nations Development Programmes, 9 July 1988; Dr. Nahid Toubia, 22 July 1988; and Fawzia Hammour, Women's Studies Coordinator and Bibliographer, Development Studies and Research Centre, University of Khartoum, 16 June 1988.

20. O'Fahey, "Islamic Hegemonies in the Sudan."

21. A Jewish community of some 100 families seemed fairly well integrated into urban society when I was in Khartoum in the early 1960s. Most of my Muslim students mistook the Jewish students around them for Copts. After the 1967 Arab-Israeli war the tolerance began to fade.

22. In "The Legal Status of Muslim Women in the Sudan" (*Journal of Eastern African Research and Development* 15 ([1985]: 125), Dina Shiekh el-Din Osman relates the process whereby the transitional constitution was amended and the Sharia Courts Act of 1967 passed, ending the subordination of sharia courts. For analyses of Sudan's pluralistic legal system, see, e.g., J.N.D. Anderson, "Recent Developments in Shari'a Law in the Sudan," *Sudan Notes* and Records 21 (1950): 82–104; C. D'Olivier Farran, *Matrimonial Laws of the Sudan* (London: Butterworth, 1963); Natalie O. Akolowin, "Islamic and Customary Law in the Sudanese Legal System," in Sudan in Africa, ed. Yusuf Fadl Hasan (Khartoum: Khartoum University Press, 1971), 279–301; and Carolyn Fluehr-Lobban, *Islamic Law and Society in the Sudan* (London: Frank Cass, 1987).

23. The tobe, a full-body wraparound worn by women, may have begun as conservative dress but by the 1970s was worn by many urban women as a form of voluntary national dress (i.e., not a "veil").

24. Osman, "Legal Status." In chapter 4 I explained the accepted use of the term "Permanent Constitution," although the 1973 document was in actuality a transitional one.

25. O'Fahey ("Islamic Hegemonies in Sudan," 32) informs us that the Ikhwan only began to operate effectively as a movement after Turabi returned from his studies abroad in 1962.

26. These events have been well chronicled, especially in a special issue of *The Middle East Journal* 44, no. 4 (1990), on Sudan.

27. On this point see Khalid Duran, "The Centrifugal Forces of Religion in Sudanese Politics," *Orient* 26 (1985): 572–600; John Esposito, *Islam and Politics*, rev. 2d ed. (Syracuse: Syracuse University Press, 1987), 282; and Mansour Khalid, *Nimeiri and the Revolution of Dis-May* (London: KPI, 1985). Khalid, for some years one of Sudan's leading political voices, mercilessly mocks Nimieri's seeming embrace of Islam.

28. Both Duran, "Centrifugal Forces," and John Esposito, "Sudan," in *The Politics of Islamic Revivalism*, ed. Shireen T. Hunter (Bloomington: Indiana University Press, 1988), 194, comment on Nimieri's "mid-life crisis" and the turn to Islam. See also Khalid, *Nimeiri and the Revolution.*

29. Esposito, *Islam and Politics*, 283.

30. Ibid., 284.

31. Khalid, *Nimeiri and the Revolution*, 257.

32. Ibid., 287.

33. The head of the University of Khartoum at the time of these debates was Dr. Omer Beleil, who had written a book that gave a religious rationalization for the fact that he had undergone a kidney transplant operation (performed in the United States), a practice that was frowned on in Sudan as un-Islamic. The book caused a mild sensation, and he was thrust into fame and a position of considerable influence. The book gave legitimacy to the interpretation of medical practice according to Islamic principles. Before Beleil's book it was unfashionable for a person of medicine or science, trained in the Western tradition with its stress on secular logic, to turn to Islam for explanations and directions. Beleil Islamized medicine at Soba Hospital, which he founded, and at the University of Khartoum. His conservative influence on the university was very strong. O.M. Beleil, in conversation with Cliff Osmond, *Two Lives: Death Odyssey of a Transplant Surgeon* (Khartoum: University of Khartoum Press, 1973).

34. See Hasan el-Turabi, "The Islamic State," in *Voices of Resurgent Islam*, ed. John Esposito (New York: Oxford University Press, 1983), 241–51.

35. Sudan Socialist Union, Section for Political and Organizational Affairs, *Summary of Working Plans for the Executive Office of the Union of Sudanese Women* (Khartoum: Sudan Socialist Union, [1980?]), 5.

36. Samira Amin Ahmed, Inaam A. Elmahdi, Belgis Y. Bedri, Samya el-Hadi el-Nagar, and Amna Badri, "Population Problems, Status of Women and Development" (paper presented at the Third National Population Conference, University of Khartoum, Khartoum, 10–14 October 1987), 37–38. Italics mine.

37. Jay Spaulding, *The Heroic Age in Sinnar* (East Lansing: Michigan State University Press, 1985).

38. Fatima Mernissi, "Muslim Women and Fundamentalism," *MERIP Middle East Report* 18, no. 4 (1988): 9.

39. Marjorie Hall and Bakhita Amin Ismail, *Sisters under the Sun: The Story of Sudanese Women* (London: Longman, 1981), 251.

40. For an analysis see Medani M. Ahmed, *The Political Economy of Development in the Sudan* (African Seminar Series No. 29, Institute of African and Asian Studies, University of Khartoum, Khartoum, 1987).

41. Hall and Ismail, *Sisters under the Sun*, 251.

42. See Nur el-Tayib Abdel Gadir, *el-Mara el-Amila fi el-Sudan* (The Working Woman in Sudan) (Khartoum: Department of Labour and Social Security, Division of Research, Information, and Media, 1984); and Samia el-Nagar, "Patterns of Women Participation in the Labour Force in Khartoum" (Ph.D. diss., University of Khartoum, 1985). Information also based on interviews with Abu Hasabu, Toubia, and Hammour, cited above.

43. Interview with anonymous doctor, Khartoum, July 8, 1988.

44. Some of this information is based on an interview with Dr. Nahid Toubia, Khartoum, 22 July 1988. She took part in the debates and is an ex-member of the Council of Surgeons and former head of pediatric surgery, Khartoum Hospital. See note 45 below for the agriculture debate.

45. Part of the agriculture debate was captured in *Sudanow* (October 1979/January 1980). In one issue, for example, Omer el-Farouk Hassan Heiba called for the "banning of girls from agricultural education." See "Letters," *Sudanow* (October 1979).

46. Interview with a male member of the NIF, Khartoum, July 1988.

47. T. Abdou Maliqalim Simone, *In Whose Image? Political Islam and Urban Practices in Sudan* (Chicago: University of Chicago, 1994), 102.

48. Ibid., 66.

49. Valentine Moghadam, "Women, Work, and Ideology in the Islamic Republic," *International Journal of Middle East Studies* 20, no. 3 (1988): 221. In Iran more women were government-employed in the mid-1980s than before the revolution, but overall the women's workforce has remained about the same size. The workforce has undergone a class transformation, however: the numbers and wage rates for working-class women have actually increased but, "Thus far, educated, Western-oriented, upper-middle-class women have borne the brunt of the regime's most retrograde policies" (239).

50. In written responses to my 3 August 1988 interview questions, Batoul Mukhtar Mohamed Taha, Republican activist niece of executed opposition leader Mahmoud Taha, described her 1983 experience of being in prison with a number of these vendors, portraying them as innocent and economically desperate women who had simply been trying to earn a living. See also her critique in the local press, "Today, No Guardian," *Sudanow* (January/February 1987): 13.

51. Suad Ibrahim Ahmed, a left feminist, is one of the leading experts on education in Sudan. Interview in Khartoum Two, 26 July 1988.

52. Ali Abdalla Abbas, "The National Islamic Front and the Politics of Education," *MERIP Middle East Report* 21, no. 5 (September/October 1991): 23.

53. Ibid.

54. Ibid., 24. English had been the language of instruction since the beginning of universities in Sudan, with only certain curricula, e.g., Arabic language, sharia, and some history and literature courses, taught in Arabic at the University of Khartoum.

55. See, e.g., Hashim Banaga el-Rayah, "We Have an Advantage: Omdurman Islamic University," *Sudanow* 9, no. 9 (September 1984): 41. The purpose of an Islamic university, he declares, is "to enrich its students with Islamic studies,

make them able to defend Islam against other secular cultures, and to revive the Islamic heritage."

56. Nafissa Ahmed el-Amin, "Education and Family," in *Change and the Muslim World*, ed. Philip Stoddard, David Cuthell, and Margaret Sullivan (Syracuse: Syracuse University Press, 1981), 87–94.

57. Sudan Socialist Union, *Summary of Working Plans*.

58. See, e.g., an interview with Nimieri's chief justice, Dafalla el-Haj Yousif, just one month after the passing of the September Laws ("Preclude Hadd Sanctions by Doubt," *Sudanow* 8, no. 10 [October 1983]: 10–12).

59. Interview with Justice John Wuol Makec, Sudan Judiciary, in Khartoum, 31 July 1988.

60. Amal Hamza Abdel Rahman and Sunita Pitamber made these observations 17 and 18 July 1988. I have put some of their terminology (e.g., "severely") in quotes to indicate their perspective.

61. Personal communication with Idris Salim el-Hassan, anthropologist, University of Khartoum, 9 July 1988.

62. The Nuba Mountains are in western Sudan, on the invisible "border" between northern and southern Sudan. Many Nuba are Muslims, some are Christians, and others are of various indigenous religions. In the 1990s the Islamist government has been highly repressive and brutal to the Nuba people.

63. I carried out a series of interviews with doctors, nurses, and workers at Abu Anja Hospital in Omdurman, 20 June 1988. Because of the repressiveness of the current regime, I have not named anyone still in the country whose views were not already written or well-known or who said anything self-incriminating against sharia, Islam, or particular political parties.

64. Women also engage in gender-exclusive rituals and ceremonies. I refer to these practices as "women's culture" and include well-known and popular practices such as the zar.

65. Zeinab Bashir el-Bakri, Fahima Zahir (el-Sadaty), Belghis Badri, Tamadur Ahmed Khalid, and Madiha el-Sanusi, "Sudanese Sub-Project: Women in Sudan in the Twentieth Century," in *Women's Movements and Organizations in Historical Perspective: Project Summaries and Evaluation*, ed. Saskia Wieringa (The Hague: Institute of Social Studies, Women and Development Programme, [post-1987]), 182.

66. Sudan Socialist Union, *Summary of Working Plans*, 5.

67. I obtained this typed registry (1985–88?) in July 1988 from the Ministry of Social Welfare in Khartoum.

68. Ministry of Social Welfare, ibid., 5.

69. Some of this information was supplied by my research assistants, Amal Hamza Abdel Rahman and Sunita Pitamber, who watched the mass wedding on television. Ellen Gruenbaum also mentioned the weddings in "The Islamist State and Sudanese Women," *MERIP Middle East Report* 22, no. 6 (1992): 29–32.

70. *Sudanow* (September 1985), 14.

71. Simone, *In Whose Image?* 125.

72. *Sudanow* (November 1984), 12.

73. Simone, *In Whose Image?* Italics mine.

74. H.A. Faris, "Heritage and Ideologies in Contemporary Arab Thought: Contrasting Views of Change and Development," *Journal of Asian and African Studies* 21, no. 2 (1986): 89–103. One exception is, of course, that women cannot head the community/state or lead prayers.

75. This is a paraphrase from Hasan el-Turabi's spouse, Wisel el-Mahdi, mentioned again below. Interview at her home in Greater Khartoum, 12 July 1988.

76. Muawiya Mohamed Ali Tambul, writing in the opinion section of "Woman at the Crossroads," *el-Sahafa* (21 June 1986), 5.

77. Interviews with doctors, nurses, and workers at Abu Anja Hospital carried out 20 June 1988. See footnote above regarding anonymous sources.

78. Ellen Gruenbaum aptly described the atmosphere in "The Islamist State and Sudanese Women."

79. The doctor, a chest specialist, said he was already not being allowed by his women patients to examine them from the neck down and expected matters to worsen. Interview at Doctors Union headquarters, Khartoum, 18 June 1988.

80. Interview, 10 July 1988, Khartoum North.

81. Batoul Mukhtar Mohamed Taha, "TheWomen Deputies/Delegates of the Muslim Brethren and Women's Representation," *el-Sahafa* (16 May 1988), 8. The Republicans (formerly Republican Brothers), liberals working within an Islamic framework for human rights, have spent years in court trying to prove the unconstitutionality of sharia. Written interview with Taha, 3 August 1988.

82. Interview with a woman professional with a Ph.D. in public administration, 14 July 1988, Khartoum.

83. The Democratic Unionist Party is a post-1968 moderate coalition of the People's Democratic Party (which has its base support from the Khatmiyya or Mirghaniyya tariqa) and the secularist National Unionist Party.

84. Quotes from the University of Khartoum students are from a 30 June 1988 group interview.

85. Both quotes are from el Badawi, "The Women Members of the Constituent Assembly," *el-Sahafa* (3 May 1986), 10. Italics mine.

86. Ibid., and from a 12 July 1988 interview (see note 87 below)

87. The following statements by Hikmat SidAhmed or Wisel el-Mahdi are from a 12 July 1988 interview at the home of el-Mahdi and her husband, Hasan el-Turabi. Nagwa Kamal Farid participated in that interview and was also interviewed alone in Khartoum 4 July 1988. Her statements are from both interviews.

88. I borrow this term from Margot Badran, "Gender Activism: Feminists and Islamists in Egypt," in *Identity Politics and Women: Cultural Reassertions and Feminisms in International Perspective*, ed. Valentine Moghadam (Boulder: Westview Press, 1994), 202–27. I am trying to avoid either imposing a "Western" concept (in this case, "feminism") or *excluding* Islamic activists from being considered feminists. That many Islamist women are very active on behalf of women cannot be denied. What name Western scholars give to the activism of Middle Eastern women is a different matter.

89. Duran, among many other sources, expressed surprise at the significance of women in the NIF. "While it is hardly surprising to have educated women seeking their emancipation through communism, outsiders are at first baffled by

the large number of prominent female activists among the ranks of the NIF" ("Centrifugal Forces," 597).

90. Information from a 17 July 1988 interview with University of Khartoum anthropology honors student Mohamed Osman, who had taken a survey of students for his unpublished paper on the social and political aspects of the veil. In 1994 I was informed that there has been a reaction to the hejab and that fewer women students are wearing it, which supports the opinions of those who said it was "just a fashion." However, a decline in Islamic dress may be related to the growing strength of oppositional students in the various university and secondary school unions. I have not confirmed this information.

91. The People's Assembly was abolished by the 1989 military junta. Though Turabi still makes reference to it, it is not an elected body.

92. For the Islamic paradigm as it relates to gender, see Barbara Stowasser, "Religious Ideology, Women, and the Family: The Islamic Paradigm," in *The Islamic Impulse* (London: Croom Helm, 1987), 262–96.

7

Culture and Transformation: Concluding Remarks

Introduction

In these concluding remarks I engage in a fuller discussion of the uses of culture (especially ritual and religion) in identity construction and change. This involves examining (1) the culture-of-resistance, (2) the (re)invention of ethnic identity (or at least the minimization of Arab identity) and the substitution (reinvention) of a pan-Islamic identity for political gain and state formation, (3) the manipulation of culture (especially religion) to marginalize women, (4) the male positioning of women as repositories of culture, intended as a conservative location for women within a revolutionary/radical transformative situation, and (5) women's resistance to and/or subverting of that positioning.

Among the significant themes in recent work on cultural transformation in the Middle East and Africa is the social construction of gender as an aspect of the development of nationalism (particularly identity politics), around which movements and states have been built. Moghadam defines "identity politics" quite simply as "discourses and movements organized around questions of religious, ethnic, and national identity."[1] Throughout this study I have treated the identity politics of Islamism as a subset of nationalism—variably referring to it as "cultural nationalism." Benedict Anderson sees nationalism as an "imagined political community"—imagined as both limited and sovereign. To him, such a social construction refers to an emotive power of mobilization.[2] Anne McClintock argues that "all nationalisms are dependent on powerful constructions of gender differences."[3] Carole Pateman asserts that women's membership in a nation is mediated through their relations with men.[4] Other scholars point out that women are designated to serve movements as biological reproducers, symbols of national difference, producers of cultural narratives, reproducers of boundaries of the nation, and as participants.[5] And I see women as the designated repositories of culture.

My research on strategies for change in potentially revolutionary situations has focused on particular institutions and organizations, especially apparatuses of the state. In general, this work has taken up the important issue in feminist scholarship of the relationship of gender to the state, integrating two areas of my research: the gender ideologies of secular and religious organizations in Sudan. Using northern Muslim ("Arab") Sudanese data, I have focused on the intersections of gender, culture (including Islam), and the state, with emphasis on the gender division of labor inside and outside political organizations. I presented some of the mechanisms that the state and political and religious interest groups have employed to achieve political and cultural hegemony. I explored the techniques of the secular left (the Sudanese Communist Party) and the religious right (the National Islamic Front), the former hiding its religious content in individual members' personal lives, the latter cloaking the political-material issues in religion. The male leaders of the NIF, for example, manipulate Islamic ideology to effect a more "authentic" culture, reiterating in the media, the school curriculum, and in political tracts the centrality of women in the effectuation of this authentication. The SCP also presents women as central: as workers, mothers, and wives; i.e., as supporters of the socialist revolution.[6]

The economic/demographic context for this study is Sudan's depressed economy—a direct legacy of British colonialism—which forced hundreds of thousands of male workers and professionals into labor diaspora, vacating jobs that women began to fill. This upheaval in the conventional gender division of labor created a quiet economic and cultural crisis that the state and, as extensions of the state, certain political and religious parties and interest groups are addressing as much through cultural agendas as through material/economic ones. All political groups—those in power and integrally connected to the state, and those in opposition—aim at stabilizing, controlling, or reshaping the gender division of labor, thereby attempting to control women's material lives. One way to control women's material lives is by controlling or eradicating "women's culture," and/or directing women's participation in Culture.

I have examined identity politics in the construction of the nation by investigating the positioning of women by men to serve the cultural agendas of the SCP and the NIF. Although differing in stated goals and strategies, both organizations, in their attempts to gain political ascendancy, have positioned women as the carriers of the moral banner. In this regard, the SCP proved to be as moralistic as the NIF about how women earned their incomes. In 1988 one of the leading ideologues of the SCP lamented that he wished the SCP had long ago done what the Islamists were doing at that moment: "cleaning out all the prostitutes, shutting down the breweries, and the like."[7]

This statement is an example of how men often refer to women. In fact, activists and scholars, men and women alike, talk as if women are there to be acted upon. Significant to my analysis is an exploration of the concept of *culture-of-resistance* or *struggle-as-culture* and the identity politics that have often resulted from it. Peteet states: "Cultures of resistance are built upon 'expressions of ethnic identity and group solidarity' ... and involve a long process of redefinition of cultural identity ... coupled with a growing awareness of the commonality of exploitative situations and of solidarity in the face of oppression."[8]

Within "women's culture" we can locate resistance as well as active, generative, positive, and forward-looking expressions of transformation. These aspects of "women's culture" exhibit a kind of consciousness some have referred to as *female consciousness*. I offer an extended example below of the contrast between *female* and *feminist consciousness*es by analyzing a ceremony in which women appropriate space and file grievances against the men in their lives. Although I have selected only the zar for the development of my argument, many other examples of women's culture in the form of rituals and ceremonies are also outside the frame of conventional Sudanese culture: saint worship, tomb visitation, and forms of keening. In general, women's behavior with each other when men are not around (as in the courtyard), although not formalized and structured, can be bawdy, lewd, rebellious, and can encourage solidarity against men. These group behaviors are usually semiprivate, spontaneous, and anarchistic, but have sometimes led to demonstrations and small, brief riots. Most Sudanese find these "outbursts" by women embarrassing and prefer to pretend they do not happen, referring to publicly angry and rebellious women as "crazy."

Many of women's potentially liberatory cultural beliefs and practices that unself-consciously encourage solidarity and rebellion are consciously thwarted by both the "conservative" right and the "progressive" left. In contrast, other aspects of culture with dubious emancipatory aspects for women (e.g., "fundamentalist" Islam) are either consciously encouraged, coerced, accepted, rationalized or ignored.

Culture, Gender (Women's) Interests, and the Sudanese Communist Party

I began exploring gender's relation to the party and state with an analysis of the SCP and its relationship to its affiliate, the Women's Union. In chapter 5 I argued that there were many problems with the relationship: the SCP dominated the ideology of the WU, using the women's group as a "Greek chorus" for the revolution; the SCP's "parent" relationship to the WU reproduced the power relationship we find in capitalism; and cadres' stress on training professional revolutionaries in accordance with "theory" rather than experience reinforced the Party's hierarchical and elitist nature.

But there were other problems as well. By relegating Islam and culture to the "private" realm, separate from politics, the SCP failed to address the arenas of women's greatest oppression: their personal and family lives. Because the SCP opted for a strategy of coexistence with Islam,[9] party methods did not call for confronting the personal status laws within sharia, for example. Many cultural practices that did address women's material and psychological needs were deemed "negative" or "backward" and were targeted by the SCP and WU for extinction.

Furthermore, from interviews with women members of the SCP and WU, I ascertained that the "secular" Marxist-Leninist movement in Sudan has for the most part not addressed gender (or women's) interests as distinct from the interests of the peasants or workers, treated as ungendered. Cadres have so far carried out very little analysis of what gender and women's issues are and whether these can or should be differentiated, opting instead for a simple plan for women: to educate them (i.e., impart literacy), to establish sewing and other cooperatives for them, and to recruit them into public life. WU leaders claim that they offer women "political education," but what women are taught all relates to SCP ideology.

As nearly as I could tell from my interviews, WU leadership has given little thought to drawing distinctions between gender issues: between, for example, *strategic* gender interests (e.g., abolition of gender division of labor, alleviation of child-care burdens, political equality, measures against male violence, reproductive freedom) and *practical* gender interests (e.g., domestic provision, such as the livelihood of their families, and public welfare). The former are deduced from an analysis of women's subordination; the latter are inferred from the concrete conditions of women's lives.[10] The gender interests of the WU, undifferentiated from women's interests, remain integrally tied to the interests of the male-dominated SCP. In short, WU leadership, hindered by being under the umbrella of the SCP, has been unable to work out its own gender ideology and requisite strategies.

Instead, WU leaders have put a lot of energy into the eradication of certain "negative customs," particularly the zar. Yet many WU members consider female circumcision even more "negative" and have called for its eradication; however, it never became a major WU and SCP agenda item. Instead, leaders saw the eradication campaign as a Western importation and left the leadership of the fight against clitoridectomy and infibulation to the liberal women of the Babiker Badri Scientific Association for Women Studies (whom they then criticized for squandering international aid on the eradication campaign) and to scholars at Ahfad University for Women.

In part the SCP and, thus, the WU were limited in their vision of what populations and what areas of society could be mobilized for the revolution or utilized as transformative mechanisms, institutions, or organizations. In this next section I suggest some of the arenas not explored by the SCP and WU, ones not noticed or deemed appropriate to be part of the organizing plans for the revolution.

Spheres of Revolutionary Potential

A number of spheres of revolutionary potential exist in all contemporary societies. The one readily acknowledged by students of leftist revolutionary strategy is composed of workers, peasants, students, intelligentsia, and disaffected "minorities" or populations living in unequally developed regions of a country.

The left has either ignored or tried to discredit or eliminate other spheres, usually dismissing them as "counterrevolutionary," "conservative," "reactionary," "atavistic," "retrogressive," "fundamentalist," and the like. One sphere of revolutionary potential eschewed by the left derives from indigenous structures: women's popular culture, networks, and struggles as workers in the home and in the neighborhood workplace—i.e., struggles around where we live, work, and interact with one another. "All classes of women understand what their society's division of labor by sex requires of them: the bedrock of women's consciousness is the need to preserve life."[11] Collective actions to gain rights and to survive may have profound revolutionary consequences in the networks of everyday life (the *practical* gender interests of Molyneux's model). Historically, women have figured prominently in these collective actions, and Sudanese women are no exception. There are, I suggest, at least four areas of women's activity that may have potential for mobilization.[12] Throughout my presentation of those areas of everyday life that I hypothesize have potential for the mobilization of women *as women*, I juxtapose Fatma Ahmed Ibrahim's contrasting strategies or perspectives.[13]

Women Workers.[14] Although they form a large portion of the labor force, Sudanese women are often not enumerated in censuses as "workers" if they are not wage-earners in the formal sector. Many of their economic activities are in cottage industries, performed at or near their residences, in the homes of others, in private, or in a closed neighborhood setting. Women are uncounted or undercounted in the large agrarian and pastoral labor force (where the United Nations claims women play the significant economic role) and in the unpaid labor of social reproduction.

Women are also brewers, street vendors, tailors, basket makers, weavers, potters, needleworkers, domestic servants, midwives, wedding ceremony and ritual specialists and functionaries, spiritual experts, healers, ritual mediators, musician/singers, beauticians, shopkeepers, bartenders, market merchants, prostitutes. Many earn irregular wages, but payment is often in kind or in goods.

Often "outside" the boundaries of Islamic decorum, these women are shunned by the SCP and other parties: organizing, recognizing, or recruiting them would be a cultural risk. No attempt has ever been made to organize or even to *recognize* these workers collectively, to institutionalize their informal networks, or to recruit them into a mass movement except as individuals.

Instead of using already established groups for transformation, the Union and the Party attempted to transform the groups—placing, according to Fatma Ahmed Ibrahim,[15] a high priority on forming new collectives where selected "uneducated" women could learn new trades. For example, instead of organizing, say, street vendors into a cooperative or union, the Union and the Party formed sewing collectives. Once women were recruited into these collectives, Union cadres attempted to educate and then recruit them into the Union.

Ibrahim commented:

> What do women want from their Union? *Although we know what they need,* it is always better to hear it from them—even if they are ignorant. What do they want, for me I think that the first thing is to educate them. If they are not convinced, I cannot do it for them. Our experience tells us this ... If you tell them you are going to teach them [literacy], they won't come. (Italics mine.)

Women Merchants. In Omdurman, a large bazaar city across the Nile from Khartoum, there was a special section of the marketplace totally controlled and regulated by women: the suq el-Niswan (women's market).[16] Many of them lived within walking distance of the market and were at their workplace most of the day, turning it into a temporary residence replete with social and kin networks that functioned as collectives. Often economically autonomous, these women merchants extended their autonomy into the domestic sphere—controlling their own incomes, using their economic power to carve out household decision-making rights, or managing woman-headed households.

The interconnections of kin, residential, and occupational networks gave the collectivity of the women's market the potential for mobilization. But this potential was never realized. One might have thought that these working-class women deserved the attention of a party pledged to serve that class. But the economic rights of the suq el-Niswan women were never enhanced or defended by the WU or the SCP. Party members generally scoffed when I mentioned the women's market; they referred to the women there as old, fat, and lazy—i.e., hardly a revolutionary vanguard. Thus, when in the mid-1980s this "women's market" was removed by Nimieri's government, part of a plan to regularize and modernize the Omdurman marketplace, no organization defended the dislocated women merchants: not the trade unions, the SCP, or the WU. It seems that everyone saw these women merchants as an embarrassment.[17]

Describing why from the time of the Abboud military regime (1958–64) until now the WU opted to struggle in the national political arena and work on *political* over *economic* rights for women, Fatma Ahmed Ibrahim contended:

during Abboud's time we studied all these rights and decided to try to put forward the easiest [to convince people]. We looked at economic rights, but saw them as very difficult. Even the workers [i.e., male unions] were not supporting us in this. The trade union movement was still busy with small demands of the working class [she is not including women in this designation]. *The majority of women are housewives*, so they can't go on strike or do anything to have these rights. We had decided it was better to postpone these economical rights—not to neglect them—but not to make a big fuss about them. (Italics mine.)[18]

The Networks. SCP and WU organizing attempts in the government schools throughout the country—where thousands of female students reside in hostels and where various self-help, consciousness-raising, emotional support networks, and collective economic activities exist—have been feeble; as have been efforts to organize the neighborhood collectives of women, for example the *sanduq* (rotating credit ring) or the *toumeen* (consumer cooperative).

Fatma Ahmed Ibrahim discussed at length the building of cooperatives for women, but did not mention extant neighborhood collectives and the possibility of building onto them or imitating their organizing strategies. Nor did she outline strategies for organizing among female students through their *daily lives* in the hostels, which the NIF has been very successful at.[19] The SCP concentrated only on organizing students *as students*, that is, part of the vanguard. The result is that students are recruited and politicized only through student unions and not where they live and interact socially. The WU could have built onto some of the domestic activities taking place in the hostels.

Women's Culture: The Zar. My last example is the most controversial, because the indigenous form I highlight, the zar, is seen by many

Sudanese as retrogressive, as an example of "negative customs."[20] However, it is from the zar, I hypothesize, that we can learn about the different kinds of organizing that raise the possibility for using indigenous prefigurative political forms upon which to build.[21]

The zar combines myth, autobiography, ritual, and bonding with the "audience"—not unlike 1970s feminist performance art in the United States. It is a gathering of women for the purpose of helping a possessed "sister" rid herself of the demons in her (and in the process make demands upon her husband or other male relatives). It is a semispontaneous occasion for consciousness-raising, self-help, and emotional, collective solidarity. The function of the zar is to help women deal with their repression and oppression within the domestic sphere. Conventionally the zar is categorized as a healing cult that specializes in women's "ailments"; but Pamela Constantinides argues that it is more: "it offers both the promise of cure and ongoing membership of a common interest, multi-ethnic group, and a widely ramifying network of zar-based contacts."[22]

Because of the behavior encouraged in the zar, women have a rare chance to engage in uninhibited entertainment in the form of comedy and drama. The zars I attended were characterized by the protagonists entering trances and being joined by other participants in trancing. The possessed engaged in bawdy or lewd behavior not acceptable in Sudanese society. Zars are often occasions for transvestism, homoeroticism, and gender role-switching. Zar specialists, most commonly older women, direct the ceremonies, but since the 1970s it has not been unusual for male homosexuals to conduct the ritual. Women play male roles—sometimes to imitate, mock, and humiliate the men in their lives and oftentimes to be erotic toward other women. The possessed may insult the men of their family and wear outlandish costumes. These activities may have healing or cathartic benefits, but there are other results:

> There is ample evidence that women actively use this network to form friendship and patron-client relationships, to promote economic transactions, and to offer and gain services. Moreover, once established, the network tends to extend well beyond the actual activities of the cult itself. The reciprocity principle is quite strongly institutionalized in the Northern Sudan.[23]

Supernatural rituals are not usually interpreted as prefigurative political forms, but such an interpretation of the zar opens our minds to the *possibility* of there being a number of extant forms upon which women may draw; some are already institutionalized acts of resistance—which is not to suggest that the revolution can or should start from the zar!—but indigenous forms such as the zar often have potential for spontaneous revolt. In addition, they can be experiential, subjective, collective, egalitarian, and affective. The zar is a mode of mitigating the internalized sexism and subordination of women by forcing men, if only temporarily, through public shaming and other methods, to submit to women's demands. A possessed woman makes these demands through the person officiating at the ritual. Through this medium the woman may demand, e.g., that her husband stop beating her, that their household budget be increased, that they take a family vacation, that he have sex with her more often, or as often as he does with a cowife. Perhaps more importantly, it also represents, if unself-consciously, an attempt at emancipation of self through sexuality. At the very least, the zar raises questions about "women's issues" that are ignored or shunned by all religiopolitical and secular political groups.

When I discussed this issue of the usefulness of the zar in teaching us about ways women organize, Fatma Ahmed Ibrahim, a longtime critic of the custom, asserted:

> The zar is the traditional culture of women and it helps in a way. But the damage is more. It encourages them to go in a direction which will not help them to realize the *real cause* of their suppression, their inequality, and their many difficulties and problems [she continued with a description of the zar, saying that she has done a study of it, indicating the cleverness of the women, the *sheikha*, who direct the ceremonies, and saying that sometimes the women get worse] ... If we encourage the zar, women will never know their problems, the roots, the cause, and they will never struggle against them ... The solidarity to which you refer [she was referring to what I had just said and to my writings about the zar], what kind of solidarity is it? Yes, they come together ... and depart. Meanwhile they come under the influence of an ignorant woman [the *sheikha*] who knows nothing about anything ... it is dangerous ... It removes them from developing a consciousness. (Italics mine.)

The theory-building potential in analyzing female consciousness, the strategies we might glean from such an enduring and successful element of women's culture—such considerations were never given the zar or any other custom defined as "women's."

"Female Consciousness," "Indigenous" and "Traditional" Culture, and Resistance [24]

In her Barcelona case study, Temma Kaplan reveals how closely social welfare and female consciousness are linked. "The capacity of local female networks to transcend the purposes for which they were originally formed appeared as women moved further and further away from their own neighborhoods and into the spaces occupied by the government and commercial groups."[25] I make the same argument here: instead of choruses for the "larger" national struggles, "conservative," nurturing collective gatherings can be transformed into "public" political actions, fueled by self-perceived women's interests.

In chapter 5 I examined contradictions within the SCP. One is in strategies. Although the SCP follows Marxist-Leninist organizational principles, there is a marked departure when dealing with the traditional religio-kinship structures of Muslims. Sudanese women—often segregated and constrained—are, nonetheless, not viewed as "structural weak points" in the traditional order, as were Central Asian Muslim women by the Soviets.[26] Neither Party literature nor my interviews indicate a view that, because of the multiple oppressions of women, the entire structure would be altered if women were mobilized. The Party and Union are not so secularized as to aim at obliterating, through administrative assault or revolutionary legalism, the social fabric on which the society is built. Besides, in all likelihood, well-informed, educated, and Russian-oriented communist leaders such as Abdel Khaliq Mahjub would have known of the resistance by Muslims to Soviet social engineering.

The SCP and the leaders of the WU strive to coexist with the traditional order, rationalizing that the Sudanese revolution will be based upon the concrete conditions of the society. At a very fundamental level, therefore, we cannot see a great deal of difference between the gender ideologies of the "Sudanese state" and of the SCP (and other various parties), because "concrete conditions" get translated into not tampering with Islam and other aspects of traditional culture.[27] Left untouched are the gender division of labor (especially domestic), personal status laws, and issues of sexuality.

Socialist revolutionary strategies for dealing with indigenous, antecedent, or traditional culture (conflated here as "traditional") have differed.[28] The Soviets had aimed at *undermining* traditional structures; the SCP, at *coexisting* with them. Feminist socialist principles suggest instead the possible efficacy of *building onto* extant traditional forms or the necessity of the movement *emanating from* them.

Following are some concluding comments on another potential sphere of revolutionary activity: *Islamism*. One certainly cannot deny that the post-1989 Islamists in Sudan—who have developed an Islamic state, with an Islamic constitution, a religiolegal framework (sharia) and economic institutions (e.g., Islamic banks), and have revolutionized various other state apparatuses (e.g., the educational system)—have created a "revolution."

Islam, the Sudanese Communist Party, and the National Islamic Front

In this section, at the risk of privileging Islam, I argue that Islamism (i.e., political Islam) is an area of revolutionary potential that the SCP ignored in its complacent coexistence strategy. I argue that a more active party vis-à-vis Islam and rising Islamism might have stemmed the revolutionary potential, or at least learned from it. But the SCP would have had to offer something to take the place of Islam, and I am suggesting the need to build onto populist and indigenous institutions.

The SCP, Culture, and the Control of Women

Most imported leftist parties of the Third World have at least paid lip service to the need to adapt to local conditions and traditions.[29] All too often, however, and as evidence of left cultural imperialism, indigenous culture (in the form of local customs) is violated or ignored. Indigenous, antecedent, and traditional customs, however, are universally observed or even *pre*served when they relate to the maintenance of the gender ideology, as in the role of women in Islamic societies that strictly apply sharia. In analyzing Islam and gender relations in revolutionary South Yemen, Molyneux maintains:

> The impact of religious orthodoxy on the juridical realm, in particular on Family Laws ... is a factor of the utmost significance: it is precisely within these religious codes that the position of women is defined as legally and socially subordinate to that of men. The religious influence and derivation of the codes has allowed the subordinate status of women to be legitimatized in terms of divine inspiration and doctrinal orthodoxy and has made it especially difficult to bring about reforms in this area. Yet given the marked gender inequality in many Muslim societies and the role of Islamic orthodoxy in sustaining it, *no government that was genuinely committed to the emancipation of women could leave the Shariah and urf (customary) codes intact.*[30]

Because the SCP and the WU were unwilling to risk losing the popular support they did have, they did very little tampering with sharia or with religious traditions as they affect women. The SCP's tendency has always been to relegate gender conflicts to the realm of culture, which cadres treat as either abstract or personal, but clearly separate from the material base and not to be tampered with.

Cadres stubbornly insisted on working within a particular kind of Islamic framework that divides the genders in many spheres of life. They were, and are, concerned that such issues as the eradication of female circumcision (which is *not* Islamic, but has become closely associated with Muslim traditionalism) would create a backlash and impede the revolution.[31]

Fatma Ahmed Ibrahim, who identifies herself as an opponent of female circumcision, asserts:

> The WU is trying to tell women that circumcision is not the cause of a problem, but is the result of a situation ... The cure is not to spend lots of money [in reference to international agencies] to convince women to stop ... The solution is to *educate* women, raise their consciousness ... so they will not feel in need to circumcise to keep respect ... there are more than 80% of Sudanese women who are ignorant and don't know what their problems are ... Which is the urgent problem to be solved—circumcision or ignorance? When you look at the percentage of women who are dying from circumcision or in childbirth, it is a very small percentage. But when you look at the percentage of women dying of hunger, it is very great. Which is more important? (Italics mine.)[32]

With regard to Islam, Ibrahim describes herself as very religious and takes pains to appear respectable and traditional in her dress on television (see chapter 5). She related an exchange she had with Abdel Khaliq Mahjub, which cleared the way for her to join the SCP:

> I told Abdel Khaliq Mahjub that I was interested in joining the Party but that I had been brought up in a religious way. For me, joining the Party would mean a contradiction. He said, "Marxism has its opinion, but as the SCP we are different. Marxism is not a belief; it is not a religion. It is a scientific ideology. We have to take from it what is suitable for us. We are not compelled to accept Marxism in its sum total ... *Politics have nothing to do with religion.* We believe that religion should be kept away from ... the Party. It is a *private* thing." (Italics mine.)

"*'Politics have nothing to do with religion* ... It is a *private* thing.'" As an addendum, Ibrahim maintained, "There is no contradiction between our struggle and the real aims of Islam." In 1969 the WU opted not to work on the reform of family laws because, she said, "They were too closely tied to religion." She said that the tactic of embracing/coexisting with Islam, which the WU decided to employ in the 1950s, was a stroke of genius and saved the organization:

> The Ikhwan opposed [women's rights in 1954] and attacked us, and the Muslim Sisters resigned from our organization ... Not only this group attacked us, but all the religious leaders, and they used the mosques to attack us ... saying that the Union was against Islam, against Sudanese traditions and customs, and should be stopped. So, we decided that the only

way to combat this was to study Islam ... and I began to discover many things. *I discovered that Islam is a progressive religion* ... The Union began to defend these ideas, through the Quran, the hadith ... We wrote in the newspapers ... that Islam is not against political rights for women ... We saw this as the only way to defeat them [the opposing groups], and we suc-ceeded in this ... We began fighting these reactionaries and those who were using Islam *by using Islam itself.* (Italics mine.)

This strategy of coexistence is significant because, as we know very well, "Much of the oppression of women takes place 'in private,' in areas of life considered 'personal.' The causes of that oppression might be social and economic, but these causes could only be revealed and confronted when women challenged the assumptions of their personal life."[33] Because the SCP has seen politics as separate from everyday life (as did the Soviets, the Cubans, and other revolutionaries), and culture, including religion, as separate from material conditions and political life, the women of the Party and the Union have led separate lives from the men. While the Party *theory* stresses production, the "real" world, and the economic base, the *practice* of its men and women members polarizes the private and public, reproduction and production, the personal and political.

The NIF, Culture, and the Control of Women

Cultural practices are key to women's oppression and emancipation. My interest in the uses and abuses of culture by political groups grew into an analysis of the Islamist strategy in Sudan. Islamists have been attempt-ing to develop a culture-of-resistance based on an authentic Islam. Women are expected to be the repositories of the culture and the Greek chorus of the revolution. NIF women are far more than the "Greek chorus" of the Islamic revolution; they have been among the central orga-nizers and socializers.

In 1988 I interviewed many leading women of the NIF. Heeding Marnia Lazreg, I did not assume oppression when I began my inter-views,[34] and I found that these women were not only learning and inter-preting Islam for themselves and other women, but were also militant, independent in spirit, and effective organizers in the movement—con-trary to popular and scholarly notions about the oppression of women under Islam and Islamic movements. NIF women are sophisticated about the goals of the Islamist movement and their position within it, and com-mitted activists on behalf of other women. My findings about NIF women organizers challenged ideas about oppression and "false consciousness," as well as the Euroamerican feminist theoretical position that Islam can explain the condition of women.

In northern Sudan some Islamist women are using Islam to construct their own identities and improve their situations. I argue, however, that there are limits on women's autonomy and independence now that the Islamic state is achieving hegemony, just as there are limits for women in identity politics in general. Moghadam asserts: "Although the quest for identity and the focus on culture is meant to differentiate one group from another, 'culture,' like 'nation,' occludes class, gender, generational, and other significant differences."[35]

In deconstructing the gender ideology of the new Islamist movement, it is clear that class interest is an underlying force. Islamism in northern Sudan, like Islamist movements elsewhere, is the product of a newly urbanized, educated middle-class; yet the NIF's appeal to traditional culture and to "native" values—the core of its ideology and the basis for its success among women—has resulted in beckoning women to serve the revolution from traditional service positions.

I analyzed a discrepancy between NIF ideological prescriptions (including the emphasis on the importance of women's domestic role) and economic and political imperatives (i.e., that women *must* enter the formal workforce) by using examples from the fields of medicine and agriculture and the debates in Khartoum about the preference for women's employment in "appropriate" fields. The entrance of women into the faculty of medicine (the most prestigious and where women were beginning to outnumber men) is being curtailed. Women doctors are being channeled into family-health clinics, general medicine, and into fields considered less taxing, less demanding, less public—and less lucrative. When the higher echelons of agriculture—the preserve of men at the university and in government positions—was being invaded by women, the NIF and its supporters effectively derailed that trend.

A similar control of labor through cultural or moral attitudes holds for women in low-income positions. We have indications that, contrary to conventional scholarship on the topic of "fundamentalists" and women's labor force participation, Islamists are not yet assaulting the numbers of women in working-class or traditionally female occupations—with the exception of those deemed disreputable, such as brewers and prostitutes (see chapter 6).

The NIF has been seeking tight control over women's access to power and privilege. This has applied to both private and public labor. Its moralizing, however, results in attempts to define women's occupations, thus controlling the material conditions of their lives regardless of their class.

Attempting to control women's morals and thus the material conditions of their lives is an age-old male pastime, but the process takes on more meaning in situations where men deem it essential, for the purposes of identity politics, for women to uphold the moral fabric of the society, as is the case in contemporary Sudan. Papanek, making the necessary link between identity politics and women, forwards the notion that "certain ideals of womanhood are propagated as indispensable to the attainment of an ideal society."[36] She presents evidence of "how and why certain institutions exercise control specifically over women's sexual and reproductive behavior in connection with group identity."[37] It is to the issue of the development of the "ideal" society based on an "authentic" culture to which we now turn.

The Invention of an "Authentic" Culture

I have said that the development of an "authentic" culture is central to the Islamist agenda, but I have only spelled out a few of the primary methods Islamists are using to effect cultural transformation. In this section I link Islamist moralism, the disaggregation of "Arab/Muslim," patriarchy and women's discontents, essentialism, and resistance to the gender dynamic surrounding the invention of an "authentic" culture.

Women as Moral Guardians and Morally Guarded

As we have seen, one way men in power create and maintain hegemony is to try to position women to serve the culture as the carriers not only of culture, but of morality as well. Yet women are seen as inherently immoral. Virginia Sapiro states:

> Regarding women as the carriers of both culture and morality but, at the same time, as having an essentially weaker grasp than men on culture and morality may appear a logical contradiction at first blush, but it is no cultural contradiction. It is a cornerstone of the views of women found in diverse pillars of cultural explanation, in Islamic, Christian, and Jewish theology, in Aristotle, and in Freud.[38]

I have argued that, in Sudan, women are positioned by men as the carriers of morality at the same time that they are guided (e.g., through religious teachings and media) and guarded (by moral guards). Such a hypothesis suggests that, to some extent, women are acted upon. Islamist women are acted upon; but they are also actors. They are creating their own identity, apart from an Arab culture that many of them see as patriarchal and oppressive. In this sense, if women are collaborating in their placement by men as the nexus and embodiment of the culture, I posit that it is only because they may see themselves as gaining from the situation. This may hold only for middle- to upper-class women, however.

Arab/Muslim

Northern Sudan's cultural identity has always been arguable (see chapter 3). The categories "Arab," "Afro-Arab," "Nubian," "African," and the like have been debated—as self-labels, as imposed categories, and as putative claims—for some time within and without twentieth-century Sudan.

To the outside world, especially the Arab areas, Sudanese have been seen as "African." Throughout the twentieth century, Sudanese have been sensitive about being thought of as marginal to pan-Arab culture and even to Islam. To make matters worse, British colonials had disallowed the peaceful spread of Islam, resulting in a very divided, *Arab-* instead of *Muslim*-oriented, Sudan.

For complex gender- and race-related reasons, new distinctions are being drawn between "Arab" and "Muslim" within the current Islamist movement. In attempting to separate the concepts of "Arab" and "Muslim," Sudanese are engaging in strategies of deconstruction, disentanglement, and dissociation. Hasan el-Turabi has made public statements distinguishing between these two identity concepts. Also, a number of the Islamist women that I interviewed for this research were adamant about making the distinction.

Kandiyoti, among others, advises against conflating cultural nationalism and Islam and Arab patriarchy and Islam ("In the Arab world ... cultural nationalism and Islam now appear as practically interchangeable terms") and quoted Mernissi's notion that in Morocco "'opting for "Arabness" was convenient in terms of finding a place and identity in the Arab world.'"[39] Kandiyoti also cautions, "Whatever the differing emphases of nationalist movements with respect to the links between Arabism and Islam, the former at the very least co-opted the latter."[40]

The Islamist women I talked with all agreed that men oppress women, and their statements usually conflated *men* and *Arabs*. Arabs (meaning "Arab men") have a low opinion of women and cannot be trusted, these women maintained. Some of them made abusive statements about Sudanese Arab men, asserting that Sudanese Arab men's ideas are "like the ideas of the Arabs before Islam [i.e., *jaahiliin*, ignorant]." One woman laid the blame for nearly everything at the feet of Arab men, ending with, "We are much against them."[41] The Islamist men I interviewed also seemed to make a distinction between "Arab" and "Muslim," but there was a certain militancy in the posture of the Islamist women, especially in their insistence that Arab customs and patriarchy (and Arab men)—not Islam—have oppressed them.

Even Hasan el-Turabi has tried to distance himself from the Arab past with regard to women and other issues. That seemed to be his goal in 1993 when he made a number of public statements about women. E.g., "The Islamic movement in Sudan chose not to allow women's liberation to be brought about by Westernized liberal elites or communists or whatever. It took the lead itself ... it evoked *religion against custom*."[42]

I interpreted the above statement to mean that, rather than have women's liberation led by Westerners, the Islamists would deconstruct their own patriarchal customs. Further appealing to women, appeasing Muslim feminist critics, and distancing himself from the (Arab) past, Turabi stated, "Segregation is definitely not part of Islam ... the *hareem* quarters, this is a development which was totally unknown in the model of Islam, or in the text of Islam; it is unjustified" (36).

The current regime's strategy to decenter Arab identity is guided by three main ideas: (1) Foregrounding Arab identity hinders north-south integration under Islam (e.g., it is easier to "become" a Muslim than an Arab, and the history of Arab slaving in the south can be minimized). (2) Women are more willing to see an "authentic" Islam as potentially liberating from certain patriarchal Arab customs. (3) Being accepted by the outside world, especially the Arab/Middle Eastern, as integral to the "Middle East" is facilitated by Sudanese becoming participants, even leaders, in the region's *Islamic* movements, whereas being embraced as "authentically Arab" was always problematic. Regarding Sudan and Arab culture, Turabi said: "the North is not Arab ... They speak Arabic, but they are not Arabs; they are part of East African people ... In fact, the Sudanese are Arab in culture. Some of them are probably Arab in descent also" (66–67). And, "The Sudan, on the whole, is probably leaning now more to Africa than to the Arab world" (68).

To serve their cause, the Islamists present an image of the NIF-led movement as populist and nonelitist. Their leaders argue that the NIF program serves women, the working-class, peasants, and marginalized ethnic groups. Turabi maintains that Sudan's Islamic movement is very democratic: "these movements are essentially grassroots movements; they are populist movements ... highly democratic" (18).[43] He presents his version of the history of Islamic movements in Sudan, making a case for the current regime by seeming to distance it and the NIF from prior Islamic/Arab movements. "The Muslim Brotherhood ... was the typical elitist movement ... The ideal, of course, is democratic Islam. Islam shuns absolute government, absolute authority, dynastic authority, individual authority" (19).

A poor country like Sudan walks a tightrope, needing Arab money whilst also needing to appease its own diverse population's gender, race, and ethnic demands. The irony in Middle Eastern studies, especially as it relates to gender arrangements, is that so many of us have privileged Islam, whereas so many Muslims have privileged Arab culture.

Women and Arab Patriarchy

In chapter 6 I quoted Judge Nagwa Kamal Farid: "Sudan is still a man's society ... Any man in the street can be your boss." The fact that

Arab culture is rife with patriarchal institutions sets the stage for the Islamist reevaluation of this national identity in their forging of a new society based on an "authentic" culture. Fluehr-Lobban, in constructing a theory of Arab-Muslim women as activists, proposes: "Arab society was more patriarchal than the religion of Islam, which introduced a number of reforms improving women's status. Thus, Arab-Islamic society needs to be regarded as a modified form of patriarchy."[44] Modified or not, treating women as the embodiment of culture is a primary mechanism of control used by patriarchs. Kandiyoti is succinct in her description of patriarchy as it relates to Islam:

> a serious weakness in our current analyses stems from a conflation of Islam, as ideology and practice, with patriarchy ... many of the uniformities we observe with respect to gender may be due to the workings of a generic system of male domination that I [have] characterized as "classic patriarchy" ... distinct systems of male domination, evident in the operations of different kinship systems, exercise an influence that inflects and modifies the actual practice of Islam as well as ideological constructions of what may be regarded as properly "Islamic."[45]

Wisel el-Mahdi was confident and satisfied when I interviewed her in 1988 that the Islamists would come to power in Sudan, that they would ban the Permanent Constitution, that sharia would be enforced, and that the plight of women would improve immensely.[46] After all, she reasoned, it was Arab customs and traditions, not Islam, that had been oppressing women.

Other Islamist women expressed similar views, all of them convinced that under sharia women would have a higher status, be more respected, and at the same time, be able to maintain their differences from men, e.g., their emotionality, their sentimental nature, and their "femininity." Islamist women operated under the assumption that women could have it both ways. So long as they dressed respectably and acted appropriately, they could work and have a career, and yet be dutiful wives and mothers, the cruxes of the family.[47]

Essentialism, Resistance, and the Modern(ist) Woman

Sudanese society has experienced many shifts in *essentialist* views of women and men and their relationships to each other. A Sudanese notion of "woman" as an autonomous entity, a female being, separable from men and from family, has no reference in preindependence Sudan. British colonial discourse introduced the concept of Woman as other than Man (a central idea in modernist discourse), which generated gender-identity politics. *Mother* emerged as an essentialized category, and *Motherhood*, a glorified state. Later, the colonial state and its successors constructed (through radio and then television) the *Working Woman*, a modern role for the modernizing/modernist Sudan.

Islamists today are attempting to abrogate some elements of colonial and postcolonial state gender ideologies while retaining others. While they interpret the relationship of men and women in sharia as complementary, because of the state's need to control the gender division of labor and to repudiate Western values and deny Western imported goods, the representation of woman as a separate entity is now conflated into woman/family and sometimes woman/family/umma. These parallel representations of women may be contradictory: The modern woman as the embodiment of the Islamic nation (bearing and rearing children, tending the hearth) must also carry out the tasks of nation-building (earning wages, holding office, driving a car, getting an education). Thus, she becomes the *modern Islamic woman*, in line with NIF ideology. But these are not always roles of complementarity.

Any discussion of moral guards, coercion, and state apparatuses to enforce hegemony raises the issue of resistance. The obverse of the rule to never assume oppression is to always assume resistance. From the start, the Islamist regime has been very repressive, banning the People's Assembly, trade unions, political parties and associations, women's organizations, all nongovernment media, and the like. Government opposition is considered dangerous.[48] Organized resistance is rare, but individual resistance to these attempts to remold Sudanese women into a Muslim ideal is considerable.

I interviewed a longtime communist activist critical of the WU. Her dissident voice, now relatively quiet for reasons of health and personal safety, railed against the insidious gender resocialization obvious by the 1950s in the national secondary school curriculum. An educator active in school reform, she pointed out that there was Ikhwan influence on school curricula even before independence. The spirit of Islamism existed much earlier than the period we associate with its rise. But because what was being promulgated was mostly directed at women, not much notice was taken, even by the SCP. In a society where males and females attend segregated schools until university, manipulating the curriculum to direct women toward Islamic ideals is relatively easy. Other feminist interviewees expressed disappointment that there had been so little resistance to the "take-over" of the schools by the Islamists. Even in the 1980s when it was more obvious what was happening, very little organized opposition emerged.

However, the most striking fact of the mid-1980s was that those opposed to the imposition of sharia and the molding of the Ideal Muslim Woman offered no alternative, no oppositional construction of the contemporary Sudanese woman, except in the vague liberal terms of the WU (e.g., "women must be educated"). With the image(s) of contemporary Sudanese women in the hands of the Islamists, there was no longer an opportunity for an image of a modern socialist woman to emerge.

Image invention was, therefore, co-opted by politically active Islamist women such as Suad el-Fatih el-Badawi, quoted in chapter 6: "It was an obligation for women [to make] the representation of women *authentic* and *real.*"[49] The image of the Muslim woman represented on television and projected by the people I interviewed is modern, forward-looking, dutiful, and enlightened—yet moral and authentic.

But there was a dilemma: How to reconcile the image of devout and dutiful Muslims with the oppression of women by men through various patriarchal customs. A strategy had to be worked out whereby Islam could be the method for rescuing women from oppression. To do that, it would be more effective to demonize some aspect of the population: not necessarily *men*, but a *category* of men.[50]

Women receive a great deal of praise and attention for the work of socializing the young with Islamic values. The resuscitation of the complementarity approach to gender increases the NIF state's labor-pool flexibility, i.e., its ability to move women in and out of the workforce and in and out of appropriate and inappropriate jobs in the guise of helpmates, but also in the image of women as creators of life and nurturers of the society. Women also receive a great deal of praise and attention for the work of building a new society along Islamic lines, i.e., being modern women. The NIF can point to its women's public activity to answer the clichéd charge that the NIF will send women back into the home.

Having "moral" women staff the household economy gives men the freedom of "biculturality," i.e., they can dirty their hands in a modern society with its banks, insurance companies, political parties, and government agencies, then return to a "stable" household that is authentic, moral, and legitimate.

Joan Smith places the above dual image of women (complementary to men and autonomous modern(ist) woman) and the "biculturality" of men within the world-economy:

> the subordination of women in colonized situations where we now find new movements for cultural, religious and national identity was in fact the product of a very modern division of labor on a world-scale. Women producers were subordinated in household production that itself was a product of the world-economy. The upshot is that the so-called traditional patriarchal relationships that are said to characterize the household are in point-of-fact the very modern creations of the world-economy; subject to its dictates and interpreted by state policy.[51]

Women are not prohibited from working for wages outside the household economy, but the jobs they have are circumscribed; they should be "appropriate" jobs, extensions of their domestic labor (see chapter 6). Right now these appropriate roles are monitored by Islamic guards. The Islamists believe that women themselves will adopt appropriate roles without persuasion or coercion once they fully realize and understand their rights and duties in Islam, i.e., once they have a raised consciousness about the correct role of women in Islamic societies.

Hasan el-Turabi claims that Islam is very democratic about women in public life. He maintains:

> With respect to the status of women generally in [Sudanese] society, we don't have any more problems ... In the Islamic movement, I would say that women have played a more important role of late than men ... Of course, I don't claim that women have achieved parity, for example, in business ... There is a question whether women will ever be present in equal numbers in all domains of public life ... but there is no bar to women anywhere, and there is no complex about women being present anywhere.[52]

The Problematics of Emancipation

What does northern Sudanese women's studies contribute to our understanding of women's emancipation? Has this exploration of religion, party, and state in the Sudanese context given us information about gender—or vice versa? Considering that anthropologists, in particular, have devoted volumes to defining, describing, and analyzing "culture," can such an elusive concept yield fresh insights into the identity politics we see at work in Sudan? Does religion, as part of culture, contain special qualities that entice those in power to use it as an instrument for domination? Or is it just one more institution of everyday life and no more manipulatable than the others? In the uses of culture to forward a movement based on identity politics, are women actors, acted upon, or both? Can women be the progenitors of their own revolution/emancipation/liberation? These are among the questions I have tried to answer.

I have presented some of the problematics of the role of culture in the emancipation or oppression of women in general and Sudanese women in particular. Oftentimes conflating state and party, I have presented various maneuverings by those in control of the party and/or the state (and its apparatuses) to position women within the culture.[53]

Above I mentioned various uses of culture in revolutionary situations. In Muslim Soviet Central Asia, the Communist Party, in an attempt to consolidate the revolution of 1919, aimed at undermining indigenous structures in order to emancipate women. The Sudanese Communist Party has aimed at coexisting with most (but not all) traditional structures, especially Islam.[54] Islamists in Sudan and elsewhere in North Africa and the Middle East are manipulating Islamic culture and ideology to put women at the forefront and at the service of the Islamic revolution. Feminist strategy, by contrast, suggests building onto extant indigenous forms ("women's culture"). The above are four theories of change. Based on my observations of the endurance and effectiveness of indigenous women's culture in Sudan, I opt for using an emancipatory theory of culture that centers women and gives them agency to generate a culture-of-resistance.

Using subtle forms of defiance and resistance, Sudanese women, I have found, consciously and unconsciously can (and do) reshape men's expectations. Like feminist theorists Temma Kaplan (women in anarchist Spain), Maxine Molyneux (Sandinista women in Nicaragua), and Julie Peteet (Palestinian women in Lebanon), I have explored women's consciousness(es) about their struggles in terms of a contrast between "feminist consciousness" (self-conscious goals to act on behalf of women, *as women*) and "female consciousness" (unself-conscious and more spontaneous actions *by women* for the community and their families).[55] I have historically contextualized this women-centered analysis within a political-economic framework. As a consequence, women—SCP, NIF, and zar activists alike—and not Islam, etc.—become the subjects of the analysis.

It is rewarding to consider the potential for a mass movement based on the principles and organizational characteristics implicit in some traditional forms, just as some students of Middle Eastern and North African societies are suggesting we look at Islamic movements with fresh eyes, seeing in them some potential for "shaking off"[56] the hindrances of colonialism and capitalism. In most Third World and Western leftist parties and movements and in most Islamic movements, women have been primarily the nurturers, the substitute soldiers, or the choruses of the revolution. It is dubious whether such a strategy of substitution and traditionalism would ever lead to a totally transformed society.

Sudanese women's movement(s) that had not been established as helpmate organizations or "wings" might have been more effective. I have proposed the potentiality of a movement emerging from extant forms "to resist an oppression which comes from inequalities of power and confidence in interpersonal relations, and from a hierarchical division of labour."[57] I assume that women are potentially "sensitive and self-conscious about inequality and hierarchy in the creating of [their] organizational forms."[58] That statement must remain an assumption at this point in the development of women's movements throughout the world.

A women's movement emanating from, but radically transforming indigenous formations (prefigurative political forms) and conflicts (e.g., women's popular culture and networks and their struggles as workers in the home and neighborhood), and emanating from strategic *and* practical gender interests, might have enabled Sudanese women to invent their own forms of resistance. I assume that once women build onto these prefigurative forms, and once they move to change their situation, they may profoundly affect other structures of exploitation. To play on some phrases from Massell, Sudanese women would then be the structural *strong* points, rather than the "weak points" to be subverted or assaulted, and would no longer serve as another movement's surrogate.[59] Considering the generalized failure, to this point, of most revolutions and liberation movements, I suggest that instead of politically and epistemologically privileging only apparatuses of the state, we consider these prefigurative political forms in developing strategies for change and endurance in potentially revolutionary situations.

Notes

1. Valentine Moghadam, "About the Book," in *Identity Politics and Women: Cultural Reassertions and Feminisms in International Perspective*, ed. Valentine Moghadam (Boulder: Westview Press, 1994), 446.

2. Benedict Anderson, *Imagined Communities: Reflections on the Origin and Spread of Nationalism*, rev. (New York: Verso Books, 1991), 4–6.

3. Anne McClintock, "No Longer a Future Heaven: Women and Nationalism in South Africa," *Transition* 51 (1991): 105.

4. Carole Pateman, *The Sexual Contract* (Stanford: Stanford University Press, 1988).

5. Nira Yuval-Davis and Flora Anthias, *Woman-Nation-State* (London: Macmillan, 1989).

6. Mervat Hatem also raised the question of whether secularist and Islamist views on gender really differ. "Egyptian Discourses on Gender and Political Liberalization: Do Secularist and Islamist Views Really Differ?" *Middle East Journal* 48, no. 4 (1994): 661–76.

7. This cadre's comments were made following my lecture on the NIF and women, at the Institute for African and Asian Studies, University of Khartoum, 3 August 1988. Such a stance from a highly educated (Ph.D.) secular left scholar underscored what women of the SCP (and women who had been rejected as members) had told me through the years: the SCP recruited only women with "good moral reputations." Assuming that this important theorist represented a common SCP stance on prostitution, we can propose that this is an outdated and unself-critical position. Furthermore, his view is typical of the stereotyping of working-class women whose professions involve prohibited or scorned beverages, personal services (hair styling, body-hair removers, and the like), public vending, and entertaining as "prostitutes."

8. The term "culture-of-resistance" is my own, but it is based on Peteet's reading of Caulfield. They used the term "cultures of resistance." Julie Peteet, *Gender*

in Crisis: Women and the Palestinian Resistance Movement (New York: Columbia University Press, 1991), 31; Mina Caulfield, "Culture and Imperialism: Proposing a New Dialectic," in *Reinventing Anthropology,* ed. Dell Hymes (New York: Vintage Books, 1974), 203–4.

9. This is not to suggest that the SCP advocated coexisting with "radical" or political Islam or any Islamic party (such as the NIF) that advocated an Islamic republic. My comments refer to freeing individual members to be religious in their private lives, and not confronting the increasing importance of sharia or the growing institutionalization of Islam over the last few decades.

10. Maxine Molyneux, "Mobilization without Emancipation? Women's Interests, the State, and Revolution in Nicaragua," *Feminist Studies* 11, no. 2 (1985): 227–54.

11. Temma Kaplan, "Female Consciousness and Collective Action: The Case of Barcelona, 1910–1918," in *Feminist Theory: A Critique of Ideology,* ed. Nannerl O. Keohane, Michelle Z. Rosaldo, and Barbara Gelpi (Chicago: University of Chicago Press, 1981), 56.

12. These ideas are part of feminist discourse and have been discussed by only small numbers of Sudanese feminists in Khartoum. The delineation of the spheres is my own.

13. As I mentioned in an earlier chapter, Fatma Ahmed Ibrahim has not always been head of the WU, but her views could be said to have been the most influential for over thirty years. I contend that her views validly represent the WU's.

14. The fullest account of the Sudanese woman urban (Khartoum) worker, including the informal sector, is by Samia el-Nagar, "Patterns of Women Participation in the Labour Force in Khartoum" (Ph.D. diss., University of Khartoum, 1985).

15. Interview at her home in Omdurman, 12 July 1988. Fatma used the term "ignorant women" throughout the interview and stressed education, primarily literacy, as the central strategy of the WU. Unless otherwise indicated, all of Ibrahim's quotes are from this interview.

16. For similar information on Khartoum women merchants, see Alawiya Osman M. Salih, "Women in Trade: Vendors in Khartoum Area Markets," *The Ahfad Journal* 3, no. 2 (1986): 37–40.

17. I was informed that many of the old women still cluster in smaller groups as street vendors.

18. It is simply not true that "most Sudanese women are housewives." They are agricultural workers, informal-sector workers, and members of the formal workforce. It is difficult, however, to find this data simply and clearly laid out. Liberal sources are keen to show that women are *not* represented in certain sectors of the economy and do not play an equal role in development. Their calculations are, therefore, skewed to make that argument. One has to glean the information on women's economic roles in Sudan from random and obscure sources, among them a number of unpublished or difficult to obtain documents, e.g., Amna Rahama and A. Hoogenboom, "Women Farmers, Technological Innovation and Access to Development Projects" (Workshop No. 5, [post-1987]); Susan Holcombe, "Profiles of Women Agricultural Producers ... A Sudan Example," Occa-

sional Paper No. 7, United Nations Development Fund for Women, 1988; Amna el-Sadik Badri, *Women in Management and Public Administration in the Sudan* (Khartoum: Conference of Business and Administrative Sciences Education in the Sudan, University of Khartoum, 15–18 November 1987); Samira Amin Ahmed et al., "Population Problems, Status of Women and Development" (Khartoum: Third National Population Conference, University of Khartoum, 10–14 October 1987); Zeinab B. el-Bakri and el-Wathig M. Kameir, "Women and Development Policies in Sudan: A Critical Outlook" (paper no. 46, 2d OSSREA Congress, Nairobi, 28–31 July 1986); Salih, "Women in Trade: Vendors in Khartoum Area Markets," *The Ahfat Journal* 3, no. 2 (1986): 37–40; Samia el-Nagar, "Patterns of Women [sic] Participation in the Labour Force in Khartoum" Ph.D. diss., University of Khartoum, 1995; Nur el-Tayib Abdel Gadir, *el-Mara el-Amila fi el-Sudan* (The Working Woman in Sudan) (Khartoum: Department of Labour and Social Security, Division of Research, Information and Media, 1984); Diana Baxter, ed., *Women and the Environment in the Sudan* (Environmental Research Paper No. 2, Institute of Environmental Studies, University of Khartoum, Khartoum, 1981); Sondra Hale, "'Private' and 'Public' Labour: The Sudanese Woman Worker in the 1980's—A Pilot Study," *The Ahfad Journal: Women and Change* 2, no. 2 (1985): 36–40; Food and Agriculture Organization of the United Nations, *National Conference on the Role of Women in Agriculture and Rural Development in the Sudan: Interim Report* (Shambat, Khartoum North: Khartoum Polytechnic and FAO-Project GCP/SUD/030 [FIN], 18–22 January 1987); and International Labour Organisation, Growth, *Employment and Equity: A Comprehensive Strategy for the Sudan* (Geneva: International Labour Office, 1976).

19. A University of Khartoum woman student informed me in 1988 that she was almost intimidated into joining the National Islamic Front (or at least into wearing Islamic dress) by the zealousness of the NIF women students who organized by visiting and haranguing other students in their hostel rooms.

20. Fatma Ahmed Ibrahim classifies the zar as a "negative custom" and in the 12 July 1988 interview refused to hear anything from me to the contrary.

21. By "prefigurative political forms" I am referring to informal organizations, collectivities, or gatherings that may have the potential to develop into a formal group. They do not, on the surface, appear "political"; they may, in fact, appear the opposite. However, they contain hidden or coded qualities that are, in fact, political. For example, they may involve resisting authority, unsettling the status quo, and taking oppositional stances. These are "prefigurative" because they have not coalesced into formal groups or collective endeavors and are not necessarily acting, in their entirety, according to their ideas. The consciousness of the participants/members may or may not be raised about their situations.

22. Pamela Constantinides, "Women's Spirit Possession and Urban Adaptation," in *Women United, Women Divided: Cross-Cultural Perspectives on Female Solidarity*, ed. Patricia Caplan and Janet Bujra (London: Tavistock, 1978), 195.

23. Ibid., 198.

24. We have an inadequate vocabulary for defining and distinguishing among aspects of culture, or even defining "culture." Mainly I have tried to use the expressions that Sudanese themselves used. The most common expression was "according to our traditions." Invariably this included Islam and customs thought

to be Islamic. In sections of this book I have used "indigenous," "authentic," and "traditional" culture somewhat interchangeably, but there are subtle distinctions. "Antecedent" culture is a term I introduce in this chapter because, although inexact, it is somewhat more neutral than the other terms. It refers to the culture that has come before. "Indigenous culture" (in its regional variations referred to as "local customs") is the culture of an area or society that existed before external intervention (colonialism, neocolonialism, cultural imperialism) and still exists in some form. The same may be said for "traditional culture," which was not necessarily "there before" (i.e., before Islam and Christianity), but existed prior to European (and other) colonial intervention. It still exists in some changed and changing form as an oppositional, populist, parallel, revived culture. "Indigenous culture" is thought of as populist, i.e., as the culture of the people. "Traditional culture" is variably referred to by Sudanese as old-fashioned, established, the status quo, orthodox. Whether accurate or not (in the anthropological sense), northern Sudanese referred to customs that preceded Islam as "antecedent customs"; to culture associated with non-Arab and/or with southern Sudanese as "indigenous"; to the zar and related rituals and ceremonies as "indigenous"; and to Islam as "traditional."

25. Kaplan, "Female Consciousness and Collective Action," 74.

26. Gregory Massell, *The Surrogate Proletariat: Moslem Women and Revolutionary Strategies in Soviet Central Asia, 1919–1929* (Princeton: Princeton University Press, 1974).

27. See note 24 for comment on including Islam within traditional culture.

28. See note 24 for definitions of these terms.

29. See note 24.

30. Maxine Molyneux, "Legal Reform and Socialist Revolution in South Yemen: Women and the Family," in *Promissory Notes: Women in the Transition to Socialism*, ed. Sonia Kruks et al. (New York: Monthly Review Press, 1989), 201. Italics mine.

31. We see the same trepidation with regard to reproductive rights in the relationship of revolutionary movements to the Catholic Church in Central America, for example.

32. Although Ibrahim may oppose circumcision, clearly it is not a high priority for her. She resents the outside interference and maintains that the problem is exaggerated by outsiders (i.e., Westerners). She is also critical of any monies given the Babiker Badri Scientific Association for Women Studies to work on eradication.

33. Sheila Rowbotham, Lynne Segal, and Hilary Wainwright, *Beyond the Fragments: Feminism and the Making of Socialism* (London: Merlin Press, 1979), 13.

34. Marnia Lazreg, *The Eloquence of Silence: Algerian Women in Question* (New York: Routledge, 1994).

35. Valentine Moghadam, "Introduction: Women and Identity Politics in Theoretical and Comparative Perspective," in Moghadam, *Identity Politics and Women*, 12. See also my "Gender Politics and Islamization in Sudan," *South Asia Bulletin* 14, no. 2 (1994): 51–66.

36. Hanna Papanek, "The Ideal Woman and the Ideal Society: Control and Autonomy in the Construction of Identity," in Moghadam, *Identity Politics and Women*, 45.

37. Ibid., 46.

38. Virginia Sapiro, "Engendering Cultural Differences," in *The Rising Tide of Cultural Pluralism*, ed. Crawford Young (Madison: University of Wisconsin Press, 1993), 52.

39. Deniz Kandiyoti, "Introduction," in *Women, Islam and the State*, ed. Deniz Kandiyoti (Philadelphia: Temple University Press, 1991), 5.

40. Ibid.

41. See chapter 6 for references to the interviews.

42. Arthur L. Lowrie, ed., *Islam, Democracy, the State and the West: A Round Table with Dr. Hasan Turabi* (Tampa: The World and Islam Studies Enterprise, Monograph No. 1, 1993), 46–47. Italics mine.

43. Although Turabi has made this comment and many others about Islam's populism, his spouse, Wisel el-Mahdi, a member of the land-owning Mahdist aristocracy, extolled the virtue of the speed of sharia law in removing resistance groups, e.g., squatters: "[English common law] takes a long time. I don't want to wait all my life to get my land from somebody who is a squatter on it!" (Interview, 12 July 1988.)

44. Carolyn Fluehr-Lobban, "Toward a Theory of Arab-Muslim Women as Activists in Secular and Religious Movements," *Arab Studies Quarterly* 15, no. 2 (1993): 103. Like Hatem, in "Egyptian Discourses on Gender," and myself, here, Fluehr-Lobban maintained a continuity—both historically and culturally/ideologically—between the activism of "secularist" and "Islamist" women.

45. Deniz Kandiyoti, "Women, Islam and the State: A Comparative Approach," in *Comparing Muslim Societies: Knowledge and the State in a World Civilization*, ed. Juan Cole (Ann Arbor: University of Michigan Press. 1992), 238.

46. The permanent constitution, which had never been formally approved by the parliament/People's Assembly, was banned as soon as the Islamists came to power in 1989; an Islamic constitution is still being developed.

47. That such a life was possible only for those who could afford servants was rarely ever mentioned. The class-interested nature of the movement gets obscured by the populist and nationalist tinge.

48. Ellen Gruenbaum gives us a taste of the fear and intimidation that have pervaded Sudan since 1989 in "The Islamic State and Sudanese Women," *MERIP Middle East Report* 22, no. 6 (1992): 29–32.

49. From *el-Sahafa* (3 May 1986), 10. Italics mine.

50. A rejection, condemnation, or denouncement of men would contradict an Islamist criticism of Western feminism: that it divides the genders.

51. Joan Smith, "The Creation of the World We Know: The World-Economy and the Re-creation of Gendered Identities," in Moghadam, *Identity Politics and Women*, 35–36.

52. Lowrie, *Islam, Democracy, the State and the West*, 46–47.

53. These maneuverings are similar to those used by Sudanese Nubian leaders during the Nubian relocation period of the 1960s and 1970s; i.e., placing women

at the service of the "Nubian cultural renaissance." See Sondra Hale, "The Changing Ethnic Identity of Nubians in an Urban Milieu: Khartoum, Sudan" (Ph.D. diss., University of California, Los Angeles, 1979), and "Elite Nubians of Greater Khartoum: A Study of Changing Ethnic Alignments," in *Economy and Class in Sudan*, ed. Norman O'Neill and Jay O'Brien (Avebury, England: Gower Publishing Company, 1988), 277–88.

54. See note 24 for definitions.

55. Kaplan, "Female Consciousness and Collective Action"; Molyneux, "Mobilization without Emancipation?"; and Peteet, *Gender in Crisis*.

56. *Intifada* means, literally, "shaking off."

57. Rowbotham et al., *Beyond the Fragments*, 12.

58. Ibid., 13.

59. Massell, *The Surrogate Proletariat*.

Glossary

aatifiyya. Empathy, compassion, sentimentality.

Ansar, Ansari. Sufi Brotherhood or order. Followers (Ansari) of the Mahdi, the chosen one. *See also* **tariqa.**

Ansar el-Sunna. Ultraconservative Islamic group in Sudan.

burqa. Particular style of veil or headdress, especially in Oman.

cartona. Term used to refer to shantytown where houses can be made of cardboard (cartons).

faqi. Interpreter of religious law.

futuwwa (pl. futuwwat). Local urban strongmen or women (especially Cairo).

hadith. The written traditions of the sayings of the Prophet Mohamed.

harem. Women's segregated quarters.

hasham. Propriety.

hejab. Women's modest Islamic dress. Now usually refers to conservative dress such as a head covering, a scarf, and/or a veil.

hudud. Sacred frontier. Used in sharia to refer to trespassing the moral boundaries/frontier. Hudud offenses are drinking alcohol, apostasy, adultery, violation of chastity, armed robbery, and capital theft.

Ikhwan, el-Ikhwan el-Muslimun. Muslim Brotherhood.

el-Ikhwan el-Jumhuriyun. Republican Brothers (changed to Republicans).

intifada. Uprising, in Sudan case refers to 1985 overthrow of military regime.

Islamism. Political Islam. A movement using Islamic ideology.

Islamist. A person who supports or leads an Islamist movement.

ijtihad. Legal interpretation of the holy sources, i.e., the Quran and Sunna.

jahiliin. Ignorant. Refers to a time before Islam (**jahiliyya.** A time of ignorance).

Jaaliyyin. An Arab ethnic group (tribe) in riverain Sudan.

jallaba. Northern Sudanese merchants. Reference is to the apparel of male northerners (**jallabiyya.** A long, usually white, gown).

jihad. Holy war.

khalwa. Quranic school.

Khatmiyya. Major Sufi order (along with the Ansar). Also referred to as **Mirghaniyya**, after founder, Ali el-Mirghani.

kisra. A type of flat bread.

el-Mahdi. The chosen or expected deliverer in Messianic traditions. In Sudan the reference is to Mohamed Ahmed, nineteenth-century religious/political figure and his successors.

mahr. Bridal gift made from husband to wife as part of the marriage contract. Islamic dower, bride-price.

mahram. Male guardian for women, especially while traveling.

marifa. Concept of divine knowledge in Sufi Islam.

mawali (sing. mawla). Arabized clients to Arab patrons.

mazoon. A man who draws up marriage contracts.

el-Mirghaniyya. Political party offshoot of the People's Democratic Party. After 1968, in coalition with National Unionist Party to form Democratic Unionist Party.

nafaqa. Maintenance responsibilities of the husband as part of marriage contract, e.g., food, shelter, and clothing.

Nagadiyya. Group of Christians of Egyptian descent whose name refers to their profession of dyers of blue cloth.

nisba. Genealogy.

qadi. Judge in an Islamic court.

Quran. Muslim holy book. The word of god through Mohamed, the messenger.

sheikh. Head of a religious order or village head.

sheikha. Woman sheikh. Also a colloquial term for woman who presides over particular women's ceremonies or rituals.

shamasa. Homeless street children (usually boys) in Khartoum, who wash cars and beg.

sharia. Islamic law.

Shaygiyya (anglicized pl. Shaygis). An Arab ethnic group (tribe) in riverain Sudan, or individuals of that group.

Sufi. Mystical Islam. **Sufism** is the practice, and a **sufist** is a member of a Sufi order.

Sunna. The words and practice of the Prophet Mohamed, during his lifetime.

Sunni. The largest of the two major branches of Islam; the other branch is **Shia**.

suq el-Niswan. Women's market in Omdurman.

tahkim. Quranic principle of arbitration. Used to settle family disputes.

tarha. Light head covering for a young girl.

tariqa (pl. turuq). Sufi religious brotherhood or order:

> Ahmediyya
> Ansar (see Mahdi)
> Hindiyya
> Idrisiyya
> Ismailiyya
> Khatmi, Khatmis, Khatmiyya (same as Mirghaniyya)
> Mahdi, Mahdist, Mahdiyya, Mahdism (Ansar order)
> Mirghaniyya (same as Khatmiyya)
> Qadiriyya
> Rashidiyya
> Sammaniyya
> Shadhiliyya
> Tiganiyya.

tobe. Sudanese women's traditional/national dress. Full-length cotton wrap-around gown.

toumeen. Neighborhood or community economic cooperative. Common among women.

ulama. The "clergy" of Islam. Official interpreters of sharia and the holy sources.

Umma. Muslim nation or world community of believers. In Sudan also the name of the political party of the Ansar brotherhood, the Mahdists.

urf. Customary law.

zakat. One of five pillars of Islam—obligatory alms-giving. Now seen as a tax to support the Islamic state.

zar. Spirit-possession ceremony, usually by and for women.

zowag el-kora. Refers to putting all the people "in a bowl" for group weddings that were held in a stadium.

References

Abbas, Ali Abdalla. "The National Islamic Front and the Politics of Education." *MERIP Middle East Report* 21, no. 5 (September/October 1991): 22–25.

Abd el-Rahim, Muddathir. *Imperialism and Nationalism in the Sudan*. Oxford: Clarendon Press, 1969.

Abdel Azim, Munira Ahmad, et al. *Women in Public Administration and Management: Upward Mobility and Career Advancement*. Omdurman: School of Organizational Management, Ahfad University, 1984.

Abdel Gadir, Nur el-Tayib. *El-Mara el-Amila fi el-Sudan* (The Working Woman in Sudan). Khartoum: Department of Labour and Social Security, Division of Research, Information, and Media, 1984.

Abdel Haleem, Asma M. "Claiming Our Bodies and Our Rights: Exploring Female Circumcision as an Act of Violence." In *Freedom from Violence: Women's Strategies Around the World*, edited by Margaret Schuler, 141–56. New York: United Nations Development Fund for Women, 1992.

Abdel Kader, Soha. "A Survey of Trends in Social Sciences Research on Women in the Arab Region, 1960–1980." In *Social Science Research and Women in the Arab World*, 139–75. London: UNESCO, 1984.

Abu Hasabu, Afaf Abdel Majid. *Factional Conflict in the Sudanese Nationalist Movement, 1918–1948*. Graduate College Publications No. 12, University of Khartoum, Khartoum, 1985.

Abu-Lughod, Lila. "A Community of Secrets: The Separate World of Bedouin Women." *Signs* 10, no. 4 (1985): 637–57.

———. *Veiled Sentiments: Honor and Poetry in a Bedouin Society*. Berkeley: University of California Press, 1986.

———. *Writing Women's Worlds: Bedouin Stories*. Berkeley: University of California Press, 1992.

Abu-Nasr, J. *The Tijaniyya*. London: Oxford University Press, 1965.

Abu-Zahra, M. "On the Modesty of Women in Arab Muslim Villages: A Reply." *American Anthropologist* 72 (1970): 1079–92.

Accad, Evelyne. *Veil of Shame*. Sherbrooke: Naaman, 1978.

Adams, William Y. "Ethnohistory and Islamic Tradition in Africa." *Ethnohistory* 16, no. 4 (1969): 277–88.

———. *Nubia: Corridor to Africa*. Princeton: Princeton University Press, 1977.

el-Affendi, Abdelwahab. *Turabi's Revolution: Islam and Power in Sudan*. London: Grey Seal, 1991.

The African Communist. London.

Ahmed, Abdel Ghaffar M. "Some Remarks from the Third World on Anthropology and Colonialism: the Sudan." In *Anthropology and the Colonial Encounter*, edited by Talal Asad, 259–70. London: Ithaca Press, 1973.

Ahmed, Abdel Ghaffar M. and Gunnar M. Sorbo, eds., *Management of the Crisis in the Sudan: Proceedings of the Bergen Forum, 23–24 February, 1989*. Bergen: Centre for Development Studies, University of Bergen, 1989.

Ahmed, Leila. [Review of Margot Badran's translation and editing of Huda Shaarawi's *Harem Years: The Memoirs of an Egyptian Feminist (1879–1924)* (New York: Feminist Press, 1987)] "Women of Egypt," *Women's Review of Books* 5, no. 2 (1987): 7–8.

———. "Western Ethnocentrism and Perceptions of the Harem." *Feminist Studies* 8, no. 3 (1982): 521–34.

———. *Women and Gender in Islam*. New Haven: Yale University Press, 1992.

Ahmed, Medani M. *The Political Economy of Development in the Sudan*. African Seminar Series No. 29, Institute of African and Asian Studies, University of Khartoum, Khartoum, 1987.

Ahmed, Samira Amin. "The Impact of Migration on Conjugal Relationships: A Study of Sudanese Migrants in Riyadh (Saudi Arabia)." Ph.D. diss., 1986.

Ahmed, Samira Amin, Inaam A. Elmahdi, Belgis Y. Bedri, Samya el-Hadi el-Nagar, and Amna Badri. "Population Problems, Status of Women and Development." Paper presented at the Third National Population Conference, University of Khartoum, Khartoum, 10–14 October 1987.

Akolowin, Natalie O. "Islamic and Customary Law in the Sudanese Legal System." In *Sudan in Africa*, edited by Yusuf Fadl Hasan, 279–301. Khartoum: Khartoum University Press, 1971.

Ali, Haidar Ibrahim. *Azmat el-Islam el-Siyyasi fi Sudan* (The Crisis of Political Islam in the Sudan). Cairo: Centre of Sudanese Studies, 1991.

Alloula, Malek. *The Colonial Harem*. Minneapolis: University of Minnesota Press, 1986.

Altorki, Soraya. *Women in Saudi Arabia: Ideology and Behavior among the Elite*. New York: Columbia University Press, 1986.

el-Amin, Nafissa Ahmed. *The Sudanese Woman throughout the History of Her Struggle*. Khartoum: Government Press, 1972.

———. "Education and Family." In *Change and the Muslim World*, edited by Philip Stoddard, David Cuthell, and Margaret Sullivan, 87–94. Syracuse: Syracuse University Press, 1981.

Amin, Samir. "Underdevelopment and Dependence in Black Africa: Historical Origin." Revised version of working paper prepared for United Nations African Institute for Economic Development and Planning, Dakar, Senegal, 1971.

———. *Unequal Development*. Brighton: Harvester Press, 1977.

Amrouche, Fadhma. *My Life Story: The Autobiography of a Berber Woman*, translated by Dorothy S. Blair. New Brunswick: Rutgers University Press, 1988 (1968 in French).

Anderson, Benedict. *Imagined Communities: Reflections on the Origin and Spread of Nationalism*. Revised. New York: Verso Books, 1991.

Anderson, J.N.D. "Recent Developments in Shari'a Law in the Sudan." *Sudan Notes and Records* 21 (1950): 82–104.

Anderson, Jon. "Social Structure and the Veil." *Anthropos* 77 (1982): 397–442.

Anderson, Lisa. "The State in the Middle East and North Africa." *Comparative Politics* 20, no. 1 (1987): 1–18.

Anderson, Perry. *Lineages of the Absolutist State*. London: New Left Books, 1974.

———. *Passages from Antiquity to Feudalism*. London: New Left Books, 1974.

Antoun, Richard. "On the Modesty of Women in Arab Muslim Villages: A Study in the Accommodation of Traditions." *American Anthropologist* 70, no. 4 (1968): 671–97.

el-Arifi, Salih. "Urbanization and Economic Development in the Sudan." In *Urbanization in the Sudan*, edited by el-Sayed el-Bushra, 56–71. Khartoum: Philosophical Society of the Sudan, 1972.

Asad, Talal, ed. *Anthropology and the Colonial Encounter*. London: Ithaca Press, 1973.

———. *The Kababish Arabs: Power, Authority, and Consent in a Nomadic Tribe*. New York: Praeger, 1970.

el-Azmah, Aziz. "Arab Nationalism and Islamism." *Review of Middle East Studies* 4 (1988): 33–51.

el-Badawi, Suad el-Fatih. "The Women Members of the Constituent Assembly." *El-Sahafa* (3 May 1986), 10.

Badran, Margot. "Gender Activism: Feminists and Islamists in Egypt." In *Identity Politics and Women: Cultural Reassertions and Feminisms in International Perspective*, edited by Valentine Moghadam, 202–27. Boulder: Westview Press, 1994.

Badran, Margot, and Miriam Cooke, eds. *Opening the Gates: A Century of Arab Feminist Writing*. Bloomington: Indiana University Press, 1990.

Badri, Amna el-Sadik. "Women in Management and Public Administration in Sudan." Paper presented at the Conference of Business and Administrative Sciences Education in the Sudan, School of Business and Administrative Sciences, University of Khartoum, Khartoum, 15–18 November 1987.

Badri, Amna el-Sadik, Mariam Khalf Alla Shabo, Elhan el-Nujumi, Maarwa Ahmed el-Obeid, and Majda Mustafa Hassan, "Income Generating Projects for Women." In *Women and the Environment*, edited by Diana Baxter, 30–35. Environmental Research Paper Series No. 2, University of Khartoum, Institute of Environmental Studies, Khartoum, 1981.

Badri (aka Bedri), Balghis Yousif. "Food and Differential Roles in the Fetiehab Household." In Susan Kenyon, ed., *The Sudanese Woman*. Khartoum: Graduate College Publications No. 19, University of Khartoum, 1987, 67–91.

Bakheit, J.M.A. *Communist Activities in the Middle East Between 1919–1927, with Special Reference to Egypt and the Sudan*. Khartoum: Sudan Research Unit, University of Khartoum, 1968.

el-Bakri, Zeinab. "On the Crisis of the Sudanese Women's Movement." The Hague: ISIS, in press.

el-Bakri, Zeinab, and el-Haj Hamad M. Khier. "Sudanese Women in History and Historiography: A Proposed Strategy for Curriculum Change." Paper presented at the Workshop on Women's Studies in Sudan, National Council for Research, Sudan Family Planning Association, Khartoum, 7-9 February 1989.

el-Bakri, Zeinab B., and el-Wathig M. Kameir. "Women and Development Policies in Sudan: A Critical Outlook." Paper no. 46, presented at the 2d OSSREA Congress, Nairobi, 28–31 July 1986.

———. "Aspects of Women's Political Participation in Sudan." *International Social Science Journal* 35, no. 4 (1983): 605–23.

el-Bakri, Zeinab Bashir, Fahima Zahir (el-Sadaty), Belghis Badri, Tamadur Ahmed Khalid, and Madiha el-Sanusi. "Sudanese Sub-Project: Women in Sudan in the Twentieth Century." In *Women's Movements and Organizations in Historical Perspective: Project Summaries and Evaluation*, edited by Saskia Wieringa, 175–85. The Hague: Institute of Social Studies, Women and Development Programme, [post-1987].

el-Bakri, Zeinab, el-Wathig Kamier, Idris Salim el-Hassan, and Samya el-Nagar. *The State of Women Studies in the Sudan*. Khartoum: Development Studies and Research Centre, Faculty of Economic and Social Studies, University of Khartoum, 1985.

Barclay, Harold. *Buurri al Lamaab: A Suburban Village in the Sudan*. Ithaca: Cornell University Press, 1964.

———. "Process in the Arab Sudan." *Human Organization* 24 (1965): 43–48.

Barker-Benfield, Ben. "Sexual Surgery in Late-Nineteenth-Century America." *International Journal of Health Services* 5, no. 2 (1975): 279–98.

Barnett, Tony. "Introduction: The Sudanese Crisis and the Future." In *Sudan: State, Capital, and Transformation*, edited by Tony Barnett and Abbas Abdelkarim, 1–17. London: Croom Helm, 1988.

———. "The Gezira Scheme: Production of Cotton and the Reproduction of Underdevelopment." In *Beyond the Sociology of Development: Economy and Society in Latin America and Africa*, edited by I. Oxaal, T. Barnett, and D. Booth, 186–207. London: Routledge and Kegan Paul, 1975.

Batrawi, A. "The Racial History of Egypt and Nubia." *Journal of the Royal Anthropological Institute* 75 (1945): 76, 81–101, 131–56.

Baxter, Diana, ed. *Women and the Environment*. Environmental Research Paper Series No. 2, University of Khartoum, Institute of Environmental Studies, Khartoum, 1981.

———. "Introduction—Women and Environment: A Downward Spiral." In *Women and the Environment in the Sudan*, edited by Diana Baxter, 1–7. Environmental Research Paper Series No. 2, University of Khartoum, Institute of Environmental Studies, Khartoum, 1981.

Beck, Lois, and Nikki Keddie, eds. *Women in the Muslim World*. Cambridge: Harvard University Press, 1978.

Bedri, Nafisa Salman, and Lee G. Burchinal. "Educational Attainment as an Indicator of the Status of Women in the Sudan." *The Ahfad Journal* 2, no. 1 (1985): 30–38.

Beleil, O.M., in conversation with Cliff Osmond. *Two Lives: Death Odyssey of a Transplant Surgeon*. Khartoum: University of Khartoum Press, 1973.

Bernal, Victoria. "Losing Ground—Women and Agriculture on Sudan's Irrigated Schemes: Lessons from a Blue Nile Village." In *Agriculture, Women and Land:*

The African Experience, edited by Jean Davison, 131–56. Boulder: Westview Press, 1988.

Berreman, Gerald. "'Bringing It All Back Home': Malaise in Anthropology." In *Reinventing Anthropology,* edited by Dell Hymes, 83–98. New York: Vintage, 1972.

———. "Is Anthropology Still Alive?" In *Reinventing Anthropology,* edited by Dell Hymes, 391–96. New York: Vintage, 1972.

Beshir, Mohamed Omer. *The Southern Sudan: Background to Conflict.* London: C. Hurst, 1968.

Betteridge, Anne. "To Veil or Not to Veil." In *Women and Revolution in Iran,* edited by G. Nashat. Boulder: Westview Press, 1983.

Boddy, Janice. *Wombs and Alien Spirits: Women, Men, and the Zar Cult in Northern Sudan.* Madison: University of Wisconsin Press, 1990.

Bouhdiba, Wahab. *La Sexualité en Islam.* Paris: Presses Universitaires de France, 1975.

Bowen, Elenore Smith (pseud. for Laura Bohannan). *Return to Laughter.* New York: Harper & Row, 1954.

Brenner, Louis. "Introduction: Muslim Representations of Unity and Difference in the African Discourse." In *Muslim Identity and Social Change in Sub-Saharan Africa,* edited by Louis Brenner, 1-20. Bloomington: Indiana University Press, 1993.

———, ed. *Muslim Identity and Social Change in Sub-Saharan Africa.* Bloomington: Indiana University Press, 1993.

Briggs, Jean. *Never in Anger.* Cambridge: Harvard University Press, 1970.

Burr, J. Millard and Robert O. Collins. *Requiem for the Sudan: War, Drought, and Disaster Relief on the Nile.* Boulder: Westview Press, 1995.

el-Bushra, el-Sayed. "Occupational Classification of Sudanese Towns." *Sudan Notes and Records* 50 (1969): 75–96.

———. "Sudan's Triple Capital: Morphology and Functions." *Ekistics* 39, no. 233 (1975): 246–50.

Caspi, Mishael Maswari. *Daughters of Yemen.* Berkeley: University of California Press, 1985.

Caulfield, Mina. "Culture and Imperialism: Proposing a New Dialectic." In *Reinventing Anthropology,* edited by Dell Hymes, 182–212. New York: Vintage Books, 1974.

Clark, Gordon, and Michael Dear. *State Apparatus: Structures and Language of Legitimacy.* Boston: Allen and Unwin, 1984.

Clifford, James. *The Predicament of Culture: Twentieth-Century Ethnography, Literature, and Art.* Cambridge: Harvard University Press, 1988.

Cloudsley, Ann. *Women of Omdurman: Life, Love and the Cult of Virginity.* London: Ethnographica, 1983; New York: St. Martin's Press, 1985.

Cole, Sally. *Women of the Praia: Work and Lives in a Portuguese Coastal Community.* Princeton, New Jersey: Princeton University Press, 1991.

Collins, Carole. "Sudan: Colonialism and Class Struggle." *Middle East Research and Information Project* (MERIP) no. 46 (1976): 3–17, 20.

Constantinides, Pamela. "Women's Spirit Possession and Urban Adaptation." In *Women United, Women Divided: Cross-Cultural Perspectives on Female Solidarity,* edited by Patricia Caplan and Janet Bujra, 185–205. London: Tavistock, 1978.

Cunnison, Ian. *Baggara Arabs: Power and the Lineage in a Sudanese Nomad Tribe.* Oxford: Clarendon Press, 1966.

Daly, M.W. *Imperial Sudan: The Anglo-Egyptian Condominium, 1934–1956.* Cambridge: Cambridge University Press, 1991.

el-Dareer, Asma. *Woman, Why Do You Weep? Circumcision and Its Consequences.* London: Zed, 1982.

de Waal, Alex. "Turabi's Muslim Brothers: Theocracy in Sudan." *CovertAction,* no. 49 (1994): 13–18, 60–61.

Dorsky, Susan. *Women of 'Amran: A Middle Eastern Ethnographic Study.* Salt Lake City: University of Utah Press, 1986.

Duran, Khalid. "The Centrifugal Forces of Religion in Sudanese Politics." *Orient* 26, no. 4 (1985): 572–600.

Eickelman, Dale. *The Middle East: An Anthropological Approach.* Englewood Cliffs: Prentice-Hall, 1981.

Engels, Friedrich. *The Origin of the Family, Private Property and the State.* New York: International, 1972.

Eprile, Cecil. *War and Peace in the Sudan, 1955–1972.* London: David and Charles, 1974.

Esposito, John. *Islam and Politics.* Rev. 2d ed. Syracuse: Syracuse University Press, 1987.

———. "Sudan." In *The Politics of Islamic Revivalism,* edited by Shireen T. Hunter, 187–203. Bloomington: University of Indiana Press, 1988.

———. "Supplement: The Sudan and Lebanon." In *Islam and Politics,* edited by John Esposito, 282–91. Syracuse: Syracuse University Press, 1987.

———. *Women in Muslim Family Law.* Syracuse: Syracuse University Press, 1982.

Farah, Amna. "Enhancing Women's Participation in Agriculture and Rural Development." Paper presented at the Conference on the Contributions of Women to Development, Development Studies and Research Centre, University of Khartoum, Khartoum, 11–14 April 1984.

Faris, H.A. "Heritage and Ideologies in Contemporary Arab Thought: Contrasting Views of Change and Development." *Journal of Asian and African Studies* 21, no. 2 (1986): 89–103.

el-Farouk Hassan Heiba, Omer. "Letters." *Sudanow* (October 1979).

Farran, C. D'Olivier. *Matrimonial Laws of the Sudan.* London: Butterworth, 1963.

Fawzi, Saad ed-Din. *The Labour Movement in the Sudan, 1946–1955.* London: Oxford, 1957.

Fernea, Elizabeth, director. *A Veiled Revolution.* New York: First Run/Icarus Film, 1982.

———, ed. *Women and the Family in the Middle East: New Voices of Change.* Austin: University of Texas, 1985.

———. *Guests of the Sheik: An Ethnography of an Iraqi Village.* New York: Doubleday, 1969.

Fernea, Elizabeth, and Basima Qattan Bezirgan. *Middle Eastern Muslim Women Speak.* Austin: University of Texas, 1977.

First, Ruth. *Power in Africa*. London: Pantheon, 1970.

Fluehr-Lobban, Carolyn. *Islamic Law and Society in the Sudan*. London: Frank Cass, 1987.

———. "Islamization in Sudan: A Critical Assessment," *The Middle East Journal* 44, no. 4 (1990): 610–23.

———. "Toward a Theory of Arab-Muslim Women as Activists in Secular and Religious Movements." *Arab Studies Quarterly* 15, no. 2 (1993): 87–106.

———. "Women and Social Liberation: The Sudan Experience." In *Three Studies on National Integration in the Arab World*. Information Paper No. 12, Association of Arab-American University Graduates, North Dartmouth, Mass., 1974.

Food and Agriculture Organization of the United Nations. *National Conference on the Role of Women in Agriculture and Rural Development in the Sudan: Interim Report*. Shambat, Khartoum North: Khartoum Polytechnic and FAO-Project GCP/SUD/030 (FIN), 18–22 January 1987.

Forster, Peter. "A Review of the New Left Critique of Social Anthropology." In *Anthropology and the Colonial Encounter*, edited by Talal Asad, 23–38. London: Ithaca Press, 1973.

Freilich, Morris, ed. *Marginal Natives: Anthropologists at Work*. New York: Harper and Row, 1970.

Freire, Paulo. *Pedagogy of the Oppressed*. New York: Seabury Press, 1970.

Friedl, Erika. *Women of Deh Koh: Lives in an Iranian Village*. Washington, D.C.: Smithsonian Institution Press, 1989.

Gadant, David. *Women of the Mediterranean*, translated by A.M. Berrett. London: Zed, 1986 (1984).

Galaleldin, Mohamed el-Awad. *Some Aspects of Sudanese Migration to the Oil-Producing Arab Countries During the 1970's*. Khartoum: Development Studies and Research Centre, University of Khartoum, 1985.

Gilligan, Carol. *In a Different Voice: Psychological Theory and Women's Development*. Cambridge: Harvard University Press, 1982.

Gilmore, David. "Anthropology of the Mediterranean Area." *Annual Review of Anthropology* 11 (1982): 175–205.

Gluck, Sherna Berger. *An American Feminist in Palestine: The Intifada Years*. Philadelphia: Temple University Press, 1994.

Golde, Peggy, ed. *Women in the Field: Anthropological Experiences*. Berkeley: University of California Press, 1970.

Gough, Kathleen. "Anthropology: Child of Imperialism." *Monthly Review* 19, 11 (1967): 12–27.

Graham, Hilary. "Do Her Answers Fit His Questions? Women and the Survey Method." In *Public and Private*, edited by Eva Gamarnikov, June Purvis, Daphne Taylorson, and David Morgan, 132–46. London: Heinemann, 1983.

Gramsci, Antonio. *Selections from the Prison Notebooks*. London: Lawrence and Wishart, 1971.

———. *Selections from Political Writings, 1910–1920*. London: Lawrence and Wishart, 1977.

———. *Selections from Political Writings, 1921–1926*. London: Lawrence and Wishart, 1978.

Gran, Judith. "Impact of the World Market on Egyptian Women." *MERIP Reports* no. 58 (1977): 3–7.

Gray, Richard. *A History of Southern Sudan, 1839–1889.* London: Oxford University Press, 1961.

———. "Some Obstacles to Economic Development in the Southern Sudan, 1839–1965." In *Nations by Design,* edited by Arnold Rivkin, 121–34. Garden City: Doubleday, 1968.

Gresh, Alain. "The Free Officers and the Comrades: The Sudanese Communist Party and Nimeiri Face-to-Face." *International Journal of Middle Eastern Studies* 21 (1989): 393–409.

Gruenbaum, Ellen. "The Islamic State and Sudanese Women." *MERIP Middle East Report* 22, no. 6 (1992): 29–32.

———. "Medical Anthropology, Health Policy and the State: A Case Study of Sudan." *Policy Studies Review* 1, no. 1 (1981): 47–65.

———. "Nuer Women in Southern Sudan: Health, Reproduction, and Work." Working Paper No. 215, Michigan State University, East Lansing, Mich., 1990.

———. "Reproductive Ritual and Social Reproduction." In *Economy and Class in Sudan,* edited by Norman O'Neill and Jay O'Brien, 308–25. Avebury, England: Gower, 1988.

Gunning, Isabelle. "Arrogant Perception, World-Travelling and Multicultural Feminism: The Case of Female Genital Surgeries." *Columbia Human Rights Law Review* 23, no. 189 (1991/92): 189–248.

Hale, Sondra. "Arts in a Changing Society: Northern Sudan." *Ufahamu* 1, no. 1 (1970): 64–79.

———. "The Changing Ethnic Identity of Nubians in an Urban Milieu: Khartoum, Sudan." Ph.D. diss., University of California, Los Angeles, 1979.

———. "Elite Nubians of Greater Khartoum: A Study of Changing Ethnic Alignments." In *Economy and Class in Sudan,* edited by Norman O'Neill and Jay O'Brien, 277–90. Avebury, England: Gower, 1988.

———. "The Ethnic Identity of Sudanese Nubians." *Meroitica* 5 (1979): 165–72.

———. "Feminist Method, Process, and Self-Criticism: Interviewing Sudanese Women." In *Women's Words: The Feminist Practice of Oral History,* edited by Sherna Gluck and Daphne Patai, 121–36. London: Routledge, 1991.

———. "Gender Politics and Islamization in Sudan." *South Asia Bulletin* 14, no. 2 (1994): 51–66.

———. "Gender, Islam, and Politics in Sudan." Working paper no. 10, The G.E. von Grunebaum Center for Near Eastern Studies, University of California, Los Angeles, Los Angeles, 1992.

———. "The Impact of Immigration on Women: The Sudanese Nubian Case." In *Across Cultures: The Spectrum of Women's Lives,* edited by Emily K. Abel and Marjorie L. Pearson, 53–56. New York: Gordon and Breach, 1989.

———. "The Nature of the Social, Political, and Religious Changes among Urban Women: Northern Sudan." *Proceedings of the Third Graduate Academy of the University of California, UCLA, 11–12 April 1965.* Los Angeles: The UCLA Graduate Student Association, 1966, 127–40.

———. *Nubians: A Study in Ethnic Identity.* Khartoum: Institute of African and Asian Studies, University of Khartoum, 1971.

———. "Nubians in the Urban Milieu: Greater Khartoum." *Sudan Notes and Records* 54 (1973): 57–65.

———. "The Politics of Gender in the Middle East." In *Gender and Anthropology: Critical Reviews for Research and Teaching,* edited by Sandra Morgen, 246–67. Washington, D.C.: American Anthropological Association, 1989.

———. "'Private' and 'Public' Labour: The Sudanese Woman Worker in the 1980's—A Pilot Study." *The Ahfad Journal: Women and Change* 2, no. 2 (1985): 36–40.

———. "A Question of Subjects: The 'Female Circumcision' Controversy and the Politics of Knowledge." *Ufahamu* 22, no. 3 (1994): 26–35.

———. "The Return." *Africa Today* (special issue on *The Sudan: 25 Years of Independence)* 28, no. 2 (1981): 98–100.

———. "Southern Sudanese: Strangers in a Plural Society." Paper presented at the Southwestern Anthropological Association, San Francisco, 1966.

———. "Sudan Civil War: Religion, Colonialism, and the World System." In *Muslim-Christian Conflicts: Economic, Political, and Social Origins,* edited by Suad Joseph and Barbara L. K. Pillsbury, 157–82. Boulder: Westview Press, 1978.

———. "Transforming Culture or Fostering Second-Hand Consciousness? Women's Front Organizations and Revolutionary Parties—The Sudan Case." In *Arab Women: Old Boundaries, New Frontiers,* edited by Judith Tucker, 149–74. Bloomington: Indiana University Press, 1993.

———. "The Wing of the Patriarch: Sudanese Women and Revolutionary Parties." *MERIP Middle East Report* 16, no. 1 (1986): 25–30.

———. "Women and Work in Sudan: What Is Alienated Labor?" *Proceedings, Conference on Women and Work in the Third World,* 245–50. Berkeley: Center for the Study, Education and Advancement of Women, University of California, 1983.

Hall, Marjorie, and Bakhita Amin Ismail. *Sisters under the Sun: The Story of Sudanese Women.* London: Longman, 1981.

Hammami, Reza, and Martina Rieker. "Feminist Orientalism and Orientalist Marxism." *New Left Review* no. 170 (1988): 93–106.

Hammour, Fawzia. "Sudanese Professional Women Series: Who—Is—Who in Women Studies." Paper presented at the Workshop on Women's Studies in Sudan, National Council for Research, Sudan Family Planning Association, Khartoum, 7-9 February 1989.

Haraway, Donna. "Situated Knowledges: The Science Questions in Feminism and the Privilege of Partial Perspective." *Feminist Studies* 14 (1988): 575–99.

Hartmann, Heidi. "The Unhappy Marriage of Marxism and Feminism: Towards a More Progressive Union." In *Women and Revolution: A Discussion of the Unhappy Marriage of Marxism and Feminism,* edited by Lydia Sargent, 1–41. Boston: South End Press, 1979.

Hasan, Yusuf Fadl. *The Arabs and the Sudan.* Edinburgh: Edinburgh University Press, 1967.

Hassan, Amna Abdel Rahman, Sakina Mohamed el-Hassan, Nawal Ahmed Adam, Afaf Ali Rehiman, Shahowa el-Gizouli, Mahasin Khider (el-Sayed), Ehsan Hussein, Asha Abdulla, and Ibrahim Ahmed Osman. *Woman Strategy for the Year 2000: Submitted to the Arab League in December, 1986.* Khartoum:

Sudan, Ministry of Social Welfare and Elzakat, Department of Social Welfare, 1986.

el-Hassan, Idris Salim. "On Ideology: The Case of Religion in Northern Sudan." Ph.D. diss., University of Connecticut, 1980.

Hassan, Kamil Ibrahim. "Women's Contribution to the Economy." In *Women and the Environment in the Sudan*, edited by Diana Baxter. Environmental Research Paper Series No. 2, University of Khartoum, Institute of Environmental Studies, Khartoum, 1981.

Hatem, Mervat. "Class and Patriarchy as Competing Paradigms for the Study of Middle Eastern Women." *Comparative Studies in Society and History* 29, no. 4 (1987): 811–18.

———. "Egyptian Discourses on Gender and Political Liberalization: Do Secularist and Islamist Views Really Differ?" *The Middle East Journal* 48, no. 4 (1994): 661–76.

———. "Lifting the Veil." *Women's Review of Books* 2, no. 10 (1985): 13–14.

Hayes, Rose. "Female Genital Mutilation, Fertility Control, Women's Role and the Patrilineage in Modern Sudan." *Ethnologist* 2, no. 4 (1975): 617–33.

Hegland, Mary. "The Political Roles of Iranian Village Women." *MERIP Middle East Report* 16, no. 1 (1986): 14–19, 46.

el-Hibri, Azizah. *Women and Islam.* Oxford: Pergamon Press, 1982.

Hijab, Nadia. *Women and Work*, A Special MERIP Publication on Women in the Middle East, *MERIP Middle East Report* no. 3 (1994).

Hill, Richard. *Egypt in the Sudan, 1820–1881.* London: Oxford University Press, 1959.

Hoffman-Ladd, Valerie. "Polemics on the Modesty and Segregation of Women in Contemporary Egypt." *International Journal of Middle East Studies* 19, no. 1 (1987): 23–50.

Holcombe, Susan. "Profiles of Women Agricultural Producers...A Sudan Example." UNIFEM occasional paper no. 7, United Nations Development Fund for Women, 1988.

Holt, P.M. *The Mahdist State in the Sudan, 1881–1898.* Oxford: Clarendon Press, 1958.

———. *A Modern History of the Sudan.* London: Weidenfeld and Nicolson, 1961.

Horner, Norman A. *A Guide to Christian Churches in the Middle East.* Elkhard, Indiana: Mission Focus, n.d.

Human Rights Watch/Africa. *Civilian Devastation: Abuses by All Parties in the War in Southern Sudan.* New York: Human Rights Watch, 1994.

Hymes, Dell, ed. *Reinventing Anthropology.* New York: Vintage, 1972.

Ibrahim, Fatima Ahmed. "Arrow at Rest." In *Women in Exile*, compiled by Mahnaz Afkhami, 191–208. University Press of Virginia, 1994.

———. *el-Mara el-Arabiyya wal Taghyir el-Ijtimai* (The Arab Woman and Social Change). Khartoum: el-Markaz el-Tibai, 1986.

———. *Tariqnu ila el-Tuhasur* (Our Road to Emancipation). Khartoum: n.p., n.d.

International Labour Organisation. *Growth, Employment and Equity: A Comprehensive Strategy for the Sudan.* Geneva: International Labour Office, 1976.

International Labour Organisation, United Nations High Commissioner for Refugees. *Labour Markets in the Sudan.* Geneva: International Labour Office, 1984.

Ismail, Ellen. *Social Environment and Daily Routine of Sudanese Women: A Case Study of Urban Middle Class Housewives.* Berlin: Dietrich Reimer, Kolner Ethnologische Studien, Band 6, 1982.

Jahn, Samia el-Azharia. "Traditional Methods of Water Purification of Sudanese Women." In *Women and the Environment in the Sudan,* edited by Diana Baxter, 49–57. Environmental Research Paper Series No. 2, University of Khartoum, Institute of Environmental Studies, Khartoum, 1981.

James, Wendy. "The Anthropologist as Reluctant Imperialist." In *Anthropology and the Colonial Encounter,* edited by Talal Asad, 41–69. London: Ithaca Press, 1973.

Jessop, Bob. *The Capitalist State: Marxist Theories and Methods.* New York: New York University Press, 1982.

———. "Recent Theories of the Capitalist State." *Cambridge Journal of Economics* 1 (1977): 353–73.

Joseph, Suad. "Women and Politics in the Middle East." *MERIP Middle East Report* 16, no. 1 (1986): 3–7.

———. "Working Class Women's Networks in a Sectarian State: A Political Paradox." *American Ethnologist* 10, no. 1 (1983): 1–22.

Jowkar, Forouz. "Honor and Shame: A Feminist View from Within." *Feminist Issues* 6, no. 1 (1986): 45–65.

Kandiyoti, Deniz. "Introduction." In *Women, Islam and the State,* edited by Deniz Kandiyoti, 1–21. Philadelphia: Temple University Press, 1991.

———, ed. *Women, Islam and the State.* Philadelphia: Temple University Press, 1991.

———. "Women, Islam and the State: A Comparative Approach." In *Comparing Muslim Societies: Knowledge and the State in a World Civilization,* edited by Juan R. Cole, 237–60. Ann Arbor: University of Michigan Press, 1992.

Kaplan, Temma. "Female Consciousness and Collective Action: The Case of Barcelona, 1910–1918." In *Feminist Theory: A Critique of Ideology,* edited by Nannerl O. Keohane, Michelle Z. Rosaldo, and Barbara C. Gelpi, 55–76. Chicago: University of Chicago Press, 1981.

Kapteijns, Lidwien. "Islamic Rationales for the Changing Social Roles of Women in the Western Sudan." In *Modernization in the Sudan: Essays in Honor of Richard Hill,* edited by M.W. Daly, 57–72. New York: Lillian Barber Press, 1985.

el-Karsani, Awad el-Sid. "Beyond Sufism: The Case of Millennial Islam in Sudan." In *Muslim Identity and Social Change in Sub-Saharan Africa,* edited by Louis Brenner, 135–153. Bloomington: Indiana University Press, 1993.

Kashif-Badri, Hagga. *el-Haraka el-nisaiyya fiel-Sudan* (The Women's Movement in the Sudan). Khartoum: University Publishing House, University of Khartoum, 1980.

———. "The History, Development, Organization and Position of Women's Studies in the Sudan." *Social Science Research and Women in the Arab World.* Paris: UNESCO, 1984, 94-112.

Keddie, Nikki. "Problems in the Study of Middle Eastern Women." *International Journal of Middle East Studies* 10 (1979): 225–240.

Keddie, Nikkie, and Beth Baron, eds. *Women in Middle Eastern History: Shifting Boundaries in Sex and Gender.* New Haven: Yale University Press, 1991.

Khalid, Mansour. *Nimeiri and the Revolution of Dis-May.* London: KPI, 1985.

Khalidi, Ramla, and Judith Tucker. *Women's Rights in the Arab World.* A Special MERIP Publication no. 1 (1994).

Kheir, el-Hag Hamad Mohammed. "Women and Politics in Medieval Sudanese History." In *The Sudanese Woman,* edited by Susan Kenyon, 8-39. Graduate College Publications No. 19, University of Khartoum, Khartoum, 1987.

Kheir, el-Hag Hamad Mohammed and Maymouna Mirghani Hamza. "A Case Study of Mahdist Historiography." Khartoum, Conference on Mahdist Studies, 1981.

Khider, Mahasin. "Women in Sudanese Agriculture." In *The Sudanese Woman,* edited by Susan Kenyon, 116–33. Graduate College Publications No. 19, University of Khartoum, Khartoum, 1987.

Kirwan, L.P. "Nubia—An African Frontier Zone." *The Advancement of Science* 19, no. 80 (1962): 330–37.

Klein, Renate Duelli. "How to Do What We Want to Do: Thoughts about Feminist Methodology." In *Theories of Women's Studies,* edited by Gloria Bowles and Renate Duelli Klein, 88-104. London: Routledge and Kegan Paul, 1983.

Kok, Peter Nyot. "Hasan Abdallah al-Turabi." *Orient* 33 (1992): 185–92.

Kronenberg, Andreas and Waltraud. "Preliminary Report on Anthropological Field-Work 1961–62 in Sudanese Nubia." *Kush* 12 (1964): 282–90.

Kruks, Sonia, Rayna Rapp, and Marilyn Young, eds. *Promissory Notes: Women in the Transition to Socialism.* New York: Monthly Review Press, 1989.

Lazreg, Marnia. *The Eloquence of Silence: Algerian Women in Question.* New York: Routledge, 1994.

Leacock, Eleanor. "Women, Development, and Anthropological Facts and Fictions." *Latin American Perspectives* (special double issue on women and class struggle) 4, nos. 12/13 (1977): 8–17.

Lee, David. "Space Levels of a Sudanese Villager." *The Professional Geographer* 29, no. 2 (1977): 160–65.

Leiris, Michel. "L'Ethnographe devant le Colonialisme." *Les Temps Modernes* 58 (Paris: Mercure de France, 1966).

Los Angeles Times. "World Report" section (29 June 1993).

Lowrie, Arthur L., ed. *Islam, Democracy, and the State and the West: A Round Table with Dr. Hasan Turabi.* Tampa: The World and Islam Studies Enterprise, Monograph No. 1, 1993.

Lusk, Gill. "Democracy and Liberation Movements: The Case of the SPLA," *MERIP* 22, no. 1 (1992): 30–31.

Lutsky, V. *Modern History of the Arabs in the Sudan.* 2 vols. Cambridge: Cambridge University Press, 1969.

MacLeod, Arlene Elowe. *Accommodating Protest: Working Women, the New Veiling, and Change in Cairo.* New York: Columbia University Press, 1991.

MacMichael, H.A. *A History of the Arabs in the Sudan.* Cambridge: Cambridge University Press, 1922.

Mahjub, Abdel Khaliq. *Lamahat min tarikh el-hizb el-Shuyui el-Sudani.* N.p. Dar el-fikr el-ishtiraki, 1960.

Mahmoud, Fatima Babiker. "Capitalism, Racism, Patriarchy and the Woman Question." *Africa's Crisis*, 79–86. London: Institute for African Alternatives, 1987.

———. *The Sudanese Bourgeoisie: Vanguard of Development?* London: Zed and Khartoum: Khartoum University Press, 1984.

Makhlouf, Carla. *Changing Veils: Women and Modernization in North Yemen*. Austin: University of Texas Press, 1979.

Malti-Douglas, Fedwa. *Woman's Body, Woman's World: Gender and Discourse in Arabo-Islamic Writing*. Princeton: Princeton University Press, 1991.

Marcus, G., and M. Fischer. *Anthropology as Cultural Critique: An Experimental Moment in the Social Sciences*. Chicago: University of Chicago Press, 1986.

Massell, Gregory. *The Surrogate Proletariat: Moslem Women and Revolutionary Strategies in Soviet Central Asia, 1919–1929*. Princeton: Princeton University Press, 1974.

Maybury-Lewis, David. *The Savage and the Innocent*. Cleveland: World Publishing Company, 1965.

McClintock, Anne. "No Longer a Future Heaven: Women and Nationalism in South Africa." *Transition* 51 (1991): 104–123.

McLoughlin, Peter. "Economic Development and the Heritage of Slavery in the Sudan Republic. " *Africa* 23 (1962): 355–91.

Mernissi, Fatima. *Beyond the Veil*. Cambridge: Cambridge University Press, 1975.

———. "Muslim Women and Fundamentalism." *MERIP Middle East Report* 18, no. 4 (1988): 8–11.

———. *The Veil and the Male Elite: A Feminist Interpretation of Women's Rights in Islam*. Reading: Addison-Wesley, 1991 (1987).

el-Messiri, Sawsan. "The Changing Role of the Futuwwa in the Social Structure of Cairo." In *Patrons and Clients*, edited by Ernest Gellner and John Waterbury, 239–54. London: Duckworth, 1977.

The Middle East Journal 44, no. 4 (1990). Special issue on Sudan.

Middleton, John. *The Study of the Lugbara*. New York: Holt, Rinehart, and Winston, 1970.

Minces, Juliette. *The House of Obedience*. London: Zed, 1980.

———. "Women in Algeria." In *Women in the Muslim World*, edited by Lois Beck and Nikki Keddie, 159–71. Cambridge: Harvard University Press, 1978.

Mitchell, Timothy, and Roger Owen. "Defining the State in the Middle East." *Middle East Studies Association Bulletin* 24 (1990): 179–83.

Moghadam, Valentine. "About the Book." In *Identity Politics and Women: Cultural Reassertions and Feminisms in International Perspective*, edited by Valentine Moghadam, 446. Boulder: Westview Press, 1994.

———, ed. *Gender and National Identity: Women and Politics in Muslim Societies*. London: Zed, 1994.

———, ed. *Identity Politics and Women: Cultural Reassertions and Feminisms in International Perspective*. Boulder: Westview Press, 1994.

———. "Introduction: Women and Identity Politics in Theoretical and Comparative Perspective." In *Identity Politics and Women: Cultural Reassertions and Femi-*

nisms in International Perspective, edited by Valentine Moghadam, 3–26. Boulder: Westview Press, 1994.

———. *Modernizing Women: Gender and Social Change in the Middle East.* Boulder: Lynne Rienner Publishers, 1993.

———. "Women, Work, and Ideology in the Islamic Republic." *International Journal of Middle East Studies* 20, no. 3 (1988): 221–43.

Mohamed Ali, Taisier. "Towards the Political Economy of Agricultural Development in the Sudan 1956–1964." Ph.D. diss., University of Toronto, 1983.

Mohamed, Yagoub Abdalla. "An Overview of the Water Situation in the Sudan." In *Women and the Environment in the Sudan,* edited by Diana Baxter. Environmental Research Paper Series No. 2, University of Khartoum, Institute of Environmental Studies, Khartoum, 1981.

Molyneux, Maxine. "Legal Reform and Socialist Revolution in South Yemen: Women and the Family." In *Promissory Notes: Women in the Transition to Socialism,* edited by Sonia Kruks, Rayna Rapp, and Marilyn Young, 193–214. New York: Monthly Review Press, 1989.

———. "Mobilization without Emancipation? Women's Interests, the State, and Revolution in Nicaragua." *Feminist Studies* 11, no. 2 (1985): 227–54.

Morsy, Soheir. "Toward the Demise of Anthropology's Distinctive-Other Hegemonic Tradition." In *Arab Women in the Field: Studying Your Own Society,* edited by Soraya Altorki and Camilla el-Solh, 69–90. Syracuse: Syracuse University Press, 1988.

Mubarak, Khalid. "The Fundamentalists: Theory and Praxis." *el-Hayat* (30 June 1992).

Muhammad Sa'id, Bashir. *The Sudan: Crossroads of Africa.* London: Bodley Head, 1965.

Mustafa, Asha. "Role of Women in the Traditional Food Systems of Drought-Affected Environments—A Study of Kordofan Region—Sudan," *Research Report.* Khartoum: Women in Development Programme, Development Studies and Research Centre, University of Khartoum, [1985–88?].

———. "Women and Water in Western Kordofan." In *Women and the Environment in the Sudan,* edited by Diana Baxter, 67–69. Environmental Research Paper Series No. 2, University of Khartoum, Institute of Environmental Studies, Khartoum, 1981.

Nader, Laura. "Up the Anthropologist—Perspectives Gained from Studying Up." In *Reinventing Anthropology,* edited by Dell Hymes, 284–311. New York: Vintage, 1972.

el-Nagar, Samia. "Patterns of Women [sic] Participation in the Labour Force in Khartoum." Ph.D. diss., University of Khartoum, 1985.

———. "Women and Spirit Possession in Omdurman." In *The Sudanese Woman,* edited by Susan Kenyon, 92–115. Graduate College Publications No. 19, University of Khartoum, Khartoum, 1987.

An-Na'im, Abdullahi Ahmed. Translator's introduction to *The Second Message of Islam,* by Mahmoud Mohamed Taha, 5–6. Syracuse: Syracuse University Press, 1987.

———. "The Elusive Islamic Constitution: The Sudanese Experience." *Orient* 26, no. 3 (1985): 329–40.

Nash, Dennison, and Ronald Wintrob. "The Emergence of Self-Consciousness in Ethnography." *Current Anthropology* 13 (1972): 527–42.

Nelson, Cynthia. "Public and Private Politics: Women in the Middle Eastern World." *American Ethnologist,* 1 (1974): 551–63.

———. "The Voices of Doria Shafik: Feminist Consciousness in Egypt, 1940–1960." *Feminist Issues* 6, no. 2 (1986): 15–31.

Niblock, Tim. *Class and Power in Sudan: The Dynamics of Sudanese Politics, 1898–1985.* Albany: State University of New York, 1987.

———. "Islamic Movements and Sudan's Political Coherence." In *Sudan,* edited by Herve Bleuchot, Christian Delmet, and Derek Hopwood, 253–68. Exeter: Ithaca, 1991.

O'Fahey, R.S. "Islamic Hegemonies in the Sudan: Sufism, Mahdism, and Islamism." In *Muslim Identity and Social Change in Sub-Saharan Africa,* edited by Louis Brenner, 21–35. Bloomington: Indiana University Press, 1993.

O'Neill, Norman. "Class and Politics in the Modern History of Sudan." In *Economy and Class in Sudan,* edited by Norman O'Neill and Jay O'Brien, 25–59. Avebury, England: Gower, 1988.

O'Neill, Norman, and Jay O'Brien, eds. *Economy and Class in Sudan.* Avebury, England: Gower, 1988.

Oakley, Ann. "Interviewing Women: A Contradiction in Terms." In *Doing Feminist Research,* edited by Helen Roberts, 30–61. London: Routledge and Kegan Paul, 1981.

Osman, Dina Shiekh el-Din. "The Legal Status of Muslim Women in the Sudan." *Journal of Eastern African Research and Development* 15 (1985): 124–42.

Papanek, Hanna. "The Ideal Woman and the Ideal Society: Control and Autonomy in the Construction of Identity." In *Identity Politics and Women,* edited by Valentine Moghadam, 42–75. Boulder: Westview Press, 1994.

Pateman, Carole. *The Disorder of Women.* Stanford: Stanford University Press, 1989.

———. *The Sexual Contract.* Stanford: Stanford University Press, 1988.

Peristiany, J.G., ed. *Honour and Shame: The Values of Mediterranean Society.* Chicago: University of Chicago Press, 1966.

Perkins, Kenneth J. *Port Sudan: The Evolution of a Colonial City.* Boulder: Westview Press, 1993.

Peteet, Julie M. *Gender in Crisis: Women and the Palestinian Resistance Movement.* New York: Columbia University Press, 1991.

Polantzas, Nicos. "The Problem of the Capitalist State." *New Left Review* 58 (1969): 119–33.

Powdermaker, Hortense. *Stranger and Friend.* New York: W.W. Norton, 1966.

"'Preclude *Hadd* Sanctions by Doubt.'" Interview with Chief Justice Dafalla el-Haj Yousif, *Sudanow* 8, no. 10 (October 1983): 10–12.

Rabinow, Paul. *Reflections on Fieldwork in Morocco.* Berkeley: University of California Press, 1977.

Rahama, Amna and A. Hoogenboom. "Women Farmers, Technological Innovation and Access to Development Projects." Workshop No. 5, post-1987.

Rassam, Amal. "Towards a Theoretical Framework for the Study of Women in the Arab World." *Cultures* 8, no. 3 (1982): 121–37.

————. "Unveiling Arab Women." *The Middle East Journal* 36, no. 4 (1982): 583–87.

el-Rayah, Hashim Banaga. "We Have an Advantage: Omdurman Islamic University." *Sudanow* 9, no. 9 (September 1984): 41.

Remy, Dorothy. "Underdevelopment and the Experience of Women: A Nigerian Case Study." In *Toward an Anthropology of Women*, edited by Rayna Reiter, 358–71. New York: Monthly Review Press, 1975.

Riessman, Catherine Kohler. "When Gender Is Not Enough: Women Interviewing Women." *Gender & Society* 1, no. 2 (1987): 172–207.

Roden, David. "Regional Inequality and Rebellion in the Sudan." *Geographical Review* 64, no. 2 (1974): 498–516.

Rouleau, Eric. "Sudan's Revolutionary Spring." *MERIP Reports* 15, no. 7 (1985): 3–9.

Rowbotham, Sheila, Lynne Segal, and Hilary Wainwright. *Beyond the Fragments: Feminism and the Making of Socialism*. London: Merlin Press, 1979.

Ruete, Emily. *Memoirs of an Arabian Princess from Zanzibar*. New York: Markus Wiener, 1989.

el-Saadawi, Nawal. *The Hidden Face of Eve*, translated by Sherif Hetata. London: Zed, 1980.

————. *Woman and Sex* (in Arabic). Beirut, 1972.

Sabbah, Fatna (pseud.). *Woman in the Muslim Unconscious*. New York: Pergamon Press, 1984.

Sacks, Karen. "An Overview of Women and Power in Africa." In *Perspectives on Power: Women in Africa, Asia, and Latin America*, edited by Jean F. O'Barr, 1–10. Durham: Duke University, Center for International Studies, 1982.

————. "A Two-Way Street: Gendering International Studies and Internationalizing Women's Studies." Working paper no. 24, Southwest Institute for Research on Women, Tucson, 1987.

Saghayroun, Atif A. "Women in Demographic Trends." Paper presented at the Workshop on Women's Studies in Sudan, National Council for Research and Sudan Family Planning Association, University of Khartoum, Khartoum, 7–9 February 1989.

Said, Edward. *Orientalism*. New York: Pantheon, 1978.

Salih, Alawiya Osman M. "Women in Trade (The Case of the Sudan)." Paper presented at the Workshop on the Conceptualization and Means of Measuring Female Labour Force Participation, Khartoum, March 1985.

————. "Women in Trade: Vendors in Khartoum Area Markets." *The Ahfad Journal* 3, no. 2 (1986): 37–40.

Salih, M.A. Mohamed. "'New Wine in Old Bottles': Tribal Militias and the Sudanese State." *Review of African Political Economy* no. 45/46 (1989), 168–74.

el-Sanousi, Magda M., and Nafissa Ahmed el-Amin. "Sudan." In *Women and Politics Worldwide*, edited by Barbara Nelson and Najma Chowdhury, 674, box. New Haven: Yale University Press, 1994.

————. "The Women's Movement, Displaced Women, and Rural Women in Sudan." In *Women and Politics Worldwide*, edited by Barbara Nelson and Najma Chowdhury, 675–89. New Haven: Yale University Press, 1994.

Sanyal, B.C., L. Yaici, and I. Mallasi. *From College to Work: The Case of the Sudan*. Paris: UNESCO, International Institute of Educational Planning, 1987.

Sapiro, Virginia. "Engendering Cultural Differences." In *The Rising Tide of Cultural Pluralism*, edited by Crawford Young. Madison: University of Wisconsin Press, 1993.

Schneider, Jane. "Of Vigilance and Virgins: Honour, Shame and Access to Resources in the Mediterranean Societies." *Ethnology* 10 (1971): 1–24.

Scholte, Bob. "Toward a Reflexive and Critical Anthropology." In *Reinventing Anthropology*, edited by Dell Hymes, 430–57. New York: Vintage, 1972.

Seligman, C.G. *Races of Africa*. 3d ed. London: Oxford University Press, 1957.

Shaarawi, Huda. *Harem Years: The Memoirs of an Egyptian Feminist*. Translated and introduced by Margot Badran. New York: Feminist Press, 1987.

el-Shahi, Ahmed. *Themes from Northern Sudan*. London: Ithaca, 1986.

Sharabi, Hisham. *Neopatriarchy: A Theory of Distorted Change in Arab Society*. New York: Oxford University Press, 1988.

Shoaee, Rokhsareh. "The Mujahid Women of Iran: Reconciling 'Culture' and 'Gender.'" *The Middle East Journal* 41, no. 4 (1987): 519–37.

el-Shoush, Ibrahim. *Some Background Notes on Modern Sudanese Poetry*. Khartoum: University of Khartoum Extra-Mural Studies, 1963.

Sidahmed, Awatif. "Interview with Nafissa Ahmed el-Amin." *Sudanow* (January 1981): 41–42.

Simone, T. Abdou Maliqalim. *In Whose Image? Political Islam and Urban Practices in Sudan*. Chicago: University of Chicago, 1994.

———. "Metropolitan Africans: Reading Incapacity, the Incapacity of Reading." *Cultural Anthropology* 5, no. 2 (1990): 160–72.

Smith, Joan. "The Creation of the World We Know: The World-Economy and the Re-Creation of Gendered Identities." In *Identity Politics and Women*, Valentine Moghadam, 27–41. Boulder: Westview Press, 1994.

Sommer, John. "The Sudan: A Geographical Investigation of the Historical and Social Roots of Political Dissension." Ph.D. diss., Boston University, 1968.

Spaulding, Jay. *The Heroic Age in Sinnar*. East Lansing: Michigan State University Press, 1985.

Stacey, Judith. "When Patriarchy Kowtows: The Significance of the Chinese Family Revolution for Feminist Theory." In *Capitalist Patriarchy and the Case for Socialist Feminism*, edited by Zillah Eisenstein, 299–353. New York: Monthly Review Press, 1979.

Stowasser, Barbara. "Religious Ideology, Women, and the Family: The Islamic Paradigm." In *The Islamic Impulse*, edited by Barbara Stowasser, 262–96. London: Croom Helm, 1987.

Sudan Democratic Gazette, no. 19 (December 1991).

Sudan, Department of Statistics. *First Population Census of Sudan 1955/56. Final Report*. 3 vols. Khartoum: Sudan Government, 1962.

———. *First Population Census of Sudan 1955/56: Town Planners Supplement* 1. Prepared by D.G. Climenhaga. Khartoum: Sudan Government, 1960.

———. *Household Income and Expenditure Survey, 1978–80*. Khartoum: Sudan Government, 1981.

———. *National Census 1983*. Khartoum: Sudan Government, 1988.

———. *Population and Housing Survey 1964/65: Khartoum*. Khartoum: Sudan Government, 1965.

"Sudan: Finding Common Ground," *MERIP Middle East Report* 21, no.5 (1991).

Sudan Government, Ministry of Social Welfare. "Women's Organisations Registered under the Ministry of Social Welfare." Unpublished government document. Khartoum, [1985–88?].

Sudan Government, Population Census Office, Department of Statistics. *National Census.* Preliminary report. Khartoum, 1989.

———. *Second and Third Population Census.* Khartoum: Sudan Department of Statistics, 1979, 1987.

Sudan, Ministry for Social Affairs, Population Census Office. *21 Facts about the Sudanese: First Population Census of Sudan, 1955/56.* Prepared by Karol Jozef Krotki. Khartoum: Sudan Government, 1958.

Sudan. *Report of the Commission of Enquiry into the Southern Sudan Disturbances during August, 1955.* Khartoum: Sudan Government, 1956.

Sudan Socialist Union. *Summary of Working Plans for the Offices of the Executive Office of the Union of Sudanese Women.* Khartoum: Section for Political and Organizational Affairs, [1980?].

Sudanow (October 1979, January 1980, November 1984, September 1985, and January/February 1987).

"Sudan's Revolutionary Spring." Special Issue, *MERIP Reports* 15, no. 7 (1985).

Sudanese Communist Party Publications. *El-Midan.*

———. *Marxism and Problems of the Sudanese Revolution* (in Arabic). Khartoum: Socialist Publishing House, 1968.

———. *Thawrat Shaab* (A People's Revolution; in Arabic). Khartoum: Socialist Publishing House, 1967.

Sulaiman, Mohamed. *Ten Years of the Sudanese Left* (in Arabic). Wad Medani: Alfagr Books, 1971.

Taha, Batoul Mukhtar Mohamed. "Today, No Guardian." *Sudanow* (January/February 1987).

———. "The Women Deputies/Delegates of the Muslim Brethren and Women's Representation." *El-Sahafa* (16 May 1988), 8.

Tambul, Muawiya Mohamed Ali. "Woman at the Crossroads." *El–Sahafa* (21 June 1986).

el-Tayeb, Salah el-Din el-Zein. *The Student Movement in Sudan, 1940–1970.* Khartoum: Khartoum University Press, 1971.

Tillion, Germaine. *The Republic of Cousins: Women's Oppression in Mediterranean Society.* London: Al Saqi Books, 1983.

Tinker, Irene, ed. *Persistent Inequalities: Women and World Development.* New York: Oxford University Press, 1990.

Toubia, Nahid, ed. *Women of the Arab World: The Coming Challenge.* London: Zed Press, 1988.

———. *Female Genital Mutilation: A Call for Global Action.* New York: Women, Ink., 1993.

———. "The Social and Political Implications of Female Circumcision." In *Women and the Family in the Middle East,* edited by E. Fernea, 148–59. Austin: University of Texas, 1985.

Toubia, Nahid, ed. with Amira Bahyeldin, Nadia Hijab, and Heba Abdel Latif. *Arab Women: A Profile of Diversity and Change.* Cairo: Population Council, 1994.

Trimingham, J.S. *Islam in the Sudan.* New York: Barnes and Noble, 1965 (1949).

Tucker, Judith, ed. *Arab Women: Old Boundaries, New Frontiers.* Bloomington: Indiana University, 1993.

———. "Insurrectionary Women: Women and the State in 19th Century Egypt." *MERIP Middle East Report* 16, no. 1 (1986): 9–13.

———. "Problems in the Historiography of Women in the Middle East: The Case of Nineteenth Century Egypt." *International Journal of Middle East Studies* 15 (1983): 321–36.

———. *Women in Nineteenth-Century Egypt.* Cambridge: Cambridge University Press, 1985.

el-Turabi, Hasan. "The Islamic State." In *Voices of Resurgent Islam,* edited by John Esposito, 241–51. New York: Oxford University Press, 1983.

United Nations, Department of Economic and Social Development, Statistical Department. *Demographic Yearbook, 1991.* New York: United Nations, 1992.

Urdang, Stephanie. *Fighting Two Colonialisms: Women in Guinea-Bissau.* New York: Monthly Review Press, 1979.

Voll, John O. "A History of the Khatmiyya Tariqa in the Sudan." Ph.D. diss., Harvard University, 1969.

Waines, David. "Through a Veil Darkly: The Study of Women in Muslim Societies." *Comparative Studies in Society and History* 24, no. 4 (1982): 642–59.

Warburg, Gabriel. *Islam, Nationalism and Communism in a Traditional Society: The Case of Sudan.* London: Frank Cass, 1978.

———. "Mahdism and Islamism in Sudan." *International Journal of Middle East Studies* 27 (1995): 219–36.

———. "The *Sharia* in Sudan: Implementation and Repercussions, 1983–1989." *The Middle East Journal* 44, no. 4 (1990): 624–37.

Waterbury, John. "Twilight of the State Bourgeoisie?" *International Journal of Middle East Studies* 23 (1991): 1–17.

Wax, Rosalie. *Doing Fieldwork: Warnings and Advice.* Chicago: University of Chicago, 1971.

Weinbaum, Batya. *The Curious Courtship of Women's Liberation and Socialism.* Boston: South End Press, 1978.

Westkott, Marcia. "Feminist Criticism in the Social Sciences." *Harvard Educational Review* 49 (1979): 422–30.

Wikan, Unni. *Behind the Veil in Arabia.* Baltimore: Johns Hopkins University Press, 1982.

———. *Life among the Poor in Cairo.* Translated by Ann Henning. London: Tavistock, 1980 (in Norwegian, 1976).

Williams, Nick B. Jr. "In Mideast, a Christian Exodus." *Los Angeles Times* (10 August 1991), A16.

Woodward, Peter. *Sudan, 1898–1989: The Unstable State.* Boulder: Lynne Rienner, 1990.

Yuval-Davis, Nira, and Flora Anthias. *Woman-Nation-State.* London: Macmillan, 1989.

Zahir (el-Sadaty), Fahima. "Women and Their Environment: An Overview." In *Women and the Environment,* edited by Diana Baxter. Environmental Research

Paper Series No. 2, University of Khartoum, Institute of Environmental Studies, Khartoum, 1981.

Zein el-Din, Nazirah. "Removing the Veil and Veiling" (1928, translated by Salah-Dine Hammoud). In *Women and Islam,* edited by Azizah el-Hibri, 221–226. New York: Pergamon, 1982.

Zenkovsky, Sophie. "Marriage Customs in Omdurman: Part I." *Sudan Notes and Records* 26, no. 2 (1945): 241–55.

———. "Marriage Customs in Omdurman: Part II." *Sudan Notes and Records* 30, no. 1 (1949): 39–46.

Zuhur, Sherifa. *Revealing Reveiling: Islamist Gender Ideology in Contemporary Egypt.* Albany: State University of New York, 1992.

Index

About the Book and Author

Focusing on the relationship between gender and the state in the construction of national identity politics in twentieth-century northern Sudan, the author investigates the mechanisms that the state and political and religious interest groups employ for achieving political and cultural hegemony. Hale argues that such a process involves the transformation of culture through the involvement of women in both left-wing and Islamist revolutionary movements. In drawing parallels between the gender ideology of secular and religious organizations in Sudan, Hale analyzes male positioning of women within the culture to serve the movement. Using data from fieldwork conducted between 1961 and 1988, she investigates the conditions under which women's culture can be active, generating positive expressions of resistance and transformation. Hale argues that in northern Sudan women may be using Islam to construct their own identities and improve their situation. Nevertheless, she raises questions about the barriers that women may face now that the Islamic state is achieving hegemony, and discusses the limits of identity politics.

Sondra Hale is adjunct associate professor in anthropology and women's studies at the University of California, Los Angeles.